Early Praise for H

"Never in recent history has there bee
their hearts together in holy, passion
centric. *His Prayers and Mine* will challenge users to look at and learn from Jesus and His life of prayer. It will also challenge believers to pray as Jesus prayed.

His Prayers and Mine is a 365-day devotional commentary that combines a daily teaching on the subject of prayer with a daily devotional and prayer challenge for each particular day. Rick Astle understands the desperate need for believers not only to pray but to be a people of unceasing prayer that focus on God's Kingdom purposes. Because of this, by using *His Prayers and Mine*, believers are challenged to study devotionally for one entire calendar year on the subject of prayer from a biblical and Christ-centered perspective. Such a study should prove invaluable in the development of a life of consistent biblical prayer that is focused on Jesus and His mission." (excerpt from the Foreword)

J. Chris Schofield, Ph.D.

"How would you describe your prayer life? Do you ever use your Bible when praying to your Heavenly Father? In my experience as a Christian speaker and teacher over many years, I have discovered that the two basic areas that most impede a believer's daily walk with the Lord are biblical illiteracy and prayerlessness. Rick Astle's book, *His Prayers and Mine*, is a powerful teaching tool written to help guide and challenge the reader into a closer relationship with the Master through biblically-based prayer and following the example of Jesus— who literally taught His disciples how to pray. Find new joy and power in praying as you learn from Jesus Himself in this wonderful devotional commentary."

Phyllis Elliott Elvington
Christian Speaker & Author

"Prayer is the Lifeline to abiding in Christ. Everything we can do to encourage our people to pray has to be priority with pastors. Thank you, Rick, for this valuable resource to help our people be challenged each day of the year to focus and spend time with our Lord in prayer. I have discovered through over 40 years of ministry there is nothing more important than time in God's Word and time in prayer. This book is a helpful tool in helping us equip and encourage our people."

Rev. Michael Barrett, Pastor
Pleasant Garden Baptist Church, Pleasant Garden, NC

A 365 DAY DEVOTIONAL COMMENTARY

HIS Prayers AND MINE

RICK ASTLE

FOREWORD BY J. CHRIS SCHOFIELD

PUBLISHING
MASTERDESIGN
MAKING A DIFFERENCE ONE BOOK AT A TIME
FULTON, KENTUCKY

Published by Master Design Publishing
  an imprint of Master Design Marketing, LLC
  789 State Route 94 E, Fulton, KY 42041
  www.MasterDesign.org

For information about special discounts available for bulk purchases contact Rick Astle at Rick@RickAstle.com.

Cover and interior design by Faithe F Thomas
Cover image copyright - Pacific Press - Goodsalt.com, used with permission
Published in the United States of America
978-1-941512-37-1 Softcover
978-1-941512-38-8 Hardcover
978-1-941512-39-5 Ebook

Foreword

I believe that the Lord is calling His people toward prayer that focuses more on Him and the bigger picture of His Kingdom perspective and purposes. The crucial question that needs to be asked is this: what is God's perspective on all the circumstances and condition of the American church and how can we join Him through strategic Biblical prayer? In John 17:1 Jesus prayed, "Father, the hour has come." He understood the Father's time and He knew the Father's desire to redeem a lost humanity through the Christ. His prayer was timely and strategic. It flowed out of His relationship and desire to fulfill His Father's purposes despite the personal and painful circumstances, even dangers that were before Him. That's the kind of praying that brought transformation through Jesus to a pagan and lost world. That's the kind of Kingdom-oriented prayers that are needed today.

Never in recent history has there been such a great need for believers to unite their hearts together in holy, passionate, one-accord prayer that is Christocentric. That is why I believe that Rick Astle has served the body of Christ well by writing this devotional commentary on the prayers and prayer teachings of Jesus for such a time as this.

His Prayers and Mine is a 365-day devotional commentary that combines a daily teaching on the subject of prayer with a daily devotional and prayer challenge for each particular day. Rick understands the desperate need for believers to not only pray but to be a people of unceasing prayer that focus on God's Kingdom purposes. Because of this, by using *His Prayers and Mine*, believers are challenged to study devotionally for one entire calendar year on the subject of prayer from a biblical and Christ-centered perspective. Such a study should prove invaluable in the development of a life of consistent biblical prayer that is focused on Jesus and His mission.

Rick Astle is a personal friend and co-laborer in Christ. We have known each other for over three decades now and I have watched Rick live a life of consistent prayer that is focused on Christ and His mission. He has also maintained a deep burden to come alongside believers, pastors, churches and various Christian ministries to equip and challenge them toward Kingdom-oriented prayer. God has used him greatly to sharpen and challenge my personal life of prayer.

His Prayers and Mine will challenge users to look at and learn from Jesus and His life of prayer. It will also challenge believers to pray as Jesus prayed. As you read and work your way through this devotional commentary, may your prayer be similar to the prayer of the early disciples in Luke 11:1, "Lord, teach us to pray." To God be the glory!

J. Chris Schofield, Ph. D.
Wake Forest, NC

Introduction

People are often intrigued when they listen to previously classified personal conversations, such as the release of Oval Office tape recordings, or of 911 emergency calls. Of far more interest and value to the *Christian*, should be the Bible's authentic disclosure and record of the conversations between God and His Son, Jesus Christ.

We know the record of Jesus' prayers to be authentic, for the inspired writers received the Holy Spirit's supernatural aid to *remember* the words they personally heard Jesus pray while they were in His presence. Jesus told His disciples, ***"But the Helper, the Holy Spirit, whom the Father will send in My name, He will teach you all things, and bring to your remembrance all things that I said to you"*** (see John 14:26). This would, of course, include the words the disciples heard Jesus say to God in prayer. In addition, the Holy Spirit clearly provided the disciples with confirmation of when and what Jesus prayed *away* from their presence.

How then, should this devotion book be used for your greatest benefit? You may know that there is a temptation to Believers who use daily devotion books to be satisfied with receiving merely a "quick inspiration." Yet all Christians need renewal that comes as the result of intimate, daily communion with God as He speaks through His Word. Therefore, a "devotional commentary" seeks not only to encourage and challenge, but also to provide a valuable Bible *knowledge and understanding* – a great need for all who are in the Body of Christ. The Apostle Paul said, ***"For whatever things were written before were written for our learning, that we through the patience and comfort of the Scriptures might have hope"*** (see Romans 15:4).

That said, there are three things that I purposely *left out* of the book. First, in order to keep the focus of the book entirely on the life and teaching of Jesus Christ concerning prayer, I have not included any personal stories or illustrations from my own life and ministry. Second, I do not provide the Scripture reference *every* time I quote a verse within a devotion so that the reader can benefit from searching for some of the references on his own. (*All* of the Scripture references are provided in the back of the book as an aid to that exercise.) Finally, there is no "title" provided for each devotion, because many of the devotions address more than one topic.

Exactly one hundred of this book's devotions are focused on "The Model Prayer," a title I prefer over "The Lord's Prayer," because Jesus could not have prayed this prayer Himself (being without sin, He would be unable to pray, ***"Forgive us our debts"***). So one of the purposes of this book is to help you learn to pray *rightly* through an imitation of the Master's own prayer habits, the content of His prayers, His perfect instruction provided through the Model Prayer, and His warnings regarding unacceptable prayer. For to qualify as "prayer," must not your prayers be in agreement with Jesus' teaching and personal example?

Here are a few suggestions that may help you receive greater blessing from this book. First, understand that devotion books and devotional commentaries are *never* intended to be a "substitute" for a disciplined reading and study of God's Word. Therefore, you should make time to read and study the Bible *in addition to* your use of this book. Second, have your Bible next to you as you read and pray through each devotion. In your Bible, mark the verses you need to remember or memorize. You should take an extra minute to actually *locate and read* each Bible verse mentioned within the devotion, beginning with the "focus verse" provided at the top of each page. By doing so, your learning experience will be greatly enhanced. Third, read each devotion *slowly.* Be receptive to the convicting work of the Holy Spirit that leads you to repentance.

In conclusion, and to offer a compassionate challenge, I cannot improve on the following words of Alexander Whyte, found in his work, *The Walk, Conversation, and Character of Jesus Christ Our Lord* (Reprinted 1975 by Baker Book House):

> My brethren, will nothing teach you to pray? Will all His examples, and all His promises, and all your own needs, and cares, and distresses, not teach you to pray? Only pray, O you prayerless people of His, and the heaven will soon open to you also, and you will hear your Father's voice, and the Holy Ghost will descend like a dove upon you. Only pray, and your joy will soon be full.

"In this manner, therefore, pray"

– Jesus Christ

"And when He had sent the multitudes away, He went up on the mountain by Himself to pray." Matthew 14:23

When we think of Jesus experiencing temptation, it is easy to think only of the occasion when the Spirit led Him into the wilderness. But we believe the words of Hebrews 4:15 to be true, that Jesus *"was in all points tempted as we are,"* and so He must have been tempted to sin on numerous additional occasions. Bible scholars see *this* occasion *"up on the mountain,"* as a time when the devil may have "renewed" one of his wilderness assaults, tempting Jesus again regarding the kingdoms of the world and the glory of them. The Gospel of John tells us that as a result of the impression made on the multitudes by the miracle of feeding the crowd of over five thousand people the desire was present to take Jesus by force and to make Him a king.

So instead of thinking of repentance and *spiritual* change following the miracle, this crowd was thinking of *political* change, which they hoped would better their circumstances. Even the disciples displayed a touch of earthliness from time to time, so they may have gotten caught up in all this worldly enthusiasm, too. Watching the reaction to this miracle then, from both the multitude and from His disciples, could have tempted Jesus to overwhelming discouragement and frustration. *People were just not seeing the main thing!*

Do we grieve Him today in the same way? Do we understand what God is saying and doing?

In life, we experience circumstantial "seasons" or periods when there comes a major change or turn in the course. A serious turn was taking place in Jesus' life and ministry at this time. And this communion with the Father, among other things, was likely a preparation for major struggles that lay ahead – struggles that would include rejection, controversy, opposition, and even desertion.

There is much to pray about concerning a new year, this new season in *your* life. Whether you sense that a change may be on the horizon, or that you are exactly where God wants you right now – pray for courage to be obedient, regardless of the cost.

January 2

"'While I was with them in the world, I kept them in Your name. Those whom You gave Me I have kept; and none of them is lost except the son of perdition, that the Scripture might be fulfilled.'" John 17:12

Jesus had previously told the disciples, *"You are those who have continued with Me in My trials"* (see Luke 22:28). When He was in trouble, so were they. When He was offended, so were they. When He was neglected, so were they. When He was hated, so were they (*"If the world hates you, you know that it hated Me before it hated you."*). And when He was rejected, so were they. So it was then, and so it is today.

Even though the disciples had numerous shining moments, only a *divine* One could have *"kept them"* from falling away. This required a day-to-day, continuous watching over them; the Greek language clarifies Jesus' care more specifically as "to keep watch over" or "to keep an eye upon" the disciples. *"I was with them in the world,"* Jesus prayed, even when they did not fully understand all that was taking place or all that He was doing.

Christ had kept them against the world, the flesh, and the devil (and Satan did make attempts, *"Simon, Simon! Indeed, Satan has asked for you, that he may sift you as wheat. But I have prayed for you, that your faith should not fail."*) The disciples were neither killed nor drowned due to His keeping (*"'Lord, save us! We are perishing!' Then He arose and rebuked the wind and the sea."*) Jesus maintained an exact care of their bodies as well as their souls. *Remember, dear reader, the devil does not fear us – he fears the Guard that is around us!*

Bodily wants are more pressing to us. We find it easy to believe in Christ for salvation, but difficult to trust Him for daily bread and provisions God gives to birds. We should give pause to Scripture such as Luke 22:35, where it is recorded that Jesus asked His disciples, *"'When I sent you without money bag, knapsack, and sandals, did you lack anything'? So they said, 'Nothing.'"*

Pray that you will remember throughout this New Year that your Father who *keeps* you - enters in with wonderful and unexpected ways of supply.

> *"And Jesus lifted up His eyes and said, 'Father, I thank You that You have heard Me.'"* John 11:41, 42

In His brief earthly ministry, Jesus displayed great power because of prayer. Clearly, Jesus had already prayed in secret to the Father concerning the raising of Lazarus – possibly when He first heard the news concerning His friend. Therefore, the reason that Jesus could assure the disciples that He would awaken Lazarus (see John 11:11) was that He had already prayed for Lazarus' resurrection and had received the Father's answer.

So on this occasion, Jesus is giving thanks for *answered* prayer because the miracle had already been granted: **"I thank You that You have heard Me."** *Powerful faith, deep faith, is not believing that God "can," but that He "has!"* It is the difference between having "confidence" or "hope," and having *certainty.* With this in mind, we see our need for increased faith.

One of the purposes for this *audible* prayer of Jesus at the tomb was to convince the multitude of His divine commission in partnership with the Father. This prayer was about the *absolute unity* between the Father and the Son "on mission together." The Father had sent His Son on mission, the Son accepted that mission from the Father, and is here engaged in carrying out the mission. The Father's conception of the mission and the Son's conception of the mission, are identical.

It is of great importance to know the life mission God has given to each one of us. Only then can we experience the oneness, the perfect harmony, and the *agreement* the Father desires to have with His children. About that oneness, harmony, and agreement, Jesus would later pray concerning us: **"That they all may be one, as You, Father, are in Me, and I in You, that they also may be one in Us, that the world may believe that You sent Me."**

Like Jesus, you are in partnership with the Father on a divine mission. Fulfilling that mission is the reason you exist. Pray today that your understanding of that mission is *the same as His,* and ask Him to tell you everything you need to know in order to complete that mission.

January 4

"And He lifted up His hands and blessed them. Now it came to pass, while He blessed them, that He was parted from them and carried up into heaven." Luke 24:50, 51

Opinions about the exact location of Jesus' Ascension abound. There is a point on the Mount of Olives where the road forks – one branch continuing on to Jericho and the other leading to Bethany – and this is probably the best analysis of where this important and historic event took place. Jesus and the disciples had often walked over this piece of road.

Jesus was in His glorified body on this occasion. He was probably seen only by the disciples whom He desired would see Him. As Jesus spoke words of blessing, He separated from the disciples while they watched intently (see Acts 1:9, 10), His visible body rising higher and higher in a wondrous manner. This was different from His manner of departing from them during the previous forty days when He simply vanished.

The disciples witnessed the "end" of the Resurrection (not its "beginning," inside the tomb), and now they are seeing the "beginning" of the Ascension (not its "end," when Jesus was enthroned). And what a privilege to *see* this beginning! Imagine being able to personally witness Jesus' final going to the Father, and then to anticipate the promised coming of the Holy Spirit upon them, to aid in the great work ahead! The last time the disciples heard the sound of His voice, Jesus was pronouncing a compassionate blessing upon *them*.

In previous prayers, Jesus had lifted His "eyes" toward heaven. *Here, as the Priest about to ascend to His throne, He lifts the nail-scarred hands toward heaven!* Hallelujah! Behold the victorious King of Kings!

And so our Savior's public ministry on earth *began* at His Baptism with prayer and *ended* at His Ascension with prayer. Of course, that was no coincidence. All of us need to be following His example of how life *really can be* an experience of prayer without ceasing. Prayer is about your intimate *relationship* with the Father. May God place the desire within you to make time for Him - to simply *enjoy His presence!*

Pray a prayer of praise and thanksgiving, that Jesus "modeled" a life of continuous communion with the Father.

"'I do not pray for these alone, but also for those who will believe in Me through their word.'" John 17:20

When Jesus prayed, *"those who will believe in Me through their word,"* He was referring not only to those who heard the apostles preach and teach in person but also to those who would hear and read what they wrote later under the direction of the Holy Spirit. The Bible mentions important truths regarding that "word" and its relationship to man's salvation.

First, *the hearing of the preached Word is a necessity.* The Bible says, *"How then should they call on Him in whom they have not believed? And how shall they believe in Him of whom they have not heard? And how shall they hear without a preacher?"* (Romans 10:14). Yes, you can and should read the Bible at home. But *hearing* Christ's "spokesmen" is the means that pleased God for the opening of our hearts.

Second, *the power of the Word is amazingly great.* The Gospel Word *"is the power of God to salvation for everyone who believes"* (see Romans 1:16). *The first Gospel sermon that was preached after the pouring forth of the Spirit resulted in the addition of three thousand souls to the Church!* Clearly, it pleases God for men to be saved when they hear His Word preached with power: *"It pleased God through the foolishness of the message preached to save those who believe"* (see 1 Corinthians 1:21).

The assumption could be made that you would not be using this book daily, unless you have *already* accepted God's offer of salvation by believing in His Son, Jesus. But *no* assumption about a matter as serious as eternity is a safe one! If you take God at His Word, the responsibility of *fulfilling* His promises regarding salvation does not lie with you, but with God, who made the promises. At this very moment, His offer of salvation from your sins is made to you through His Word. Please, *"Confess with your mouth the Lord Jesus and believe in your heart that God has raised Him from the dead,"* and be saved (see Romans 10:8-13).

Pray for the salvation of unconverted people reading today's devotion.

January 6

"Jesus spoke these words, lifted up His eyes to heaven, and said: 'Father, the hour has come. Glorify Your Son, that Your Son also may glorify You.'" John 17:1

This prayer of Jesus is a continuation of the long discourse He had just shared with His disciples. An important change takes place when it comes time to pray: the Teacher becomes the Intercessor, and the Prophet becomes the High Priest. This prayer may very well be the "purest revelation" of the mind of God's *"Son"* in Scripture and is therefore so worthy of our careful study.

Many evidences of Christ's thinking and attitude are manifested in this prayer, but today we will focus only on one: His attitude of confidence toward the disciples. The greatest portion of this prayer was offered on behalf of the disciples. Given the circumstances He was facing at the moment, it is likely we can rely on the honesty and genuineness of the feelings He expresses for them in this prayer. Jesus was *grateful* for the men the Father had given Him (see John 17:6-8).

Not overlooking our own spiritual shallowness and ignorance, let us reflect on whom Jesus had to work with! The disciples often misinterpreted who Jesus was and misunderstood His mission. At the Last Supper, just moments before this prayer, they were arguing over who was going to be the greatest. Vulnerable Peter's faith was about to fail him. Very soon they would all flee and leave Him to face His enemies alone.

Yet Jesus had confidence in these men! Though their understanding was far from being full, He still placed His future work on their confused shoulders. Think of it - the authentic record of Jesus' words and ministry would come to mankind through the inspired writings of some of these followers!

This examination of how Jesus viewed the disciples should cause us to humble ourselves. The fact is, God uses feeble, sinful, proud, spiritually confused men to accomplish His work – men like us! Still, He is thankful for us. Still, He has confidence in us. Oh, that this truth would encourage our hearts today! What a privilege to be "instruments in His hands" for the furthering of His kingdom.

Thank Him now in prayer, that He is thankful for you.

"'In this manner, therefore, pray'" Matthew 6:9

This prayer is "The Model Prayer," because it guides us toward the *"manner,"* order, and spirit in which we should pray. As to the "manner," notice its *brevity*. The measure of a prayer is never its "length," but rather its sincerity and earnestness. Just as there is a great difference between the length of a sermon and the strength of a sermon, so there is a great difference between the length of a prayer and the strength of a prayer.

Sadly, many still "enjoy listening" to long, spectacular prayers. Therefore, we still hear church members make comments like, "That was a beautiful prayer," or, "I wish I could pray like him." Augustine noted that much speaking is one thing, and much praying is quite another; the shortest prayers are often the most eloquent. Thomas Binney used to say, "A little prayer may bring a large answer, and bring it soon if sincerity and faith give it wings. A short word may be made long enough to span the distance between earth and heaven if it be struck off from the living heart."

In addition to its brevity, notice also the *specificity* of the prayer. Here are a number of distinct and definite petitions, each stated clearly and plainly. There is no need to "elaborate" when we pray! Finally, notice the *simplicity* of the model prayer. Even a little child can understand it. But its simplicity is not shallowness.

As to the "order" in which we should pray, notice that in all true prayer, *God's glory* is to occupy *first* place. First things first - first God's glory, *then* our personal wants. *This may be the hardest lesson of all to learn about true prayer!* It is the man who overlooks this order who often complains of "unanswered" prayers. To conclude, the power of a prayer depends upon the "spirit" in which we offer it. We come to the Father as His *children*, believing that He is more ready to give good things to us than we are to give good things to our children.

Pray today with these lessons in mind.

January 8

"Jesus spoke these words, lifted up His eyes to heaven, and said: 'Father, the hour has come. Glorify Your Son, that Your Son also may glorify You.'" John 17:1

In this prayer, we are looking at the deep burden on Jesus' heart regarding the subject of "unity." Yet there is a tension within us as we read this prayer, namely the tension of just how to interpret His prayer for unity, when His desire seems to our eyes, dare we say, unrealistic, or at best, a "stretch." Knowing the nature of men the way He did, was Jesus overconfident? Does the prayer for unity represent merely a "goal" for all of His disciples? Has this prayer gone unanswered?

No, His prayer was and continues to be, answered. But we are *partially responsible* for the answer by *contributing* to that unity. First, we who are His disciples are to *behave* as one, in the "essentials" of a common faith. And second, like this prayer teaches, we are to demonstrate the faith and confidence Jesus had in God and in men.

Look closely at the entirety of this prayer in John 17, and you will easily see the faith Jesus had in God. See His manner of praying to the Father, see His humility, see the way He used God's name, see His deep respect and reverence for the Father, see the trust Jesus had in God, and see the close relationship between the Father and the Son. It is all recorded there for our benefit.

Look further into this prayer, and you will clearly see how Jesus never doubted that His disciples would indeed carry on the work He had planned for them. Twelve Galilean peasants sufficed. The way people view success today, there would be no hope for Christianity under these circumstances. *But twelve ordinary men dependent on the Master and operating in the Spirit have changed the world!* We realize that we are to have a greater confidence in God than in men, but the lesson is that *both* are needed.

Jesus knew when He prayed this prayer, that in a short time these men were going to abandon Him. We, too, have abandoned Him numerous times. Thank Him now for the confidence He still has in you.

If the praying of Pharisees was "hypocritical" and the praying of pagans was "mechanical," then the praying of Christians should be *real.* *"Therefore,"* the praying of Christians must be sincere and thoughtful; their hearts and minds must be *involved* in what they are saying. Their prayers should never be a meaningless repetition of words, nor should they be a means to their own gain; prayer should be a true union and sincere communion with our heavenly Father. *The praying of Christians should have as its priority concern God's name, kingdom, and will!*

The essential difference between pharisaic, pagan, and Christian praying lies in the "kind of God" we pray to. Other gods may accept mechanical incantations, but not the one, true *living* God revealed in Jesus Christ. As C.S. Lewis put it, "our" God may be "beyond personality." In other words, God is just as personal as we are, in fact, *more* so! In addition, "our" God is motivated by His desire to be the perfect, loving *Father.* Therefore, it was not because of a concern for proper "protocol" or "etiquette" that Jesus taught us to address God as *"Our Father,"* but rather because of the truth!

Religious people approach Him as "God," but Believers approach Him as "Father." So, *before you begin to pray,* Jesus is saying that you are to spend time "realizing" to whom you are speaking, and also to check and see if your prayer will be according to the "manner" taught by the One who said, *"I always do those things that please Him"* (see John 8:29).

This realization will prompt you to make *God's* concerns, *God's* agenda, your priority. Interestingly, Calvin may have been the first person to point out a parallel between this Model Prayer and the Ten Commandments – for both are divided into two portions: the first section outlining your duty to God, and the second section has regard for yourself and for your neighbor. Praying *"in this manner,"* the first thing you are saying is, "Father, your name be sanctified and set apart."

Pray today with a focus on this *manner.*

January 10

"Jesus spoke these words, lifted up His eyes to heaven, and said: 'Father, the hour has come. Glorify Your Son, that Your Son also may glorify You.'" John 17:1

Luther said of this prayer of Jesus, "Plain and simple as it sounds, it is so deep and rich and broad that no man can fathom it." It is deep, too deep to comprehend fully, for a variety of reasons. For example, consider the "theology" of this prayer. Represented in this one prayer are such doctrines as His deity (John 17:1), His pre-existence (John 17:5), the inspiration of the Scriptures (John 17:8), and God's electing grace (John 17:2).

Another unique aspect of this prayer is that, although the act of Calvary has not yet taken place, Jesus prays this prayer as One who thinks of His work as already done: *"I have finished the work which You have given Me to do."* Therefore, as He prays, He is already consumed with re-entering His Father's presence: *"Now I am no longer in the world."*

Again looking at the uniqueness of this prayer, it is the longest recorded *public* prayer of Christ. This and the Old Testament's prayer of Solomon at the dedication of the Temple, are the only "long" public prayers in the Bible. Jesus' public prayers tended to be short in length, while His private prayers tended to be longer in length – sometimes lasting an entire night. You will remember that He cautioned His disciples, *"Do not use vain repetitions"* and that they should not desire their prayers to be heard for their many words.

Notice that all of Jesus' petitions in this prayer were for *spiritual* benefits. These men had practically nothing by way of financial resources, yet they were being called on to head up *world evangelism!* And for what did Jesus ask on their behalf? *Spiritual protection and sanctification!*

One final lesson from this prayer – notice how *specifically* Jesus prays. There is no hint of generality or vagueness. And not only did He make His requests specific, but He also shared His heart with His Father as to *why* He desired these things. This is truly a model for us to follow when we pray.

Be specific, as you bring your petitions to the Father in prayer today.

"Jesus also was baptized; and while He prayed." Luke 3:21

Adedicated Christian desires to determine and obey the will of God, whether about specific circumstances or about His overall plan for his life. He may find God's will in a variety of ways: through Bible reading and study, through the illumination of the Holy Spirit, through the counsel of mature Christian friends or family members, through circumstances that do or do not occur, through God's still small voice, through the preaching and teaching of God's Word, through prayer, fasting, or meditation – or through any combination of the above.

Once a Christian believes he has an indication of God's will, the Father may provide "confirmation." Confirmation provides assurance when natural questions arise such as, "Have I missed it?" "Did I misinterpret anything?" "Has the devil deceived me through a counterfeit, or through someone who meant well but was wrong?" "Am I at least on the right track?" The matter is too important; he must be certain.

Jesus' act of obedience through baptism may have been preceded by a time of questions, reflection, and processing accompanied by the desire to be absolutely sure He was beginning His earthly ministry according to God's plan. Was our Lord asking specifically for that confirmation on the occasion of His baptism? Possibly, but clearly, the Father provided Jesus with confirmation and assurance, by declaring, **"You are My beloved Son; in You I am well pleased."**

God's confirmation always agrees with His Word! **"You are my Son"** (from Psalm 2:7) and, **"In whom My soul delights!"** (from Isaiah 42:1, with connection to Isaiah 53) were words that would have had special meaning to Jesus. The Father was telling His Son that He was indeed the Messiah (the anointed King) and that this was all going to lead to suffering and to a Cross. The fact that Jesus willingly accepted this painful yet critical role in God's plan would affect you and the rest of mankind forever!

Jesus desired confirmation of God's will in order to distinguish it from His own will (see John 6:38-40) Ask the Father today for confirmation concerning His will for your life.

January 12

"Jesus spoke these words, lifted up His eyes to heaven, and said: 'Father, the hour has come. Glorify Your Son, that Your Son also may glorify You.'" John 17:1

Our Lord Jesus was, is, and ever will be *the* Intercessor! Intercessors "stand in the gap" for people in need. Christ stood in the gap and redeemed us to God when we were in our most desperate need. And at the Father's right hand, He continues to intercede for us.

Many of Jesus' prayers were "intercessory" in their content, and this prayer is the best example. Intercessory prayer is prayer that earnestly petitions God for someone other than ourselves. In this prayer, Christ prayed thoroughly, fervently and specifically for His followers. His prayer was for their sanctification (continued spiritual growth), deliverance from the devil, joy, and unity.

The High Priestly Prayer recorded in John 17 is a sort of "specimen" of the praying for us in which Jesus is *now* engaged. He is our Advocate before God, who prays with us and for us. For three and one-half years He was a Prophet, speaking to men for God. For twenty centuries He has been High Priest, speaking to God for men. And when He returns, it will be as King – to reign over men for God!

In Isaiah 59:16 we find these pitiful-sounding words, **"He saw that there was no man, and wondered that there was no intercessor."** We are to be interceding for others for a reason. Do we now exaggerate? Do we make entirely too much over this business of remembering to pray for one another? Ought we not deny ourselves some time of rest or pleasure to engage in heartfelt intercession for each other? *Without a doubt, the ministry of intercessory prayer is sorely needed in these days of casual Christianity!*

We can agree that **"Pray for one another,"** is more than just a nice thought or suggestion. When someone is praying for us, we *know* it, we *feel* it! So, the next time God looks for an intercessor, may it please Him to see *you* standing in the gap for someone in need. Just now, will you ask the Holy Spirit to place some soul on your heart for whom He desires you to pray?

"'Therefore, pray'" Matthew 6:9

When Jesus assured Ananias of the conversion of Saul of Tarsus, He said, *"Behold, he is praying"* (see Acts 9:11). It took the miracle of grace upon Saul before *Jesus* could say he was "praying," for only a person who has been born again can graduate from "saying" prayers to pouring out their heart before God.

Now in verses eight and nine, Jesus uses the word *"Therefore,"* to connect with *warnings* that are given in verses five through seven. In this first recorded teaching of Jesus on the subject of prayer, it is important to note that He begins with a warning against *hypocrisy* – the seeking to attract the "notice" of others with the purpose of gaining the reputation of great spirituality. A hypocrite is one who assumes a character that does not belong to him. All of us have been a hypocrite, at one time or another. Prayer is so important that the devil makes it one of his primary targets.

But we must be careful not to read too much into this warning. Jesus was *not* condemning the physical posture of "standing" in prayer (kneeling can be just as reprehensible when the motive is wrong), nor was He forbidding His disciples to "pray in public." Rather, our Lord was speaking to the motive and manner of prayer. Motive is everything in the kingdom of God. And this warning should prompt us to examine the question: "What sort of creatures are we that *need* this kind of caution?" Yes, we are men with evil hearts, that we would ever use the precious opportunity to speak to *God*, in order to impress other *men!*

Many of us when attending church services, for example, have heard preachers and other individuals pray to the *congregation* instead of praying to God or pray using a *tone of voice* that is out of the ordinary. *Praying with the desire to charm the ears of men is hypocrisy!* No doubt our public prayers would be simpler and shorter if we were *alone* with God.

With His warnings in mind, pray in sincerity and in truth.

January 14

"Jesus spoke these words, lifted up His eyes to heaven, and said: 'Father, the hour has come. Glorify Your Son, that Your Son also may glorify You.'" John 17:1

It was the practice of the high priest to make atonement for himself and his house, after which he did the same for the priesthood and for all the people (see Leviticus 16:6, 33). That is why this particular prayer of Jesus has come to be known as the "High Priestly Prayer," for in it, Jesus assumes the priestly role (see John 17:19).

Some have called this prayer of Jesus "the greatest prayer ever prayed." Such a statement must be backed up with sound reasoning, and there are certainly some good arguments to support this claim. First, this is a great prayer because Jesus covered every Family member through His petitions: Himself, His disciples, and the disciples of the future (the Church). He specifically asks for glory, security, sanctity, and unity. Keeping those four petitions in mind can help us to deepen our own praying.

A second reason this is a great prayer is due to the incredible circumstances in which the prayer took place. Every human being was to be affected for eternity by the events that followed this prayer. And this prayer continues to have a powerful effect on people, because of the blood that was shed at Calvary. But probably the biggest reason why this prayer is great is because it was prayed by the Savior of the world! *Only Jesus Christ, God the Son, could pray using these words!* The very *manner* in which Jesus prayed this prayer demonstrates that He is God.

As an aid for people learning to pray, we sometimes suggest neatly designed "acrostics" and "alliteration" to help them remember to include various aspects such as praise, adoration, confession, thanksgiving, and supplication. While such tools can be useful, the most important prayer guide for *any* occasion is the leadership of the Holy Spirit. This prayer flowed from and revealed the heart of Jesus Christ.

Jesus said, **"Out of the abundance of the heart the mouth speaks"** (Matthew 12:34). Our greatest prayers are what we say from a clean, honest, humble heart. Pray now in *freedom and comfort,* realizing that God knows your heart.

"'Therefore, pray'" Matthew 6:9

The Model Prayer is short, making it easy to learn and remember. It contains all things pertaining to life and godliness.

The word *"Therefore"* here in Verse 9, relates to Jesus' previous warnings regarding prayer recorded in Verses 5-8; we must give consideration to those words to receive the full teaching of the model prayer. Verse 5 mentions hypocrites who pray *"standing"* in the synagogues and on the corners of the wide streets. The practice of "sitting" while praying is not generally supported by Scripture, except possibly when King David *"sat before the Lord"* in prayer (see 2 Samuel 7:18). The three "postures" of prayer most often mentioned in Scripture are standing, kneeling, and prostration on the face.

Standing, then, was a common posture of prayer. The Talmud of Babylon states that people would sometimes stand for three hours in prayer, so we must understand that Jesus was not condemning the "posture" of the hypocrite, but rather their *display*, their desire to "shine" before men. To pray like that is to put on a self-righteous performance. These hypocrites did not really pray; they only imitated prayer. *Because true prayer is such a high and holy thing, the devil likes to ruin it in as many ways as he can!*

Neither was Christ condemning "praying in public." When the motive and the heart is right, intercessory prayer at a hospital, or with someone who is clearly in distress, or prayer-walking a location where you are asking God to work mightily, or interceding from the side of the road for the occupants in vehicles, or gathering to pray with others on the National Day of Prayer – all of these prayers can be fruitful for the kingdom of God. There is most definitely a place for public prayer when the motive is not the desire for an *audience*.

When Jesus said, *"And when you pray"* in Verse 5, the grammar indicates that He expects us to be praying *regularly*. Jesus was taking our *necessity* of prayer for granted, but sadly, we are only gradually realizing that necessity.

As you pray, realize the necessity.

January 16

"Jesus spoke these words, lifted up His eyes to heaven, and said: 'Father, the hour has come. Glorify Your Son, that Your Son also may glorify You.'" John 17:1

"These words"** refer to Jesus' words recorded in the previous four chapters of John, not to the words of the prayer before us. These were words of teaching, promises, warnings, and revelations spoken in the Upper Chamber that led up to and *connected with,* the prayer.

These were not just "casual" words spoken; none of the Savior's words were. These were *magnificent* words like, **"A new commandment I give to you, that you love one another"** (John 13:34) and **"In My Father's house are many mansions; if it were not so, I would have told you. I go to prepare a place for you. And if I go and prepare a place for you, I will come again and receive you to Myself; that where I am, there you may be also"** (John 14:2).

"These words" provided *comfort* like, **"The Helper, the Holy Spirit, whom the Father will send in My name, He will teach you all things, and bring to your remembrance all things that I said to you"** (John 14:26), **"Peace I leave with you, My peace I give to you; not as the world gives do I give to you. Let not your heart be troubled, neither let it be afraid"** (John 14:27) and **"By this My Father is glorified, that you bear much fruit; so you will be My disciples"** (John 15:8).

"These words" were *glorious* words like, **"These things I have spoken to you, that in Me you may have peace. In the world you will have tribulation; but be of good cheer, I have overcome the world"** (John 16:33). "These words," are indeed precious, and spoken to all of us. But when we come to the prayer – it was spoken to the Father. It is not to us that He speaks now, but like the disciples, we may listen.

Brethren, whether it be the words Jesus spoke to men, or the words He spoke while praying, we are grateful for the Holy Spirit bringing to the disciples' remembrance all that Jesus said – that we might be helped! Give thanks for the Word of God.

"And when He had given thanks." John 6:11

In the eighth chapter of Deuteronomy, we find these words, **"Beware that you do not forget the Lord your God ... who brought water for you out of the flinty rock; who fed you in the wilderness with manna."** Every provision of food is an evidence of God's mercy. Jesus did not forget this fact and paused to give thanks. The other three Gospel writers note that, on this occasion, Jesus literally looked up to heaven while giving thanks for the Father's provision.

But there is another reason why Jesus looked up to heaven. The Father and His Son were in *partnership* – another fact Jesus did not overlook. Ministers have that same partnership with the Father. Paul expressed it this way in 1 Corinthians 3:9, **"For we are God's fellow workers."** "We" refers to Paul, to Apollos, and to those in Christian ministry. *Oh, for more ministers who look vertically rather than horizontally!*

So here we have our Lord setting the example of "saying grace" at mealtime. He may have spoken words that specifically fit this occasion, but it is believed that He spoke a customary table prayer. John uses the word, "eucharistesas," which brings a sacramental atmosphere to the occasion, and corresponds to the function of the head of a household.

When you eat at a restaurant, the blessing at mealtime provides an opportunity to show your server the compassion of Jesus. When you place your order, you might say, "We are about to ask God to bless our food – is there something we can ask God to do for you?" Many "divine appointments" await you in restaurants.

Placing a blessing upon food is something *God* does, not man. We often mistakenly ask the pastor, a fellow believer, or a family member at mealtime to "bless the food," when they are, in fact, incapable of doing so! It is God who blesses the food at our "request," with thanksgiving.

Jesus asked the Father to bless the food before He ate. Slow down long enough today to give thanks not only for food but for all of His merciful provisions.

January 18

"Jesus spoke these words, lifted up His eyes to heaven, and said: 'Father, the hour has come. Glorify Your Son, that Your Son also may glorify You.'" John 17:1

The disciples listened as Jesus prayed out loud so as to be heard. And the Holy Ghost, true to the promise of Jesus (see John 14:26), saw to it that not one petition should be lost to the Church.

Jesus speaks "to" us in the Word and "for" us in prayer. All things come "from" God "to" us "through" Christ. The "red print" in some of our Bibles is more than just an easy way to notice the things that Jesus said. That red print offers praise to the Holy Spirit, for helping the disciples to remember the words spoken by the only sinless man who will ever walk on earth!

It is humanly impossible to reproduce with integrity human words spoken during a period of over three years when all the words are *understood* perfectly. But it is much more impossible, to reproduce with exactness the many words of Jesus which the disciples *failed to grasp* when they heard His words. The Spirit enabled them to recall every utterance of Jesus, and in its true meaning. How marvelous, then, the record of the four Gospels (especially the Gospel of John) that contains the extended discourses of Jesus. *The Holy Spirit is behind it all!*

Two examples from this very Gospel give testimony. In John 2:22 we are told, **"Therefore, when He had risen from the dead, His disciples remembered that He had said this to them; and they believed the Scripture and the word which Jesus had said."** And again in John 12:16 we read, **"His disciples did not understand these things at first; but when Jesus was glorified, then they remembered that these things were written about Him and that they had done these things to Him."**

You, too, can rely on this wonderful promise concerning the ministry of the Holy Spirit! Whether during a sleepless night, or prior to teaching a Bible class, or when on a bed of sickness, or when sharing the Gospel with someone – ask Him to bring back to your remembrance words of Holy Scripture. Remember God's promises as you pray right now.

January 19

"'Therefore, pray'" Matthew 6:9

We shut the door to our room when we wish to be alone, or when there is something urgent that needs to be done that cannot be postponed. *Before* giving us "The Model Prayer," Jesus described a "setting" for prayer that all of us can understand: ***"Go into your room, and when you have shut your door, pray to your Father."*** Jesus is clear, although He does not say how "often" or how "long." He leaves all that to each man to discover for himself.

Although God is present at the family altar and *wherever* men diligently seek Him, He is present to His children in a most special way when they enter their closet and shut the door. It is not that God is one thing on one side of a door of wood, and another thing on the other side of that same door; it is that *we* differ so much depending on which side of that door *we* are on. Given enough time and opportunity, your Father and you will be the whole world to one another once you have "shut your door!"

Notice that Christ assumes here, that the circumstances and the correspondence connected with your relationship to Him will need some time and will take some trouble! It is here that the Holy Spirit may bring conviction. Your distaste for secret prayer and a shut door (and consequently your treatment of your heavenly Father) absolutely *horrifies* you, when you "come to yourself" and consider your priorities and this matter of secret prayer!

So it is that the *extreme spirituality* of secret prayer is what sets it apart from all other prayer. Communion with the Father in your room with the door shut will provide you with a revelation of your closeness to Him. At the end of a day, for example, where is your focus? Is it on music, movies, books, or family – and then to bed? How *easily* seemingly "good and harmless" things can rob you from your nightly fellowship with *God!*

Pray that you will not be too occupied to *be* with Him.

January 20

"Jesus spoke these words, lifted up His eyes to heaven, and said: 'Father, the hour has come. Glorify Your Son, that Your Son also may glorify You.'" John 17:1

"Jesus spoke these words" recorded in the previous chapters of John's Gospel, and then, with the simplicity of a child, **"lifted up His eyes to heaven."** Before He begins to speak the prayer, Jesus looks upward to the One who knows, wills, and loves with a tenderness that cannot be imagined. We cannot conclude, as some commentators do, that He was somewhere "outdoors" between the Upper Chamber and Gethsemane when He prayed this prayer; He may have prayed while still indoors.

The disciples did not "overhear" the prayer; Jesus *intended* for them to hear it, therefore He did not pray silently. There are advantages and blessings attached to vocal prayer – whether offered in public or in private. We know that the mind is prone to wander. Psalm 39:3 says, **"My heart was hot within me; while I was musing, the fire burned. Then I spoke with my tongue: 'Lord, make me to know my end, and what is the measure of my days, that I may know how frail I am.'"**

This moment marked the first and only occasion when Jesus could have expressed the content of *this* particular prayer. Earth had been like a wilderness to Him; *heaven* was the place of His rest and of His throne (see Psalm 103:19). He looks there now with longing eyes as He begins to pray. The disciples took notice of Jesus' eyes looking upward; gestures often reveal the feelings of the heart. Prayer is the elevation of the heart to God.

Looking up to heaven was a reverent consideration of God's majesty. Solomon wrote, **"Do not be rash with your mouth, and let not your heart utter anything hastily before God. For God is in heaven, and you on earth"** (Ecclesiastes 5:2). There is a distance! If for no other reason, prayer is necessary for *submission* to God. *Whether we fall on our face to the ground or lift up our eyes to heaven, we are to pray in awe of this amazing God!*

He who made the heavens can accomplish your desires. Have *confidence* in God as you pray today.

"Then little children were brought to Him that He might put His hands on them and pray." Matthew 19:13

The persons bringing children to Jesus were evidently parents, fathers, and mothers. Luke 18:15 describes these children as *"infants."* Even today there are parents who, lacking a personal relationship with Jesus themselves, want their children to belong to Him.

Placing the hand upon someone in connection with prayer is a symbolical act still used today, invoking divine "blessing." The Jews valued the blessing of a prophet or rabbi and brought their young children to the synagogue for this purpose. It was thought that this physical touch established a "personal relationship" between the good man and the child.

Jesus held a babe in one arm and placed His other hand upon its head. But the blessing did not flow through the Master's hands, but rather through His words. The actual words that Jesus spoke to each child, we are not told. On this occasion, the curtain falls while Jesus is busy with His blessings.

Just think of having the childhood memory of physically being held by Jesus Christ! And whether these adults knew Jesus or not, it must have been quite a moving experience to hear the voice of Jesus speak the name of their child in prayer, and to see Jesus hold their child in His arms. Little did these parents know that these same arms would soon be stretched out on a cross for their sake, making it possible to *truly* know the Savior of the world!

Children are ready to come to Jesus and to accept the gift of grace, and men should let them do so. "As the flower in the garden stretches toward the light of the sun, so there is in the child a mysterious inclination toward the eternal light." If only the children will *see* Jesus, they will instinctively be after Him! And this same receptivity is necessary for the adult to experience regeneration and justification by the operation of the Holy Spirit and of the Word of God.

Jesus welcomed the opportunity to pray for little children. Ask the Father to show you a child who needs to be brought to the Savior.

January 22

"Jesus spoke these words, lifted up His eyes to heaven, and said: 'Father, the hour has come. Glorify Your Son, that Your Son also may glorify You.'" John 17:1

Six times in this prayer Jesus uses the tender word, *"Father."* Earlier, John had written, *"But as many as received Him, to them He gave the right to become children of God, to those who believe in His name."* So this word, "Father" is dear to the believer's heart, because he hears in this word the assurance that he is *"accepted in the Beloved"* (see Ephesians 1:6).

There is no precedent for the use of this particular word for "Father" in Old Testament prayers, in first-century Jewish liturgies, or at Qumran. That is because this word *Abba* means "Daddy," or, "my own dear father." It is the word of address by a tiny child to its male parent, and therefore, was considered an over-familiar and inappropriate term for addressing the Almighty. Jesus, however, used it constantly as a witness to His unique sense of intimacy with the Father.

In olden times, the High Priest went into the *Holy of Holies* alone, and no one else was allowed. But for the believer, *"the veil of the temple was torn in two"* and the way into the "Holiest of All" is now made manifest. When the believer sincerely tries to *allow* God to decide for him, it changes his perspective. This is because God explains to us: *"'For My thoughts are not your thoughts, nor are your ways My ways,' says the Lord"* (Isaiah 55:8).

How quickly we go astray in our thinking! We *still* want the Word of God to justify or testify to our way of thinking, instead of allowing God's Word to *teach* us His way. We *still* create our plans and strive to carry them out, without as much as a thought toward God. And worse, oh, may God have mercy, we *still* ask for His blessing on, and His help carrying out *our* plans! Consequently, the blessing of just "learning" God's standards and His ways is still out ahead of us.

Do you have intentions of your own, over which you are asking the blessing of your Father? Surrender your will to His right now, in prayer.

January 23

"'Therefore, pray'" Matthew 6:9

The verses just ahead of Verse 9 provide instruction about true prayer that must not be disregarded, thus the *"therefore."* Again we will consider the words recorded in Verse 6, *"go into your room"* or "closet." *Jesus understood the tendency of our minds to wander, and so He is instructing us to get away from everything and anyone that could disturb or distract us!* This calls for a secluded spot, a place where we can be *intentional* about reducing, if not eliminating, interruptions. The "inner chamber" may be located in the solitude of nature; we know that Jesus often chose the solitude of a mountain or garden to pray.

The Greek word for "closet" originally referred to a "store-room" or a separate "apartment," but in the Septuagint, it is frequently applied to a "bed-chamber." In Matthew 24:26, it is translated *"inner room."* "Closet" is an old English word that means "private bedchamber" or bedroom. But we should consider what this word would suggest to a Jew. The closet is simply a closed place, shut in for privacy, shut out from interruption. To those listening to Jesus teach, the word might remind them of the innermost section of the temple where Jehovah had His special dwelling in the holy of holies – a closet from which the people were excluded.

The holy of holies was a place marked by silence and secrecy, seclusion and separation. It had a unique design; there was no door, no window, and no skylight. None of the Levites were permitted to enter except the high priest, who went there as the representative of the nation to meet with God. The holy of holies contained only one piece of furniture – the sacred ark covered by the mercy-seat. Thus this Holy "closet" was where man spoke to God and where God spoke to him.

Wherever your "room," remember that unless God meets with you there, you will not profit. If you carry the distractions of the world with you into your secret place, it will be difficult to converse with Him. Go now and meet Him in secret.

January 24

"Jesus spoke these words, lifted up His eyes to heaven, and said: 'Father, the hour has come. Glorify Your Son, that Your Son also may glorify You.'" John 17:1

This is *"the hour"* appointed by the Father, about which Father and Son have always had an understanding, and of which none but they have had any knowledge. All the light of the past streaming forward was focused on this hour, and all the light of the future streaming backward is focused on this same hour – and the two met! There in the spotlight of the centuries stood Jesus Christ, lifting up His eyes to heaven and praying.

Earlier in John's Gospel we read, *"They sought to take Him; but no one laid a hand on Him, because His hour had not yet come"* and again, *"These words Jesus spoke in the treasury, as He taught in the temple; and no one laid hands on Him, for His hour had not yet come."* The word "hour" refers not just to a specific time of day; it refers to much more than that – it refers to the eternal side of things, a time fore-willed, the hour perfectly established in the wisdom of God. It's working out into *fact* was perfectly harmonized and protected through the circumstances occurring in *each day* of Jesus' life! Who but Almighty God could have accomplished *that?*

And who but Almighty God can accomplish the same work in our lives? The fact that He has a will for each of our lives means that He is continuously intervening, as He did with Jesus. Often without our knowledge, He is continually protecting us from people and events that might send us down some wayward path away from realizing His "plan" (see Jeremiah 29:11). Our sin can cause twists in the journey – but this amazing God will find a way - to bring us to "the hour" in which we accomplish His purpose.

There is a place you need to reach. It is the place of *trust*, where you are so aware of what the Father wants to do in your life, that you surrender all. It is the place of *rest*, knowing that He does all things well, and with perfect timing. Pray that He will help your "unbelief."

> *"And when Jesus had cried out with a loud voice, He said, 'Father, into Your hands I commit My spirit.'"* Luke 23:46

Although Jesus *"cried out with a loud voice"* at the beginning of this prayer, we should be careful not to interpret that fact as evidence that this statement is of more "importance," more "worth," than any of the other statements He made throughout His life. The fact of the matter is, God uses the same will in speaking His last word that He uses in speaking His first.

What was the purpose, then, for the "loud voice" in this third and final prayer from the Cross? First, He spoke loudly that everyone would hear, especially His enemies, who believed Him to be forsaken of God forever. That separation was only temporary, and now He declared loudly that He was confidently placing His spirit into the Father's hands. The intense satisfaction and joy in Jesus' soul over His reunion with His Father were not to be kept secret, but rather *deserved a shout!*

Second, it was not to place emphasis on His dying, but rather, it was an affirmation of uninterrupted life! The vigor of His voice evidenced the vigor of *His thoughts of service to God;* **"My food is to do the will of Him who sent Me, and to finish His work."** The Father's will had been done, and the Son is *going home!*

Here is the lesson for us today; *there are no pauses in the kingdom of heaven.* Jesus made His departure from life on earth the *continuation of God's work. This prayer was a declaration that Christ was going forward, with His eyes fixed upon God!* The Nazarene's departure becomes God's progress. The work must go on. The work *will* go on!

Do you understand, my dear reader, *your* place, *your* role, in the continuing work of God? Is it your food to do the will of He who saved you by His grace? Are you "sidelined" because you have allowed the circumstances and cares of this world to determine your course? Let this time of prayer in your closet be a time of Holy Spirit revelation to you, regarding your part in God's ongoing work.

January 26

"Jesus spoke these words, lifted up His eyes to heaven, and said: 'Father, the hour has come. Glorify Your Son, that Your Son also may glorify You.'" John 17:1

It was *"the hour"* in which Jesus would be made an offering for sin. Yet it was still Satan's hour; *"Your hour, and the power of darkness"* is how He described it when speaking to His enemies at Gethsemane. And so it can be truthfully said that this was *God's* hour, *Jesus'* hour, *Satan's*, His *enemies'* hour, and the *world's* hour! It was the hour for which Jesus had come into the world, for He said, *"For this purpose I came to this hour"* (John 12:27) – not the hour for merely His death, but for His death, resurrection, and ascension *combined*.

This was the hour that Jesus had referred to constantly, beginning way back at Cana when He said to His Mother, *"My hour has not yet come"* (John 2:4). *Christ had been looking forward to this hour from the beginning, preparing His listeners for it through His teaching, preaching, and actions!*

Throughout this entire prayer, Jesus has His own death in mind. Yet the reward of saving a whole world was so great, that He *"for the joy that was set before Him endured the cross."* On a far lesser scale, we experience the brevity of suffering in *our* hour. Our sufferings seem long but are generally very short. Jesus taught, *"A woman, when she is in labor, has sorrow because her hour has come; but as soon as she has given birth to the child, she no longer remembers the anguish, for joy that a human being has been born into the world"* (John 16:21).

Imagine the "natural" ways by which Jesus could have *escaped* all of this, not to mention the supernatural possibilities. Remember, Christ was in numerous situations throughout His ministry when He escaped. Sometimes He escaped in order to find the privacy to pray, and other times He just needed rest from the demands of the crowds. There were times when He escaped political plots and the ill will of religious leaders, and times when people sought to actually kill Him.

Praise Him now for not escaping "the hour" that was meant for you.

"'Therefore, pray'" Matthew 6:9

It is imperative that we get alone with God. The word, *"Therefore"* takes us back to previously given instruction regarding prayer, such as the words, *"shut your door."* Jesus was teaching a lesson here regarding *privacy* – the intentional "getting away" from all sights and sounds that could disturb or distract us in prayer. *The verb used here denotes that the "door" is to not only be shut but fastened – providing the most complete privacy!*

Verse Six says that God will *"reward"* those who pray as He instructs. Perhaps His reward will be in our children's eternal salvation, to which they might never have attained but for our secret, unceasing prayer. *What would heaven be for us, if our children were not there with us?* Or, perhaps His reward will be the joyful surprise of learning what our intercession for others actually accomplished for their benefit.

God often rewards those who pray rightly in secret, by removing their fear of praying in public. Many sincere Believers avoid praying out loud in the presence of others, some of them going to the extreme of saying that these words of Jesus show His dislike for public prayer! But Jesus was here condemning public prayer made *with the motive of calling attention to ourselves.* Christ, Himself, prayed publicly on numerous occasions, and said regarding prayer, *"Where two or three are gathered together in My name, I am there in the midst of them"* (see Matthew 18:20). Acts 1:14; 2:42; 6:4; 12:5 and 16:13 describe how the early Christians practiced public prayer.

And Verse Six is grammatically interesting, in that no less than eight times in this one verse is the second personal pronoun used in the singular number: "But *you,* when *you* pray, go into *your* room, and when *you* have shut *your* door, pray to *your* Father who is in the secret place; and *your* Father who sees in secret will reward *you* openly." Christ makes it clear; we have the responsibility to *find* this private place of prayer, and then to shut the door.

Enjoy Him, as you meet together in private.

January 28

"Jesus spoke these words, lifted up His eyes to heaven, and said: 'Father, the hour has come. Glorify Your Son, that Your Son also may glorify You.'" John 17:1

The request of Jesus, *"Glorify Your Son,"* expressed His sense of relationship to the Father. It was answered on several occasions that were to follow, such as through the angel sent to strengthen Him at Gethsemane, through the testimony of Pilate: *"I find no fault in Him at all,"* through the salvation of the dying thief on the cross next to Him, through the rending of the temple veil, through the confession of the centurion: *"Truly, this Man was the Son of God,"* and then through His resurrection and the ascension.

We cannot separate Calvary from the resurrection, because the resurrection guaranteed that all that Jesus had spoken was indeed true (see Romans 1:4) – nor can we separate Calvary from the ascension, since the ascension was a type of the ascension of the believer in Christ (see Ephesians 2:6). The first request of this prayer, then, was for the Father to help Jesus through the agony of Calvary, but also that His resurrection and His ascension would make the salvation that He came to accomplish *real* to men. By this, both the Father *and* the Son will be glorified.

Jesus knew that the Father would grant His request. But we are to *ask* in prayer, even though God knows our needs, that we might be assured – for usually, the Father is already at work. Daniel understood by books the number of the years, and then he became earnest in prayer. When Elijah heard the sound of the rain, he prayed. *Prayer promotes the continuation of things that the Father has already set in motion!*

Jesus desired glory that came from the Father. We are to "seek" the *honor* that comes from the only God, more than the honor we receive from one another (see John 5:44) - and we are to love the *praise* of God, more than we love the praise of men (see John 12:43).

Any honor that we may receive in this life, God has permitted. Pray that the desire of your heart will always and forever be, to turn such recognition into the glory of the Father.

*"Now in the morning, having risen a long while before daylight,
He went out and departed to a solitary place; and there He prayed."*
Mark 1:35

Luke says it was a "deserted" place where Jesus went to pray, but the most accurate translation is that it was a "lonely" place. Bible scholars note that this was a busy period in Jesus' life when He made time to get alone with the Father in prayer.

The previous day had been exhausting for the Lord Jesus - teaching in the synagogue, interrupted by a demon-possessed man, the healing of Peter's mother-in-law, then at sunset a crowd of diseased and demonized individuals to heal and restore. And now a new day is upon Him when He will be going into the next towns to preach.

Notice how Jesus responded to Peter when the disciple brought the news that many people wanted to see Him. Jesus replied calmly but *decisively,* **"Let us go into the next towns, that I may preach there also, because for this purpose I have come forth."** It appears that this particular prayer time had, among other things, provided Him with a firm determination to be obedient to His divine mission.

Possibly this prayer was a time to ask the Father what to do next, a time to seek the Father's blessing or a time of praise over the miracles and victories of the previous day. We are not told what Jesus prayed about on this occasion. Maybe that was not the point Mark wanted to make. *Perhaps Mark wanted us to see how Jesus, exhausted as He had to have been, still made time to be alone with God in prayer!* No excuses. Communion with the Father was a priority of His. He would *make* time.

Jesus understood that each day would provide opportunities to be used by His Father for the furthering of the kingdom. Spending an entire night, or the better part of a night *in prayer* was His method of preparing Himself for doing whatever things the Spirit led Him to do.

No matter how tired, no matter how busy you may be today and in the days ahead, may you be this determined, this committed, to meet with God in prayer.

January 30

"Jesus spoke these words, lifted up His eyes to heaven, and said: 'Father, the hour has come. Glorify Your Son, that Your Son also may glorify You.'" John 17:1

There are many petitions for the people of God in this prayer, but Jesus asks only one thing for Himself – recorded here in verse 1, and then repeated and expanded in verse 5. When Jesus prayed, **"Glorify Your Son,"** He was asking the Father to enable Him to fulfill His ministry, so that the salvation of men for which He had come, would be fully accomplished. **"To open blind eyes, to bring out prisoners from the prison, those who sit in darkness from the prison house"** (Isaiah 42:7). This was the work Jesus was about to accomplish, and to *finish* it, was the "glory" He desired from the Father.

Christ urgently desired to be glorified, but He was not seeking honor for His own sake; He quickly gives the reason: **"that Your Son also may glorify You."** The "glory" of the Son of God will rest in His being the Savior, in addition to His being the Son. And so, "Glorify Your Son" is Jesus saying, "Father, let Me become glorious in Your sight and in the sight of My redeemed in all the ages, as Him who died, the Sacrifice. Give Me the cup of trembling, that I may become eternally the cause and the means between them and You. Glorify Your Son by enthroning Him at Your right hand, by crowning Him as head of the Church, and by sending down the Holy Ghost."

Galatians 6:14 says, **"God forbid that I should boast except in the cross of our Lord Jesus Christ."** *For the Christian, the Cross is essential to Jesus' holy dignity; He would not be the King to us that He is, except for the shame and agony through which He went for us!* The effect of the Cross, *for* and *in* the believer, cannot be stated more adequately. Indeed *all* of His suffering, beginning with the sweat of blood in Gethsemane, contributes to His being named, **"the Lamb who was slain."**

Pray that God will help you see the Cross in the same fullness with which it filled the eyes and the words of Paul.

"'Therefore, pray'" Matthew 6:9

Jesus specifically singled out **"*vain repetitions*"** and **"*many words*"** as something to avoid when we pray publicly (see verse 7). But what exactly did He mean? Certainly, that we are to avoid any type of praying that is mechanical or lifeless. **"*As the heathen do*"** or "like the Gentiles" is more than a reference to the custom of the pagans in their praying, for the Jews often prayed in the same way. Since the context in which these words are used is Jewish, it is important to consider them in the light of Hebrew literary practices.

The Greek words used here should not be interpreted as "stuttering;" rather, they refer to a Jewish system of speaking alphabetically (using words, clauses, or sentences) when praying in the Synagogue. Worship of this kind became mechanical and came to be regarded as an end in itself. These memorized Synagogue prayers were passed on from generation to generation, and are today present in the Service Books used by the Jews. To be fair, Catholics also have such prayer "formulas" in the form of their rosary.

Returning to the text, the *emphasis* should be placed on the word "vain" instead of on the word "repetitions." Jesus was not prohibiting *all* repetition in prayer, for He repeated Himself in prayer at Gethsemane (see Matthew 26:44). *"Vain" repetition is, simply put, speaking without thinking, which can hardly pass when speaking to God!*

Long public prayers spoken in an unordinary tone, are not the mark of true spirituality. They are often babbling prayers of self-interest and self-righteousness, made with the motive of manipulation. **"*Bring no more futile sacrifices,*"** God said through Isaiah (see Isaiah 1:11-15). We may have advanced beyond the days of sacrificing animals, but some of the prayers we offer today reveal our belief that there are still "secret formulas" that will hopefully work to our advantage. For example, prayers that twist the Scriptures for the purpose of gaining "prosperity" merely obscure the *true* purpose of prayer.

Pray sincerely and with care. Pray with a focus on *His* agenda, rather than on your own agenda.

February 1

"Jesus spoke these words, lifted up His eyes to heaven, and said: 'Father, the hour has come. Glorify Your Son, that Your Son also may glorify You.'" John 17:1

The ultimate aim of Jesus, our great Intercessor, is *to glorify His Father,* **"that every tongue should confess that Jesus Christ is Lord, to the glory of God the Father."** The Son will make the many and glorious attributes of the Father shine forth throughout the world, through the work of the Spirit in the Gospel and in the Church. The *greatest* glory of God is the giving of eternal life to men by bringing them to Himself by faith in Christ. The deepest passion of Jesus' heart was not the saving of men, but the glory of God *first*, and then the saving of men – because salvation is *for* the glory of God.

Notice that Jesus refers to Himself in the *third* person, saying, **"Your Son."** This demonstrates that Christ is rising out of Himself and into the consciousness of God, "losing Himself" in the Father. We honor the Father when we lose ourselves in Him and behave ourselves (and not just in times of convenience) with the realization that we are before a great God, when we make Him glorious in our own hearts, and when we think of Him as more excellent than all things.

Here, an important lesson from the school of prayer claims our attention. When we pray, we should ask that our Heavenly Father would glorify us, so that we would glorify Him; that we, who have come short of the glory of God, may still *illustrate* that glory day by day. *When we pray, we should plead His finished work, say that we are one with it, say that we trust in it, and then live in it!*

There is power when we pray in the Name, and with the very words, of Jesus! To pray in the Name of Jesus is to pray in unity and in sympathy with Him. Stop everything, and enter into the closet! Pray right now, that you will finish the work that the Father has given you to do. Pray that you will live only for His glory. Pray that the Son will be glorified in you.

> *"Now in the morning, having risen a long while before daylight,*
> *He went out and departed to a solitary place; and there He prayed."*
> Mark 1:35

Luke refers to the location as a "deserted" place (Luke 4:42). This is not the only occasion when Scripture records Jesus praying in lonely places. Matthew 14:23, Luke 5:16 and Luke 6:12 mention similar locations for prayer. Whether alone with the disciples or alone by Himself, Jesus found a place where He would be undisturbed. That is how we treat a "priority" in our life, isn't it? We do whatever it takes to guard the time it requires.

Sometimes the Master withdrew for a time of refreshing and renewal. There were times when these solitary moments provided the perspective needed from the Father when man's interpretations of His ministry were so misguided. At other times, He needed to literally escape from the crowds and their demands, due to His popularity. These are some of the more obvious reasons why Jesus made the effort to get alone with God.

Less obvious is the benefit of prayer that He had learned as a child. Luke 4:16 says that it was Jesus' *"custom"* to go to the synagogue and read the Scriptures. It is likely that during His childhood years Jesus also learned the practice and value of prayer because we see Him as a man of prayer from the very beginning of His ministry. He had *already* learned to be dependent on the Father for all things.

Some of us are still discovering the necessity of spending time alone with God each day. *And when we reach this awareness − that prayer is not simply "important," but that prayer is "essential" − we make one of the greatest discoveries of our Christian lives!*

People often say, "Prayer is where the power is." But actually, prayer is not where the power is; *God* is where the power is, and prayer intimately connects us to Him. Jesus knew that He must get alone with God to pray, but He also knew *why*. As you spend time alone in prayer today, tell Him *why* you need Him.

> "I need thee every hour, teach me thy will;
> Thy promises so rich in me fulfill."
> - Annie S. Hawks

February 3

"As You have given Him authority over all flesh, that He should give eternal life to as many as You have given Him.'" John 17:2

Verse 2 being a continuation of Verse 1, we have Jesus asking for a *"glory"* mentioned in Verse 1 that is suitable to the *"authority"* mentioned in Verse 2. When God glorifies Jesus in order that Jesus may glorify Him, this is in perfect harmony with what God did when He gave Jesus authority *"over all flesh."* Therefore, what Jesus now requests is in absolute accord with this past act of God.

And so in order to carry to completion what God began in the past, He will now glorify Jesus. *What we learn, then, is that Jesus and God are in absolute harmony, on all points, of this great mission regarding the world!* This mutual "glorification" of Father and Son is to the fulfillment of the divine purpose, for only by means of this glorification can the gift of *"eternal life"* be given.

Jesus came to reveal the Father, which He will do – if we let Him (*"Have I been with you so long, and yet you have not known me, Phillip? He who has seen Me has seen the Father"*). Therefore, our spiritual growth will be stunted if we think of Jesus apart from, or instead of, His Father. Paul wrote to the church at Corinth: *"Now when all things are made subject to Him, then the Son Himself will also be subject to Him who put all things under Him, that God may be all in all."*

In summary, all that Jesus says to us He has *heard* from the Father, all that Jesus gives to us He has *received* from the Father, and what Jesus has come to do is to *show* us the Father. If we miss those truths, then we miss what Jesus desires most to tell us. Jesus came to tell us and to show us that God constantly loves and cares for us. He has set God forth; He has *revealed* the Father – His being, His love, His mercy, His grace, His salvation. All is ours if we will receive.

Pray that you may receive *all* He desires to give you today.

"'Therefore, pray'" Matthew 6:9

Is there such a thing as "bad prayer?" If there is, Jesus defined it in Matthew 6:5-8. The Model Prayer is preceded by the word, *"Therefore,"* which draws our attention back to these four verses of caution. When a prayer contains *"vain repetitions"* or *"many words,"* it is not acceptable to the Father, when prayed with the wrong motive. In fact, this kind of prayer *dishonors* Him. Ecclesiastes 5:2 says, *"Let not your heart utter anything hastily before God. For God is in heaven, and you on earth."*

A bit of history may be helpful here. Occupied with the "letter" rather than with the "spirit," the Rabbis in Jesus' day piled up terms of supplication and thanksgiving during Synagogue worship. Eventually, a liturgical "system" was developed, the chief characteristic of which was a wealth of repetition of thoughts that was both wearying and sterile.

No doubt this feature of Synagogue worship was in Jesus' mind when He spoke against the use of vain repetitions and much speaking during prayer. The Gentiles had also developed this worship habit. (In sharing this history, we are in no way intending to be critical or unloving toward the Jewish people; we are merely clarifying our Lord's preface to the Model Prayer.) And so in the time of our Lord, prayer in Israel had often ceased to be a means of blessing, and had become instead a mechanical formalism.

We must remember not to make a "show" of prayer. When communing with God, we should give regard to *intent*, in addition to *content*. And, it is not "much praying," but rather, "much *speaking*" in prayer, that Jesus condemned. Christ, Himself, spent *whole nights* in prayer! *When religion is a formality, then a prayer that is also a formality - even if uttered "quickly" - will satisfy!* A pastor or group leader may fall into this temptation, saying to those before him, "Let us pause for *a quick word of prayer.*" How easy it is to become careless about *speaking to God!*

Take the time you need, and allow the Holy Spirit to prompt your prayer.

February 5

"As You have given Him authority over all flesh, that He should give eternal life to as many as You have given Him."' John 17:2

The *"authority over all flesh"* means the rule and dominion over all men. Jesus' mission was to the entire world of men, and so when He came on this mission, He received this authority. According to His *divine nature,* the Son already had this authority – He could not be given what He already had. But *as man,* He could and did receive this gift of authority. So Jesus prays here in an "official capacity," in the office of God-man Mediator, for as God He could not pray. It is important to note that, during His humiliation, Jesus had this authority over all flesh, but did not exercise it except to a very limited degree.

Ephesians 1:22 says, *"And He put all things under His feet, and gave Him to be head over all things to the church."* This *"authority"* that Jesus has in the world is exercised for the good of His Church. And so even though we who belong to Christ appear weak at times, we *still* have a great Champion!

These truths lead us into a time of worship, do they not? *He is worthy!* His is the *authority* in heaven and in earth! His is the *authority* over all our enemies! And *nothing* is able to hinder or interfere with His mission to *"give eternal life."* With Paul as our "worship leader," we agree and proclaim: *"For I am persuaded that neither death nor life, nor angels nor principalities nor powers, nor things present nor things to come, nor height nor depth, nor any other created thing, shall be able to separate us from the love of God which is in Christ Jesus our Lord."*

We who are in Christ Jesus are as secure as the love of God! *"Now to Him who is able to keep you from stumbling, and to present you faultless before the presence of His glory with exceeding joy, to God our Savior, who alone is wise, be glory and majesty, dominion and power, both now and forever. Amen."*

Eternal life is a gift. Have you received it? Prayerfully continue to worship.

"Now in the morning, having risen a long while before daylight,
He went out and departed to a solitary place; and there He prayed."
Mark 1:35

Christians sometimes ask, *"How long* should I spend each day for my Quiet Time?" The answer that Jacob gave to God as they wrestled (see Genesis 32:26) is a good one: **"I will not let You go unless You bless me!"** When you need to be alone with the Father, a clock is not as important as your determination to be blessed. *Read God's Word and pray until His Spirit satisfies your heart!*

Considering both the time (**"a long while before daylight"**) and the place (**"a solitary place"**), it is clear that Jesus felt the need to be alone on this occasion. This was a prayer time of some significant length because, when the disciples finally found Him, Jesus was *still* praying.

A hurried Quiet Time has a large, even a dangerous risk attached to it: the risk of missing a new blessing God desires for you for that day. Lamentations 3:23 states that His compassions **"are new every morning."** What an amazing truth! God wants to lovingly communicate with us in a fresh way at the beginning of *every* day. Think of the consequences if we should miss what He has to say!

Just as Jesus learned that the solitary place was a place of true rest for Him, this same Jesus invites us to find rest for our souls in Him. He says, **"Come to Me, all you who labor and are heavy laden, and I will give you rest."** Joseph Scriven put it this way:

"Have we trials and temptations? Is there trouble anywhere?
We should never be discouraged, take it to the Lord in prayer."
"Are we weak and heavy laden, cumbered with a load of care?
Precious Savior, still our refuge; take it to the Lord in prayer."

Let these words of Peter encourage your heart today: **"Therefore humble yourselves under the mighty hand of God, that He may exalt you in due time, casting all your care upon Him, for He cares for you."**

How many minutes should you spend today alone in prayer? Until the burden is lifted! Until the blessing has come!

February 7

"As You have given Him authority over all flesh, that He should give eternal life to as many as You have given Him." John 17:2

Jesus has authority over all flesh! He can subdue it, and He can control it. There are times, oh, too many times, when we are unwilling to restrain the rise of corruptness in our hearts – but Christ can. We read in Romans 14:9, *"For to this end Christ died and rose and lived again, that He might be Lord of both the dead and the living."*

There were two reasons for this petition in Christ's prayer, the first being the glory of God, and the second being the salvation of men. We know that the salvation of man depends on the resurrection, *"And if Christ is not risen, your faith is futile; you are still in your sins!"* In seven different places in this prayer, Jesus speaks of His Father's "gift" of His people to Him: in Verses 2, 6 (twice), 9, 11, 12, and 24. This frequency reveals the delight Jesus has in the possession of this gift.

Martin Luther said that the most damnable heresy that has ever plagued the mind of man was the idea that somehow he could make himself good enough to "deserve" to live with an all-holy God. The Gospel, the good news of the Christian faith, is that God offers eternal life to us as a gift! *Heaven is free to us because it was paid for by Christ!* *"Eternal life"* is the life of the kingdom of God, now and hereafter. That fact teaches us an important truth about prayer: Prayer is not only related to an eternal God but is communication with Him based on *our* eternal life.

And so, dear reader, as you consider the words, *"as many as You have given Him,"* are you describing yourself? Have you received His Word? Do you know for certain that He came forth from God? Have you believed that the Father did send Him? If not, I plead to God that you would do so right now! If so, pray for Jesus to overcome your fleshly appetite today, to cleanse your thoughts, kindle your faith, brighten your hope, and deepen your love.

February 8

Of course there are exceptions, but generally speaking, you should keep your public prayers short and your private prayers as long as necessary! Jesus condemned the prayer offered in public that should be offered in secret. He taught that hypocrites and prayer don't mix. The hypocrite wanted the reputation of being a man of prayer, and so he stopped to pray in the public square where he could impress the most people and be **"seen by men"** (see Verse 5).

Still, there are people who interpret long public prayers as a sign of spirituality. According to John A. Broadus in his *Commentary on Matthew*, Buddhist monks have been known to cry aloud for entire days the sacred syllable "Um." There are Mohammedans who "turnabout in a circle and pronounce the name of God until they drop down," and in some countries at Mohammedan funerals, devout men assemble and repeat "Allah el Allah" ("God is God") three thousand times! Roman Catholics occasionally count prayer repetitions by slipping rosary beads – a Buddhist practice which came through the Mohammedans to the Spanish Christians.

Jesus' teachings regarding prayer made mention of "hypocrites" on yet another occasion. Christ said, **"Woe to you, scribes and Pharisees, hypocrites! For you devour widows' houses, and for a pretense make long prayers"** (see Matthew 23:14). The word "pretense" is the translation of the Greek word for "cloak," suggesting "the show of something" so as to disguise one's *real* self or motives. The fact that Jesus pronounced a "woe" upon these people is a sure warning for the need to *examine your motive* before you begin to pray publicly!

So, for example, if you are in the presence of others and ask God to bless the food at mealtime, don't get so caught up in the opportunity that you pray about everything you can think of, and in the process, forget to thank God for the food. *Always remember, that whenever you speak with God – even at mealtime – you are engaged in the highest activity of the human soul!*

Pray for as long as you need to, in private.

February 9

"As You have given Him authority over all flesh, that He should give eternal life to as many as You have given Him." John 17:2

*"**That He should give eternal life**"* is a grace intended for *all* men, with no indication here of any limitation. *Only by excluding themselves* do unbelievers bar themselves from the gift of Jesus, and from receiving the gift of life. Anyone (*"**whoever believes in Him**"*) who hears may believe and is welcomed by Christ. The clear connection to Verse 1 is that the greatest glory of God is the impartation of eternal life to men, by bringing them to God in faith.

When we consider Jesus' *"**authority over all flesh,**"* it is important to know that, as Creator, Jesus also has His kingdom by "right," and not by mere authority. On the other hand, Satan may be prince of the world, but he is a robber and a thief. His hold is not due to a grant from the Father, but by limited power. He may actually possess many nations, but he has no right to them.

Jesus knows *you*, even though you do not know yourself as well as you may think. Are you not startled on certain days when you learn a new *truth* about yourself - even though you have lived many years? You assumed you could explain to someone if asked, who you really are, and then you are shocked to discover something about your heart that you neither knew nor understood. Yet *Jesus* knew! And still, He *values* you, gave Himself for you, and rules heaven and earth for your interests. Do you understand what He is going to do – He is going to present you *"**not having spot or wrinkle or any such thing ... holy and without blemish.**"* Hallelujah!

For *your* sake Jesus was incarnate. For *your* sake, the office of Mediator was appointed. For *your* sake, Christ died and rose from the grave. For *your* sake, all authority is committed to Him and exercised by Him. *The Word of God confirms every bit of it!*

Having considered these truths, how easy it is to pause now in humble gratitude to sincerely seek His *face,* instead of presenting Him with a "want list."

*"And at the ninth hour Jesus cried out with a loud voice, saying ...
'My God, My God, why have You forsaken Me?'"* Mark 15:34

Jesus spent nearly six hours on the Cross. The last three of those hours were spent in darkness, and Christ was silent during that period of time, even though He was still suffering extreme anguish of spirit and physical pain.

Those three hours of total darkness were a sign from God signifying the historical, unusual, and unique nature of this event. It pleased God to make Nature sympathize visibly with the passion of His Son, and the effect upon the consciences of the crucifiers and witnesses had to have been profound. *This was a darkness which science has been unable to explain!* Here is what we know. It was not the darkness of night, for it began at twelve o'clock in the day. It was not the darkness of an eclipse, for it was then full moon, and it is only at the new moon that eclipses of the sun can take place.

The darkness was connected to the cry that hung over Jesus' spirit at this time. The cry, the second of three prayers from the Cross, came from feeling the mystery of sin-bearing. That was the cup "tasted" that, in the Garden, He had prayed would pass, if possible. It was a cry that had been foretold in Psalm 22. Jesus was crying to His Father, "My Strength, My Strength," while He was being crucified in weakness.

Jesus did not address God in the usual manner as "Father" on this occasion, but we are certain that He knew the following verses: **"The Lord is the strength of my life"** (Psalm 27:1), and **"God is our refuge and strength, a very present help in time of trouble"** (Psalm 46:1). Even though the Father was unable to look upon the Son and to see the sins of the world upon Him, there was no doubt in Jesus' mind where to look for the only level of strength that would be sufficient for His need.

"Have you not known? Have you not heard?" God is the strength of your life! Thank Him that His strength is sufficient for your need today.

February 11

"And this is eternal life, that they may know You, the only true God, and Jesus Christ whom You have sent." John 17:3

"This is eternal life" is the same as saying, "this is what it *means* to have eternal life." He has spoken of "giving" eternal life, and now Jesus states what "receiving" and "having" it mean.

Jesus did not say, "Here is what eternal life will be like *someday.*" He said, "This *is* eternal life." It is a life we may have *now.* It is to know God as revealed in and through Christ (**"I am the way, the truth, and the life. No one comes to the Father except through Me"**). Corrie ten Boom said, "Eternal life does not start when you go to heaven. It starts the moment you reach out to Jesus."

We often think of "eternal life" as "quantity" of life, instead of as *quality* of life. Yes, eternal life is "endless," but that is not its most important feature. It is life *knowing God.* That is why Augustine said, "You have made us for Yourself, and our hearts are restless till they rest in You." Such an intimate, personal knowledge of God is the promise of the new covenant recorded in Jeremiah 31:34, **"No more shall every man teach his neighbor, and every man his brother, saying, 'Know the Lord,' for they all shall know Me, from the least of them to the greatest of them, says the Lord."** Knowing God means knowing *all* of the Godhead-Father, Son, and Holy Spirit. For this, we were made, and this is life indeed.

Plainly speaking, God is looking for men who know Him well, fear apathy and comfort supremely, and hate sin immensely! Knowing God is not that complicated. Peter's statement from Luke 5:5 is revealing: **"Master, we have toiled all night and caught nothing,"** for anything that begins with "we" will usually end with "nothing." Knowing God through Christ means, among many things, learning to depend upon the One who said, **"Without Me you can do nothing."**

Is it possible you are missing the joy of eternal life "in the present," due to much *striving?* Pray for conviction as to what you should *surrender* today.

February 12

It must bless the Lord whenever He sees us *really* praying! Before giving us the Model Prayer, Jesus took time in Verses 5-8 to explain that all prayer is not "real" prayer. The hypocrites of Jesus' day, for example, loved **"to pray standing in the synagogues and on the corners of the streets"** (see Verse 5). They actually adopted a pose and struck an attitude – like an actor! Christ said that these people **"have their reward."** The word that is translated "have" was the word associated with a receipt process, where payment was *completely* made and received, with no further consideration of the matter. In other words, the hypocrites prayed in order to be commended of men, and after they got what they desired, that's all there was to it - as far as God was concerned!

The only verse in the Bible where we are commanded to pray in a particular "location" is Verse 6, where we read, **"When you pray, go into your room."** Our "room" is a place of silent retreat from this noisy world.

Is there such a thing as "religious jargon" when we *pray?* Are we ever guilty of using "roundabout words or phrases" when we talk to God? Or, is it even possible to pray while letting one's mind wander? Jesus is warning us against any kind of prayer when the mind is not engaged, and therefore, any words will do! Religious jargon these days might include, "Bless this food to the nourishment of our bodies," "Bless the gift and the giver," or "Lead, guide, and direct us" (not exactly examples of intimacy, but it "gets the job done")!

Jesus said, **"Do not use vain repetitions as the heathen do"** (see Verse 7). The key word here is "vain," for Christ, Himself used genuine, Holy "repetitions" when He prayed in Gethsemane (see Matthew 26:44). When praying, repetitions might refer to the constant use of certain *words* or of certain *phrases* that resemble "chatter" more than anything else. *Prayer is simply not the time to repeat or to say idle things!*

Pray words of intimacy.

February 13

"And this is eternal life, that they may know You, the only true God, and Jesus Christ whom You have sent." John 17:3

There is "natural life," and there is "spiritual life," and then there is *"eternal life."* Natural life, spiritual life, and eternal life all flow from God; He *created* natural life, He *inspires* spiritual life, and He *gives* eternal life. As all life flows from God, He supports and maintains it.

Salvation is a matter of life. This life is eternal life. No person has eternal life by natural birth or life. There has to be a *new* birth, as told to Nicodemus by Jesus, when He said, *"Most assuredly, I say to you, unless one is born again, he cannot see the kingdom of God."* On the other hand, there is an "ignorance" of God that results in the death of the soul: *"Having their understanding darkened, being alienated from the life of God, because of the ignorance that is in them"* (Ephesians 4:18). Jesus came to dispel this ignorance of God, and to impart to us the knowledge of Him.

The more we know God through Christ, the more we will love Him. The more we know God, the more this eternal life we are experiencing here on earth will energize our souls, and the more happiness and peace and joy and power and holiness and love we will realize. If you want to love God more deeply and obey Him more readily, you will need to begin with knowing Him more intimately. *Here is a formula of truth: Priority time given to Bible study and prayer moves you to know God, knowing God moves you to love God, and then loving God moves you to worship and obey Him!*

Your Father in heaven wants to reveal Himself to you. Allow Him to do so! Walk with God! Perhaps it is time to put this book down right now, and to pray this prayer: "Father, abide with me that my heart might *burn* within me as we commune together! Reveal more of Your heart to me, so that my prayers might truly express Your kingdom priorities, *for Yours is the kingdom and the power and the glory forever. Amen."*

> *"Now in the morning, having risen a long while before daylight,*
> *He went out and departed to a solitary place; and there He prayed."*
> Mark 1:35

Read about the great missionary to China, Hudson Taylor, and you will find that he had powerful times of prayer during the *very early* morning hours. He learned this practice from Jesus.

Some of us call ourselves "morning persons," which means we feel far more alert in the morning than at night. Of course, most people can rise early when they absolutely have to for something like an early doctor's appointment or an early departure at the airport. But getting out of bed during the *very* early hours of the day - just for the purpose of prayer - is a blessing many a saint continues to miss. We can produce plenty of excuses, plenty of reasons, for not establishing *that* discipline!

"Very early, while it was yet very dark" is a more accurate translation of Mark's account; the word used here actually means "in the night." So it was toward morning but still far from dawn when Jesus left the house, left the city, and reached the ***"solitary place"*** where He desired to pray.

There are very good reasons for having an undisturbed prayer time in the morning. God should be put first in our lives, which means He should be first in our thoughts and considerations for each day. *He deserves that level of attention – ahead of the sensational headlines, physical exercise, breakfast, social media, or any other activity!* If the world's Christians all began their day in this manner, surely we would see a powerful, glorious change!

Not only does the morning time of prayer honor and glorify God by giving Him the level of attention He deserves, but it also gives us the perspective, strength, and cleansing *we* need for the facing of each day. Each new day brings the expected and the unexpected, the planned and the unplanned experience. We are much more prepared for all that will come our way after we have spent time with the One Who loves us and knows all that we are about to face.

Dear reader, pray that you will put God *first* in your thoughts and considerations today.

February 15

"And this is eternal life, that they may know You, the only true God, and Jesus Christ whom You have sent.'" John 17:3

The Greek verb used here for, *"that they may know,"* means *continuance* and *progress*. It does not mean a once-and-for-all gain of knowledge; it translates, "should keep on knowing." The phrase suggests knowledge by *living contact*, and not just the learning of "information." It is interesting that Jesus refers to Himself in the grammatical "third person," perhaps due to the solemn occasion in which the prayer is offered.

The Scriptures were written that we might attain this *knowledge of God*. The Holy Spirit came down from heaven to enable us to study and understand the Scriptures. 2 Peter 1:3, 4 explains, *"His divine power has given to us all things that pertain to life and godliness, through the knowledge of Him who called us by glory and virtue, by which have been given to us exceedingly great and precious promises, that through these you may be partakers of the divine nature."*

Without the Holy Spirit and prayer assisting as we actually read the Scriptures, we will not *fully* understand what we are told about God through His Word. The Holy Spirit is the best interpreter. *Just as every preacher and teacher should pray before and after "proclaiming" the Word, every Believer should pray before and after "reading" the Word!* Psalm 119:18 says, *"Open my eyes, that I may see wondrous things from Your law."* And Jeremiah 33:3 says, *"Call to Me and I will answer you, and show you great and mighty things, which you do not know."*

Therefore, not only is the Holy Spirit the best "interpreter," He is also the best One to enlighten and open the heart of the reader. How is it that, amazingly, we see more than we have ever seen before when we read and study the Word of God? It is because of the ministry of the Holy Spirit! We should cry for knowledge and lift up our voice for understanding with the same intensity as did the blind man who cried to Jesus, *"Rabboni, that I may receive my sight."*

Cry out to God for Holy Spirit-given knowledge and understanding of God's Word.

"'Therefore, pray'" Matthew 6:9

Jesus understood the human inclination for prayer, yet prayer is not a need that Christianity has created. We are like Abraham, Moses, David, and Elijah in that we all pray. Wherever you find man, you find that his heart and flesh cry out for the living God. Christ taught us that prayer should be made *rightly*.

"Therefore, do not be like them" when you pray (see Verses 5-7). Instead of letting the wrong example of others mislead you, let their behavior serve as a *warning*. Verse 8 says, **"Your Father knows the things you have need of before you ask Him."** *To talk to God in prayer as though you need to "inform" Him of anything – as though by your omitting some detail He would be left in ignorance – is an insult to an omniscient God!*

For example, prayers like, "Father, bless my neighbor Mr. Jones who was in a car accident yesterday and is in the hospital with two broken legs," become unnecessarily long, because God already knows Mr. Jones' whereabouts and his condition. And, when you are praying in the presence of others, you should not use prayer as an opportunity to inform your prayer partners of detailed "information" you want *them* to know; share the necessary facts *prior* to your prayer to God.

Then why pray at all? *Not* to pray, is to reject both the commands and the promises of God, and to ignore the means by which He has appointed for us to secure His blessings. The purpose of prayer is not to make us feel relieved or more comfortable; prayer is our opportunity for an *intimate relationship* with Almighty God, to intercede for others, and to focus on *His* agenda rather than on our own. Thus the error of **"the hypocrites"** is *selfish* prayer, whereas *true* prayer is a preoccupation with God and His glory. The error of **"the heathen"** is *mechanical* prayer that is virtually mindless. It is a false image of God, along with an inward degeneration, that produces false prayer.

Pray for the Holy Spirit to convict you of false prayer.

February 17

"And this is eternal life, that they may know You, the only true God, and Jesus Christ whom You have sent.'" John 17:3

Why are there so many tears, why so much fear, and why do we lack joy? It is because our faith in what we have already come to know of God, and our desire to learn still more of God, is so feeble. Jesus prayed these words in the hearing of the disciples, in order to increase their faith and ours. The "knowledge" of God that Jesus mentions here is not the intellectual or even doctrinal type, but rather an intimate and close relationship with the only true God and His Son. *The man who does not know God may eat, drink, even accumulate a fortune – but he has not begun to live!*

In Philippians 3:10, Paul expresses His desire, **"that I may know Him and the power of His resurrection."** In order to truly have *that* desire, we must reach a certain level of intimacy with God where little else matters except to **"gain Christ."** Jesus' desire is to remove anything that comes between us and intimacy with, or knowledge of, the Father - whether it is the influence of another human being, or the influence of our own stubbornness, pride, ignorance or unbelief.

And so there must be many benefits to our knowing God for Jesus to be so desirous, even protective, of our opportunity to have it. The Scriptures speak clearly of those benefits; we will **"be strong, and carry out great exploits"** (Daniel 11:32), we will receive **"the spirit of wisdom and revelation"** (Ephesians 1:17), **"grace and peace multiplied"** (2 Peter 1:2), and we will **"be neither barren nor unfruitful"** (2 Peter 1:8). Because God alone is eternal, we will receive enduring satisfaction beyond human limits. In addition, this knowledge will remind us continually of who He is, what He has done for us, and what He offers us.

This knowledge of God is the final expression of the triumphant Christian! Paul did not write, "I know *what* I have believed;" he said, **"I know whom I have believed"** (2 Timothy 1:12). Pray from a position of triumph today, because you know God through Jesus Christ.

*"And do not lead us into temptation, but deliver us
from the evil one"'* Matthew 6:13

From past sins, the Model Prayer turns now to possible *future* sins. This can be a difficult petition to understand because ***"temptation"*** is a "continual" experience while we remain in the flesh (see James 1:2-4, 12 and 1 Peter 4:12, 13). This is a petition primarily for protection. It recognizes the danger of temptation, confesses our weakness in dealing with it, and asks for our deliverance from it.

The Greek word for "temptation" (*peirasomos*) is difficult to translate. Usually, it means to "test" or to "prove." God subjects His children to testing, but it is Satan who seduces them into sin. While God will never deliberately do anything to draw a child of His into sin, temptation is one of the "God-permitted" ways of toughening our Christian character and consequently can be a good thing, if handled and understood properly.

So we make this request asking that we would not be left overwhelmed, presumptuous, or in a state of false security with the experience of temptation. *We are asking God to keep us out of certain situations when our lack of faith and trust in Him would bring sure defeat – all of this while we are growing to the place where the fear and love of God frees us from all coveting and lust!*

In the New Testament, *prayer* is shown as the proper response to "testings" and "temptations." Jesus provided the example when He prayed that Peter might not ultimately fall while *experiencing* temptation (instead of praying that Peter would not enter into Satan's temptations). When you pray this prayer, you are praying that, with God's help, you may *overcome* temptation rather than "avoid" it.

One Bible scholar paraphrases this petition to mean, "Do not allow us so to be led into temptation that it overwhelms us." This is "real" prayer, "humble" prayer, "Christian" prayer, in comparison to the prayers of Pharisees, hypocrites and heathen. True prayer warriors are obsessed with His name, His kingdom, and His will; they are "preoccupied" with God and His glory!

As you pray, bring a humble, honest heart to God concerning your weaknesses.

February 19

"And this is eternal life, that they may know You, the only true God, and Jesus Christ whom You have sent.'" John 17:3

Today we consider a most powerful and important phrase from this verse, the phrase, *"You, the only true God."* If only all of the people of all religions throughout the world knew these five words to be the undeniable truth! *May our most fervent prayers and actions bring them to that knowledge!*

Let us consider two questions. First, how can the Father be said to be the "only" true God, to the exclusion of Jesus and the Holy Spirit? The answer is that one person of the Trinity does not exclude the rest. With reference to salvation, the Father is always represented as the supreme of the three personalities of the Trinity, because He is the "Originator" of salvation; *"For God"* so loved the world."

Therefore, Jesus is seen praying here, not as the "second person in the Trinity," but as *Mediator.* So Christ used this phrase for two reasons; first, to note His Father's supreme role in salvation, and second, to distinguish His Father from the fake gods of pagan polytheism, from Jewish unbelief, and from all other idols and false gods of the Gentiles (see 1 Thessalonians 1:9).

Second, if there is "only" one true God, why do *we* behave so badly? That is, why do *we* have idols and false gods, why do *we* worship Him with less than a whole heart, and why do *we* practice selective obedience? Clearly, we are capable of spending hours, even days, without behaving like we *personally know* this "only" true God! Too often, our behavior has the appearance that we are still wandering as one who is "lost," or, at times, as one who obeys two masters.

Let us each one ask for the convicting work of the Holy Spirit upon our hearts at this very moment! What should it mean to us today (and every day), that there is "only" *one* true God – and that *we have come to know Him?* God forbid that we would live today or tomorrow or *any* day, without the *amazement* that comes from knowing the "only" true God!

Pray like you know Him.

"'Therefore, pray'" Matthew 6:9

A merica has ceased to be a praying nation, which has resulted in people feeling isolated, alone, and "to themselves" – while still trying to
deal with the cares of this world. A prayer-less America has led to the
fields growing dry, our hearts filling with hate, and God's blessings melting
away. For when we lose our fellowship with the Father, we fall out among
ourselves. And we are seeing this deterioration *increase* all across America
today. What, then, shall we say? And what shall we do?

"Therefore, pray" but **"your Father knows the things you
have need of before you ask Him"** (Verse 8). While it brings us comfort to learn that He already has this knowledge of our needs before we
pray, it also raises the question, "Then, why pray?" After all, the Bible says
that we ask and do not receive because we ask amiss (see James 4:3), and
that, **"we do not know what we should pray for as we ought"** (see
Romans 8:26). That is because, on our own, we neither know our *real needs*
nor the *remedies* to fix our issues. *Imprisoned by our passions and favorite sins, we
pray for plush carpet in our cell!*

Here we pause to learn a most valuable truth about prayer. Prayer is
not so much about "asking for things" as it is about entering into and maintaining an intimate *relationship* with the Father. If all I do is pray sincerely,
"Father," the most important part of prayer has *already happened!* Therefore,
the greatest blessing of prayer does not consist in whether or not we receive
the specific "things" we have prayed for, but rather in receiving "communion" with the Father as He gives us His whole heart.

And this truth frees us to pray, not in sad resignation but in childlike
trust, **"Not my will, but Yours, be done."** Pray, then, with a calm
spirit; you don't need to concern yourself with whether or not you "sound
right." Instead, pray and thank God that your prayers do not depend on
your making a correct diagnosis of your needs.

February 21

"'I have glorified You on the earth. I have finished the work which You have given Me to do.'" John 17:4

"I," Jesus Christ Your Son, *"have glorified You,"* He prayed. Jesus was God and man in one person, the eternal Son of the Father, the Word of God by whom all things were made, the brightness of the Father's glory, the express image of His person; His majesty, preciousness and holiness our words cannot express (see John 1:14, Colossians 2:9, and Hebrews 1:3). Reverently, we listen in and ask the Holy Spirit to teach us as we examine another prayer offered by the God-man.

Jesus' entire life was a continued manifestation of the glory of the Father. When Phillip asked Christ to show him the Father, Jesus replied, **"Have I been with you so long, and yet you have not known Me, Phillip? He who has seen Me has seen the Father."** How did Jesus glorify the Father? By making God known to His creatures, and by revealing the Father's true nature. There is nothing that we can do to *add* to God's glory, but we can make that glory *known*.

Making God's glory known was the "work" of the Hebrew prophets, yet they could only reveal a small part of God's nature. The prophets would sometimes introduce what they had to say using the words, "Thus says the Lord," because they knew that their words were not theirs, but God's. Their teachings were wonderful, beautiful, powerful – but incomplete, because *only in Christ is God fully revealed.* 2 Corinthians 4:6 says, **"For it is the God who commanded light to shine out of darkness, who has shone in our hearts to give the light of the knowledge of the glory of God in the face of Jesus Christ."**

What can be said of church groups, mission organizations, or mission endeavors that merely inflate statistics or human egos? *They stand self-condemned!* The motivation for doing *His* work should be to *give Him* glory! **"And He died for all, that those who live should live no longer for themselves, but for Him who died for them and rose again."**

Pray for the desire to *deliberately* glorify God in all that you do.

"*Our Father in heaven*" Matthew 6:9

Y ou are not alone when you call God, "Father." You go to Him in prayer along with, and on behalf of, other Sisters and Brothers in *the rest of the Family of God.* One of the great secrets of the very first Believers was the enjoyment of continuing **"steadfastly in the apostles' doctrine and fellowship, in the breaking of bread, and in prayers"** (see Acts 2:42). And the Rabbis in Jesus' day required that, when man prayed, he should "associate himself with the Congregation," praying in the plural number rather than in the singular. Both in your life and in your prayers, you should remember and practice the Fellowship.

He is **"our"** Father - thus prayer as *intercession* is taught in the very opening word of the Model Prayer. In fact, not once is the word "I" mentioned throughout the entire Prayer! Jesus is teaching you to think not simply of yourself as you pray, but also of others – of blessings *shared.* Therefore, when you pray, "Our" Father, you do much more than simply acknowledge God's Fatherhood; you also proclaim *your brotherhood.* You are not to lose concern for that great company of fellow Believers who share your sorrows, anxieties, pains, needs, and sins. Prayer that forgets the whole Family of God is selfish, reckless prayer.

Intercession, then, is the most beautiful expression of Christian love. You are a member of a Body. When you begin to grasp and believe this truth, you will begin to think differently, behave differently, and pray differently. Intercessory prayer is neither a mechanical thing nor an automatic thing; it is the *fruit* of true, deep communion with the Father. *You must be very near to God in order to faithfully stand in the gap for others!*

Andrew Murray wrote, "We have far too little conception of the place that intercession, as distinguished from prayer for ourselves, ought to have in the church and the Christian life. Through it alone we can do our work, and nothing avails without it."

Is there a Believer who has asked you for prayer? Spend time interceding for him.

February 23

"'I have glorified You on the earth. I have finished the work which You have given Me to do.'" John 17:4

Today we will consider the many different ways by which Jesus glorified the Father.

"I have glorified You on the earth" means, "I have performed all that was in Your heart, all that You have required of me for the accomplishing of the salvation of Your people given to Me. I have expressed Your eternal and everlasting love to poor sinners, I have manifested how perfectly faithful You are to Your promises, I have displayed the riches of the grace You have bestowed on a lost world, and I have made known the holiness of Your nature."

Scripture is specific about how Jesus glorified God, a few examples being through the image of His life (*"the express image of His person"* Hebrews 1:3), through His perfect obedience (*"Which of you convicts Me of sin?"* John 8:46), through His doctrinal teaching (*"And so it was, when Jesus had ended these sayings, that the people were astonished at His teaching, for He taught them as one having authority, and not as the scribes"* Matthew 7:28, 29), and through His divine miracles (*"Now when the multitudes saw it, they marveled and glorified God"* Matthew 9:8).

"These things I have done," Christ was saying, "and now I am prepared to glorify You through My suffering that is yet to come." The hours ahead would be rough; indeed abhorrent to flesh and blood, but it was the way His Father had appointed. *"My Father is greater than I"* said Jesus, so it was a privilege to glorify Him, even in these circumstances.

This brief examination of the various ways by which Jesus *glorified* the Father, brings to light how the Master was so "intentional" about accomplishing this primary objective. *The desire and determination to glorify God had to have been constantly on His heart, every single day!* Jesus was a focused man; He knew that there were certain matters of priority that simply must be remembered, in order to further the kingdom of God.

Pray that when your life on earth comes to an end, you can honestly say, "I have glorified You on the earth."

"So He Himself often withdrew into the wilderness and prayed."
Luke 5:16

The literal meaning of this word *"withdrew"* describes an activity that Jesus *kept doing;* it was a habitual thing. At every opportunity, He would slip quietly and secretly away from needy crowds of people to pray. Even Jesus could not be constantly in public, performing miracles and ministry without ceasing. That was not the reason He had come to earth. Therefore, He had to *make opportunity* to get alone with the Father. These prayer times enabled Him, among other things, to maintain His focus.

If simply having an "attitude" of prayer were sufficient, Jesus could have prayed as He went about ministering. There are far too many ministers who take that approach to prayer today. Supposing that specific "activities" of the ministry are the most important use of their time, they do not make opportunity for intense set-apart prayer as we see Jesus doing here. And they rationalize that "God understands" their lack of time spent in intense prayer since they are so busy doing His work. Our ministers need our prayers.

Jesus' life was like ours – busy! *He had less opportunity to get alone than we do, and Scripture does not even record all of His activities (see John 21:25)!* Yet communion with the Father was never neglected. Seeing faces rather than numbers, surely He prayed for the souls of these crowds that they would enter the kingdom. Our Lord's many prayers in the lonely place were kingdom-focused and fruitful.

Prayer connects us with the God who is our strength, our help, and provider of escape in temptation, our source of all true joy and gladness in a world that daily seeks to render us profane, depressed and common. "O God, help us! Let us see the *privilege* of coming into your Holy presence, that the evil in this world would not find an echo or agreement in our needy hearts. Forgive me for saying that I do not have enough time for intimate prayer when an analysis of how I spend my time reveals so much waste."

Make opportunity today, for undistracted prayer time with your Heavenly Father.

February 25

"'I have glorified You on the earth. I have finished the work which You have given Me to do.'" John 17:4

Notice the location, *"on the earth."* Christ came down from *heaven* that men would glorify God. God sent His Son to earth to give man further manifestations of His glory. The great errand of Jesus was to glorify God "on the earth," where so few are mindful of God's glory. Earth is instead a place where men seek their own glory, profit, and personal contentment.

Earth - the place of our trial, temptations, and difficulties! The saints in heaven glorify God, but without any difficulty. It costs them no shame, no trouble, no pain, no tears. But to men on earth, Jesus said, *"Whoever confesses Me before men, him I will also confess before My Father who is in heaven"* (Matthew 10:32). According to Jesus, it is not wishes that glorify God, but *practice;* *"Let your light so shine before men, that they may see your good works and glorify your Father in heaven"* and *"By this My Father is glorified, that you bear much fruit; so you will be My disciples."*

Only here on earth do we have this present missionary service. Only here on earth can we *"Go therefore and make disciples of all the nations, baptizing them in the name of the Father and of the Son and of the Holy Spirit, teaching them to observe all things"* that He commanded us. And then there is the awful *urgency* on the earth, where *"the night is coming when no one can work."*

The most useful thing you can do for others is to care for your own soul! Each one of us reveals something of God's glory to others, to the extent that we manifest something of the likeness of Jesus. The best thing you can do for your neighbor is to pass on to him some rays of the glory of God. Looking back over your life, you will recognize that the people you remember with gratitude are those who have made God a reality to you. They, like Jesus, have glorified God upon the earth.

Pray that you will reveal God's glory to someone today.

"'Our Father in heaven'" Matthew 6:9

We do not find that Jesus Himself used the Model Prayer that He gave to His disciples. For one thing, being without sin, He could never have prayed the words, "Forgive us our debts." So when Christ prayed, He began by saying, "Father," *without* the "our," showing Himself (as in other respects) to be separate from sinners. Jesus also addressed God in prayer as "Abba, Father," "Holy Father," or "Righteous Father."

The name "Father" occurs a few times in the Old Testament, where it refers to a "national" (not a personal) relationship. It was left to Jesus Christ to reveal God's best and truest name because no one *but* Jesus the Son could have revealed that name to men. One of the main reasons for which Jesus came to earth was to give us this new name for God. *It was vitally important for man to know that God is more than power, more than justice – but that God, above and beyond everything else, is Love!*

Even though countless thousands of men have forgotten God and rebelled against Him, the *reality* of His Fatherhood is unaffected. Though men still sin against Him, God still loves them. So praying the words "Our Father," reminds us that God is our Father and we are His children. Christ told Mary Magdalene, **"Go to My brethren and say to them, 'I am ascending to My Father and your Father'"** (see John 20:17).

But though God is the Father of all men, all men are not "sons." The right to become a child of God is given to the person who receives Jesus and believes in His name. We must, first of all, believe that God *is* – in a spirit of childlike confidence; to many, God is just a "word" and nothing more. So it is that Jesus puts the word **"Father"** at the very front of the Model Prayer, that we might begin our prayers with a childlike expectancy and trust.

Is there any lack of *confidence* as you prepare to pray? Pray and realize the *meaning* and the *power* of that word "Father."

February 27

"'I have glorified You on the earth. I have finished the work which You have given Me to do.'" John 17:4

The words, *"I have finished,"* or, "having finished," do not merely mean, "It is ended;" they mean, "It is *completed.*" These words represent triumph!

Yet how could Jesus make this declaration *just yet?* It was because our Lord had determined to undergo death, which was now at hand. In the consent and full determination of His will, it was *done.* Looking back, it had been an adventure hazardous beyond words – but now, He could say that it had been carried through fully and thoroughly.

He had laid down His life in compliance with His Father's command, *"This command I have received from My Father."* It was time to pass on to the next stage – first to the Cross, and then to heavenly exaltation. Philippians 2:8 declares, *"He humbled Himself and became obedient to the point of death, even the death of the cross."* While much suffering at the hands of men (including more conflict with evil) was still ahead, Jesus was triumphant.

Notice the accountability Jesus demonstrates! *It mattered* that He had been obedient to the point of death. We, however, can live for days, for weeks, without caring that we are accountable in any way to our Creator. In fact, the thought of giving account to Him one Day may be one of the furthest things from our minds.

Imagine being able to make such a claim about your life, much less being able to make it to *God!* Many of us, if standing before Him now, would be able to bring Him only little of what *we* had intended – but then, there is what *He* had intended for us to accomplish for His glory and His kingdom. *Here is our life as God planned it at the moment of our creation; here is our life as we have pitifully lived it!*

Pray that when you reach that Day, that Day of perfect and just evaluation of the one life you were given to live, that you will be able to stand before the Father and say, "I have finished the work which *You* have given me to do."

"*Our Father in heaven*" Matthew 6:9

While an earthly father may *want* and *know* what is best for his children, our heavenly Father is in position to *actually do* what is best. Therefore, we come to our heavenly Father with the simple trust and confidence with which a little child comes to his earthly father, whom he knows and loves and trusts.

Sometimes we address our prayers to the Lord Jesus, and sometimes we address our prayers (particularly in hymns and songs of praise) to the Holy Spirit. Neither address can be "wrong," since both Jesus and the Holy Spirit are God. But the more "precise" way to begin a prayer is to address the **"*Father,*"** *through* the Son, and *by* the Spirit.

Only people who have **"*received*"** Jesus and **"*those who believe in His name,*"** have the right to address God as **"*our*"** Father (see John 1:12). Galatians 3:26 says, **"*For you are all sons of God through faith in Christ Jesus.*"** The Apostle Paul did agree that, in a sense, we are *all* His offspring (see Acts 17:28). But on that occasion, Paul was speaking only of God's relation to man as his Creator (as is described also in Malachi 2:10).

Man is not now what he *was* when God created him. We need a "second birth," because all of Adam's offspring are born in sin (see Psalm 51:5 and Romans 5:12). That second birth occurs when a believing sinner trusts Christ for salvation. Jesus told some of the religious leaders of His day, **"*You are of your father the devil*"** (see John 8:44). *The Bible simply does not support the politically correct idea of the "universal fatherhood" of God!*

You can become a member of the *actual* family of God and begin your prayers confidently with the words, "Our Father in heaven." **"*For there is one God and one Mediator between God and men, the man Christ Jesus.*"** Trust Jesus now for your salvation. God has brought you *this very devotion,* desiring that you will be born again! Believer, pray for those who need to trust Him, who are reading this devotion today.

March 1

"'I have glorified You on the earth. I have finished the work which You have given Me to do.'" John 17:4

Go d is to be the great scope of our lives, meaning He is our first consideration in all that we are, all that we do, and all that we desire, **"For of Him and through Him and to Him are all things."** Glorifying Him is the ultimate end for all of our actions, **"Therefore, whether you eat or drink, or whatever you do, do all to the glory of God."** Certainly, it is **"work"** that glorifies God when that work is God-honoring; **"Let your light so shine before men, that they may see your good works and glorify your Father in heaven."**

Having said that (and the statement ahead may sound strange at first), certain "limitations" were placed on Jesus! For example, *geographically,* His entire earthly life was confined within the boundaries of central Palestine. He never saw Rome, or Athens, or Alexandria – to say nothing of other locations around the globe. Even within the sphere of His teaching and healing ministries, there were multitudes of people in Palestine to which He never ministered. *Yet His ministry was perfect and whole because He did all that He was* **"given"** *to do!*

A similar limitation is upon each of us who are His disciples. No one person is called to reach the *entire* world, or to minister to *every* need that exists. We each have a specific work to do, and doing *that* work, along with its limitations, brings our fulfillment and our peace. The truth is, resisting temptation, exercising mountain-moving faith, and practicing kingdom-focused prayer (to name only a few disciplines) are all *work!* Honoring God, then, is not only the doing of a project but also the faithful *completion* of it. Therefore, every servant of Christ covets Paul's testimony: **"I have finished the race"** (2 Timothy 4:7).

And so His work, while it was for the redemption of men, also involved a *higher purpose* – the glorification of God. Pray that you will identify your "mission" on earth, for it is in the doing and the completing of *that* work, that you will find fulfillment, and God will receive glory.

"Our Father in heaven" Matthew 6:9

"T"he Lord's Prayer" may not be the best *name* for this prayer, since the Lord Jesus could never have prayed it. It has long been called by that name because it is the Prayer that Jesus taught to His disciples. Perhaps "The Disciple's Prayer," or "The Daily Prayer," or "The Family Prayer" would be more fitting. But the title *most* appropriate is, "The Model Prayer," for Jesus prefaced the prayer by saying, **"In this manner, therefore, pray."**

We can believe that God has truly "connected" Himself to us because of the *relationship* we have to Him as **"Our Father."** When we enter into that relationship through Christ, we cease to be homeless and a wanderer upon the earth. On our own in this world, we are unstable and uncertain. As a child of God, we find a hold and a hope; we can pray to Him and feel, "It is good for me to be here." Therefore, the only prayer Jesus taught begins with the words, "Our Father."

The "Father" is the One mentioned because He is "first in order." Jesus said, **"My Father is greater than I"** (see John 14:28). But the Son and the Holy Spirit are *included* because, in essence, they are the same. The name Father carries two important attributes with it: *mercy* and *love.* He made us His "children" by a miracle of mercy. **"Behold what manner of love the Father has bestowed on us, that we should be called children of God!"** Praise the Lord!

Religious people may approach Him as "God," and the unbeliever may call Him his "Creator," but only a man *born again* may call God his "Father." The best of our earthly fathers excel in areas such as strength and tenderness, but our heavenly Father is *infinitely* more satisfying to us. Martin Luther said, "If I could only truly believe it, that God, the Creator of heaven and earth and all things, is *my Father.*" And all of us can acknowledge that lack of belief!

Pray that you will "truly believe" that the Creator of all things is *your* Father.

March 3

"'I have glorified You on the earth. I have finished the work which You have given Me to do.'" John 17:4

Observe from this verse that **"the work"** was **"given"** to Jesus by God. Christ took work upon His shoulders as a *servant*. That is why Paul wrote that Jesus took **"the form of a bondservant"** (see Philippians 2:7). Jesus did not die as a "disappointed" man; He died as the successful "Servant Messenger" from God to men.

We glorify God when we obediently set ourselves to finish the work He has given us to do. It is indeed amazing that Almighty God would "give" *any* of us a work to do! Probably the hardest thought for our egos and our sin-damaged minds to entertain is the truth that God does not "need" our help. To admit the existence of a need in God is to admit that He is incomplete or inadequate. All that God is He is in Himself.

It may well be true that thousands of people enter the work of the ministry, supposing that *they* will deliver *God* from an embarrassing situation! Sadly, some people hold on to that view throughout many of their years in Christian service. But the truth about the matter is clearly provided in the fifteenth chapter of John. We are **"branches"** connected to Jesus who is the true Vine. We are to *abide* in Him so that we will bear fruit, much fruit, fruit that remains.

Also in that glorious chapter are six words spoken by Christ that may be the most easily forgotten words of all in Christian ministry: **"Without Me you can do nothing."** Although most of us say that we "know" that, it is not clear that we operate as though we *believe* it. *How easily we lose our humility and declare, "Look what I have done!"*

As you consider the work that you are doing, the work you believe was "given" to you by the Father, be certain that it is *real work* you are doing for Him, in Him, and to Him – whether it be work in your family, in your business, or something you have undertaken for the church.

Pray that you will *finish* that work.

"So He Himself often withdrew into the wilderness and prayed."
Luke 5:16

Being fully Man and fully God did not prevent Jesus Christ from having priorities in His life or from having a personality. When we read through the four Gospels, we meet Jesus the Savior and Teacher, but we also meet Jesus, the *person. How wonderful, and what an honor, to get to know The Savior of the World intimately!* Here are some of the things we notice about His personality that provide valuable ministry lessons for today.

For one thing, the Savior was not impressed by popularity. Crowds, multitudes of people, were seeking Him daily with wild enthusiasm, following Him everywhere He went – but popular demand did not excite Him. When a ministry generates "excitement," there is a present danger of carnality replacing spirituality. Jesus saw people as souls, not as His "fans."

And Jesus was a Man of worship. The word translated **"prayed"** here is a word that has deeper meaning than to just ask God for things. This word actually reveals that Jesus was engaged in *worship* as He prayed. For Him, communion with God was a priority over the performance of various ministry activities. Oh, for the Church today to come to the place where it realizes that prayer is more than just "important" – it is *vital!*

One of the greatest deceptions before today's church is the lie that "service to God" should take priority over prayer. Sad but true, many ministers today say that they cannot find time to pray because the "responsibilities" of the pastorate demand so much of their time. Consequently, too much of our ministry activity is carried on in the energy of the flesh. Only service that has grown out of *prayer* will demonstrate the power of the Holy Spirit.

What do your spiritual priorities look like? Take a moment to examine your heart; see if you are more comfortable doing things *for* God than spending time alone *with* God. When you pray today, do not miss the opportunity to *worship* God. That time spent in communion *with* Him, will accomplish more than any activity you may perform today "for" Him.

March 5

"And now, O Father, glorify Me together with Yourself, with the glory which I had with You before the world was."' John 17:5

"And now,*"* that the earthly part of the work has been completed, the heavenly part may begin. The heavenly part is the Father's will, just as was the earthly part now completed. *Therefore, this very point in time marked a "milestone" in God's plan!*

Heaven is now in full view, including the glory Jesus enjoyed in the bosom of the Father before His incarnation as God's eternal Son. The time has come when His work of dispensing the blessings of salvation can be best carried forward by His being lifted up. The reason Jesus does not say, "with the glory which I had with You before You sent me into the world," or, "before I came into the world," is because He wanted to be clear about the nature of the glory He had in mind.

He had in mind the glory of the Godhead – the eternal, divine glory that extends back into all eternity. In the incarnation, Jesus "veiled" this glory, and did not use it according to His human nature during His humiliation, because of His work among men. But now that the work is completed, He requests to be glorified according to His human nature, with the glory that was His before the world began.

There are specific reasons why Jesus made the request, **"Glorify Me."** He did not make the request from vanity, egotism, or assumption. He wanted to provide comfort to His disciples who were listening to His prayer, and who were troubled over what was about to take place. He wanted to teach *us*, that suffering for God is the path to glory. And finally, that His Church would prosper as the result of His glorification.

The Father's *answer* to Jesus' prayer is described in the second chapter of Acts, where we read, **"This Jesus God has raised up ... therefore let all the house of Israel know assuredly that God has made this Jesus, whom you crucified, both Lord and Christ"** (see Acts 2:32, 36).

Pray a prayer of praise, that God has given Jesus **"the name which is above every name."**

"'Our Father in heaven'" Matthew 6:9

Jesus often drew attention to childhood, where many of us have a secret feeling of affection in our memories. By bringing before us the *mind* of little children, Christ shows us a part of our nature that makes us regard childhood with tenderness. He was the first who set a child in the midst of His disciples, providing a revelation of the heavenly mind.

The influences of the world can lead us far away from the spirit of our childhood. Such things as the pursuit of wealth, career successes and disappointments, and emerging health issues distract us away from the humility and unassuming peace of children. A child is earnest, even in awe, as he listens to any description of something marvelous. He is so ready to believe things unseen, so reverent when he hears of God and of heaven, so expectant of answers to prayer. A child is frank and honest. How different from children we become in our "mature" years!

Yet a child is no specimen of perfection. The Bible tells us (and we know from our experience) that a child's heart is bound up in folly. As we are born in sin, sin manifests itself in our lives very early on. And as children of God, we cannot cover up the fact that we are often lacking in our communion with fellow members of the Body of Christ, and in our communion with the Father in prayer. *"Prone to wander,"* we stray easily!

The full revelation of humility and a childlike spirit is evidenced in Jesus Himself. He was *"gentle and lowly in heart."* When in Christ we call God *"Our Father,"* we are reminded of this loving union between child and father. Jonathan Edwards wrote, "The strong and lively exercises of a spirit of childlike, evangelical, humble love to God, give clear evidence of the soul's relation to God as His child; which does very greatly and directly satisfy the soul."

Are there evidences of a childlike spirit in your life? Imagine you are a child, as you pray to your Father who is in heaven.

March 7

"And now, O Father, glorify Me together with Yourself, with the glory which I had with You before the world was.'" John 17:5

John begins his Gospel with this powerful statement: ***"In the beginning was the Word, and the Word was with God, and the Word was God."*** The word "incarnation" means, "taking flesh." 1 John 4:2 says, ***"Every spirit that confesses that Jesus Christ has come in the flesh is of God."*** That God Himself would care so much for you and me as to come to earth, to take our nature upon Him, and to die upon the Cross – is no small matter at all.

God did not bring Jesus into heaven, as we are brought into heaven – merely to rest from labor and to enjoy the reward of glory. God brought Jesus into heaven that He would sit in the throne of majesty and authority, to have power to send the Spirit and to gather the Church (see Psalm 68:18).

On the occasion of this prayer of Jesus, the disciples were dejected and in need of comfort. In a moment as Jesus continues with the prayer, He will say in their hearing, ***"These things I speak in the world, that they may have My joy fulfilled in themselves."***

But it was also for *our* hearing and for *our* profit that Jesus prayed these words because He knew it could not go well with the Church unless it went well with Himself. Rejoice! While our Head is so highly magnified, and made Lord of all, He will rule all for the best! Psalm 110:1 declares, ***"The Lord said to my Lord, 'Sit at My right hand, till I make Your enemies Your footstool.'"*** *There will come a time when those who hindered the Church will curse themselves that they ever resisted the Church!*

Jesus loved the Church and gave Himself for it. Frankly, the Church today has no greater need than to fall in love with Jesus all over again! And my Christian friend, each one of us is either contributing to the "pollution" or to the "purity" of His dear Church!

Pray now with brokenness, for a fresh move of the Holy Ghost in your heart and in your church.

"He went out to the mountain to pray, and continued all night in prayer to God. " Luke 6:12

Jesus saw the work yet to be accomplished and knew that the hour had come to set apart the men to do it. Bible scholars calculate that the time of this prayer was about a year before the Savior's death. This was a period when there was both growing popularity as well as growing hostility toward our Lord's ministry.

The Twelve would be elected not for the reason of "excluding" others, but *for the sake of others* and for the sake of the Father's kingdom. During and after praying the entire night, it became clear to Jesus that His choice was in accord with His Father's will. Therefore, it is likely that Jesus prayed specifically for the men He was about to choose, for their work in the world, for their preparation for that work, and for all that would be accomplished in the future as a result of their work.

The Master **"continued all night in prayer to God."** Who can breeze past *those* remarkable words without pause? *We pause not only to be amazed at the Savior's prayer habits, but also to come under conviction regarding our own!* What shall we say, then? "I am weak and cannot continue in prayer as He did?" "It is impossible for those who live a busy life to have long devotions?" "We need our natural rest and a good night's sleep to take care of our bodies and our health?" "God does not require such a thing of us?" God forbid that we should have *any* of these thoughts!

Though His life on earth was short by today's standards, it is unlikely that there has been a man whose life was so interrupted, so diverse, so demanding, so "busy" than that of Jesus Christ. And yet, look at this! He is praying all night! We think little of traveling through the night for an event concerning business, family or amusement. But it hardly seems necessary to the majority of us that *prayer* should keep us up all night.

Ask the Father to give you *Holy Spirit conviction* concerning your prayer habits.

March 9

"'I have manifested Your name to the men whom You have given Me out of the world. They were Yours, You gave them to Me, and they have kept Your word.'" John 17:6

The verb translated as *"I have manifested"* actually means, "to make visible and clear." So Jesus did more than just "teach" about God; He "revealed" the nature of the Father, in all that He was, said, and did. One of the ministries of the Son was to declare the Father: *"No one has seen God at any time. The only begotten Son, who is in the bosom of the Father, He has declared Him"* (John 1:18). That word "declared" means, "to unfold, to lead, to show the way."

Jesus did not instantly reveal the Father "all at once;" His disciples could not have handled that kind of revelation. And so He revealed the nature of God to the disciples *gradually,* as they were able to bear it, by His words and deeds (see John 16:12). The same thing is taking place with us. Our God is simply too magnificent, too high, to be understood at once; we learn the facts of His holiness and attributes over time, as we are able to grasp them.

One of those facts is that of *His perfection as a Father.* Those of us who have children know that each child has a *secure* place in our heart; a place that nobody except that child can ever fill. Jesus taught us that our welfare matters to God. Our Heavenly Father is well aware of our foolishness and weaknesses as children, yet He will see that we benefit from His divine understanding, patience, and forgiveness.

Is not the ability of God to see everything, think of everything, coordinate everything, address everything - while simultaneously and personally loving us and providing for us, simply amazing? Just stop and think for a moment, about all that God is able to accomplish in these five seconds throughout the world! *He is dealing with you, He is speaking to your heart right now – and at the same time, He is dealing with and manifesting His love toward every person on earth!*

As you pray now, *"To whom then will you liken God? Or what likeness will you compare to Him?"*

"'Our Father in heaven'" Matthew 6:9

The words, ***"in heaven,"*** indicate that He who is ***"Our Father,"*** is also, in reality, "heavenly." God, who is present *everywhere*, is represented in Scripture as making His special abode in heaven. It is there that He has prepared His throne. This thought was not strange to Israel, for in the Old Testament writings, God was described as ***"Possessor of heaven and earth"*** and ***"the God of heaven."*** So it became the confidence of His people, that in the most desperate of circumstances, whether national or personal, God would ***"hear in heaven Your dwelling place."*** But these words refer to much more than God's "postal address."

When you pray to your Father who is "in heaven," you are making a reference to His *glory. Jesus is teaching you to consider "His majesty" before naming "your petitions!"* Moses put his shoes off his feet, and Solomon advised that God is in heaven while you are on earth. And prayer to your Father "in heaven" also makes reference to His *power, dominion, and authority.* Fathers on earth cannot always help us, because they are on our level – learners by trial and error. But your Father in heaven has both the power and the vantage point, from which He can influence all that happens.

Jesus knew, that if you would pause long enough to consider these things when you begin to pray, you would understand the reason why you should ***"pray without ceasing;"*** you would give God the *reverence* due His name. Now you are lifting up your heart from earth and things earthly to another and a higher world. *You* are coming into His presence with combined feelings of love, awe, humility, and adoration, while *He* is looking down on you and on all of His children, observing your needs, your supplies, and your life. He is "at the helm!"

Heaven is a high and exalted place, and you should address your heavenly Father as one who is infinitely above you. Be *amazed* when you pray, that He who is "in heaven," is actually, *your Father!* Pray today in awe of Him.

March 11

"'I have manifested Your name to the men whom You have given Me out of the world. They were Yours, You gave them to Me, and they have kept Your word.'" John 17:6

These Jewish fishermen and businessmen had been chosen by Jesus, even with the knowledge of all their limitations. Christ then taught them by His own life and by His words. To make known the Father's name was to reveal Him, to manifest His character, and to display His perfections. *The Son alone was competent for this task.* Christ had manifested the Father's perfections in His perfect life, in His amazing miracles, and in His sublime teaching. Outward teaching was necessary, for the mystery of the Gospel was only sparingly revealed by former prophets.

It has been said that the greatest possible blessing which even Jesus Christ could bestow upon His people, is to manifest the Father's name to them. In the brief listing Jesus makes here as He prays, He places *first* the fact that He has **"manifested Your name."** Apparently, Christ felt like this manifestation included everything else because all the rest flows *from* it. In other words, if Jesus manifests God to you, every blessing that eternity can supply must follow!

When Jesus prayed, "I have manifested Your name," He was saying to the Father, "I have interpreted and poured light upon the meaning of the prophetic names that You took for Yourself long ago." In the earlier chapters of Genesis, we find four names for God that describe who He is: "God" (in Hebrew, Elohim), "Lord" (or Jehovah), "Almighty" (El Shaddai) and "Most High" (El Elyon). These same four names are constantly repeated in the Psalms for our rest and comfort.

Our families should be to us as a little flock, a little church! When we stand before God, how sweet it will be if we can say concerning our families, "I have manifested Your name, and they have kept Your word." True, some family members are only taught by the clergy. But each one of us who is saved must consistently behave in a Christ-like manner before the people who are often said to be the hardest to reach – our family members.

Pray to be convicted concerning your role in manifesting God's name to your family.

"He went out to the mountain to pray, and continued all night in prayer to God. " Luke 6:12

Jesus never had a house, so He could not go into a room and shut the door as He instructed us to do when we pray. Instead, He made the mountain his private place.

Life is full of "eves," and it was on the eve of the election of the Twelve that we find Jesus praying all night on a mountain. This selection was one of the most important decisions ever made in history! The whole history of the Christian Church begins right here. We may reverently assume that the selection of the men to whom He was to entrust the salvation of the world, was made and confirmed by the Father during this prayer time. *Oh, that today's Church would spend this much time in prayer before selecting its leaders!*

A Greek word found only once in the entire New Testament is found in this verse. The word literally means, "to pass the night in watching." This was a medical term, used to describe the all-night vigil of a medical doctor waiting at the bedside of a patient. Therefore, we see a picture of compassion and of urgency as Jesus prays on this mountain. It was a prayer time wrapped around the intense contemplation of God's presence. It was a time of profound communion between Father and Son.

Samuel Chadwick spoke of the *absence* of this kind of prayer when he described the prayers of today's Church by saying, "There is much phrasing, but little pleading. Prayer has become a soliloquy instead of a passion. The powerlessness of the Church needs no other explanation; to be prayerless is to be both passionless and powerless."

It is humility that brings us to God's grace and power. 2 Chronicles 7:14 says, "If My people who are called by My name will humble themselves, and pray ...". Too often our helplessness is what we do not see, because of blindness that is caused by pride.

Let us humble ourselves!

Ask the Father today for humility, coupled with a spiritual alertness and passion in prayer, such as what we see here in Jesus.

March 13

> *"'I have manifested Your name to the men whom You have given Me out of the world. They were Yours, You gave them to Me, and they have kept Your word.'"* John 17:6

In the Bible, names were often given to reveal something special or unique about that person's nature. The reason Jesus prays, **"I have manifested Your name"** instead of praying, "I have manifested You," is because the "name" is the revelation by which God's divine nature and purpose is brought to us, that we may receive Him into our hearts.

Let us try to understand further the importance of understanding the name. Jesus' priority work toward man was to reveal the nature of God as Father. You may immediately react by saying, "Wait a minute! Jesus' priority work toward man *must* have been, to bring about our *salvation*." And here is the explanation: *Jesus' work was not to reconcile God to the world, but rather to reconcile the world to God!*

How, then, did Jesus Christ persuade sinful men to accept a loving God? He did it by revealing God as Love. It is the *love* of God, revealed in the Cross, that breaks sin-hardened hearts and brings men to repentance. For, **"God demonstrates His own love toward us, in that while we were still sinners, Christ died for us"** (Romans 5:8).

The Old Testament Jew knew his God as "Jehovah," the great "I AM." So Jesus took that sacred name and made it meaningful to His disciples, for example: **"I am the Bread of Life,"** **"I am the Light of the world,"** and **"I am the Good Shepherd."** In this way, Christ revealed the Father's name by showing His disciples that He was *everything* they ever needed.

The devil will lie to you and tell you that Jesus is "something" you need in your life, but not *everything* you need. If the enemy succeeds in persuading you with this lie, you will be a "religious" person, who occasionally displays Christ-like characteristics. You will desire much of what Jesus has to offer, but you will also desire some of what the devil has to offer. If Satan can't "own" you, he will gladly "rent" you from time to time.

Pray for increased faith to believe that Jesus is *everything* you need.

"'Our Father in heaven'" Matthew 6:9

We are reminded of two things about God when we pray the words, *"Our Father in heaven:"* He is *holy*, and He is *powerful. This is comforting to us because while we are occupied in this world, we can petition the One who is not only "above" it, but who is also uncontrolled by it!* When the best skills and strength of a child have come up short, he runs to his father — never doubting that with him, is more skill and sufficient strength. And when we keep God's holiness before us, we find strength to overcome temptation and to resist desires inconsistent with His purposes.

Because our Father is in heaven, we are reminded of His sovereign power. Psalm 115:3 says, *"But our God is in heaven; He does whatever He pleases."* We are reminded of His glory and majesty; *"O Lord my God, You are very great: You are clothed with honor and majesty"* (see Psalm 104:1). And we are reminded of His omniscience, for *"all things are naked and open to the eyes of Him to whom we must give account"* (see Hebrews 4:13).

Childhood has no problem with thinking of heaven as a *locality*. Such things as the throne of God, Jesus at the right hand of the Father, a multitude of angels, and the glorified saints, are easily received by the minds of children. They readily accept God as "high above" — seeing all, and ruling over all. In their mind's eye, children can easily picture Jesus coming again with a cloud. They do not understand heaven to be a "state of mind."

Scripture teaches the *omnipresence* of God, but the word "omnipresence" is inadequate. We do not have a word in our language that, like "eternal" in relation to "time," describes God's infinity above space. But the Bible makes it clear that there is definitely a heavenly sanctuary, a throne of grace, where the Most High dwells.

Join now with the cherubim and seraphim, and cry, "Holy, holy, holy, Lord God of hosts." As a blood-bought member of the Family, pray, "Our Father in heaven."

March 15

"'I have manifested Your name to the men whom You have given Me out of the world. They were Yours, You gave them to Me, and they have kept Your word.'" John 17:6

When Jacob was about to die, he blessed his sons; here, Jesus blesses His disciples only hours before His death. Jesus viewed the disciples as God's gift to Him. The phrase *"the men whom You have given Me"* (or a similar expression) is found twice here in verse 6, and once in verses 9, 11, and 12. Jesus chose them *after* the Father granted them. The disciples had been given to Jesus to receive from Him the knowledge that is eternal life, and the men present that night had kept to the end the divine message that they had heard from Him.

Jesus prays chiefly for these eleven who received His special grace and revelations; the men who in seeing saw, who in hearing heard, and who by divine grace and having been taught of God, came to Christ. Of course, more than the eleven belong to this group of which Jesus speaks; there are the 120 persons mentioned in Acts 1:15, and the more than 500 persons mentioned in 1 Corinthians 15:6. But the eleven are "singled out" from this larger group as the ones *especially* in need of prayer, as they have been sent out into the world as the apostles of Jesus (*"I also have sent them into the world"*).

How *gracious* Jesus is as He speaks to the Father about the eleven! Christ presents them to the Father almost as though they were consistent, faithful and compassionate - when, in truth, these men were a company of needy, weak, failing, unworthy sinners whose knowledge was very dim, whose faith was often very feeble, and whose trust was both earthly and sensual. Yet when Jesus prays for His disciples, He says, *"they have kept Your word."* *Precious Intercessor!*

You have already made the connection, haven't you? We are just as feeble as His disciples. Even those with theological education know very little about the Word of God. The ones of us who have had the most years knowing Him, know Him with only a little intimacy.

Pray a prayer of praise and thanksgiving for your gracious Intercessor.

"He took bread, blessed and broke it." Luke 24:30

The table was set for an evening meal, and the risen Jesus had reclined for dining in the Jewish manner. Reclining with Him were two disciples who had not been present at the Lord's Supper. It is interesting that the Savior did not act as a "guest" at the meal, but as the *host* – taking the bread in His hands and pronouncing the blessing on the food.

Evidently, during the moments when Jesus blessed and distributed the bread, the eyes of the two disciples were opened. This was a supernatural illumination, following a supernatural occurrence in which **"their eyes were restrained"** from recognizing Him (see verse 16).

There are those who believe that the two disciples recognized Jesus at the moment they received the bread because their hands were within inches of the *nail prints.* Some believe the recognition was prompted by the *manner* in which Jesus took and broke the bread. Others believe it was the recognition of His manner of *pronouncing* the prayer of blessing. But when they looked again, **"He vanished from their sight."**

As we see here, although Jesus prayed at Calvary, Calvary was not the end of His prayers. And, praise God, He *still* prays for us continuously! Hebrews 7:25 assures us that **"He always lives to make intercession"** for us. Intercessory prayer is His main occupation in relation to His Church. Jesus' earthly life was devoted to prayer, and His ascension life is devoted to prayer!

It is possible that the prayers of people who sometimes pray for you are "hindered" by reasons that are named in Scripture. But when *Jesus* is praying for you, there is no hindrance at all. You can believe that His prayers for you are unhindered and that they are heard. And so we have two Persons of the Godhead, Jesus and the Holy Spirit, praying for us (see Romans 8:26) – and we have the Father *hearing* their prayers! *It can't get better than that!*

Pray a prayer of thanksgiving for the truth that you have the Father, the Son and the Holy Spirit covering you now in prayer.

March 17

"'I have manifested Your name to the men whom You have given Me out of the world. They were Yours, You gave them to Me, and they have kept Your word.'" John 17:6

The more we understand about the Father's interests in us, the greater our confidence when we go to Him in prayer. If we realize that the Father's heart has been set upon us from the beginning of all things, what assurance will be ours when we approach the throne of grace! The Psalmist declared, **"It is good for me to draw near to God."**

All creatures belong to the Father by creation, but this is not what Jesus means in this prayer. **"They were Yours, You gave them to Me"** means, each of the eleven were given to Jesus as former members of the old covenant. What that covenant promised, they had found in Jesus.

"You are not your own" says God's Word. Who we belong to, is of eternal importance. To reach the point where you realize that you are not your own is a place belonging to the spiritually mature. Do not assume that you (or anyone else) have reached that place, simply based on a *knowledge* of Jesus. *Many believers do not believe that pride is one of their sins, which is exactly what the devil wants them to think!*

Christians have actually come into God's possession; we **are a chosen generation, a royal priesthood, a holy nation, His own special people"** (1 Peter 2:9). We have been "bought at a price," when on Calvary God paid the blood of His own Son. *To be His!* Psalm 73:25, 26 declares, **"Whom have I in heaven but You? And there is none upon earth that I desire besides You. My flesh and my heart fail; but God is the strength of my heart and my portion forever."** Is that the cry of your heart? Before you pray, it will be a blessing to you if you spend time meditating on the thought that *you are actually His!*

But if you do not believe that you are His, or if there is uncertainty, understand that the convicting work of the Holy Spirit has come to you through the words on this page. Make haste! Draw near to God in prayer.

"'Our Father in heaven'" Matthew 6:9

The Model Prayer is found in *two* places in the Bible (Matthew 6:9-13 and Luke 11:2-4), and those two "versions" of the prayer are different. (1) Luke omits the phrases, **"Your will be done on earth as it is in heaven,"** **"As we forgive our debtors,"** and **"But deliver us from the evil one."** (2) Luke uses the phrase, **"Forgive us our sins, for we also forgive everyone who is indebted to us,"** while Matthew's version says, **"Forgive us our debts, as we forgive our debtors."** (3) Luke omits the benediction, **"For Yours is the kingdom and the power and the glory forever. Amen."**

The Word of God does not contain error! The reason that the two versions differ is because Jesus shared the Prayer on *two different occasions*. Matthew gives us the Prayer in its fullness, on the occasion when Jesus was teaching on the subject of prayer. (Although Jesus gave the prayer in Hebrew, it is written in Greek.) Luke, on the other hand, simply gives us the "main points" of the Prayer, when it was given at a subsequent time in our Lord's ministry in response to a request by **"one of His disciples."** Presumably, the disciple who made this request was not present on the earlier occasion. All of that said, having been twice given by our Lord, the Prayer demands careful attention.

The Model Prayer contains "petitions" – most interpreters list six in number, while some name seven petitions by dividing the phrase, **"And do not lead us into temptation, but deliver us from the evil one"** into two separate petitions. Almost everyone agrees that the first three petitions have to do with God and His glory. In true prayer, the Father and His glory claim top priority. *Everything a Christian does* should be for the glory of God (see 1 Corinthians 10:31), and prayer is a Believer's highest exercise. The last three petitions have to do with man and his needs.

These petitions in the Model Prayer are not merely your desires, but His desires *for* you! They are *His* petitions. Pray each of them today.

March 19

"'I have manifested Your name to the men whom You have given Me out of the world. They were Yours, You gave them to Me, and they have kept Your word.'" John 17:6

Jesus regards the apostles as the Father's gift to Him. Christ spent the entire night in prayer before He chose them (see Luke 6:12, 13), with the desire to be in agreement with the Father concerning this all-important selection. He prays now primarily for those disciples, who were "His" since they were the first to believe in Him.

All comes from God and is conveyed to us through Christ by the Spirit. So all God's flock are put into Christ's hands, and Christ leaves them to the care of the Spirit, that they may be enlightened and sanctified. God has given us to Jesus to be subjects of His kingdom. Jesus is Lord of all the world, and He is *"King of the saints"* (Revelation 15:3) to rule as Lord in the Church.

Two important truths about Believers emerge now because we have been given to Christ. First, we are to be students, even scholars, in His school. Jesus is the great prophet and doctor of the Church. Christ came to show God's mind and heart. Hebrews 3:1 says that Jesus is *"the Apostle and High Priest of our confession."* Even though He is Lord of the Church, Jesus is an Apostle who considers it an honor to be a preacher and teacher of the Gospel. Unlike many teachers, Christ teaches the heart rather than the ear. Therefore, the Scripture is our book, but Jesus is our Master – *and we see wondrous things when He opens our spiritual eyes!*

Second, because God gave us to Jesus, we are to be faithful members of His body. Jesus is *"the head of all principality and power"* (Colossians 2:10) for the Church's sake: *"And gave Him to be head over all things to the church"* (Ephesians 1:22). Therefore, knowing these things, we are to walk as *clean* members of His body. *"And you are Christ's, and Christ is God's"* (1 Corinthians 3:23). We are here as His body, for God's glory.

If you are a Christian, you have given up yourself for Him! As you pray, invite the Holy Spirit to convict your heart.

"'Our Father in heaven'" Matthew 6:9

Like children, we start speaking at once about our cares. But when we pray, we would do well to begin by just covering our mouths for a moment! This would provide the opportunity to consider what we are about to do. The essence of true prayer is found in these two words, **"Our Father."** There is a sense in which, just by being able to say from the heart these two words, regardless of our circumstances, our prayer is already answered! Sadly, we lack an acute awareness of the *reality of our relationship* to God.

Turn in your Bible to the ninth chapter of the Book of Daniel. In his prayer that begins at Verse 4, notice that Daniel does not begin immediately with a petition; rather, *he starts by praising God.* **"O Lord, great and awesome God,"** he prays. *This is the manner that people begin their prayers who belong to God, and who know Him intimately – they hallow His name and praise Him before and above anything else!*

The Bible makes a very clear distinction between those who belong to God and those who do not. Jesus makes this distinction in the High Priestly Prayer when He prays, **"I do not pray for the world but for those whom You have given Me, for they are Yours"** (see John 17:9). Only those who are in the Lord Jesus Christ are truly the "children" of God the Father.

When we are born of flesh, we are "the children of wrath," "the children of the devil," "the children of this world." So in order to become "the children of *God,*" we have to be taken out of that realm and translated into another realm. This occurs only by believing on the Lord Jesus Christ when we receive **"the Spirit of adoption."** Not all men care for this doctrine and believe instead that we are *all* the children of God. But when those men pray, they have no real *assurance* that they are speaking to their "Father."

As you prepare to pray, consider the reality of your relationship to our Father.

March 21

"'I have manifested Your name to the men whom You have given Me out of the world. They were Yours, You gave them to Me, and they have kept Your word.'" John 17:6

"**They**," speaking of the disciples, at least held on to the message of the Father, with the one exception of Judas (see John 17:12). Therefore, as Jesus prays, He claims loyalty and fidelity but not perfection in the eleven - for there were occasions when they doubted and wavered.

Notice that Jesus makes no distinction between one disciple and another in His prayer, although some of them were clearly more instructed, more faithful, and closer to Him than others. Instead, He speaks of them as one group that has kept God's word. The disciples did not have much, but what they had, they left behind to follow Jesus. With all their failures and shortcomings, they did trust Him – still, they could not have said of themselves what *He* said so graciously of them: **"They have kept Your word."** Jesus is referring to their faith, without placing emphasis on their failures. *That's how love behaves!*

When **"many of His disciples went back and walked with Him no more,"** Jesus asked the Twelve, **"Do you also want to go away?"** Peter answered, **"Lord, to whom shall we go? You have the words of eternal life."** Keep in mind, Jesus had just told the disciples before this prayer, **"The hour is coming, yes, has now come, that you will be scattered, each to his own, and will leave Me alone."** Still, His plea to the Father is, "They have kept Your word." Christ makes no mention of them forsaking Him. And rejoice, this same Intercessor is pleading for *you* at this moment! Satan is an accuser and speaks evil of us. Jesus is our Advocate and speaks well of us.

Whenever you intercede for someone in prayer, do your best to speak well of him – especially if he has wronged or disappointed you. Speak to God of his good attributes, rather than emphasizing his failures. What you say to *God* about someone reveals your heart toward that person – and more importantly, toward God.

As you pray, speak well of someone to God. Tell the Father how well this person has kept His word.

"When Jesus had spoken these words, He went out with His disciples over the Brook Kidron, where there was a garden." John 18:1

It was a full moon and near midnight. The households were either at Passover feast, or asleep. Jerusalem was still. Jesus now leads the small band of disciples from the upper room, out of the city gate, across the swift, muddy *"Brook Kidron"* and into the small, enclosed grove of olive trees known as "Gethsemane." Eventually, they will reach the stone shelter housing the "oil-press" from which the Garden received its name. (In the later Roman siege, the garden trees that often provided cover over Jesus - as well as the trees for ten or twelve miles around the city - were destroyed, so that mounds could be built around the walls.)

You may recall the occasion when King David passed over this same stream while experiencing extreme sorrow (see 2 Samuel 15:23). Bible interpreters offer various explanations for Jesus' sudden change from calmness at the Paschal feast to His awful struggle at Gethsemane. One interpreter notes that the color of the water in the Brook Kidron would have been red that night because the blood of the lambs that were slain for the Passover drained into a channel that emptied there – providing a startling "visual" reminder to Jesus of His own blood that would soon be shed!

Judas was absent, but the remaining eleven disciples were with the Master. During the walk from the upper room to Gethsemane, Jesus delivered the lessons that are recorded in the fifteenth and sixteenth chapters of John's Gospel. He also stopped and prayed the prayer known as the "High Priestly Prayer" recorded in John 17, which would have been for Him an experience similar to what He felt on the Mount of Transfiguration.

The disciples must have felt strengthened as they saw Jesus lift up His eyes to heaven, and then heard His voice praying for *them* in such a way: *"Keep through Your name those whom You have given Me, that they may be one as We are. Keep them from the evil one. Sanctify them by Your truth."*

And Believer, Jesus is interceding for you right now! Thank Him! Be strengthened! Be encouraged!

March 23

"'I have manifested Your name to the men whom You have given Me out of the world. They were Yours, You gave them to Me, and they have kept Your word.'" John 17:6

Jesus told the Father that the disciples had **"kept"** His word, meaning that they had "guarded," "held to," and "watched over" it. The Greek word actually means, "to give heed to," "to watch narrowly" and "to take care of." In other words, they did not lose the word from their hearts, nor violate it in their lives, nor did they let anyone else tamper with it. They remained loyal to God's earlier revelations in Scripture, by recognizing its completion in the revelation of Jesus.

Today our focus is on this small word, "kept," as it relates to what God has taught us and shown us since our new birth. How easy to read this prayer of Jesus, and to miss this little word and its important meaning! *May the Holy Spirit do His convicting work in our needy hearts right now!* God expects to be believed in what He has revealed to us over the years, and He expects to be obeyed in what He has commanded. Are we guarding His word?

Jesus loves us, and He delights in the *evidence* of our love for Him. He has said, **"If you love Me, keep My commandments"** and **"If anyone loves Me, he will keep My word."** Oh, for grace to keep His word! It is all we really need while we are here below. Today's Church and Christian organizations must come to the realization that obedience to the Lord and to His Word, *remains* the greatest single "strategy" that has ever been discovered for effective kingdom work.

When we keep His Word, we discover that it can keep, enlighten, comfort, strengthen, and establish us. Andrew Murray wrote, "The blessedness and the blessing of God's Word is only to be known by doing it." When we keep His word in our memory as *sacred treasure*, and in our hearts by *believing*, and in our lives through steadfast *obedience* – then, even now, the Lord Jesus can say to the Father on our behalf, "They have kept Your word."

Pray for the grace and power of God to help you *keep* His word.

"Hallowed be Your name" Matthew 6:9

When you pray, regardless of your circumstances at the time, you must never *begin* with yourself and your own wants. This is the teaching of Jesus. Even your concern for the salvation of souls, your concern for God's blessing on the preaching of the Word, or your concern for the needs of others who are dear to you – even these things should not be given the *very first* place when you pray. Instead, you are to remember that you are in the presence of *God!* You are to remember that *He is right there*, looking upon you as your ***"Father."***

The word ***"hallowed"*** means to *sanctify*, to *revere*, or to *make and keep holy*. The Jews in Old Testament times had a marvelous sense of the greatness and the majesty and the holiness of God. Jesus is teaching you to pray that the whole world may come to *know* the Father in this way – that the whole world may come to *honor* God like that! Your Savior had that passion; He was filled with this sense of the glory of God, and His one desire was that all mankind might come to know it.

David wrote, ***"Oh, magnify the Lord with me, and let us exalt His name together"*** (see Psalm 34:3). David did not mean that you can actually add to the greatness of God; that is impossible! He meant that his desire was to see the greatness of God appear to be greater among men. "Hallowed be Your name" means a burning desire that the entire world may bow before God in adoration, reverence, praise, worship, honor, and thanksgiving. Do *you* have that burning desire?

If you want to know God, if you want to be blessed of God, the place to start is by *worshipping* Him. *Before mentioning any concern about yourself when you begin to pray, before getting to your "want list," seek His face before you seek His hand!* Every great person of prayer has learned this lesson from Jesus.

Hallow His name *first* as you pray today. He is worthy of adoration and praise.

March 25

"'I have manifested Your name to the men whom You have given Me out of the world. They were Yours, You gave them to Me, and they have kept Your word.'" John 17:6

*N*othing *is more striking than to see how, in the course of history, the full meaning of Jesus' teaching grows clearer and clearer!* The word is like seed; it grows and continues to grow while producing new branches.

If we listen, we will hear God speaking to us in a variety of ways – in the silence of our hearts as we pray, in the things we hear while gathered with the saints under sound preaching, in a word of wisdom from a Christian friend, to name just a few. But we must do more than simply hear; we read in Luke 11:27, 28, ***"A certain woman from the crowd raised her voice and said to Him, 'Blessed is the womb that bore You, and the breasts which nursed You!' But He said, 'More than that, blessed are those who hear the word of God and keep it!'"*** As Prophet, Jesus spoke to people in such a way that they would see the difference between something "special" and something of *great importance.* That is what God's prophets do.

When will we *value* the word as we ought? To keep His ***"word,"*** among other things, means to read it slowly, mark it, learn it, memorize it, and digest it. To do so is not a painful chore, but rather a delightful blessing. Furthermore, if we are not established in the *keeping* of that "word" today, we have no security against the deceitful doctrines, rationalizations, and lies circulating everywhere. Yet in addition to these hindrances from the "outside," we battle against our own flesh when attempting to keep the word.

Our minds wander too often when we open up God's word to read or when we listen to preaching. We are too often accurately described by these words in Ezekiel: ***"So they come to you as people do, they sit before you as My people, and they hear your words, but they do not do them; for with their mouth they show much love, but their hearts pursue their own gain."***

Pray that you will cherish, obey, and keep the word of God.

"'Now I am no longer in the world, but these are in the world, and I come to You. Holy Father, keep through Your name those who You have given Me, that they may be one as We are.'" John 17:11

What did Jesus mean when He prayed, *"Now I am no longer in the world?"* Surely He did not mean that He was withdrawing His presence forever from the universe. Instead, He meant that He was no longer now in the human world under visible and audible conditions, as before. He was to be taken away from the eyes and ears that had grown so used to Him.

Therefore, no longer would Jesus be sought and seen by friend or foe, on the hillside, and on shore, in temple-court, by the well, morning and night. No longer would His disciples be able to consult Him about each and every incident of need, or to get His personal answer about such things as food for a multitude or about the meaning of a parable. Such bodily presence "in the world" was just about to cease, meaning that the disciples were about to be deprived of His personal care, thus exposing them more to "the world."

Can we imagine how the disciples *felt* when faced with this realization? Would not Satan have bombarded their vulnerable minds with fear and imaginations regarding the thought of dealing with the world and self and the devil without Him at their side? The disciples had enjoyed three years of going in and out with this perfect Companion; would they survive?

In the Acts and in the Epistles, we learn of the light, liberty, and the divine companionship that they continued to enjoy. Evidently, the memories of their own unfaithfulness to Him never "depressed" them to the point of hindrance. The present was lit up by the *triumph* of their redeeming Lord! And they believed these words, *"I will fear no evil; for You are with me."*

Somehow, even with their different personalities and temperaments, they entered upon an existence in which the highest happiness which they had enjoyed alongside the "visible" Jesus *continued.* How did they do so? *Because of the truth of a Risen Savior and a living and indwelling Paraclete!*

Pray that you will have a powerful sense today of His living presence with you.

March 27

"'I have manifested Your name to the men whom You have given Me out of the world. They were Yours, You gave them to Me, and they have kept Your word.'" John 17:6

Let us recognize the sweet way in which Jesus refers to His far-from-perfect disciples. When we speak of a fellow saint, we should imitate Christ rather than Satan, the accuser. We often commend others while making exceptions; we may begin with praise but then finish with a "but," and proceed to blast the good with a little evil at the end. We should be more tender like Jesus, who tells the Father in His prayer, **"they have kept Your word."**

What is involved in "keeping" God's word? First, it involves *knowledge* of the word: **"He who received seed on the good ground is he who hears the word and understands it"** (Matthew 13:23). Second, it involves *embracing the promises* of the Gospel: **"Having heard the word with a noble and good heart, keep it and bear fruit with patience"** (Luke 8:15). Third, keeping God's word involves displaying the fruits of love and obedience: **"He who says, 'I know Him,' and does not keep His commandments, is a liar, and the truth is not in him"** (1 John 2:4). And lastly, it involves constant profession and perseverance: **"My son, hear the instruction of your father, and do not forsake the law of your mother"** (Proverbs 1:8).

If we will keep the word of God, we must *watch over it. In other words, we must feel the force of it in our hearts!* Knowing the word, we must keep it and feel the virtue of it. Also, the word must be "expressed" in our life. There needs to be motion that follows the "notion."

One of the most striking verses in the Bible is 1 Thessalonians 2:13, **"For this reason we also thank God without ceasing, because when you received the word of God which you heard from us, you welcomed it not as the word of men, but as it is in truth, the word of God, which also effectively works in you who believe."** Oh, that we may receive His word *as* His word! That is how to "keep His word."

Pray for God to help you *reverence* His word.

"'Hallowed be Your name.'" Matthew 6:9

How might we take a word like *"hallowed,"* and make it understood today? Exactly what are we asking when we pray, "Hallowed be Your name?" Today's young people might express this petition by saying, "Go God! Set the record straight! Get up close and personal with those who ignore You! Show Yourself and Your glory! Demonstrate how *awesome* You are! Make Yourself famous!"

A Christian is a person who wants the whole world to see how supreme and loving and good God really is! More than anything, a Believer wants to love God and to see Him loved by everyone. The Christian wants *his own life and words* to proclaim who God really is. He seeks to glorify God's name (instead of seeking honor for himself) and wants His name to be sanctified and set apart.

Jesus is not teaching us to praise or adore God by using these particular words, but rather to "petition" Him – to ask Him to *do* something that will *result in* His name being hallowed. The word "hallowed" means to "set apart" or to "sanctify." To ask God to hallow His name, then, means to strongly desire for men to revere and esteem His name to be far above ordinary. It is something that *must be done!* Therefore, Christ taught His disciples to start their prayers by *worshipping* God. We are to **"Give to the Lord the glory due His name"** (see Psalm 96:8).

God's name should never be "profaned," which means to desecrate or degrade. When you pollute God's name, you cross over the line that separates the holy from the unholy. Usually, such profanity comes forth out of the mouths of unbelieving men. But there is a blasphemy of the sanctuary that is *even more* tragic, whenever professing Christians gather to worship, preach, or sing with unclean hearts!

You must remember that "behind" this and the following five petitions, is God Himself – so God will certainly do what you are asking Him to do in this prayer! So prize, honor, reverence, adore as divine, yes, *hallow* His name, as you begin to pray.

March 29

*"'Now they have known that all things which You have
given Me are from You. '"* John 17:7

"Now,*"* at this time, Jesus can make this statement about the disciples. Previously, their knowledge was incomplete; *"For they had
not understood about the loaves, because their heart was hardened"* (Mark 6:52), and, *"Why do you reason because you have no
bread? Do you not yet perceive nor understand? Is your heart
still hardened? Having eyes, do you not see? And having ears, do
you not hear? And do you not remember?"* (Mark 8:17, 18)

But "now," in His intercession to His Father, Jesus mentions neither
their previous hardness of heart nor their lack of understanding. He says
nothing of their weak faith, their slender knowledge, their shallowness, or
their faint hearts. It is clear from this sentence in Jesus' prayer that our
Lord sees far more in His Believers than they see in themselves, or than
others see in them. Although weak, the disciples loved and believed their
Master when thousands refused Him. So Christ places a garment over
their nakedness.

We are reminded of the parable of the lost son, and of his older brother's reaction to the celebration over his return. Our merciful Father is ready
to see us at our best, while too often we are busy disrobing our brother of
his robe of honor. May we be so gracious to fellow believers who, despite
the limitations of their understanding, are beginning to grasp the fundamental truths of Christianity. It is this kind of thing that distinguishes the
saint from the world, and that demonstrates the compassion of Christ.

Do you get frustrated easily when someone in your Bible study group
or someone among your Christian friends reveals their lack of understanding about the things of God? Like the older brother of the lost son in the
parable, our feelings can get in the way of our realizing the bigger picture.
Instead of noticing what God is doing, too often we focus on disappointments and failures. *Jesus was demonstrating the fact that love always makes room
for growth!*

Pray that you will be patient, encouraging, and kind toward someone
you know who lacks maturity in the faith.

"Then an angel appeared to Him from heaven, strengthening Him." Luke 22:43

The writer of Hebrews was almost certainly referring to Jesus praying at Gethsemane, when he says Christ *"offered up prayers and supplications with vehement cries and tears"* (see Hebrews 5:7). Clearly these prayers of Gethsemane were not "normal" prayers but were literal beggings and pitiful pleadings.

Interestingly, the four Gospel writers say nothing about the "tears" of Jesus, as their accounts are brief. We cannot believe that the writer of Hebrews merely pictured the scene at Gethsemane and "imagined" that there must have been tears. One or more of the three disciples must have reported that tears were shed, and then the fact was preserved orally.

In the midst of Jesus' agonizing prayer, suddenly, like a meteor from the midnight sky, there flashes before Him a bright spirit that came straight from the throne of God to answer His prayer and to minister to Him! What did the angel say; what did he do? Maybe the angel whispered words of encouragement. Perhaps the angel reverently bowed before the Lord. It is possible the angel spoke words of sympathy to Jesus since the disciples had failed to do so. We do not know the answers to these questions.

It is worthwhile for us to pass through rough places – *very* rough places – to have angels to bear us up. An angel appeared to Joseph when Herod was seeking Jesus' life. Angels ministered to Christ after the devil tempted Him in the wilderness. Here at Gethsemane, when Satan was loose during the hour of the powers of darkness, an angel of war came from heaven to strengthen Jesus. *Our God is able!*

We are at war for the souls of men. Will you think at this moment of someone for whom you care, who has not trusted Jesus for salvation? That person has sorrow at times, but without comfort that completely satisfies. He has the cup of agony but without the angel. He has the painful experiences of life, without consolation from the messengers of heaven.

Pray now for the Holy Spirit to bring that person under conviction today. Pray for his salvation.

March 31

"'Now they have known that all things which You have given Me are from You. '" John 17:7

J esus told a group of Jews in the temple one day, *"If anyone wills to do His will, he shall know concerning the doctrine, whether it is from God or whether I speak on My own authority"* (John 7:17). *"Now we are sure,"* the disciples had recently told Jesus, *"that You know all things, and have no need that anyone should question You. By this we believe that You came forth from God"* (John 16:30).

Jesus here tells the Father, *"Now they have known,"* or have come to understand by the grace of God, the significance of a glorious phenomenon! The disciple's knowledge came sometimes supernaturally, and also from experience, as they began to comprehend that Jesus' teaching *actually worked.* But the term Jesus uses here in His prayer is emphatic, and includes everything in and about Jesus that would have enlightened the disciples. The eleven believed in Jesus from the start, but the longer they were in contact with Him, the more they arrived at the realization that *everything about Him* was from the Father.

If you would glorify God, you must live neither according to your own will nor for your own interest. If you would glorify God, you must study and obey the Scriptures. *And if you would glorify God, you must do as these disciples, and learn of Jesus Christ!* From the first day that you ever heard the name, "Jesus," until today, you have been learning about Him. Your knowledge may have been gained through a Christian family member, a compassionate pastor, a dedicated Sunday School teacher, a close friend, a gifted author, or through your own Bible reading.

My friend in Christ, can Jesus tell the Father yet concerning you, "Now he has known that all things which You have given Me are from You?" Given the number of years you have spent with Jesus, are you truly "abiding" in Him? Do you recognize readily when something that is said or done has come forth from God?

Pray that your thirst and desire to know and to obey His Word will be *strong* today.

"'Hallowed be Your name.'" Matthew 6:9

Did you know that there is an "order of precedence" – a *priority* – which we should observe when we pray? *The very first (and maybe the most important) lesson Jesus taught us in giving us the Model Prayer is, "first things first!"* Christ knew that our prayers would tend to be focused first on our own wants and desires, so here the Master makes it clear that the acceptable order of prayer is "God first."

Today, we are approaching an important subject – the matter of *how to* "hallow" God's name. We should say from the start, that if we suppose that by abstaining from the vulgar and wicked practice of *swearing* we have **"hallowed"** God's name, we are much mistaken. And what is the use of bowing at the name in church, if we go home to be selfish and unkind, or to the office to be hard and unfair, or into society to be gossips and busybodies? For "hallowing, God's name" means honoring the *character* of God, as that character has been made known to us in Jesus Christ.

Here are three do-able, practical ways by which you can hallow God's **"name."** First, you can *trust* Him. Fear, suspicion, distrust – such things are an insult to fatherhood! Men who, in spite of the Cross, think that God can be unkind, are insulting His love. As a child of your heavenly Father, you cannot hallow His name better than to practice a quiet, simple trustfulness.

Second, you can *obey* Him. God was weary of the outward marks of respect that the Jews paid Him because those outward marks of reverence were accompanied by gross disobedience. Jesus hallowed His Father's name by being about His Father's business, and by obeying Him always. Make it your meat and drink to do His will and to finish His work.

Finally, you can *represent* Him. Refuse to "believe" in anything or to "practice" anything that contradicts His love. Show men the true picture of God; represent Him *accurately!* Cherish beautiful, gracious thoughts of God in your mind.

Pray for strength today, to hallow His name.

April 2

"'For I have given to them the words which You have given Me; and they have received them, and have known surely that I came forth from You; and they have believed that You sent Me.'" John 17:8

Every time Jesus spoke, every word was divine. In the utterances of Jesus, the people of His day and the disciples were listening to God's voice. Of course, His listeners did not always understand what they were hearing.

In John 8:43 we read where Jesus said to some Jews, ***"Why do you not understand my speech? Because you are not able to listen to My word."*** Jesus appeared as a "foreigner" to the Jews, so far were they from receiving Him. No matter how much truth Jesus presented to them, they were "not able to hear" a bit of it. Jesus may as well talk to deaf men. They did not "recognize" the language of God.

The disciples eventually came to realize that they were hearing the very voice of God when Jesus spoke in their presence! By grace, the disciples entered into that of which the world was completely ignorant, namely, that the Father was the Source of all that was given to the Son. There were some who "wondered" at His words and works, and others who were ***"astonished"*** at His understanding, even at the age of twelve. There were others who even attributed His words to Satan. But the disciples learned not only that Jesus had come out from the Father, but also that ***"the words"*** were of the Father.

Therefore, all of Jesus' words, revelations, warnings, and promises – like Christ Himself – came from the eternal Father. And the question for our consideration today is this: if these were the days, the unique and remarkable days when Jesus was walking about the earth – would we be among those who "missed" the words, or among those who "received" them? Would we be among those who heard the very voice of God when Jesus spoke? Of this we can be certain: One day we will hear the sound of Jesus' voice, but on *that* day, there will be no question as to who is speaking!

Today, God desires that you recognize His voice. He is with you now, and He speaks truth and comfort. Welcome His voice in prayer.

> *"'O My Father, if it is possible, let this cup pass from Me.'"*
> Matthew 26:39

If Jesus had died while He was in Gethsemane, then we would have no saving Gospel! The Gospel is that Christ died for our sins *"according to the Scriptures,"* and that He was buried, and that He rose again the third day *"according to the Scriptures"* (see 1 Corinthians 15:3, 4).

That means (to name only a few examples) Jesus *must* have His beard plucked out (Isaiah 50:6), He *must* be beaten with many stripes (Isaiah 53:5), they *must* pierce His hands and His feet (Psalm 22:16), and the mocking of the chief priests and the people *must* be fulfilled (Psalm 22:7, 8). If Jesus did not die literally "according to the Scriptures," then He could not be our Savior. Were it not for an angel from heaven (see Luke 22:43) *"strengthening Him,"* Jesus would surely have died in the Garden that night.

The words, *"if it be possible,"* mean, "if it be possible within the Father's purpose of redeeming the world." There was no question in Jesus' mind of the Father's "ability" to cause the cup to pass from Him. It was all about the Father's *will*, as Luke writes it, *"Father, if it is Your will."*

"Let this cup pass from Me" means, "do not put this horrible cup to my lips." The "cup" was a common image for great suffering. This is the human will of Jesus speaking. Jesus died under sin and its curse, the sting of death *torturing* Him with all its power! It was the cup of *the wrath of God against sin* from which He shrank. The fact that Jesus asked if there was any other way to accomplish the same result was no disappointment; the fact that He fully accepted the Father's manner, crowns Him Christ the King!

God will not always take the cup of suffering from us. For our own good or for the good of others, it may be necessary for us to suffer in order to accomplish His purposes. Pray that you will be "willing" to drink from this cup, in order to accomplish His will for you.

April 4

"When He rose up from prayer, and had come to His disciples, He found them sleeping from sorrow." Luke 22:45

This terrible agony over, as a result of prayer, Jesus proceeds to take the necessary steps toward Calvary. He returns to the disciples and finds them asleep. Great sorrow and continued heaviness of soul had brought an inner dullness of mind to the disciples, resulting in the physical reaction of sleep. The disciples were already stirred up from listening to Jesus speak sad words at the Last Supper, and they were not indifferent but rather very much aware that sorrowful hours were still ahead.

Their sleep in Gethsemane was also the result, however, of the influence of Satan. Their sorrow, in its heaviness, kept them off their guard and presented the enemy with easy opportunity. Jesus had warned them that the devil was on the prowl. But they failed to watch and pray as instructed, which led to numerous subsequent failures to overcome temptation. Satan saw their vulnerability and wasted no time. Still, the Master showed compassion and explained to them that their spirits were willing, even though their flesh was weak.

All of that said, we must hold *ourselves* accountable when we commit such sin as did the disciples. The sin they committed was the failure to obey the Lord's plea to watch with Him at a time when His soul was exceedingly sorrowful, out of sheer love for Him and out of the great confidence and trust He had placed in them. And we know that, throughout our lives, we have committed the same sin numerous times when Christ has plainly asked us to keep His commandments.

"He found them sleeping." Like the disciples, we have been taught to know Him, we have grown to love Him, we have been taught to believe in Him, and we have trusted Him for our very salvation. *Yet we still need to break our slumber and be aroused to prayer!* We make excuses and sleep when we ought to watch and pray – as Christ's Church is suffering, His cause is suffering, His people are suffering.

Pray today that you will awaken to, and then obey, what He is asking of you.

"'Nevertheless not My will, but Yours, be done.'" Luke 22:42

Man's *"will"* is not only a reflection of the divine image within him, but it is also the essential expression of his real self. When God made man in His own image, His desire was not to make a machine. Instead, He gave man the divine gift of free will, so that man would be able to choose God for himself. Therefore, "will" was given to man so that man would *freely* give it back to God.

If we should search for the root of sin, however, we would find it in the preference of our own will to the will of God. Sin is the result of men unwilling to be what God created them to be, and unwilling to do what He desires them to do. When we give in to temptation, we say, "*My* will, not Yours, be done."

The moment Jesus prayed this one word, *"Nevertheless,"* He wasn't thinking of one single act; He was submitting to an *entire course* of actions that were to follow. Jesus was praying, "Let it all come! May Your will keep on being done!" This is absolute submission to the Father: when we learn to continuously say under serious discouragement, exhausting pain, deep disappointment, or heavy loss – "Father, do with me as Your wisdom and love direct."

That is the spirit in which we are to pray. We are to lay all our wants before our Father, and by faith, remember the lessons of Gethsemane. Let your only desire be what you are certain God desires, and cheerfully reject whatever you are certain your Father in heaven rejects. *There is nothing too small in life for practicing oneness with the will of God!*

Are you abiding in the Son as He is revealed in Gethsemane? The will implies a struggle – a deliberate setting before us two courses, and a choice of one. Are you choosing God or that which is opposed to God? Every action of our lives needs to be put to that test. Pray that you will both know and choose to obey the will of God today.

April 6

"And He began to be troubled and deeply distressed." Mark 14:33

You may want to have some tissue paper nearby.

The most expressive words in the English language do not come near describing anything about the life of the Lord Jesus Christ. This verse probably illustrates that fact better than any other in the Bible. Literally translated, Mark tells us that Jesus began to be *sore amazed.* Luther said that, to him, these words of Mark about our Lord were the most astonishing words in the entire Bible. The difficulty for us is that, at Gethsemane, we are invited to look at Jesus' human soul, and it is more than we can see or imagine.

Consider all of the theories about what could have "amazed" the Son of God and only one explanation satisfies us: it was *sin!* Sin is so unspeakably evil that, even for Jesus at this moment, it sore amazed Him. You will remember that He had previously seen sin making angels of heaven into devils of hell. Throughout His ministry, He had studied and seen the manifestations of ugliness and wickedness from the heart of man. But *this* was a new thing: to have all of that wickedness poured in *upon Himself.* To be "made sin" amazed, absolutely overwhelmed, our Lord.

To look at pure sin – to conceive of "the sinfulness of sin" – our eyes have to be sufficiently anointed and our hearts continually broken! To look at "pure" sin, you, too, will need an angel from heaven to strengthen you. Honestly, this matter of pure sin has not cost any of us even an hour's sleep.

Yes, we can identify with Paul who wrote, **"For the good that I will to do, I do not do; but the evil I will not to do, that I practice."** Paul probably understood the seriousness of sin better than any of us. But even Paul did not experience this sore amazement over sin that Jesus felt in the Garden. Even though we "wrestle," we do not truly *hate* sin, because we do not understand the seriousness of it.

Pray to be *sore amazed* over your favorite sins, and repent.

"'For I have given to them the words which You have given Me; and they have received them, and have known surely that I came forth from You; and they have believed that You sent Me.'" John 17:8

Alll three Persons of the Trinity take part in these *"words"* Jesus mentions here: the Father *gives* them, the Son *executes* them, and the Holy Ghost *reveals, applies and communicates them.* Christ is telling the Father that now the apostles *"received"* the words. Later they *preached* them and *wrote* them. And the same Holy Spirit that revealed the words to them reveals them to *us* and keeps them in our hearts.

Next to God Himself, there is nothing greater, nor more precious than the Word - which, by the Spirit, reveals God and His Son our Savior. Therefore, the steps of *communication* of the word are as follows: from the Father to the Son, from the Son (through the Holy Spirit) to the apostles, and from the apostles (as inspired by the Holy Spirit) to ourselves. These are words of promise, words of power, words of salvation; they are spirit, and they are life.

May we hide "the words" in our hearts for His name's sake who gave them to us! Listen to the words, yes! Talk about them, yes! Profess the words, yes! But until the words which the Father gave to Christ, and which Christ has given to us, are *received* by us - that we *believe* on Him whom God has sent - we have never profited.

Romans 10:17 says, **"So then faith comes by hearing, and hearing by the word of God."** The word is God's *instrument:* **"For I am not ashamed of the gospel of Christ, for it is the power of God to salvation for everyone who believes."** All the angels in heaven, if they joined all their forces together, could not convert one soul to God. The power is of God, but it is wonderfully joined to the Word. Jesus delights, then, in telling God that the disciples have received the words that originated with the Father.

You may have purchased this book out of a desire to draw closer to God day by day.

But you must still *believe* on Him whom God has sent. Please, settle the matter regarding eternity *today.*

April 8

"'Hallowed be Your name.'"   Matthew 6:9

This first petition of the Model Prayer, "Hallowed be Your name," is the priority request. Every other request must not only be of lesser importance to this one but be in harmony with and in pursuance of it. None of our prayers are "right," unless the honor of God is dominant in our hearts. Even such important petitions as the prosperity of His Church or the spreading of the Gospel must be subordinated to the hallowing of His great and wonderful name!

His *"name"* signifies God as He is *revealed* – in the Scriptures, in our lives, in His various titles, in His attributes, and most supremely, in Jesus. He makes Himself known so that we may honor Him in all situations and circumstances. However low we may feel, we are to glorify the Father. This was demonstrated so perfectly by Jesus when He said, *"Now my soul is troubled, and what shall I say? 'Father, save me from this hour?' But for this purpose I came to this hour. 'Father, glorify Your name'"* (see John 12:27, 28).

You have an immense responsibility because you bear His name! James 2:7 makes reference to *"that noble name by which you are called."* If you do not dishonor it, people may come to Him for what they see of Him in you.

What are some ways you might hallow God's name today? First, *by the thoughts of your heart.* *"Unite my heart to fear Your name. I will praise You, O Lord my God, with all my heart, and I will glorify Your name forevermore"* (see Psalm 86:11, 12). A second way you can hallow God's name today is *by the words that you speak.* *"O Lord, open my lips, and my mouth shall show forth Your praise"* (see Psalm 51:15). And you can hallow God's name today *by the work of your hands.* *"Therefore, whether you eat or drink, or whatever you do, do all to the glory of God"* (see 1 Corinthians 10:31).

Pray that you will recognize and use the opportunities the Father gives you today to hallow His name.

"'Watch and pray, lest you enter into temptation.'" Matthew 26:41

Eight disciples were stationed like sentinels at the Garden gate at Gethsemane while Jesus prayed. Their task, most likely, was to watch lest Jesus be caught by surprise by those who were going to handle and arrest Him. Further inside the Garden, it was to Peter, James, and John that Jesus spoke these words. But these three men were instructed to **"watch"** for a different reason.

Peter, James, and John were placed in position to watch the actions and hear the words of Jesus while He prayed. In addition, it was hoped that these three disciples might encourage or express sympathy to the Master in His time of severe agony. But what was the **"temptation"** Jesus was concerned might come to the three disciples?

Jesus knew that His Passion and all that went with it was going to bring deep sorrow to the disciples. The devil would tempt them to sin, resulting in further multiplication of their sorrow. If they became withdrawn in their gloom, if they were to neglect communion with Christ, they would become vulnerable to the enemy's attack. Satan would accuse the disciples of "hypocrisy" in the midst of their despair.

The three disciples were to watch Jesus closely while He agonized in prayer. You and I need to do the same. We need to enter the Garden with Him, and then move right up to the Cross and "watch." Abide with Him there as the Holy Spirit brings the Scriptures alive. *We must not turn our heads the other way, no matter how uncomfortable we become by the sight!*

If you have not done so already, *now* is the time to trust Him. He will save you! The sin burden that was on your shoulder when you began reading this devotion can all be gone! Look now at Him in the Garden, look now at Him on the old, Rugged Cross, look now at Him on the Throne! He is alive! He is risen! Trust Him completely for your salvation!

Watch and pray today. Think about Jesus in Gethsemane and at Calvary. Be there for Him.

April 10

"'O My Father, if it is possible, let this cup pass from Me.'"
Matthew 26:39

The *"cup"* is a mystery about an infinite sorrow that we cannot understand. It refers here to the bitter agony of Jesus' Passion and approaching death, although a variety of other explanations exist from authors we
respect. This cup refers to the Cross and to all the anguish that would be
involved with it, both physical and spiritual. The thought of being made
sin on behalf of all of *us* had to be horrible!

A cup is a natural metaphor for a personal portion of sorrow. All sorrow, all suffering, even if it includes agony, is a "cup." It is an exposure, at
varying levels, to Satan's limited but existing power. *For Jesus, the cup included
rejection – one of Satan's most powerful weapons still to this day!* Our Lord experienced rejection at different points throughout His earthly life, and He is
still rejected by men today - but the *intensity* of rejection He experienced
from men during the period between Gethsemane and the Cross, was like
no other.

You are familiar with these words of Paul recorded in Galatians 5:17,
**"For the flesh lusts against the Spirit, and the Spirit against the
flesh; and these are contrary to one another."** That statement comes
as close as any to describing the agony *we* experience as His disciples, the
struggle *we* face daily whenever we share in **"the fellowship of His sufferings."** As for the *depth* of pain, and shame, and tears, and blood – that
has to be hid away with Jesus among the wine presses and the crosses. We
cannot describe what we do not know.

If you evaluate your spiritual life as it is today, are you wrestling against
flesh and blood, or have you come to your own Garden where you wrestle
**"against principalities, against powers, against the rulers of the
darkness of this age, against spiritual hosts of wickedness in
the heavenly places?"** Wrestling of this kind requires the use of every
ounce of energy available.

Pray now concerning the level of your *willingness* to drink of His cup,
and to share in the fellowship of His sufferings.

"'Watch and pray, lest you enter into temptation. The spirit indeed is willing, but the flesh is weak.'" Matthew 26:41

It is important to understand what Jesus was referring to when He used the words, *"spirit"* and *"flesh"* in this statement. Regeneration has produced "the spirit" in all true disciples. This is the new divine life that is open to God and to Christ and is therefore ready to respond to their promises and directives. The spirit is what we often refer to as the "heart" or "will" that is illuminated by the grace of God.

But the Christian still has in himself "the flesh," which refers not to the fleshly body but rather to the old sinful nature that still clings to us after conversion. It is our fallen state with all of its affections and lusts, so far as they still remain, even in the regenerate. *The flesh opposes the spirit (see Galatians 5:17) and would delight in regaining complete control of the personality!*

By sleeping and by giving way to sleep-producing sorrow, the three disciples closest to Jesus in Gethsemane were yielding to the flesh. The flesh in us *"is weak,"* completely helpless under temptation, and a constant handicap to the working of the spirit in us which *"is willing"* to endure and to overcome the temptation.

Unfortunately, followers of Christ sometimes yield to the temptation to use this very statement by Jesus, not as a loving "warning," but as an excuse to proceed in sin! The devil may introduce thoughts at the moment of temptation such as, "Go ahead and sin! You cannot resist this; you're too weak!" Or he may tempt us to have good "intentions" without a desire to carry those intentions out. Yet even in our weakness, divine purposes in the spiritual world can be fulfilled.

Is it the spirit or the flesh that most often inspires your behavior when you are tempted to sin? Amidst the weakness of your flesh, is your spirit *really* willing? Is it possible that your weaknesses and faults are left to abide in you, that you may learn the perfection of hating what God hates?

Pray for your spirit to gain ground over your weak flesh today.

April 12

"And being in agony, He prayed more earnestly. Then His sweat became like great drops of blood falling down to the ground." Luke 22:44

The root meaning of this word *"agony"* comes from the struggle, conflict, and pain when taking part in an athletic contest. The "contest" here was indeed spiritual warfare. At this moment Satan is pressing Christ harder than ever before, but *Jesus prayed hardest when it was hardest to pray.*

It is quite possible that the disciples saw the evidence of bloodstained skin when Jesus returned to them. Luke's medical language testifies to how the intensity of this struggle caused such a physical reaction, as to make the sweat of Jesus become bloody. We know that severe mental distress and strain drive out sweat from the human body to the point that, when tiny blood vessels of the skin are ruptured, blood mingles with sweat. This mixture of blood and sweat thickened the globules, resulting in it *"falling down to the ground"* as clots or as *"great drops."*

While we may draw parallels to the agonizing of athletes or to the pain experienced by heroes and martyrs, what we reverently consider now as we observe Jesus in the torment of Gethsemane has no equal. The torture of His Spirit, the agony of His soul, the anguish of His mind, the intensity felt in His body, the burden of His heart – all of this was so terrible, that every vein and blood vessel swelled to the bursting point!

It is one thing to cry, "Lord, teach us to pray." But it is quite another thing to be willing to learn, much less practice, *this* type of prayer! *How powerfully this type of prayer rebukes our own cold and heartless ritual!* We make our speeches to God, repeat meaningless phrases, and then hurry on to the next activity. My dear friend, do you react proudly and negatively to these written words, arguing that this type of agonizing prayer is unrealistic and unnecessary?

May the convicting work of the Holy Spirit come upon you right now, to reveal the "distance" between your prayer life and the prayer life of Jesus. Pray now for a new and sincere willingness to learn and practice *agonizing* prayer.

"And He began to be troubled and deeply distressed ... He went a little farther, and fell on the ground, and prayed." Mark 14:33, 35

At Gethsemane, the Savior now begins to be *visibly* sorrowful, the fulfillment of the Isaiah 53:3 prophecy that He was **"a Man of sorrows and acquainted with grief."** The *inward* beginning came to Jesus earlier, but He had concealed His anguish until only these three could observe it. The vivid sense of what it all meant came upon Him at this time in a manner that was surely disturbing for the disciples to watch. Jesus had not previously shown *this* level of anguish to the crowds or to those closest to Him.

As He walked with them beyond earshot of the other eight disciples, Peter, James, and John saw Jesus' strong agitation before He even began to speak. Being faithful to the end was costly, even for Jesus. Mark uses two strong verbs in his description of the Lord; the first verb is translated, "to be completely upset by distress," and the translation for the second verb is, "to be filled with uneasiness and dread" – even "amazement!"

Many explanations for why Jesus was experiencing this level of anguish in the Garden have been offered over the years, some difficult to believe such as the fear of pain, regret over His decision to go forward, the realization that death was near, a nervous breakdown or a period of self-pity. It is possible that a previous temptation – to set up a kingdom that would not involve the Cross – may have been revisited by Satan (see Matthew 4:8-9).

So here is the Savior of the world, crushed and beaten down. The blackness of the deep has been let loose, the horrors of hell grip His soul, and the most vicious wolves of the pit are upon Him. *Yet one resource remains, and it is the most supreme of all: He braces Himself by prayer to His Father!*

Consider reverently this picture of perfect communion between Jesus and His Father. The Son is telling His Father everything, even about the shrinking of His own soul – but concluding with this all-important desire: **"Nevertheless, not what I will, but what You will."** Make that your prayer.

April 14

"'For I have given to them the words which You have given Me; and they have received them, and have known surely that I came forth from You; and they have believed that You sent Me.'" John 17:8

The High Priestly prayer of Jesus names seven things that God had given Him as Mediator. In verse 2, three of these are listed: a *people* given to Him, *eternal life* to bestow upon that people, and *power over all flesh*. Verse 4 mentions that He has been given a *work* to do (to do the Father's will and to die), and verse 6 mentions that *the Father's name* has been given to Him. Our verse for today, verse 8, mentions **"the words"** that have been given Him, and verse 22 mentions the *glory* that has been given Him.

Those seven things make up no easy load! Praise be to God that He gave them to *Jesus*, who would take care of them, and make no mistake about the use of them. Many others spurned the gift of the words, but the disciples accepted and appropriated in their hearts the words. In doing so, they received spiritual knowledge, discernment, and understanding – all fruits of "receiving" God's words.

A "carnal" Christian enjoys God's grace and His promises but is not as happy about His commands and His conditions. In fact, he labels the latter as "pushy" or "narrow-minded." But the same God who requires that we love Him with all our hearts, also requires that we *believe* in Him with all our hearts, by receiving the entirety of His word. There is not only a believing with the mind but also a believing with the heart. Paul wrote, **"For with the heart one believes."**

We often speak of Bible verses that contain important truths that are easily overlooked or "passed over." In the portion of Jesus' prayer provided in this eighth verse, there is such a truth easily missed. *Consider this: the very foundation of the Church of Jesus Christ was laid, because Jesus gave the disciples the words the Father provided, and then the disciples* **"received"** *those words because they believed that Jesus came from God!*

Pray a prayer of thanksgiving for the "process" that took place (and *continues* to take place!) by which we learn the truth we need.

"'Hallowed be Your name.'" Matthew 6:9

The Model Prayer has also been called, "The Missionary Prayer," and for good reason. The Prayer was obviously designed for missionaries like the disciples. The opening petitions of the Model Prayer deal with advancing the cause of God, and should, therefore, be on the heart of all disciples of Jesus. So to men who were missionaries, He gave a missionary prayer.

The word "hallowed" is clearly not a "household word" today and might prompt thoughts of mournful music or of ancient sanctuaries. "Hallowed" comes from the Greek word *"hagios,"* which is also the word for "holy." Jesus is teaching us to pray with a desire for God's name to be holy on earth as it is holy in heaven. *We are to put God on the throne of our lives on earth, as He sits upon His throne in heaven!* Hallowing His name means giving Him the honor He deserves and desiring to lift up His Person and His attributes.

One explanation of what **"Hallowed be Your name"** means, is to think and to speak well of Him from the heart and to praise Him with sincerity. When this takes place, the more practical things such as glorifying God in life and representing Him as holy to the world will follow. The desire of the person praying this prayer, then, is that the whole world may come to know as holy, **"Our Father in heaven."**

When you pray, "Hallowed be Your name," your missionary heart goes out in pity to those who do not know God and who are ignorant of Him. You are praying with the desire for **"the Lord of the harvest to send out laborers into His harvest;"** you are praying realizing that *you* are an answer to your own request, so that wherever you may go, His name may be seen in you and on you, "known and read of all men."

Pray this petition from the Model Prayer. It will help you realize how meaningful the Father is to you. Allow this particular request to lift you to a new level of reverence for God.

April 16

"'Simon, Simon! Indeed, Satan has asked for you, that he may sift you as wheat. But I have prayed for you.'" Luke 22:31, 32

"**B**ut I" changed everything! The One mighty to save, stronger than the strong, had changed the circumstances by His intervention. The One with perfect knowledge and perfect love had entered the picture. Those who were in need were now wiser and stronger because He was personally involved. Get your Bible and circle those two words, "But I." *Those two little words make all the difference!* Those words placed Jesus' action in direct contrast to the devil's action. And so it was on that Easter morning recorded in Acts 13:29, 30, *"Now when they had fulfilled all that was written concerning Him, they took Him down from the tree and laid Him in a tomb. But God raised Him from the dead."*

Satan was granted opportunity to sift the disciples, but Jesus knew that the devil would gain only a temporary victory. Why? Because He had prayed, and His prayer would hold Peter. On this occasion, Jesus modeled "intercessory" prayer – when we pray for a third party with reference to a definite, spiritual need. He prayed for Peter specifically. We can be certain that He did not casually pray, "Father, be with Peter" in the manner we often pray for someone. True intercession is serious business; your unhurried, sincere prayer for someone today can result in his being changed for *eternity!*

Jesus regards us with tender interest. He monitors the advances of the enemy toward us. He follows the choices we are making. When He sees us wander from the way of wisdom, He is grieved. When He sees us take the upward path, He rejoices in us and over us.

One of God's names is "Jehovah-Jireh," which means, "the Lord will provide." He will meet the needs of your heart. He will meet the needs of your life. He will come to your rescue at just the right moment. He wants you to stop looking at your circumstances, and to start looking *only to Him.* "Only trust Him."

Pray today that when you feel helpless or overwhelmed by your circumstances, you will think of Jesus who says to *you*, "But I."

> *"'For I have given to them the words which You have given Me; and they have received them, and have known surely that I came forth from You; and they have believed that You sent Me.'"* John 17:8

Jesus says that the disciples have **"known surely"** that He came from the Father. This certainty on their part came primarily through receiving His words, and they are now persuaded that Jesus' origin and mission are both divine.

The term "Incarnation" is of Latin origin, and means "becoming-in-flesh." It is not a biblical word, but it does convey a biblical truth – that Jesus, who had His being eternally within the unity of the Godhead, became man at a point in time, without relinquishing His oneness with God. Jesus testified to the Incarnation in a conversation with some Jews recorded in John 8:58. He said, **"Before Abraham was, I AM."** The Jews took the statement to mean blasphemy.

When the Bible says, **"The Word became flesh,"** it means that God Himself took on the form of a man. Before He ever became "Jesus of Nazareth," Christ was the Son of God, existing from all eternity. Because our Lord Jesus Christ lived before He came into this world, He could not be born in the ordinary way. It is recorded in Matthew 1:23 and in Luke 1:27, that Jesus was born of a virgin.

It is important to believe that Jesus came out from God and that God sent Him. If we were to somehow lose faith in the Incarnation, the rest of Christianity would be of little value. 1 John 4:3 says, **"Every spirit that does not confess that Jesus Christ has come in the flesh is not of God. And this is the spirit of the Antichrist, which you have heard was coming, and is now already in the world."** The doctrine of our Lord's Incarnation is expressed throughout the New Testament.

"Who can this be" exclaimed the disciples with fear and overpowering awe, after Jesus rebuked the wind and the sea from a boat. *Almighty power was being revealed!* The disciples were not "afraid" of Jesus, but certainly wondered to themselves, "Who but God can make the raging wind and sea obey words?"

As you pray, pray *in awe* of the Father, the Son, and the Holy Spirit.

April 18

If you have a personal and saving relationship with Jesus, then the way that you "hallow His name" is to admit and confess (with trembling and praise) that your life is a bond of indebtedness that has been *canceled* in His name. So that now, ***"Hallowed be Your name"*** means that you *believe* that the bond has been canceled and that you *believe* that Jesus has paid the debt in full. Now, you *believe* that you are *His* child in *His* name. You "hallow His name" when you allow Jesus to be your *Lord!*

What a realization, this! You are back home again, back from the far country – and look! *The light from your Father's house is flooding out to meet you!* Now, nothing depends on your own outer efforts or inner progress, and everything depends on your desire to honor God and to let Him work in your life where He is put *first* - above all men and above all things. You have not become a new creation by *deciding* to become one; you have become a new creation through the fellowship and communion that you now have with the Father through Jesus His Son. If you could see Jesus as He is, you would be more like Him!

"Hallowed be Your name" is the *fundamental* petition, and therefore the first petition of the Model Prayer. When you contemplate the glory manifested in your redemption and your adoption in Jesus, and when you rejoice in the hope of His inheritance – how *natural* it is that you exclaim, "Hallowed be Your name!" The ultimate object of Jesus' life and death was to show you the Father and to declare His name (see John 17:6).

Luther once said that a Christian is a man who runs out of a dark house into the sunshine. Now, you know why that dark old house where you once lived was so *dark!* Because now, you know the Light. Focus your prayer time today on this – that God may become *holy* to you, and that He may occupy the *ruling place* in your life.

"'I pray for them. I do not pray for the world but for those whom You have given Me, for they are Yours.'" John 17:9

❝ **I**, on my part, make request concerning them" is the literal translation, as Jesus prays specifically for His disciples. We see here His great personal interest in these men. *"I,"* the Son of God, intercede for them! And, hallelujah! We have the same Son of God interceding for us, for it is written, *"It is Christ who died, and furthermore is also risen, who is even at the right hand of God, who also makes intercession for us"* and *"Seeing then that we have a great High Priest who has passed through the heavens, Jesus the Son of God."*

Since the Father always answers the prayers of His Son (*"And I know that You always hear Me"*), His "current" intercessory ministry helps to keep us safe and secure. *Oftentimes we forget that Jesus is praying for us!* Unexpectedly, at any given moment, comes this very recognizable awareness to the Believer that we are experiencing a supernatural refreshing. Someone, somewhere, is praying for us! We *know* it. We *feel* it. Could it be a friend? Perhaps, but it may also be *the* Friend interceding for us!

"I pray *for* them." Let's pause for just a moment, and consider what else Jesus has done "for" us. Jesus came to earth *for* us, He lived *for* us, He died *for* us, He rose *for* us, He ascended *for* us, He prepares a place *for* us, He has sent down the Holy Spirit *for* us, and He will come again *for* us – just to name a few things! *"Satan has asked for you ... but I have prayed"* *for* you," said Jesus to Peter. On how many occasions during your lifetime do you imagine the Intercessor may have prayed *for you* at such a time - and you were completely unaware?

To be blessed to have one or more Christian friends who faithfully intercede for you is a tremendous privilege. Perhaps you are so fortunate that your name appears on someone's "prayer list." But what a blessing to know that *Jesus* is praying for you, *continuously!*

Thank Jesus for His faithful intercession for you.

April 20

"'Hallowed be Your name.'" Matthew 6:9

Only God can teach us His *"name."* To "hallow" the name of God is to look to Jesus. It is a fact that all of our sins and our shortcomings arise from our forgetting some aspect of Jesus Christ our Lord. *If we could only see Jesus as He is, the name of God would be hallowed in us - and we would adore Him!*

We dishonor God's name when we engage in unholy conversation, unholy thinking, and unholy living. God's name is dishonored when men speak irreverently of Him as if He were like one of them (see Psalm 50:21). Men swear using the name of God and dishonor it by taking His name in vain. We dishonor God's name when we ignore the study of His Word. *Entire nations* dishonor His name when they make sinful decisions!

How will *you* hallow God's name? You hallow the name of God by *rejoicing in it.* Psalm 43:4 calls God *"my exceeding joy."* If you rejoice in anything else – yourself, your faith, your feelings, your works, even your prayers – your rejoicing will fluctuate. You hallow the name of God by *worshipping His complete character* (not just the attributes that you *prefer!*) – which means His justice along with His mercy, His holiness along with His goodness, and His commandments along with His promises.

You hallow the name of God when you, yourself, *manifest His heart* – by reflecting His image, demonstrating His will, and resembling His character. You hallow God's name when you *give Him high honor* and *consider His name sacred.* When you *obey* God, you hallow His name. When His name suffers in any way or is dishonored, and you *grieve* over that; when you *stand up for His truths,* you hallow His name. When you *witness to,* and when you *pray for those who are lost,* you hallow God's name.

To hallow God's name is to *trust in it* and to *love it.* The reason God's name is no more hallowed is because His name is no more loved. Ask Him for strength to hallow His name with your *life.*

> *"Coming out, He went to the Mount of Olives, as He was accustomed, and His disciples also followed Him. When He came to the place..."*
> Luke 22:39, 40

For Jesus to have already known the beauty of heaven, and then to have been attracted to a particular place of tranquility on earth, says something about the peaceful location on the Mount of Olives called Gethsemane. John writes that it was a garden across the Cedron (Kidron) valley from Jerusalem. Still today, just the mention of the name "Gethsemane," brings a sense of awe and adoration to every Believer who considers all that Jesus experienced there.

A small, enclosed property about three-fourths of a mile from the eastern walls of Jerusalem, the garden called Gethsemane probably contained a variety of olive trees, vegetables, and flowering shrubs. The only structures on the property would have been what were needed to take care of the olives – maybe a small building for tools and an oil-press. Jesus used this place because it was a quiet and secluded retreat setting.

It is a blessed minister (and Believer) who has a special **"place"** *where he can enjoy times of intimacy with the Father!* There are those who prefer the seaside or the mountains. For some, it may be a favorite swing or chair. Others may use a study or library in the house. While it is true that we can approach the Father through prayer wherever we may be, a retreat setting can provide a refreshing change of pace.

Bible scholars believe that a friend of Jesus, someone who gave Him permission to go there whenever He desired, may have owned the property at Gethsemane; some suggest Mark's father. This would be one explanation for His repeat visits there with the disciples. Generous people who bless us in such a way are often overlooked and go unnoticed. Sometimes they prefer it that way, believing that it is enough that the Father sees their gift.

Someone owned the ass for His triumphal entry on Palm Sunday, the upper room in the city for the Passover, and this Garden where He often went to pray. As you spend time in prayer today, ask the Father what He wants *you* to provide for the man of God.

April 22

The *"name"* of God is His revealed character. It is *"hallowed"* whenever His holiness manifests and when we regard it as the holy thing that it is. The *spread* of that knowledge and reverence is the way by which His kingdom comes. The name, the kingdom, and the will are *His*.

We are living in a day when lighthearted, even flippant direct and indirect references to God are common. Even Christians forget that God's name stands for His nature, and is a reference to *God Himself* – in all His attributes and holiness. Dr. G. Campbell Morgan once said, "I am more afraid of the blasphemy of the sanctuary than the blasphemy of the street." God's name should never be profaned, desecrated, or degraded. When we do so, we cross the threshold from the holy to the unholy.

The pious Jew had such reverence for the name of Jehovah that he never pronounced it! It lost its vowel points by lack of use, so that even today, Hebrew scholars differ as to how God's name ought to be pronounced.

Jesus taught right thoughts of God; everything else follows from that, for to know God is eternal life. Jesus called God, *"Righteous* Father," *"Holy* Father." There can be no increase of holiness given to God or to His name; God's name is *already* holy, in that it is separate from every other name. God and His revelation are what they are, irrespective of us. *Jesus taught us to pray that the name of God may be treated as holy – in our lives, in the Church, and in the world!*

If your behavior does not bring honor to God, so as to attract others to Him, you have missed the target. God's name should be hallowed *in* you and should be regarded as holy *in* your thoughts and words. Does your *behavior* esteem, prize, honor, reverence, and adore His name? And what about your *choices?*

As you pray, let this first petition of the Model Prayer be a commitment to total allegiance to the Father, to the Son, and to the Holy Spirit.

> *"'I pray for them. I do not pray for the world but for those whom You have given Me, for they are Yours.'"* John 17:9

"I *pray for them,"* and *"We have an Advocate with the Father,"* are words we should be thankful for every day. Romans 8:26 says, *"The Spirit also helps in our weaknesses. For we do not know what we should pray for as we ought, but the Spirit Himself makes intercession for us with groanings that cannot be uttered."* And those groans will result in joy.

Since prayers of intercession are continuously taking place in heaven, we should be encouraged to pray continuously for one another here on earth. Intercessory prayer is a spiritual act of love. "I love my pastor" we hear people say, yet they confess they spend very little time praying for their pastor. *"Brethren, pray for us"* pleaded Paul affectionately to the Thessalonians. Ministers and those who regularly share the mysteries of salvation and grace are in *desperate* need of our faithful prayers!

Your church staff, your deacons, and elders, your lay leadership, the missionaries and ministers you have sent out – should all be prayed for daily. Pray that they will be clean, holy, humble servants. Pray that they will each spend significant time daily in prayer and in God's Word. Pray for their families. *God's rule in your church will be accomplished best through leadership that listens to and relies on Him!*

The local church is under relentless attack from the enemy because of its significant role in the establishment of God's kingdom on earth. Yet even with all of its faults, the Church still has the potential and capability to do more for the kingdom of God than any other institution or organization. Let us intercede for one another!

What is the point of being apprenticed to a painter, but to learn to paint? And what is the purpose of being joined to the Intercessor if we do not learn to intercede? You may not feel the need to pray, but Jesus Christ within you does! Jesus is the only One who can take you from where you are in your prayer life, to where you need to be.

Pray fervently for your dear pastor.

April 24

"'Hallowed be Your name.'" Matthew 6:9

The *"name"* of God is important because it is a revelation of His character. There is a long list of names for God, too many to provide here. What you need to know is that every name applied to God *means* something; each name tells you something special about Him.

There are a variety of ways in which God *reveals* His name to you. He reveals His name to you *in Nature.* **"The heavens declare the glory of God; and the firmament shows His handiwork"** (see Psalm 19:1). You can see God's mark on the sky and the sea, on mountain and flower. You can see His name when you look at lightning and when you hear thunder, and when you gaze at the lilies of the field and at the birds of the air.

More plainly than in Nature, God's name has been revealed to you *in the Bible and in Jesus.* The greatest discovery that ever happens is not when you are told of a new invention of man or of a new planet in the universe. *The greatest discoveries that you ever experience are when the Holy Spirit reveals more of God to you through His Word and through Jesus the Christ!* Perhaps there are people in your family who resemble one another in "physical appearance," yet there are still striking differences among them as "individual personalities." But between God the Father and Jesus Christ the Son, there are no differences.

Underneath the surface, this first petition of the Model Prayer is a prayer of repentance – a confession of sin! Your behavior, from time to time, shows that you have other gods and that you want to be the master of your own life. Luther said, "I know of no teaching in all the Scriptures that so mightily diminishes and destroys our life as does this petition." The truth is, you cannot pray the Model Prayer to the glory of God without praying it against yourself.

Therefore, when you pray today, pray humbly, "Father, I confess that Your name plays a miserably small part in my life."

"'I pray for them. I do not pray for the world but for those whom You have given Me, for they are Yours.'" John 17:9

The biggest difficulty we face with intercession is ourselves. Until we are willing and eager to learn to intercede for others, we resemble the Pharisees. This is true because our duty is not to ourselves or to others, but to Jesus. We take *ourselves* so seriously in prayer that we cannot even see God – and therefore we "dictate" to God, instead.

Jesus is praying here for His disciples. If you feel led by the Spirit of God to begin praying for others through faithful, systematic intercession, here are some suggestions that may help you. Begin all prayer by remembering to whom you are speaking (see Matthew 6:9), with thanksgiving. Take into consideration His many attributes, and the evidences of His faithfulness. Repent from any known sin in your heart.

Transition to thanking God for this particular person for whom you are praying. You should not pray for anyone with a spirit of negative criticism. Instead, thank God for their potential, for their good qualities, for the work He is already doing in their life, and then ask for God's will to be accomplished in their life.

Now you are ready to ask the Father for your concern for this person to increase to the level of a burden. *We bring too many superficial, half-hearted requests to God in prayer!* Ask the Father to open wide this person's heart to receive His wisdom and understanding. Speak against any satanic power or influence that the Holy Spirit reveals may be affecting this person's life.

Next, you may want to connect a Bible verse or Bible promise to this person's life or circumstances, based on your awareness. Plead the truth of those Holy words over the person, and thank God for His intervention before you see Him move in answer to your prayer. Do not become discouraged, but persevere in intercession – particularly when it appears there is little or no change. Faithful, intercessory prayer is *hard work*, but it is *God's work*. He is likely accomplishing far more than you realize.

Pray right now with a burden for someone needing the Master's touch.

April 26

"And when He had sent the multitudes away, He went up on the mountain by Himself to pray." Matthew 14:23

In the previous verse, Matthew's use of the words **"made His disciples get into the boat,"** implies that the disciples may have been unwilling to leave Jesus' side. Jesus was unable to confide right now in the disciples whom He trusted most because their comprehension was not much deeper than that of the crowd. It was best, then, that the disciples also be dismissed, lest they be tempted to agree with the multitudes that wanted to make Him their king. *Ambition can be an evil thing, especially when it is related to leadership in the Church!*

Although in just a few hours the faith of Peter would be tested upon the water, the disciples did have more *faith* in Jesus than the multitude. The crowd had little if any devotion to the *person* of Jesus. Instead, they were fascinated mainly by His amazing miracles. Jesus recognized their motives and emotions, declaring, **"Most assuredly, I say to you, you seek Me, not because you saw the signs, but because you ate of the loaves and were filled."** (A careful study of the teachings of Jesus reveals that He often called attention to the "motives" of people's hearts.)

We who follow Him today too often make this same mistake, do we not? We seek His "hand" to change our circumstances or to provide for temporal needs when our more desperate need is to seek His "face," that we may *know Him more intimately*. We are often fascinated with how He answers our personal and corporate prayers, or with what we see Him "doing" - when we need to be more focused on gaining a spiritual and clear knowledge and understanding of *who He is*.

Pray that you will gain a deeper understanding of the Father beyond what is "obvious" to everyone, an understanding received from your intimate relationship with the Vine. Pray that you will seek Him and love Him and understand Him - not because of what He does – but because of who He is. Consider His marvelous attributes; seek His *face* as you pray today, and not just His hand.

> *"'I pray for them. I do not pray for the world but for those whom You have given Me, for they are Yours.'"* John 17:9

Prayer would be amazing enough if it was limited to intimate communication between man and God. Just the knowledge that it is "actually possible" to converse with the One who put the stars in place is difficult to grasp. But in this prayer of Jesus, we are reminded of another privilege of prayer - intercession. Intercessory prayer introduces a "third party" to holy communication.

Jesus interceded for His disciples during this part of His prayer, saying, **"I pray for them."** Whenever we pray on behalf of others, we take part in an activity that closely identifies us with Jesus Christ. Intercession is what Jesus *does* (see Romans 8:34). The Bible says that Jesus is **"at the right hand of God,"** interceding for the saints continuously.

Psalm 16:11 declares that it is a *pleasure* to be at God's "right hand." When we engage in intercessory prayer for others, we have the pleasure of joining Jesus at God's right hand. What is taking place in the throne room where we join Him? Life-changing, world-changing activity! The destruction of the works of Satan! Non-stop worship!

Sometimes Christians say, "I wish I knew something I could do for God that would actually make a *difference.*" They lack a basic understanding of intercessory prayer! The work of an intercessor is a privilege of the highest level because *it places us right there with Jesus* in His work of furthering God's kingdom, and of reconciling all of humanity to the Father. *That's making a difference!*

Paul explains how this can happen; **"God ... made us alive together with Christ ... and raised us up together, and made us sit together in the heavenly places in Christ Jesus"** (see Ephesians 2:4-6). Therefore God has "transported" us to a higher place of divine activity – the invisible, heavenly arena – where powerful intercession occurs.

Yet, there is "work" involved when we compassionately and sacrificially intercede for others. With the pleasures and privileges come the responsibilities to be available, to be attentive, to persevere, and to discern.

Ask the Father to reveal to you the *value* He places on intercessory prayer.

April 28

Which is worse: a man who does not pray, or a man who does not pray aright? The habit of our minds is to be so constantly focused on "our own good," that to learn how to pray *rightly* requires massive adjustment. But in reality, God's glory and our own good are so connected that we cannot desire the one without (at least indirectly) desiring the other.

The Christ has come, and has tenderly shown us how we have totally misunderstood God! *Jesus* is who *God* is - expressed in terms of human thought and speech. In Jesus, we get the full and final revelation of God's character. When Philip said to Jesus, **"Lord, show us the Father,"** Jesus replied, **"He who has seen Me has seen the Father"** (see John 14:8, 9). Jesus showed us, that while we are busy forgetting God, He is busy compassionately thinking of each of us personally. Amazingly, God would have us know Him by the name, **"Our Father."**

Jesus wants us to know that when God's **"name"** is **"hallowed"** – when His name is *declared* to all, *believed* by all, and *kept sacred* by all – the best things will be brought about in our nation and in other nations. When men learn to look devoutly to Jesus the Christ as the "image of God," then there will be saving health among all nations. If only all men had one common knowledge of God and were true worshippers of the true God, how amazing would be our world!

Pray today that all nations may come and worship before Him and may glorify His name. Because there can be no rest for the human mind, no peace for the human heart until they know that "name."

As for yourself, let these words also be a portion of your prayer: "Remove all my ignorance of You, remove all my unworthy thoughts of You, remove all in my heart that opposes or exalts itself above You, remove all my rebellious distrust of You – that my trust in You may increase, and that I may serve You in love."

"'I pray for them. I do not pray for the world but for those whom You have given Me, for they are Yours.'" John 17:9

The verb translated here as ***"pray for"*** means to "request" in Biblical Greek, or more specifically, "I make request." We should look carefully at the following words, ***"I do not pray for the world"*** to understand what Jesus meant, and what He did not mean. These words definitely do not mean that the Lord Jesus *never* "requests" on behalf of the world; only that He was not doing so at this particular moment of His prayer. At this moment He is praying for the Eleven who have been the companions of His ministry.

We can be confident that Jesus had not "forgotten" the world, even for a second. The world was on His heart, for He was in union with the God who ***"so loved the world."*** From the Cross, Jesus prayed for His crucifiers. Later in this very prayer, Christ prays for the world. Christ died for sinners, prayed for sinners, and still intercedes for sinners.

So these words Jesus prayed, "I pray for them. I do not pray for the world" meant, "In order that I may reach the world, I must pray first for *those through whom* I am going to reach the world." If these "instruments," multiplied as they will be over time, are to bring belief and knowledge to the world concerning the truth about God, then they must be one. They must be *far different* from the world, and therefore they are in much need of prayer.

Jesus said to Pilate, ***"For this cause I was born, and for this cause I have come into the world, that I should bear witness to the truth."*** Pilate replied, ***"What is truth?"*** We live in a world that is *still* in search of truth. *The present need to spread the truths of God throughout the world before lies about Him are believed, is urgent!* Perhaps we underestimate the importance to the world that, as Christians, we *actually know* the truth about life!

Pray for each person that you are aware of, who is part of the effort to share the truth about God throughout the world.

April 30

"And when He had sent the multitudes away, He went up on the mountain by Himself to pray." Matthew 14:23

We are not told what Jesus prayed about on this occasion, but we can name some possibilities. He may have expressed thanksgiving and praise for the victory over temptation when the crowd wanted to make Him king, or for the miracle that the Father had just enabled Him to perform. Perhaps He was in need of sympathy from the Father over a disappointing experience when the crowds were wild with enthusiasm, and when His own disciples were not seeing the full picture of why He came to earth.

One thing is for sure: the Master spent quite a long time that night on the mountain. Verse 25 tells us that Jesus walked on the sea to join the disciples *"in the fourth watch of the night."* The first watch is from 6pm to 9pm, the second from 9pm to midnight, the third from midnight to 3am, and the fourth from 3am to 6am. Therefore, this prayer time began *"when evening came"* and lasted until some point the next morning between 3am and 6am. - roughly nine hours. The exact translation does not confirm that Jesus spent that entire time "in the act" of praying, but only that prayer was His *reason* for going up on the mountain.

Knowing the exact number of minutes He spent in prayer here is, of course, not of great importance. Instead, we should observe that Jesus was fervent in prayer and that He needed to pray. *Jesus needed to pray!* Jesus Christ did not pray because He had sinned; He was sinless, and *still* needed to pray!

Tragically, it seems easy for us to overlook the place and the importance of prayer in Jesus' life. Recognizing the fact that He prayed *continuously* throughout His amazing ministry is not as "exciting" to us as reading that He performed miracles or cast out demons. The devil has managed to reduce our awareness that fervent, prevailing prayer is something we *must* make time for, or we perish.

Jesus allowed plenty of time for prayer because it was *essential*. May you see that same necessity when you pray today.

"And all Mine are Yours, and Yours are Mine,
and I am glorified in them."" John 17:10

The Father has **"given"** the disciples to Jesus, but not to dismiss them or to send them away; Jesus prays for the Eleven because they "belong" to the Father, and therefore are of particular *value*. We focus today on the relevance of the possessive pronouns found in verse ten: **"And all Mine are Yours, and Yours are Mine."**

Observe that the use of these possessive pronouns shows that God values His people above everything. There is nothing God lacks; the silver and gold are His, plus the cattle on a thousand hills. Yet these are no comparison with those who belong to Him. Observe that these words appear in private conversation between the Father and the Son. It is what people talk about in private, which lays bare their heart.

We do not have any notion of how much God loves us! Dear Brother, Dear Sister, you do not know *how much!* How great are our *privileges* because of this love! Because He places such value on us, our position changes from being a stranger standing far off, to drawing near and touching His kingly scepter. Because He demonstrates such love toward us, we once dared not lift up our guilty eyes but can now gaze upon our Father and Friend.

Before we belonged to Him, we hid our lips in trembling shame, but now we may open our mouths in petition and praise. Before we became His, a gaping hell and eternal anguish was below us waiting, but now hell's gates are barred to us by the precious blood of Jesus. Before we became His children, the horrors of darkness were before us, but now it is an eternity of glory that we see, now and ahead.

Yes, before we were His, everything external called for our condemnation, but in Him, these things minister to our comfort and are enjoyed with thanksgiving! Oh, how these four possessive pronouns, "Mine, Yours, Yours, Mine," speak volumes of blessing to our hearts today! Praise be to God for His **"indescribable gift"** of Jesus!

Pray a prayer of praise that you are *His*.

May 2

In the Model Prayer, the words *"in heaven"* are included when addressing *"Our Father"* so that there may be nothing "earthly" in our conception of Him. The word "heaven" should not be understood as the *only* place to where God is confined; His Spirit cannot be localized. We find these words in the Book of Jeremiah: *"'Do I not fill heaven and earth?' says the Lord."* We may conceive of a particular region where God is especially manifested, but we will miss the purpose of these words if we think only in terms of locality.

His works we see, but He is not His works. Between Him and ourselves, there are personal relations. We are His creatures, He is our Creator; we are His children, He is our Father; we are on earth, He is in heaven. *However distant the heavens, we are at the very threshold!* Our littleness always touches the infinite that reaches beyond the stars.

There are some Believers who have difficulty approaching God with *boldness* in prayer. But may we not *"come boldly to the throne of grace"* when He who sits there is our *Father?* It is with confidence that a loving child tells everything to a loving Father. We should never doubt the love that prompts, the power that executes, or the wisdom that directs.

Yet there are Believers who struggle with a relationship to God involving *intimacy* in prayer. When we are unable to put what we feel into words, and can only say, "Father!" we cry out a word that He will always hear. On the refrigerator in many homes are the *imperfectly* colored drawings made and given by the children and grandchildren. Are those pictures not precious to the parent's heart? In the same way, our Heavenly Father cherishes our gifts of intimate prayer.

Are life's storms approaching or already upon you at this time? Amid the roaring of the winds and the thunder – as well as when there is perfect calm – He is saying, "My child," and you can respond by saying, "Our Father." Be intimate with Him in prayer.

**"*And all Mine are Yours, and Yours are Mine,
and I am glorified in them.*"** John 17:10

When Jesus prayed the words, **"*All Mine,*"** the literal meaning is, "All things that are Mine," referring to everything that Jesus in any way has as His own. Examples would include souls, powers, words, and works. Although the word "all" is not included with reference to what is the Father's also belonging to the Son, it is certainly intended. Put simply, the interests of the Father and of the Son could not be separated. What belonged to the one belonged to the other.

What a place for us to occupy – think of it - to be the "subjects" of this mutual affection of the Father and of the Son! Keeping our salvation secure is the will of God, and Jesus always prays in perfect harmony with the will of the Father. As our High Priest, Jesus serves as the "anchor" of our souls, who forever keeps us from drifting away from God. As Believers, our relationship with Christ anchors us to God.

If you do not know *with certainty* that you are saved for eternity, you are likely to wonder if you are saved at all. The question for you becomes, "How long will my salvation last if it can be lost?" You may even have some genuine doubts about God's love, His mercy, and His ability to forgive. But on this we agree: either the Good News of eternal salvation is true, or it is a flawed provision that requires the continuous, futile, and desperate efforts of man to make things right.

John wrote these words, recorded in 1 John 5:13, **"*These things I have written to you who believe in the name of the Son of God, that you may know that you have eternal life.*"** Do you have that blessed assurance of eternal security today? Your security rests in the hands of a loving Heavenly Father who gave His only begotten Son to ensure your fellowship with Him *forever.* Understanding and accepting this provision gives you the assurance that your salvation is eternally secure.

Pray that you will recognize and reject Satan's lies regarding your eternal salvation.

May 4

"And when He had sent the multitudes away, He went up on the mountain by Himself to pray." Matthew 14:23

With the approach of the Passover, the moon would be almost full, providing opportunities for Jesus to watch the disciples in the boat. Mark says *"He saw them"* from the mountain, straining at rowing. Perhaps the Holy Spirit prompted Jesus to pause His time with the Father long enough to physically see the difficulty the disciples were experiencing. It is also possible that Jesus was not engaged in prayer at that very moment, for the Word does not indicate that He prayed the entire time He was on the mountain.

It may be that our Lord was praying with His eyes open, something many of us do on different occasions. Regardless of how and why Jesus saw the disciples struggling, He saw them in their danger and came to them. The Savior's compassion had to be noticed and appreciated by the disciples, who may well have been the subject of much of His praying on the mountain. Clearly, nothing was going to prevent Jesus from bringing these men the help they so desperately needed.

What a wonderful lesson we learn through a careful examination of this occasion! *How encouraging this is for us, knowing that Jesus is, at this very moment, with the Father as He was on that mountain – now watching us so closely, should we enter into difficulty!* And we are also encouraged today by the promise we find in Hebrews 7:25 that tells us, *"He always lives to make intercession"* for us.

Even though you may be doing *exactly* what God has told you to do, like the disciples in the boat, you may experience trouble. Do not worry; this is not the end of the story! Will you pray right now, "Thank you, Jesus, for your watchful eye."

"Whenever I am tempted, whenever clouds arise,
When songs give place to sighing, when hope within me dies,
I draw the closer to Him, from care He sets me free;
His eye is on the sparrow, and I know He watches me;
His eye is on the sparrow, and I know He watches me."
– Civilla D. Martin

May 5

"When He came to the place, He said to them, 'Pray that you may not enter into temptation.'" Luke 22:40

While we are in intimate communion with the Father, we do not yield to temptation! The word translated *"pray"* here refers to the full meaning of the word, which includes the experience of *worship*. Putting God at the center of attention, we take the focus of our minds off of satisfying fleshly desires. These are important truths to remember.

What was the particular temptation Jesus was concerned about enough to call the three disciples to prayer in Gethsemane? It was *not* the temptation to try and escape the ordeal of the coming hours. It was rather the temptation during the ordeal *to fall in their faithfulness to Jesus*, as Peter nearly did.

He has such compassion for us when we are tempted! The disciples, like us, were still learning about the dynamics of spiritual warfare. They knew there was a devil, and they had even successfully cast out some of his demons in other people. But there was still much to learn about when and how the enemy might strike *them*. Satan often strikes at our vulnerable places. Jesus knew that the disciples were particularly vulnerable to a fierce attack on this night, and so He called them to *prayer*.

Now look a few more verses further down at Luke 22:53. Said Jesus to the chief priests, captains of the temple, and the elders who had come to Him, **"This is your hour, and the power of darkness"** literally, "the authority of the darkness." Here, as always, the truth of Jesus' words sheds light on darkness. Other forces are operating here besides merely the human cunning of the traitor and his accomplices. Those who arrested Christ were the tools and agents of the devil, whom God *permitted* to operate.

And here is a lesson for us: The ordeals of life can become temptations if we listen to the devilish voice that says God has abandoned us, or that it is useless to cling to Jesus. Therefore, pray today "that you may not enter into temptation" to fall in your faithfulness to Jesus - in whatever circumstances you may be facing.

May 6

"**B**less US," bless OUR work," "bless MY family," "bless OUR plans," or "bless MY ministry," we often pray. We pray about OUR agenda. We pray about our friends, our own personal needs, and our circumstances. Thankfully, there are mission organizations that at least prompt us to pray for missionaries on their birthdays. Jesus teaches us to *first* pray for the advance of God's kingdom. Therefore, there is no petition more suitable to the Scriptures than *"Your kingdom come."* In the Model Prayer, Jesus shows us a more excellent way to pray. *We must learn to pray by making our petitions demonstrate our Heavenly Father's purposes!*

After all, God is "King!" David said, *"You are my King, O God"* (see Psalm 44:4). He declared, *"The earth is the Lord's, and all its fullness"* and, *"Who is this King of glory? The Lord of hosts, He is the King of glory. Selah"* (see Psalm 24:1, 10). It is to *"Our Father in heaven"* that this petition concerning the "kingdom" is addressed. Yet Christians *live* under the King who rules His kingdom. The kingdom of God is also *within* us; therefore, it does not alter or change our personal "circumstances" – *it changes us!*

People who at least "acknowledge" the name of God, who believe that He "is" what He has revealed Himself to be, expect that one day there will be a better order of things in the world than what we are now seeing. No true Believer can be satisfied with a kingdom (although temporary) that is operated by Satan.

The hallowing of God's name is closely related to the coming of His kingdom. This involves the victory of God over all His enemies. The "first fruits" of this final victory are already ours through the Holy Spirit. In the meantime, we wait for that glorious manifestation and pray, *"Even so, come, Lord Jesus!"* (see Revelation 22:20).

Are you obeying the command of Jesus, to *"seek first the kingdom of God and His righteousness"* (see Matthew 6:33)? May this particular command apply now to your *praying* as well as to your living.

> **"And all Mine are Yours, and Yours are Mine,**
> **and I am glorified in them.'"** John 17:10

Jesus said something powerful and extremely important in this prayer, when He prayed, **"And I am glorified in them,"** referring to His disciples and also to us. To be sure, the faith, ministry, and lives of the Eleven glorified Jesus. Our Lord was glorified in the disciples both because of their belief and because of what their belief was going to mean in the extension of God's kingdom.

But to confine these words as meant *only* for the Eleven, would be to ascribe to Christ but a very limited glory. Simply put, "glory" is the display of the fullness of God. We who believe on the Lord Jesus must grasp the meaning of these words as they relate to *our* lives. *Just think of it – Jesus glorified in us!*

Christ is not glorified by "what He *gets from us,*" but rather He is glorified through "what He *bestows upon us.*" We are the empty vessels into which Jesus pours *grace.* In time, having filled us with grace, He will fill us with glory too, and this results in His being glorified "in us." Our part, therefore, is to *abide* in Him (see John 15:1-17). Abiding in Him requires that we do not go beyond Him for such things as comfort, guidance, hope, peace, and forgiveness of sin.

Let's be encouraged as we consider just a few of the many things Jesus was asking the Father for, as He prayed so earnestly for His disciples then and now. Christ desires for all the blessings His disciples can contain, for all the fullness of God, for all the happiness the Holy Spirit can provide, for all the strength and love and righteousness that is possible - which a person in union with Him can possess.

We should be further encouraged that bringing glory to Jesus includes our welcoming His watchcare in our weakness, His comfort in our sorrow, His direction through our difficulties, and His union with us in His love - which provides the unity of the Spirit.

Pray a prayer of thanksgiving that your life can actually bring Jesus *glory*.

May 8

Jesus was in perfect accord and harmony with the Father, and so it was not surprising that He would look up to heaven before He healed this man. The man was *"deaf and had an impediment in his speech,"* so Jesus made certain that this man who could not understand words, *noticed* when He looked heavenward. By this action, the Master was indicating to the man that what was about to happen was from *heaven*, and was not merely a "human act."

A number of Bible interpreters believe that Jesus' look toward heaven, combined with His sigh, constituted a prayer. The deafness of this man was a sample of the miseries that fill the world due to sin. A man of profound compassion, Jesus was touched by this person's condition. It may be that the Savior's sigh was a moment of reflection during which He thought of the bliss of a place He left - in order to seek and to save the lost. Therefore, this healing may have signified the coming of God's kingdom. Any or all of these feelings may have moved Jesus to prayer.

"He sighed" – perhaps mindful that the miraculous healing that was about to take place would expose this man to new temptations to sin, for in a moment the man would be able to *hear* evil things and *speak* evil words. Yes, the devil would once again try to rob someone's joy following a work of God in his life.

The fact that prayer and spiritual warfare are strongly connected is illustrated here. The deep sigh of Jesus demonstrated the Savior's awareness that this man's illness involved a struggle against evil. This struggle is confirmed by Jesus' use of the Aramaic word *"Ephphatha,"* which means, "be opened." It was not simply about the opening of a man's ears and the loosening of his tongue. *This miracle was about the spiritual battle in which a whole person was opened up and set free with relation to God's kingly rule!*

Pray a prayer of thanksgiving that when you trusted Christ for salvation, Jesus said: *"be opened!"*

"Then an angel appeared to Him from heaven, strengthening Him." Luke 22:43

At the beginning of His ministry, angels visited Jesus *at the close of* the three temptations in the wilderness (see Matthew 4:11). In Gethsemane, *"an angel"* visited Him *during* the devil's temptation. It was night, yet one or more of the three disciples that had been selected as special witnesses to His agony, clearly saw the angel come to Jesus. We are most grateful for the record of that observation. Gethsemane's angel was a visible, miraculous answer to Jesus' prayers at the very moment when strength was most needed.

The strength was intended for the human nature of Jesus during this ordeal, and it came from the Father; the angel was only the Father's medium. Jesus' exhausted, human body was about to give way and expire in death under the terrific physical, mental and spiritual strain – thus the deep significance and necessity of the angel's visit. The visit from the angel must have also revealed to Christ that the cup could not pass away.

Remarkably, Jesus, the *Creator* of angels, is now as Man deriving strength through the *ministry* of angels. The writer of Hebrews explains that when Jesus became incarnate, He was made (like all men) a little lower than angels (see Hebrews 2:9), by assuming our human nature with its present earthly weakness.

We can only speculate, with reverence, what the angel might have said that so encouraged Jesus at that moment! The angels are usually God's messengers. But this we can say with certainty: whatever the Father said through the angel, it was effective, and it met Jesus' deepest need. So this same compassionate and perfect Father continues to come to *our* aid in the very moment that we need Him most. Wrote A.W. Tozer: "He hears prayer because He is good, and for no other reason."

Unless you can be certain that the Father *listens* to prayer, all talking, preaching, reading and teaching about prayer is useless. Repent now of any known sin in your heart (see Psalm 66:18), and then pray a prayer of praise and thanksgiving that, out of His goodness, He hears you.

May 10

He who has a *"kingdom"* can be no less than a "King!" Psalm 47:7 says, *"God is the King of all the earth; sing praises with understanding."* God is great in and of Himself, and it is written, that He is *"the great King above all gods"* (see Psalm 95:3). Our God is so great, that *"heaven and the heaven of heavens cannot contain"* Him (see 1 Kings 8:27)! *"He does whatever He pleases"* (see Psalm 115:3).

If you belong to the King of heaven, you are without question on the victorious side. When human means fail, God is never at a loss or disadvantage. It is an honor to serve a king. But it is a higher honor for you to serve *God* than to have kings serve you! What a blessing it is, for you to be able to say, *"My King and my God, for to You I will pray"* (see Psalm 5:2).

Obey the King of all the earth, when He speaks to you through the Holy Spirit! *Obey* the King of all the earth, when He speaks to you through His Holy Word! *Obey* the King of all the earth, when He speaks to you through your time of prayer! *Obey* the King of all the earth, when He speaks to you through His ministers and *"ambassadors,"* and *"be reconciled to God"* (see 2 Corinthians 5:20).

When your King pleads with you by His Spirit to flee from sin, *do it!* Repent! Obey your King *swiftly* and *willingly.* Perhaps you are wondering, "Why have you written *these* things to me for my time of devotion?" My friend, it is because of a small, little-known verse in the Psalms that says, *"If I regard iniquity in my heart, the Lord will not hear"* (see Psalm 66:18). *You do want your King to hear your prayers today, do you not?*

Make this your prayer today: "Give me the fullness of a godly grief that trembles and fears; grant that through the tears of repentance, I may see more clearly the brightness and glories of the saving cross."

"'Now I am no longer in the world, but these are in the world, and I come to You. Holy Father, keep through Your name those who You have given Me, that they may be one as We are.'" John 17:11

The physical departure of Jesus was a crisis for the disciples. His relationship to them was about to change in a fundamental way, and this reality prompted these tender words of prayer. Jesus refers to "the world" more than once, which seems to indicate the danger to which the disciples will be exposed when He leaves them there.

Now circumstances were about to be altered. When the disciples were accused, He would not be there physically to defend them. When they felt cast down, He would not be there physically to raise them up. When they were mistaken, He would not be there physically to teach them. And when they were troubled and exposed to peril and temptation, He would not be there physically as their constant, unfailing Comforter.

It is the *"Father"* who will maintain this continued separation, and will *"keep"* that which deeply concerns the disciples at this time, and for the future. We are strong, therefore, not in ourselves, but in God. Yet, by its open hostility, and by the lust of the flesh, the lust of the eyes, and the pride of life – *"the world"* is always a place of *danger*. It is a world of unsaved men and of the societies, cultures, and values that they have established. It is the world over which Satan rules as the prince and the power of the air. Jesus' prayer, therefore, was a request due to a very intense need that *we still face!*

If it pleased God to do so, He could take each saint to Heaven the very day he believed (as He did the dying thief). For many reasons, He leaves them in the world for a shorter or longer season. *By leaving us here in the world, God gets more glory, because His power is made perfect in our weakness* (see 2 Corinthians 12:9)! And we are left in this world to make us more appreciate the coming glory. We long for rest, and our desire to be at Home is deepened.

Pray for God to be *glorified* through your life in this world.

May 12

"Your kingdom come." Matthew 6:10

We are what we pray. Jesus has taught us to *prioritize*, even when we pray, regarding our desires and His will. Some things are just more urgent than others. The literal translation of **"Your kingdom come"** is, "May Your kingdom come *now!"* The kingdom is to be *our top priority*, just as it was the dominant theme in Jesus' teaching and preaching. Unfortunately, it seems that only a small percentage of Believers and churches have made the advancement of God's kingdom their *number one* ministry and prayer priority.

The "kingdom" of God is His royal *rule*. He is already "King," reigning in absolute sovereignty throughout history. To pray that His kingdom may "come," is to pray both that it may *grow* (as people submit to Jesus through the witness of the Church), and that it will be soon *consummated* (when Jesus returns in glory to take His power and reign).

There are two rival kingdoms in this world: the kingdom of God and the kingdom of Satan. Consequently, when a child of the devil becomes a child of God, there is a switch from one kingdom to another. Paul gave thanks to God, who **"has delivered us from the power of darkness and conveyed us into the kingdom of the Son of His love"** (see Colossians 1:13). However, the kingdom is still "future" for those who are currently in bondage to sin within Satan's kingdom. *"Your kingdom come,"* then, is a prayer for people who are lost!

The content of the Model Prayer demonstrates that Jesus wants you to take seriously your responsibility to establish the kingdom of God on earth. Is making God's kingdom your "first place goal" really *that* important? Try this experiment; the next time you are faced with an important decision, and you want to know God's will, focus first on God's kingdom and its relevance to your decision. *Focusing on God's kingdom is the key to discerning God's will* because God's will for your life is always connected in some way to the advancement of His kingdom.

Pray for urgency and priority regarding God's kingdom.

"'Now I am no longer in the world, but these are in the world, and I come to You. Holy Father, keep through Your name those who You have given Me, that they may be one as We are.'" John 17:11

When Jesus prays, *"I come to You,"* He does not mean, "I come to You *in prayer*." He means, "I come to be with You in glory." What were some of the *reasons* for Christ's ascension?

One reason for Jesus' ascension was so we could look upon Him in a greater capacity to do us good. Now, He is made King on the throne, King in His palace exercising every office: sending out His spirit as a Prophet, ruining His adversaries as a King, and interceding with God as a Priest. A second reason for His ascension was to prepare a place for us (see John 14:2). Die when we will, *our place is ready*, and nothing can keep us out! The Church may be tossed with waves, but Jesus has gone ashore and has secured a "landing place" for us. And yet another reason for Christ's ascension was to pour out the Spirit. *"For the Holy Spirit was not yet given, because Jesus was not yet glorified"* (John 7:39).

Notice now, how touching and sensitive these words were, *"But these are in the world, and I come to You."* Notice the contrast: "I come" (to where the river of the water of life flows from the Throne of God), *"but these are in the world;"* "I come" (where no enemy can follow Me, where no temptation can assail Me), *"but these are in the world;"* "I come" (to see Your face, to listen to the praises of angels, to where the harps are playing), *"but these are in the world." Notice how Jesus does not, and cannot, forget His poor struggling followers; He is leaving His heart behind!*

The Bible describes "the world" as *"A dry and thirsty land where there is no water"* (Psalm 63:1), a place that is *"defiled"* (Micah 2:10). The world promises much but gives little. Nothing in the world abides, corruptions are strong, foes are numerous, and, if that were not enough, the devil walks about.

Pray a prayer of praise, that Jesus is still tenderly watching and providing for you "in the world."

May 14

"Then little children were brought to Him that He might put His hands on them and pray." Matthew 19:13

Christian mothers can do what no one else can do so well – hold a small, very young child in her arms, and pray! The prayers heard from a mother's lips will long be remembered, and will have lasting effect even if her child is still in the womb or too young to understand. We naturally pray for health-related matters during pregnancy. But no child should ever enter this sinful world, without having been also prayed for regarding his soul, his life purpose, and his protection.

What a touching scene this is! These parents are thinking far beyond the period of childhood as they bring their **"little children"** to Jesus. They desire the blessing of God upon the *entire life* of this precious one. The character and destiny of many a child has been determined by prayer. Blessings on children, offered for them through prayer, will continue to bless them long after the death of the intercessor.

Jesus had just finished talking about marriage and divorce when He had the opportunity to take innocent children into His arms. Children are often the victims of disturbed home relationships. They can be the victims of unkind attitudes expressed by words such as "You are only a child," "You are in the way," or "You should be seen and not heard." But children found nothing in Jesus that made them uncomfortable. Instead, they sensed His interest and His love.

When you are in heaven, will you learn (or do you already know?) that someone prayed fervently for your salvation? When ministers are in heaven, will they learn that they "entered" the glorious work of our Lord one day praying, **"Here am I! Send me,"** because someone was obedient while reading, **"Pray the Lord of the harvest to send out laborers into His harvest"**?

No wonder Jesus stopped everything else to put His hands on little children and pray! When *you* pray individually or with others, are you more inclined to focus on adults? Do not overlook the baby in the womb or in the cradle, or the child in school as you pray today.

"'Now I am no longer in the world, but these are in the world, and I come to You. Holy Father, keep through Your name those who You have given Me, that they may be one as We are.'" John 17:11

What precious words these, *"**Having loved His own who were in the world, He loved them to the end**"* (John 13:1). Jesus' love will include two necessary things for His disciples in the world: first *protection* (from a world which has, and will continue to hate them, due to its correct perception that the disciples do not belong to the world) and (from the devil, *"**a roaring lion**"*); second *unity* (during spiritual assaults within the strategy of the evil one), for there is a huge difference between the believer being in the world, and the world being in the believer.

We are left "in the world" for several reasons. First, for the influence of the churches of God scattered over it. We are "The light of the world." We are left here to illuminate a dark world through our lives and through our families, to tell the sweet story of His love, and to honor and bring glory to His name. Second, we are left in the world to humbly learn who we truly are – and where so effectively a place than the world, to learn of our own selfishness and corruption?

Further, we are left in the world to learn the abundance of His grace. His strength truly is made perfect in our weakness and lack. We are left in this world that we would further believe in His Word. And, all praise be to Him, we are left in this world to learn of His great faithfulness. *This is the most important lesson we can learn in the wilderness – the faithfulness of our God!* He does not vary in His love toward us, as we vary in our love toward Him. He has never once broken a promise.

Jesus Christ said, *"**In the world you will have tribulation; but be of good cheer, I have overcome the world.**"* Brethren, may our cheer indeed be great, as we pray today: "O Father, grant that I may learn my wilderness lessons well, that I may remain in the hollow of Your hand – for soon the wilderness will be past forever."

May 16

"Your kingdom come"** is a prayer that God may reign *here* upon the earth, that men *here* may acknowledge Him as King, that life *here* may be regulated by His commands. It is not a prayer to remove us from the earth and deliver us into heaven; it is a prayer that heaven may come down to earth, so that earth itself may become like heaven. It is a prayer for that kingdom of God which is righteousness, peace, and joy in the Holy Spirit to be established here on earth.

What *kind* of kingdom is it? Paul said that the kingdom of God is **"righteousness and peace and joy in the Holy Spirit"** (see Romans 14:17). His kingdom is *righteousness.* Man wrongs man and the dark places of the earth are full of cruelty, but when His kingdom comes, wrong will cease. His kingdom is *peace.* Peace between men and peace between nations; the noise of war will not be heard. And His kingdom is *joy.* The tears, grief, and pain that result from the hate, oppressions, and injustices of life will end.

God wants to be King *in Jesus Christ*, meaning, He wants to be King not by virtue of His "power," but by virtue of His *love.* He wants men to obey Him not because they are "afraid" of Him, but because they *love* Him. God wants to be King not because He is "Creator," but because He is *Father.* Only when God is enthroned as King and when He is *known in reality as King*, will the matters of this earth be mended. *Still, the Lord God omnipotent reigns in spite of the "big show" being made by the forces of evil!*

God's kingdom includes His rule over men's hearts. Therefore, it spreads slowly throughout the world. It is a rule that works on men through their understandings from divine revelation. To pray for His kingdom to come is to yield ourselves to His service.

Pray that you will be conscious today of your "spiritual job description" that promotes the coming of God's kingdom to earth.

"'Now I am no longer in the world, but these are in the world, and I come to You. Holy Father, keep through Your name those who You have given Me, that they may be one as We are.'" John 17:11

*T*he time had now come, in the progress of divinely-appointed events, when Jesus was no longer to be bodily present with His disciples - a time unique in the history of the universe! The disciples were not to be left alone at the time when the world's salvation and the existence of the Church was at stake, so Christ commits them to the divine keeping of the Father.

"I come" is better translated, "I am coming." Christ will no longer be visibly present to the world, but He will be with the believers through the Holy Spirit (see Matthew 28:20). In a little while, He will go into heaven where angels and authorities and powers will be made subject to Him. Above all, Jesus was about to receive His Father's embrace, "I come **to You.**" Christ was going there to be ours forever, **"The Son of Man standing at the right hand of God"** (Acts 7:56)!

Earlier, Jesus had said to His disciples, **"If you loved Me, you would rejoice because I said, 'I am going to the Father,' for My Father is greater than I."** But as He prays at this moment, He grieves for their sakes; He grieves to be leaving them. It reminds us of when Paul said, **"For I am hard-pressed between the two, having a desire to depart and be with Christ, which is far better. Nevertheless to remain in the flesh is more needful for you"** (Philippians 1:23, 24).

Many of us have known elderly or sick people ready to depart this world, tired or perhaps weary from long periods of pain, who yet would have chosen to go on living for the sake of some child, relative, or friend. Is it rebellion against our Father's will to regret leaving friends and dear ones who may still benefit from our help? Jesus grieved to leave His own. There was nothing in human life or in human conduct (except sin) from which Christ shrank. He was tender.

What glorious words are these: "I come to You!" Pray that you will be ready when the time comes.

May 18

"'Nevertheless not My will, but Yours, be done.'" Luke 22:42

If you are a new believer or a believer who knows little about the things of the kingdom of God, today's devotion will both challenge you and teach you something very important regarding your prayer life. If you are a more mature believer, then you are already doing business in the deep waters of communion with the Father, and you are more apt to understand this prayer in all of its depth and breadth. May we *all* look at these words that Jesus prayed in Gethsemane, that we may learn from Him.

When we pray this prayer and mean it in all its fullness, we must be willing to go from the mountaintop into the valley. Just when the church seems to need us most, or at a time when our hearts are full of love towards Jesus and towards the family of God – something comes along that knocks us off our spiritual feet. It is then, that we must be prepared and willing to pray, **"Nevertheless not My will, but Yours, be done."**

If we adopt this prayer we should be prepared to suffer instead of to serve, we should be willing to lie in the trenches instead of scaling the walls, or willing to lie in the King's hospital bed instead of fighting on the front lines. Yes, this is difficult for flesh and blood – but we must do it if we dare pray these words of Jesus. We should be prepared to begin a work that seems strange or to continue toiling when we see absolutely no fruit.

There are ministers and church members who are unable to pray these words with sincerity because of the possible consequences. The days have already arrived when believers will be shamefully slandered, all manner of falsehoods uttered against us, and no opportunity to "clear our name" for the sake of our character or reputation. *Praying, "nevertheless," means you are ready to be considered the vilest of the vile because the One True God knows your heart!*

May you continue to humbly practice praying these words. Pray them now with sincerity.

May 19

"'Now I am no longer in the world, but these are in the world, and I come to You. Holy Father, keep through Your name those who You have given Me, that they may be one as We are.'" John 17:11

An inadequate, inaccurate view of sin lies at the root of perhaps every grave error in the history of the Church! If we were to raise the qualifications for membership in local churches, and especially for their leadership, we would likely find fewer members but more power. Political correctness has frequently replaced biblical church discipline.

Therefore, Jesus' use of the word, *"Holy,"* as He addresses the Father in intercession for the disciples is entirely appropriate. The disciples must be kept *pure* in faith and in practice, separate from all known error and sin, in order to be a salt to the corrupt world in which their Lord is about to leave them. They had already been taught to pray, *"Hallowed* (made holy) *be Your name"* (Matthew 6:9).

The *holiness* of God has been called the crown of all His attributes. It is the beauty and the perfection that sets off everything. The crown of the Godhead is holiness, and that is pledged to Christ, and Christ claims the pledge. Psalm 89:35 says, *"Once I have sworn by My holiness; I will not lie to David."*

The petition can be separated into two parts – that the disciples may be kept in *truth* (as the badge of distinction between His Church and the world), and that they may be *one* (separate from the world, but not divided among themselves). These two things, truth, and love, the Church of Jesus Christ must ever keep in view as of vital importance. When we get to heaven, we are going to get a new body, not a new nature – we have that already.

In Ephesians 1:18, 19, Paul prays a model prayer for the Church, asking that Believers will be enlightened, encouraged, enriched, and empowered. God is still looking for men who know Him intimately, who fear apathy supremely, and who hate sin immensely. This is the way our Holy God would have us intercede for one another who are *"in the world."*

Pray for *your* desire to be found among that few, who want to be kept in truth and who want to be one.

May 20

"'Your kingdom come.'" Matthew 6:10

How can you begin to *think and pray* with a **"kingdom"** focus? First, see the need for the kingdom to come to *your heart.* The kingdom of God is not just about foreign missions and evangelistic meetings! Are *you* allowing Jesus to "rule" and "take the throne" of your heart? Do you *honestly desire* that every cherished sin and passion be cast out of your heart? In order for the kingdom to come to your own heart, *God's* will (not your own will) must rule. So in a very real sense, when you pray the words, "Your kingdom come," you are praying for yourself.

May God give you grace today to pray this prayer in surrender! For men who love their sins too much, love their pleasures too much, love their money too much, or who love themselves too much − cannot pray these words with sincerity. May God continue to work in your heart to make you a true and loyal subject of His kingdom so that you will help extend its boundaries and further its interests by winning others to our King.

Second, see the need for the kingdom to come, not only in your own heart but *everywhere.* Do you want to see the banner of the Cross floating over every land? Do you want to see every nation acknowledge the same King? All nations are to bow down before Him and serve Him. And a third way you can begin to think and pray with a kingdom focus is to see the need for the kingdom to come in every segment of life − in business life, in social life, in political life, in art and literature, in social media, and in the home.

The truth is, you are in this world for one purpose: to look after the interests of God and of His kingdom! We are here to lift up Jesus and to tell the story of the Cross! And when we lift Him up, He will draw men to Himself and into God's kingdom. Pray for a kingdom focus in *all* areas of your life.

"'Now I am no longer in the world, but these are in the world, and I come to You. Holy Father, keep through Your name those who You have given Me, that they may be one as We are.'" John 17:11

" Why does Jesus use the title, *'Holy,"* at this point in His prayer?" When we commune with God, especially regarding such things as grace and sanctification, we must look upon Him as a *Holy* Father. God's holiness is an attribute by which we understand His essence to be perfectly just and pure. God is not "a" holy one; He is *the* Holy One. **"No one is holy like the Lord, for there is none besides You"** (1 Samuel 2:2). Not only is God holy, *He is holiness itself* – it is His very essence.

The root meaning of the word "holy" is *separation*. When applied to God, it means He is far removed from evil. But there is a "positive" side to His holiness, in that He is absolutely and essentially pure in Himself. Therefore we read in Revelation 15:4, **"Who shall not fear You, O Lord, and glorify Your name? For You alone are holy."**

Psalm 97:10 says, **"You who love the Lord, hate evil!"**

Here is an important prayer teaching. When we pray, it should be in our minds concerning the *character* of God, that we are communing with One who is pure, righteous, and sinless. God's Word says, **"Do not love the world or the things in the world. If anyone loves the world, the love of the Father is not in him. For all that is in the world – the lust of the flesh, the lust of the eyes, and the pride of life – is not of the Father but is of the world.** Jesus wants His disciples "kept" in the characteristics of the "Holy" God, and separated from the world, which refuses to follow the line of conduct for which "holiness" stands.

In all of this, we see Jesus describing what we often only "casually" refer to as *spiritual warfare*. There is, on the one hand, the kingdom of light and holiness – and then there is, on the other hand, the kingdom of darkness and evil. *All things relate in some way to one kingdom or the other!*

Pray for your hatred of evil to increase.

May 22

The kingdom of God was the great theme of the teaching of Jesus and His Apostles. It was an axiom of the Jewish schools, that "any benediction wherein there is no mention of the kingdom, is no benediction at all." To leave out all references to the thought that God is King, and that at length He will exercise universal dominion, would be to omit an essential element from Synagogue devotions. In the early Church, the kingdom of God had a significant place in preaching and in prayer. In Matthew's Gospel, it is called "the kingdom of Heaven," but in the other Gospels it is called "the kingdom of God;" the two are synonymous.

This second petition of the Model Prayer is for the full accomplishment of God's kingdom, as well as all of the events *leading up to* that accomplishment. Among other things, it is the desire that the conflict with sin and Satan may reach its end without delay. Keep in mind that the early disciples were welcomed in some towns, but were refused hospitality in others – their message received by some hearers, but bitterly rejected by others. Anticipating and longing for the day of victory, they preached and prayed, **"Your kingdom come."**

While the kingdom is established "within" us, yet it is always "to come," as it makes itself visible "without." *It is impossible for the kingdom of God to be alongside other people or things, and not increase, reverse, or in some way influence them!* One cannot carry a light through a dark room without scattering *some* darkness; the light from a candle cannot be confined to the flame. Thus the kingdom will grow and express itself until there is no room for any opposition.

The kingdom of God, therefore, does not shun the place where there is blindness, captivity, heartache, prejudice, poverty, or greed; it will appear precisely at the doorstep of such places! Pray today for yourself, that as a subject in His kingdom, aware of the charge to further that kingdom on earth through your life, you will not avoid the "uncomfortable" places.

"'Now I am no longer in the world, but these are in the world, and I come to You. Holy Father, keep through Your name those who You have given Me, that they may be one as We are.'" John 17:11

A truth such as God's holiness must be more than a fact that rests in our minds. The holiness of God must be applied to our daily lives, so as to affect our *behavior.* **"But as He who called you is holy, you also be holy in all your conduct, because it is written, 'Be holy for I am holy'"** (1 Peter 1:15, 16). Not only is our behavior affected by the knowledge of His holiness, but also our entire outlook on an understanding of life. Therefore, to say that the sudden realization of God's holiness is "emotionally violent" for a man is not an exaggeration!

The moment that Isaiah had his revolutionary vision of the holiness of God, he declared, **"Woe is me, for I am undone! Because I am a man of unclean lips, and I dwell in the midst of a people with unclean lips; for my eyes have seen the King, the Lord of hosts."** Until we have seen ourselves as God sees us, we continue living as though unholiness is the natural and expected thing. Tragically, we are not disappointed when we do not find all truth in our teachers, all purity in our ministers, all honesty in our politicians, or all trustworthiness in our friends – because unholiness is what we know best.

Hearing Jesus pray these words, **"Holy Father,"** we move into unknown territory. Holy is the way God is. Because He is holy, His attributes are holy; so whatever we think of as belonging to God must be thought of as holy. God's holiness is more than just considering the finest person we know, and then multiplying by a million. *We know nothing at all like the divine holiness; it stands apart, unique, and incomprehensible!* The natural man is blind to it. We may fear God's power and admire His wisdom, but we cannot even imagine His holiness.

What shall we say, then? Humbly pray that you may hide your unholiness in the wounds of Christ, as Moses hid himself in the cleft of the rock while the glory of God passed by.

May 24

"And it happened, as He was alone praying, that
His disciples joined Him." Luke 9:18

The setting is on a road (see Mark 8:27) near the Roman city of Caesarea Philippi, where legend had it that all the gods gathered. The temples of Baal worship, the place said to be the birthplace of the god Pan, and the place where Israel had worshiped the golden calf – were all scattered around that area. Because of the location, it may have been necessary for Jesus to pray regarding the defeat of evil spirits that were presently causing a hindrance.

The importance of the topic Jesus is about to discuss with His disciples is shown by the fact that He prays before He proceeds. It seems possible that He prayed that His disciples would be able to discern the truth about Who He was - for Matthew tells us that following Peter's confession, Christ revealed that his answer had been provided supernaturally, saying ***"Blessed are you, Simon Bar-Jonah, for flesh and blood has not revealed this to you, but My Father who is in heaven."*** In addition, it is possible that the Savior, anticipating the reaction of His disciples when He is about to tell them for the first time of His approaching death, was praying in preparation for this disclosure.

When people intercede for us in prayer, supernatural things happen. Much of the time we do not realize the exact moment when this takes place. When Jesus prayed, we can be sure that the Holy Spirit brought many things to His mind that the Father wanted to affect. How marvelous to remember, that today, Jesus is still interceding and is in touch with God on our behalf!

Oh, to be in touch with Almighty God! Today's Church is looking for ways to get in touch with a new generation. We look at statistics that seem to indicate we are not meeting that challenge well. Yet we are told that the average minister spends less than five minutes a day in private prayer!

As you pray today, intercede for your pastor – asking God to supernaturally reveal things to him that he is unable to recognize on his own.

"'Now I am no longer in the world, but these are in the world, and I come to You. Holy Father, keep through Your name those who You have given Me, that they may be one as We are.'" John 17:11

As He prays, Jesus reminds us that God is a *"Holy"* God. The Bible says that God is *"Of purer eyes than to behold evil"* (Habakkuk 1:13). God's perfection is seen in His holiness, and that perfection is the *standard* by which mankind's behavior is judged: *"For all have sinned and fall short of the glory of God"* (Romans 3:23). Sin is missing the mark of God's holiness. To be holy, God does not conform to any preconceived standard; He *is* the standard!

Because God is holy, He hates all sin and must, therefore, punish it. We have all known men who have decided to take their chances on that Day. They hope that God's mercy will override everything else when the fate of their souls is determined, and when they can remind God of their good works. But God's Word describes those men, saying, *"These things you have done, and I kept silent; you thought that I was altogether like you"* (Psalm 50:21).

In this prayer, Jesus is using God's greatest title of honor, *"Holy Father."* God's holiness was manifested at the Cross. *How hateful must sin be to God, for Him to punish it in the manner that He did!* Never has divine holiness appeared more beautiful and lovely than at the time Jesus' countenance was most marred! Consequently, this one perfection of His is the one celebrated before the Throne of Heaven, as the seraphim cry, *"Holy, holy, holy is the Lord of hosts."*

When you sin willfully – just because you want to – you tell God that you do not like Him, that He does not completely satisfy you, that you can do without Him at that moment. On the other hand, the more our hearts are in awe of His holiness, the more acceptable our approaches will be to Him; *"Serve the Lord with fear, and rejoice with trembling"* (Psalm 2:11).

Every time you think of God today, every time you pray today, remember that He is Holy. When you are tempted to sin, think of His holiness. Understand the *privilege* of being in His presence.

May 26

"'Your kingdom come.'" Matthew 6:10

It has been said that *all* prayer is, in some respect, "against the devil." The petition *"Your kingdom come,"* certainly includes the desire for the devil's kingdom to be demolished in the world. Satan got his kingdom by conquest when he conquered mankind in paradise. Nothing but sin goes on in the devil's kingdom, which is why Luke 11:24 refers to *"an unclean spirit."*

Satan's kingdom is a kingdom of slavery; he rides some men in the same way people ride horses. Interestingly, during ceremonies of the voodoo religion, spirits known as *Loa* are believed to "mount" people like horses. Tragically, the devil has more men to stand up for his kingdom than God has for His! Satan's kingdom must be thrown down before God's kingdom can flourish.

Where Jesus is, there God's kingdom and rule is! God's kingdom is the heavenly reign and rule of God through Christ in the gospel of *grace.* When you pray, "Your kingdom come," you pray that the kingdom of grace may come into your heart. When grace comes, there is a "kingly government" set up in the soul. Grace rules your will and affections. Grace brings you into subjection to Jesus. And you want to *know* that this kingdom of grace is set up in your heart.

The kingdom of grace *adorns* you; it sheds a glory and luster upon your soul like a diamond does to a ring. *Peace* is the best blessing of a kingdom, and the kingdom of grace is a kingdom of peace. And when the kingdom of grace comes, it *fixes your heart on God.* Isaiah 26:3 says, **"You will keep him in perfect peace, whose mind is stayed on You,"** and Psalm 57:7 says, **"My heart is steadfast, O God, my heart is steadfast."**

So why should you pray, "Your kingdom come," if the kingdom of grace has already come into your heart? It is so grace may be *increased,* and that His kingdom may flourish *still more* in your soul! Pray then, "Father, let Your kingdom of grace come into my heart in *more* power."

"'Now I am no longer in the world, but these are in the world, and I come to You. Holy Father, keep through Your name those who You have given Me, that they may be one as We are.'" John 17:11

Numerous times in the Old Testament, God is seen as the "Keeper" of His people who provides "protective oversight" – as a Shepherd (Ezekiel 34:11-16), as a Husbandman (Isaiah 27:2, 3), and as a Watchman (Psalm 121:3-5). As the hour approaches when Christ will leave the disciples in the world, our Lord prays with urgency for His own.

Observe the *types* of things over which Jesus knows the disciples will need such protective oversight from the Father – not finances, reputation, or influence – but rather to be kept from evil, separated from the world, qualified for duty, and then brought home safely to heaven. Jesus is asking the Father to **"keep"** these valuable things **"through"** the power of His name, as if in a "fortress" where they cannot be stolen.

The Greek word for "keep" suggests a faithful and attentive "watching" by eyes of love. Jesus was asking the Father for the "preservation" of the disciples; He was leaving them in a hostile world. They will need to be kept from evil, from being overcome by temptation, from being crushed by persecution, and from every device and assault of the enemy. The old nature, still in the disciples and still in us, required this powerful intercession from the Master.

Such was the loving intercession of Jesus for the disciples in this prayer. Day by day, year by year, until one by one they fell asleep, they would be the recipients of a secret safety that only the Father could provide, as He "kept" them spiritually. *We live day after day and lose the awareness of our secret safety!* Jesus is asking the Father to keep us.

What would you be like if you were not kept through His name? To have a lasting impact upon the kingdom of God, to bear fruit that remains, requires this divine keeping. It is, without a doubt, one of those things that is constantly happening without your giving very much thought to it.

As a Believer in the Lord Jesus Christ, you are in the Father's preservation. Pray that you will recognize His divine keeping today.

May 28

The *"kingdom"* occupied a large place in the thought and speech of Jesus; His Gospel was a Gospel of the kingdom. *But to pray "about" or "concerning" the kingdom of God, and to pray that His kingdom will* **"come,"** *is not necessarily the same thing!*

The Bible is a book of *hope;* it looks forward, not backward. It always speaks of "a best that is still to be." Man lost everything by sin, except hope. God left man with hope in order to comfort him in his grief and suffering and to save him from despair. So God gives man one glowing promise after another in His Word. "Your kingdom *come*" is a prayer for the good time *coming!*

But the kingdom of God is not only "future," it is "present." Right now, it is the world's "evil time." This earth is full of misery and pain. But you may remember that when the Pharisees asked Jesus when the kingdom of God should come, they were treating as "future" what was *already present.* The kingdom of God was *in their midst* because the kingdom is *where Jesus is.*

It was not that surprising that the Pharisees failed to discover the presence of the kingdom; at that time the kingdom was a tiny affair, consisting of only a handful of Galilean peasants. Even Jesus, speaking of the unnoticed beginning of the kingdom, said that it was like leaven that a woman took and hid in three measures of meal. In *our* day the kingdom is not hidden, for that leaven has been "working" through the centuries. It is in *our midst* – the mightiest kingdom and the most potent force on earth! Yet its *full realization* is yet to come.

Yes, the time will come when this prayer will be changed into praise, and we will be able to say, "Your kingdom *has* come!" The time will come when asylums and penitentiaries will no longer openly proclaim our shame because the drunkard and the drug dealer will be no more. So, *lift up your heart* as you pray! The King *is* coming!

> *"'Now I am no longer in the world, but these are in the world, and I come to You. Holy Father, keep through Your name those who You have given Me, that they may be one as We are.'"* John 17:11

Jesus is praying for the disciples because they are the precious fruit of His life-labor, the hope of the future, the founders of the Church, and the missionaries of the truth to the whole world. Therefore, He commends them to the Father's care, support, and maintenance. If the disciples should fail, Christ's cause, His name, His doctrine will be shipwrecked.

We can safely say that it cost Jesus far more to leave His people in the world than it cost *them* to be in the world. So vital, then, are these words of intercession: **"Keep through Your name."** Jesus had already declared, **"I have come in My Father's name"** (John 5:43), and in that name, is the power to keep those who are still in the world.

"Name" in the Bible often means "nature;" in this case, the name stands for the personal power and character of God. Paul wrote, **"If anyone is in Christ, he is a new creation;"** this, then, is that name, that nature in which Christ prays His Father to keep us. *We are to live and grow and rejoice and conquer within that name!* God provides a wonderful nearness and intimacy, a loving shelter, a place close to the voice and to the countenance of everlasting Love.

Someone once said, "The most perfect antidote to all sinning is 'nearness to God.'" The Bible says, **"But it is good for me to draw near to God"** (Psalm 73:28). Just His holy presence – welcomed and sought after – will, among many other blessings, provide that way of escape when you are tempted to sin. Do you wrestle today with a particular temptation? **"Submit to God. Resist the devil and he will flee from you. Draw near to God and He will draw near to you"** (James 4:7, 8).

When was the last time you realized that you were actually "in His Holy presence?" How long has it been since you stopped long enough to experience *only Him?* As you take time to pray, let this be your heart's desire: "Father, let me know only Your presence during these moments."

May 30

"And it happened, as He was alone praying, that His disciples joined Him." Luke 9:18

How could Jesus be praying **"alone"** if **"His disciples joined Him?"** On this occasion, the disciples were close by, but Jesus was praying separately and apart from the multitudes. Therefore, the term "alone" in no way excludes the *physical presence* of the disciples, and there is no "contradiction." We can be alone with God and be with people at the same time. How can that be?

Jesus was caught up in communion with God – something that all of us need to learn to do. True prayer means that your awareness of God "overrides" your awareness of men. Have you ever been praying aloud in the presence of others, and catch yourself choosing words that might impress people? Do you listen for people to groan, to make noises of agreement, or to say "Amen" while you are praying? *When you are seeking the approval of others as you pray, you are not praying "alone" in the manner Jesus demonstrates here!*

Should we wait to pray until we find the perfect time and place? No, because the devil will often provide distractions when we determine to commune with the Father. Satan and all of his accomplices will do everything possible to try and prevent you from enjoying the presence of the Lord. A verbal rebuke will send him away! Pray whenever and wherever the Holy Spirit leads you. When necessary, pray with your eyes open – but pray.

A popular fast-food restaurant has advertised, "Eat like you mean it." We "pray like we mean it" when we are alone praying, totally focused on *His* presence rather than on the presence of others. A man named F.W. Baller once heard missionary Hudson Taylor pray and remarked, "I had never heard anyone pray like that. There was a simplicity, a tenderness, a boldness, a power that hushed and subdued one, and made it clear that God had admitted him into the inner circle of His friendship. Such praying was evidently the outcome of long tarrying in the secret place, and was as a dew from the Lord."

Pray today, and always, like you mean it.

"'Now I am no longer in the world, but these are in the world, and I come to You. Holy Father, keep through Your name those who You have given Me, that they may be one as We are.'" John 17:11

The words, *"Keep through Your name those who You have given Me,"* bring out the *value* Jesus sets upon us, and the *deep interest* He has in us. *We are the Father's love gift to the Son!* In John 3:16 we learn of the Father's love to us, and here in John 17:11 we see the Father's love to Christ; He so loved the world that He gave His Son, and He so loved His Son that He gave Jesus a people who would, through all eternity, show forth His praises.

All that is in God, and all that is in Jesus, are for us; and we are not for ourselves. There is no serving the Son without serving the Father, and there is no glorifying the Son without glorifying the Father. Therefore, it is a terrible misuse of ourselves whenever we refuse to give Jesus the necessary and full control of our lives. Paul writes, *"I beseech you therefore, brethren, by the mercies of God, that you present your bodies a living sacrifice, holy, acceptable to God, which is your reasonable service"* (Romans 12:1) and, *"You are Christ's"* (1 Corinthians 3:23). The message is clear: whatever we have, we must give up to Him for His glory.

Paul says that God "beseeches" us to be persuaded by His mercies. These divine mercies have persuasive powers over our wills. In the case of a slave, his master owns his body, so he does what his master says, often with inner reluctance. We, on the other hand, are besought to present our bodies *willingly.* The whole matter of "want to" comes into question. We are reminded of the words of Paul recorded in 2 Corinthians 5:15, *"He died for all, that those who live should live no longer for themselves, but for Him who died for them and rose again."* This is a very powerful statement that speaks to our *motives* and our *purpose.*

As you pray, rejoice that you are the Father's love gift to His Son, and consider how you might show forth His praises and glorify Him today.

June 1

"'Your kingdom come.'" Matthew 6:10

*I*t may well be that the words **"Your kingdom come"** *represent the deepest desire of the Believer's heart!* When the disciples were instructed to announce the coming of the kingdom, they were given a task that stirred their hearts as nothing else could do. They told people that the kingdom was at hand; now they were taught to *pray* for its full manifestation to hasten.

The Apostles spoke of the kingdom as a future inheritance, and they associated it with the expected appearing of Jesus on His return from heaven. As men had looked for the coming of the kingdom, so they now looked for the coming of the King – Jesus the Christ. The prayers of God's people become more rich and urgent and specific when they understand more of the divine *purpose.*

Although we are expressly warned against being occupied with speculation regarding the day or hour of our Lord's return, we are encouraged to look forward to and to rejoice in the hope of, the coming glory (see Romans 5:2). If we pray "Your kingdom come" with regularity, our hearts will be stimulated with the desire to see His face and with a readiness for His appearing. The kingdom is on its way!

So when you pray, "Your kingdom come," you are asking for Jesus' return; you are pleading, **"Come, Lord Jesus!"** But you are also asking for the spread of the Gospel to those throughout the world who, as yet, have not trusted Jesus by faith. This is not a prayer that you hope "somebody out there" will tell lost people the Good News; this is a prayer that God would use *your* witness for the expansion of His kingdom.

Yet your deepest desire as you pray these words should be for God to rule first in *your own heart.* This is when His kingdom becomes personal; because you *love* God, you want your Master's principles to rule in your life. Therefore, praying these words expresses your "choice" in the matter – *to glorify God with your life.*

Pray for God to *expand* His rule in your heart.

> *"'Now I am no longer in the world, but these are in the world, and I come to You. Holy Father, keep through Your name those who You have given Me, that they may be one as We are.'"* John 17:11

Today we consider the connection between these words from Jesus' prayer, *"that they may be one as We are,"* and the fellowship of the Church of Jesus Christ. The New Testament never speaks of "isolated believers." When you find saints in the New Testament, you find them in fellowship - because *God's people need each other.* The safety of the Church consists in union with the Father.

Adam was not in union, and he fell. Angels that did not keep their first estate were not in union, and they fell. But there can be no fall for those who are in union with the living God. Jesus taught about the union between the branches and the Vine, and between the members of the body and its Head. But praying now, He speaks of the union in which the Deity itself rests. Jesus actually asks (therefore it must be a possibility!) that the same quality and quantity of unity that exists between He and the Father be experienced in His Church.

Looking back at the operation of the Church since the time Jesus prayed this prayer, we understand His wisdom in praying for the Father to hold us together and to help us preserve our unity. At the start, according to the Acts and the epistles, things were a bit shaky at times. To be sure, there were some wonderful examples of unity in the early church; however, church unity was frequently tested by selfish, disputing, bitter, and narrow-minded behavior.

It is important that we first keep in mind our relationship to the Father if we will have the relationship among ourselves that will impress and convince outsiders that something "new" has come. *For why would an unsaved person trade what he already has in a selfish and greedy world, to receive more of the same in the Church?* The benefits of divine unity, then, are to those both inside and outside the walls of the "building."

Pray for a divine unity to exist in the fellowship of the church you attend, that all may see your oneness with the Father.

June 3

"He took Peter, John, and James and went up on the mountain to pray. As He prayed, the appearance of His face was altered." Luke 9:28, 29

For today's devotion, let us examine the effect that the Transfiguration had on Jesus and His disciples, and then the meaning this event may still have for us today.

First, the effect on Jesus. He receives divine approval. He receives a strengthening of His faith as He prepares for the Cross, through a fore-taste of the glory awaiting Him, the assurance that His humiliation and obedience was understood and appreciated by saints in heaven, and the approving voice of His heavenly Father. Having received these things, Jesus responded by coming down off of the mountain to enter again into life.

Second, the event provided a lesson and a command for the three disciples present – and for every follower of Jesus: ***"Hear Him!"*** Pray for strength, and then walk in the direction that the Father has chosen for you. The "mountaintop" experience occurs from time to time, for the purpose of providing temporary support and encouragement for when we bravely *return* to the challenges of life.

This event took place because, and while, Jesus *prayed*. Prayer brings the transforming power of God. *When it becomes as natural as breathing, prayer will provide a glory that works out into the face and features, into the character and conduct!* The glory that shone in the face of Jesus as He prayed on this occasion was the shining forth of that which was on the *inside*.

Webster defines "countenance" as "the look on a person's face that shows his nature or feelings." Have you ever been next to a person physically at the moment that he trusts Jesus for salvation? You may have personally seen a change in his countenance. Whether the person has lived a crude, unruly, wicked life or a respectable, good, decent life – the moment he believes on Jesus for salvation, the fashion of his countenance is altered. Something that has occurred on the inside shows up on the outside!

Hear Him! Pray that you will see His glory. Pray that you will see His glory in the changed countenance of a sinner that you have brought to Jesus for salvation.

"'Now I am no longer in the world, but these are in the world, and I come to You. Holy Father, keep through Your name those who You have given Me, that they may be one as We are.'" John 17:11

Why was Jesus so *earnest* in this prayer, asking that His disciples "be one" as He and the Father are one? First, Jesus foresaw how much the Church would *need* this blessing of the Father. Divisions would surely arise within such a vital, impactful group. Satan could not prevail against the Church were it not for divisions. To this day, with reference to helping local churches at the first sign of sickness – some are for immediately starting a new church, while others are for trying all ways and all means of recovery first, and others everything in between extremes. The Holy Spirit's voice is not always heard in the matter. And with nearly everyone barking at and biting one another, Christ is dishonored. Therefore, that there might be some sparks of love fanned in the unhealthy church, Christ earnestly pleads with the Father in this prayer: **"That they may be one."**

Second, Christ would have us know that divine unity among Believers is actually a *possible* thing. He understands our lack of patience and our lack of wisdom when troubles come to the church. He knows how quick we are to criticize others, without the ability to know their hearts. He is aware that decisions are often made without prayer. On and on; but there is hope! Jesus has prayed for our unity! And John 11:42 records Him saying to the Father, **"And I know that You always hear Me."**

Finally, Jesus is encouraging us to *pray* in the same manner for His Church. We see unhealthy churches because we do not pray for unity and oneness. We wait until after the damage is done to pray. But the Scripture instructs us to, if possible, live peaceably with all men (see Romans 12:18).

What is the lesson for us? *It is God who keeps the saints together!* If God should leave us, we would immediately discover what is in our hearts. Our part is to carry on *the privilege of intercession for unity* in His Church, as modeled here by our Lord.

Earnestly pray for divine unity among the brethren.

June 5

"'Your kingdom come.'"   Matthew 6:10

When we pray this second petition of the Model Prayer, we pray that all may be brought into this kingdom and that its laws may affect all earthly governments. We are praying that a heavenly state of things will be established on earth and that King Jesus and the laws of heaven will be acknowledged on earth. *Why not* pray for God's purposes in history to be completed? Although prayer is not the *only* means of bringing in the kingdom of God, without earnest and sustained prayer for its development and advancement, what can we look for?

Let's consider, then, some specific reasons why we *should* pray these three powerful words. First, once His kingdom comes, we will see God face to face! Second, once His kingdom comes we will never sin again! Third, we should pray these words because the Lord Jesus taught us to pray them, and *intends* for us to pray them! And lastly, we should pray these words because His is a kingdom worth praying for!

"Your kingdom come" was the prayer of the apostles and martyrs in the first centuries of the Church, and it has been, and continues to be, the prayer of Believers of all ages and countries. Regardless of your theological position about the end times, almost all Christians agree that God's kingdom will not become a *complete* reality until the day Jesus comes again. It is the day to which Jesus Himself on His heavenly throne is looking, *"waiting till His enemies are made His footstool"* (see Hebrews 10:13). And so this second petition is also a prayer for the defeat of Satan's kingdom. *When the kingdom of God comes in fullness, creation will be delivered from bondage!*

"Your kingdom come" means, "let Your kingdom come actually and completely," even though it involves a *gradual* coming of His reign in the hearts and lives of men. It should give you great joy to "watch" the kingdom grow from heart to heart! Pray that the kingdom of God will triumph in you, direct your will, captivate your affections, and rule your life.

"'Now I am no longer in the world, but these are in the world, and I come to You. Holy Father, keep through Your name those who You have given Me, that they may be one as We are.'" John 17:11

One particular danger that concerned Jesus as He prayed was the breaking up of the bonds of fellowship and brotherly love that would disrupt the Christian society which He had founded in the world. The safeguard against this would be the unity of *holy love* that binds together all Believers in the Christian brotherhood. The disciples had union, but lacked unity or oneness of spirit, as was shown at the supper earlier that very evening (see Luke 22:24).

"That they may be one" or "that they may be a unity" describes a harmony profound and beautiful, in which the various parts are truly distinct, yet always perfectly related. This was, and is Jesus' intention – not only then for the Apostles, but for all His own (see John 17:20, 21). These individual souls will, by divine power, be preserved within the name of His Holy Father.

The more they all lived within that circle, the more they would mutually understand and love; the more they would endeavor **"to keep the unity of the Spirit in the bond of peace"** (see Ephesians 4:3) so that all would desire a unity that only the Holy Spirit can produce. They would experience the bond of **"one heart and one soul"** (see Acts 4:32) where all would desire to be faithful and obedient.

This unity Jesus prays for includes the bond of **"the same mind"** and of **"the same judgment"** (see 1 Corinthians 1:10), where all in the church seek to gain a scriptural understanding of things. Also included in this divine unity is **"the unity of the faith"** (see Ephesians 4:13) which encourages people to mature together. Colossians 2:2 wraps everything up that is included in this special unity Christ desires for His own, which is the unity of **"being knit together in love."** This is the secret of how the disciples will hold together through the tests and trials to come.

If Jesus was concerned enough to pray for unity as He considered the future of His Church, He must have known something! Pray, as Jesus did, for unity in the church you attend.

June 7

"He took Peter, John, and James and went up on the mountain to pray. As He prayed, the appearance of His face was altered. " Luke 9:28, 29

Jesus was preparing His disciples for the close of His earthly life and work. He selected the three disciples that He had chosen once before (see Luke 8:51) and went up on the mountain to pray. ***"Peter, John, and James"*** were the nearest to Him in understanding and in sympathy, and witnesses were needed to the event about to take place.

We are grateful to St. Luke for recording (by far more than the other Gospel writers) the numerous occasions when Jesus prayed during His ministry. On this occasion, there is no indication that Jesus prayed to be transfigured, just as there is no indication that He asked for the Spirit to descend upon Him as a dove at His baptism. Possibly He was experiencing temptations of doubt or fear regarding His coming passion. Clearly it was a prayer time of intense, yet sweet, communion with the Father.

When we truly, humbly, sincerely pray, we undergo a transformation in that we are no longer what we were before. We often speak about our worship services in the same way – that the hope is, we will "leave the service a different individual than when we arrived." It is neither unreasonable nor unrealistic to expect such results when we meet with the Father, for prayer and worship are capable of ushering in this kind of transformation resulting from the opportunity to encounter the one, true Living God.

Transfigured while praying! Jesus has said to us, ***"Follow Me."*** Surely this means we will be so desirous to be alone with Him, so eager to obey Him, so hungry for His Word – that we will more and more bear His very likeness upon our faces. When we are out in public, people should be able to look at us for the very first time and discern by our very countenance, that we belong to the One whose Name is above every name. It is *still* "no secret what God can do!"

As you pray today, instead of asking God to change your circumstances or to provide you with something, ask Him to change *you.*

"'Now I am no longer in the world, but these are in the world, and I come to You. Holy Father, keep through Your name those who You have given Me, that they may be one as We are.'" John 17:11

In this prayer, Jesus reveals and explains a huge need that will exist in the Church. He petitions the Father that His disciples *"may be one,"* being kept in love to each other, separate from the world, but not divided among themselves. The need is for truth and love to remain. "Truth" will be the badge of distinction between His Church and the world (see John 17:14), and "love" will be the bond that unites believers of that truth into a holy brotherhood. The strength of their discipleship will consist in the unity of this love.

All Believers are one spiritually by their living connection with God. The grammar here reveals two interesting notes. First, *"one"* refers to "one thing," or a "unit," "one body" over against the world. Second, *"that they may be"* one, actually means, "that they may *continue* to be" a unit, indefinitely. The disciples are already one, as shown clearly in verses 6-10. Since they are already one in the name that the Father gave to Jesus, Christ asks that the Father *guard* them, "in order that they may go on being one." The Father will accomplish this by keeping the disciples in the name, in the Word, and in the utterances of Jesus (see verse 8).

The longer we live, the more we realize that all sin is selfishness. From the book *Theologia Germanica,* a favorite of Martin Luther's, come these words, "It is said, it was because Adam ate the apple that he was lost, or fell. I say it was because of his claiming something for his own, and because of his I, Mine, Me and the like. Had he eaten seven apples, and yet never claimed anything for his own, he would not have fallen." Unfallen man ought to have remained truly "one," bound together in perfect unity by mutual love. But self crept in.

Selfishness, along with any teaching or doctrine that is contrary to the Word, endangers the oneness because it cuts into the bond that ties the disciples together! Pray that your selfish desires will not endanger this oneness.

June 9

"'Your will be done on earth as it is in heaven.'"   Matthew 6:10

There are times when praying *"Your will be done"* addresses God's overall plan for your *entire life*, as described in Jeremiah 29:11, *"For I know the thoughts that I think toward you, says the Lord, thoughts of peace and not of evil, to give you a future and a hope."* But there are also times when praying these words means you are placing your trust in God's decision-making ability to guide you in your *day-to-day* decisions. Whether for the short term or for the long term, asking for God's will to be done is trusting that His will is the *absolute best* for your life. To pray these words sincerely is to express your *priorities* as a Christian.

We are constantly tempted to conform to the self-centeredness of our secular culture, even when we pray; in fact, prayer is sometimes conceived as a means of getting *our* will done! There are times when it can accurately be said that we "boycott" His will. We resist the will of God as if our whole happiness depended on our having our own way. Is it because of a lack of perseverance that we behave this way? *No, it is because we just do not choose to trust Him!*

As a Believer, your top priority concern is *not* to promote your name, your kingdom, or your will. Your top priority concern is that *His* will would come to pass. Ask yourself: Is it not my own will that makes me so unhappy at times? Is it not my own will that causes me to want to be set free from voluntarily praying, "Your will be done?" Dear reader, pray today that it will no longer seem to you an "aggravation" to surrender your will to His, but rather something you do cheerfully. For it is then, that you will be joined to those already in heaven.

The will of God is not something to be "endured," but is rather something to be *embraced.* Pray sincerely, "Father, let Your will happen in my life. Your will, God - that's all I want, in everything."

"'Now I am no longer in the world, but these are in the world, and I come to You. Holy Father, keep through Your name those who You have given Me, that they may be one as We are.'" John 17:11

It is important to distinguish between what this "oneness" Jesus asks for *is*, and what it *is not*. Jesus does not ask that His disciples be kept in a oneness of their "opinions" by fleshly agreement. A consideration of, or focus on merely the "opinions" existing in the church, can sometimes *appear* to be spiritual oneness, but may only be the result of indifference, coincidence, or even the work of the devil. Nor is Jesus referring to the desire for an "ecumenical" church when He mentions oneness, as some have claimed.

What Jesus means when He prays, **"that they may be one,"** is that the Father would **"keep"** the disciples' hearts alive to all the attributes that constitute His **"name"** and character. Jesus desires that His disciples follow God in strict obedience - not as slaves, but as dear, loving children. Divine love, on the one hand, divine justice on the other. He is pleading in this prayer for a oneness of vital, divine union among His disciples.

This divine oneness in spirit, affection, and motive has been demonstrated and described in Acts 4:32: **"Now the multitude of those who believed were of one heart and one soul."** There will be minor differences, and the devil will always magnify them. *But there will be unity and oneness in the belief that God's Word is inspired, inerrant, and the final authority!*

The oneness Jesus asks for from the Father provides spiritual growth and comfort. Without this divine harmony of will and spirit, the witness of the disciples will fail. We must pray earnestly against carnal pride and selfish interests that so often hinder this oneness. We must pray faithfully that, through this unity, the Father will be abundantly glorified, and that the world will be attracted to Jesus by the visible oneness and love among His disciples. Jesus said, **"By this all will know that you are My disciples, if you have love for one another"** (John 13:35).

Our continued separation in a dangerous world is maintained by the Father. Pray to remember today that you are strong only in God.

June 11

"And for their sakes I sanctify Myself, that they also may be sanctified by the truth.'" John 17:19

*W*hen our Lord prayed, He prayed on a level above that of any other person! Yet His prayer, *"I sanctify Myself,"* does look a bit strange to us. And that is because this prayer reveals the very *thinking* of Jesus in the presence of His Father, immediately before His Cross. The truth is, no matter how humbly we approach it, we may never comprehend the *full* meaning of this great prayer!

Here is what we do know; God the Father had already sanctified His Son for the work of redemption, for we read in John 10:36 this reference to Jesus, *"whom the Father sanctified and sent into the world."* Jesus Christ was set apart for the purpose of redeeming lost humanity, for we also read in 1 John 4:14, *"the Father has sent the Son as Savior of the world."* Then, after Jesus came into the world, it was left up to the Son to devote Himself to that unfinished task – so He set Himself apart, in order to complete redemption's plan.

Now we should ask how all of this applies to ministers, to parents, and to you. A minister of Christ and of His Church, should look around and say, *"for their sakes,"* I sanctify myself; I dedicate and devote myself for their sakes. For their sakes, I keep myself at peace with God, and I practice the Presence of God; for their sakes, I seek more and more to please God."

A Christian parent should look every day at the children or grandchildren and say, "for their sakes, I sanctify myself; I make daily intercession before God in their behalf, that they might grow in grace, and in wisdom, and in favor with God." It would seem difficult for God to resist a parent's prayer that is sufficiently backed up by that parent's sanctification. Instead, many a sorrowful parent realizes too late, that his child has despised his counsel just as he, the parent, has despised God's counsel.

As you pray for your children or grandchildren today, pray for your intercession to be backed up with *your sanctification.*

> *"While I was with them in the world, I kept them in Your name. Those whom You gave Me I have kept; and none of them is lost except the son of perdition, that the Scripture might be fulfilled."* John 17:12

A more accurate translation of this portion of the prayer may be, "I, Myself, kept guarding them in Your name; whom You have given to Me, I also did protect." Today our focus is on the fact, the truth, that *we need* this keeping, this protection.

Believers cannot "keep" themselves secure in salvation. That is why Jesus has an individual keeping for each of us, which prevents us from perishing everlastingly. Were it possible to lose one's salvation while in His keeping, Christ would be dishonored.

And, like the disciples, we have need of being kept not only spiritually, but also physically. Scripture speaks of us as lambs in the midst of wolves; accounted as sheep for the slaughter; exposed to storms and tempests; and exhibiting the helplessness of infancy. In these dangerous circumstances, all of our individual and collective wisdom does not "keep" us for one moment. In this wicked world, all of our watchfulness and collective experience does not "keep" us through one single difficulty. And as long as the devil is permitted to roam, all of our willpower and determination does not "keep" us from giving in to one single temptation.

Even though *"The fruit of the Spirit is love, joy, peace, long-suffering, kindness, goodness, faithfulness, gentleness, self-control,"* there are still many wearied souls in the fellowship! They do not understand that they are being kept in the constant care and love of God. Where God keeps and guards, there is rest and peace. St. Augustine said that the heart of man was made for God and is restless until it finds rest in Him.

Yes, it is *still* safe to be in Christ's hands and keeping! Jesus was a faithful Shepherd when He was upon the earth, and He is still keeping His flock. Are you anxious today? When it comes to trusting Him, do not limit the One who hung the earth on *nothing! Because He is keeping you, you will have everything you need to stay in His service, further His kingdom, and glorify Him!*

Pray with thanksgiving, that you are in His keeping.

June 13

"'Your will be done on earth as it is in heaven.'" Matthew 6:10

Notice that this petition comes *before* the petitions for "personal" blessing. Our Lord Jesus has taught us an *order* in which we are to ask things of God. It is so much more important that God's will should be done than it is to have the personal "things" upon which we have set our hearts.

Yes, it is quite natural and appropriate for a child to ask his father for personal things like preserving him from trouble and loss, keeping him safe from danger or harm, helping him in sickness, and watching over those he loves. But the child of God must *first* learn to pray a prayer that requires a lot of learning, namely, **"Your will be done."** It is a difficult prayer to learn, because of the fact that it may be God's will to send him the very things he shrinks from!

The desires of the flesh and of the mind are for earthly comfort and ease. But God's will concerning us is, that whatever the cost and the pain, we should be clean and honest and true. *Therefore, scarcely a day passes but that our desires and the will of God for us come into extreme conflict!* To surrender our own wills, and to make God's will ours, means pain; it means *dying.*

The will that we are asked to make our own is *our Father's* will. Remember that! In the Garden, when He was facing the Cross and the Grave, Jesus was helped by remembering that same fact. He remembered that His Father is *love at its best* and that His Father always seeks the *highest good.* **"On earth"** means that our desire should be for God's will to be done in business life, social life, political life, public life, and family life.

Jesus has warned us by saying, **"Not everyone who says to Me, 'Lord, Lord,' shall enter the kingdom of heaven, but he who does the will of My Father in heaven."** Pray not only for more "knowledge" of God's will but also *for grace to put into practice what you already know.*

> **"*Father, forgive them, for they do not know what they do.*"**
> Luke 23:34

Every dying word uttered by Jesus Christ has been written with *exactness,* for the purpose of perfect and eternal publication. There has never been and never will be a preacher like the dying Christ, no sermon like the seven sentences spoken there, no pulpit like the Cross, and no congregation like that which was, or ever is, around it.

Here are the first words that Jesus spoke once He was on the Cross at Golgotha. It is believed that He spoke these words while the crucifixion was actually in progress. *As the nails were driven into those hands* that had constantly been used in ministries of mercy, *as the nails were driven into those feet* that had been continuously taking Him on errands of kindness – He opened His lips to pray for mercy on His executioners and enemies. To call this "remarkable" is not enough!

To forget about self *in the midst of* suffering, to think of others, to use the last gasps of breath under torture – in order to be in prayer for another soul – is not the way of common man. But it was the way and the prayer of Jesus Christ. As we listen to this prayer, we are listening to His heart. *Unrewarded, unappreciated, misunderstood, rejected, ill-treated, condemned on a totally false charge - the last beats of His big heart were pumping a forgiving spirit!*

And this very prayer of Jesus provided a model for martyrs who have followed. For example, Stephen prayed for those who were stoning him (see Acts 7:54-60), crying out with a loud voice, **"Lord, do not charge them with this sin."**

The trouble with the crowd at Calvary was the same trouble we discover in crowds today, who never clearly think out an issue. What attitude will be in our hearts when we breathe our last? We should not hope for a "sudden change of heart" when we are only moments from being in the presence of the One who prayed this incredible prayer.

Let us pray today, "Change my heart, O God, and put within me *Your* forgiving spirit."

June 15

"'Father, forgive them, for they do not know what they do.'"
Luke 23:34

Who is the source from which redemption and pardon flow? At Calvary, Jesus addressed His *"Father"* as that source. For His Father, *"desires all men to be saved and to come to the knowledge of the truth."*

This prayer of Jesus demonstrates the thought, the desire, that these men may *yet* learn just what they have done, and come to the knowledge of the truth – that this was God's own Son, the Prince of Life, the Lord of Glory – and not just another man killed by their ungodliness. He was not asking for their pardon without repentance, for that would run counter to all Scripture and to the very redemption Jesus was now accomplishing. But rather a pardon through repentance, once the truth would be made known to them. In other words, Jesus is praying that the Father may give these murderers the time, the grace, and the knowledge that may bring them the Father's forgiveness.

Some say that this prayer of our Lord went unanswered. But it was certainly answered in this way: God did not treat these men as murderers, but He opened up the possibility of salvation for them. *Therefore, it should not surprise us if, when we reach heaven, we meet the actual men who drove the nails into the hands and feet of Jesus!*

All His life, Jesus was revealing God the Father. But now His time was short, and the very highest about the Father needed to be revealed. And what was that? The truth that God is love and God can do only what love can do.

Our dear, always compassionate, Lord was looking to the end, the *eventual* state, the eternity facing His murderers. We must do the same, as we consider our enemies and those who mistreat and abuse us. Someone has written, "Wander whither thou wilt, thou must come at last to the place of a skull."

Pray now for *your* enemies. And pray now for your unsaved relatives and friends by name, that they may be saved while there is time to come to the knowledge of the truth.

"'While I was with them in the world, I kept them in Your name. Those whom You gave Me I have kept; and none of them is lost except the son of perdition, that the Scripture might be fulfilled.'" John 17:12

In a number of Bibles, a serious error in translation is made within this part of Jesus' prayer. That error is where the Greek word is incorrectly translated **"except"** previous to "the son of perdition" reference to Judas. This error has caused Bible interpreters to see Judas as some "sad exception," in whom all the guarding and protecting of Jesus failed.

In truth, Judas appeared to be, but was not, an "exception," for he, the son of perdition, was never "given" to Jesus by the Father in the first place. A correct translation would read, "None of them is lost, *but* the son of perdition," or "None of them is lost *save* the son of perdition." That is why Jesus could say truthfully, **"Those whom You gave Me I have kept."**

To clarify further, Jesus certainly labored with Judas, as He did with the Jews, and He persisted in those labors to the last. But, as in the case of the Jews, Jesus knew that Judas was not His own. Only for a time was Judas numbered among the apostles; only for a time did he have a portion in the work, **"For he was numbered with us and obtained a part in this ministry"** (see Acts 1:16, 17). God foresaw all that Judas would become and would do, in spite of all the grace given him.

Jesus kept the disciples in God's "name." Yes, **"The name of the Lord is a strong tower."** Your daily experiences have revealed a variety of "needs" that prompt you to **"run"** to that tower (see Proverbs 18:10). Only He can know the full story of your difficulties, your dangers, your enemies, and your future. *Yet you are "kept" in such a way as to be humbled, while He is glorified!* This is the way the Son of God kept His disciples then, and this is the way your dear heavenly Father keeps you now.

His keeping you means, **"Your ears shall hear a word behind you, saying, 'This is the way, walk in it"** (see Isaiah 30:21). Pray for grace to trust Him more.

June 17

"Your will be done on earth as it is in heaven." Matthew 6:10

G od has a will. To the Hebrew, the will of God was the good pleasure and holy purpose of the Creator. Doing His will was the joy of the righteous, prompting the Psalmist to write, ***"I delight to do Your will, O my God"*** and ***"Teach me to do Your will, for You are my God."***

So it is not enough that His kingdom be "established" and "enlarged;" there is an *end* for which all this is brought about, which is that the will of the Ruler may be *done. It is not merely a thing to be discussed, contemplated, or realized – it is a thing to be done by the words and works of men!* According to the seventeenth-century writer, Robert Hill, God's will is to be done "willingly, without murmuring; speedily, without delaying; constantly, without ceasing; universally, without omitting."

God's will was revealed and accomplished when Jesus Christ came to earth for the salvation of all men (see Hebrews 10:7-9; John 3:16, 6:38-40, 12:32). God's will centers in Jesus, who came to do His Father's will and who will carry it to its goal. This prayer would not be needed if no opposition ever interfered with His will, and so implied here is the undercurrent provided by "the devil, the world, and our flesh."

Our asking when we pray is based on a very limited knowledge, so it is best that we pray, ***"Your will be done,"*** literally, "Your will be done, as in heaven, just so on earth." The same sovereign heavenly Father who created us knows what's best for us, and has every detail of our lives under control. So our will is at its best when we will the same thing as God. This is easier said than done; we may gladly yield today, but find that tomorrow is a different story. Even though His will has always been accomplishing good, it is this same will that we too often resist and to which we object.

As you prepare to pray, surrender your heart and will to the One who knows what's best for you.

> *"He went a little farther, and fell on the ground, and prayed*
> *... 'Abba, Father.'"* Mark 14:35, 36

What is the meaning of the word *"Abba?"* In the New Testament, this word occurs only three times, each time in prayers. This word "Abba" is of the *Aramaic* language that Jesus spoke. Elsewhere in the gospels, the *Greek* word for "Father" is used when recording Jesus' words. "Abba" is an intensely personal and intimate word that means "my father." The intimacy of His relationship with the Father, particularly at this moment, explains the appropriate choice of this word as Jesus reached up as closely as possible to His Father's heart.

In order to describe the Believer's deep, inner sense of belonging to the Father's family, we find the Greek-speaking Christians using this word for God in Romans 8:15, and in Galatians 4:6. So in this passage, Mark simply communicates to his readers the equivalent word that they knew, for the Aramaic word Jesus used in this prayer.

Jesus knew what all of us need to know: If we can call God, "Father," then everything becomes bearable! Never is a childlike spirit so important, as when it is in regard to suffering, and in regard to prayer concerning it. Jesus' place of refuge was His Father's heart. He knew His Father's love, He knew His Father's wisdom, He knew His Father's power, and He knew *His Father's infinite ways to work* in even the most desperate situations.

God delights in being a perfect Father. There are circumstances in life when we, like Jesus in Gethsemane, need to say, "I know it's going to hurt, but You are my Father, and I know that you will be everything that I need. I choose to trust You." Similarly, the Church will be dysfunctional as a family if its members fail to see God as a good "father." It is the Father's desire that the Church function as a loving, caring, encouraging and affirming family.

"His infinite ways to work" – what a thought! Your Father has unlimited ways in which He can touch your life today. As you pray now and throughout the day, experience the comfort and joy of praying, "My Father."

June 19

"'While I was with them in the world, I kept them in Your name. Those whom You gave Me I have kept; and none of them is lost except the son of perdition, that the Scripture might be fulfilled.'" John 17:12

What are some of the things we know about Judas, *"the son of perdition?"* Of his history, we know him to be the only disciple of Jesus from the province of Judea. As the treasurer and administrator for Christ and the Twelve, Judas *"had the money box"* (see John 12:6), yet he was *"a thief"* and used to steal the money from the box! Apparently his thievery evolved over the course of time, for he must have been looked up to *initially* by the others as fit for such a position of trust. Jesus may have left Judas in the position not, of course, to ignore his sin - but to prevent the exposure of his moral decline until it was time.

We know also that, *"Those whom You gave Me"* definitely did *not* include Judas. Referring to Judas, Jesus did not say (as many Bibles inaccurately translate) *"except* the son of perdition;" He said, *"but* the son of perdition." We know this first from the Greek grammar - a disjunctive participle used here to draw contrast between those belonging to two different classes. Secondly, Jesus prayed later in this very prayer, *"I desire that they also whom You gave Me may be with Me where I am."* Jesus neither says nor implies that the son of perdition was given Him by the Father.

So we are confident that Judas was not a Believer (see John 6:64-71), that he had never been cleansed (see John 13:11), and that he had not been among the chosen (see John 13:18). Therefore, it is unscriptural to use Judas as an example of a Believer who has "lost his salvation." *Like some church-goers today, he only pretended to be saved, satisfied with a "connection" to Christ!*

Admit it or not, Judas Iscariot had passions like ourselves - in his case, covetousness and ambition. It had been thoughts of Israel's King that sparked his imagination and brought him to follow the Messiah. And, once more like ourselves, the disenchantment came gradually and increasingly.

Are your passions Godly passions? Pray for your passions to be Christ-like.

"*Your will be done on earth as it is in heaven.*" Matthew 6:10

When you pray **"*Your will be done,*"** you are praying that you will both know and actively obey God's will. Obviously, you must know God's will before you can *do* it – and knowing it without doing it, is clearly displeasing to God.

But the knowing and the doing of God's will is not the Believer's only responsibility. The *manner* of doing God's will is also very important. It has been said, "The manner of a thing is as well required as the thing itself." And so you must not only *do* God's will but *in the way* that He wants it done. God wants you to do His will as it is done **"*in heaven,*"** or, as the angels do it (meaning with a "likeness" to the manner of angels, not with an "equality" to them). Additionally, God wants you to *prefer* His will over man's will, and He wants you to do His will *spiritually*, that is, through Jesus Christ.

Praying "Your will be done," means that you are content to suffer anything because of what God has already done for you. He has given you *Jesus*, He has given you *grace*, and He has *adopted* you for His child! But praying this prayer also means that you take time to ponder and to study His will. When you do so, you will discover a number of "qualities" about His will.

God's will is both *gracious* and *good*. It may be different from your will, but it will not be without profit to you. His will is *wise*; God's wisdom and discernment determines what is best for you. God's will is *just*, in that it is holy and unerring. And the will of God is *sovereign*; He has absolute jurisdiction over you and over all of His creation, to do as He pleases.

Would it not glorify God for you to surrender your will to Him now, believing that He is truly sovereign? Pray "Your will be done," with complete confidence that the One in whose hand is your very breath will make no mistake when directing your path.

June 21

"'While I was with them in the world, I kept them in Your name. Those whom You gave Me I have kept; and none of them is lost except the son of perdition, that the Scripture might be fulfilled.'" John 17:12

The whole story of Judas, *"the son of perdition,"* raises some interesting questions, but also contains a valuable lesson. Some of the questions that are raised include: Did Jesus know, when He chose Judas, that he would prove a traitor? If what Judas did was foretold, so that by his action the Scripture was fulfilled, could he help doing it? Are some souls predestined by God to eternal damnation? Is there such a thing as eternal punishment?

But perhaps the most important use of our time today is to examine a *lesson* that comes from the story of Judas. One of the most shocking, even horrifying, passages in Scripture is Matthew 7:21-23, where we are told that *"many"* in that day will say to Jesus, *"'Lord, Lord, have we not prophesied in Your name, cast out demons in Your name, and done many wonders in Your name?' And then I will declare to them, 'I never knew you; depart from Me, you who practice lawlessness!'"*

The Lord did not "hold Judas back" when He sent forth the disciples to heal the sick, cast out devils, and preach the kingdom. Judas was right there present and ministering, along with the other disciples. Surely this same type of activity is taking place in the Church today!

The truth is, even the *constant presence* of Jesus fails to win, where the truth brought to the individual by the Spirit is not "received." Judas had unspeakable privileges; for years he had been the constant companion of Christ – he had seen Him, he had surely handled Him, and he had been taught from His own lips – but he was not saved. Oh, my! *You may have the highest office possible in the Church, you may sit under the most privileged ministry, and the Father may even use you to accomplish His purposes along the way – and you can be lost!*

The great lesson from the story of Judas is that you can connect with Godly people and even do Godly things, and be lost. Ask the Father to grant you blessed assurance of your salvation.

"'I thank You, Father ... that You have hidden these things from the wise and prudent and revealed them to babes.'" Luke 10:21

"The wise and prudent" can refer to many types of men. While the scribes and the Pharisees are the types referred to here, these people include the "great" people of the world, in the eyes of men. They include those who are held back by intellectual pride, those hindered by their love for glory, and those who consider the message of the Gospel to be beneath them. These are the men who sometimes display nearly a dozen letters following their name, who are cultured and accomplished. They are puffed up and quite satisfied with their own ideas and opinions.

On the other hand, we have men the Word of God describes as **"babes."** These are the humble instruments God uses. They have a simple yet strong faith and are sometimes men of poverty by the world's standards. *The sling of David is enough - because God is with them!* They are, in many ways, as children.

Yes, there are some men who, as the wise *or* as the babe, cling to their own foolish and incomplete understanding in spite of all the expressions of God's grace. That is why **"it seemed good"** in God's sight to arrange it so that *nothing* would be required of us, and that all should come from Him.

Who in the history of the world could suggest a better plan or method, than this that was good in His sight? Well, now and then the Father seems to "lift the veil" and allow us to see a glimpse of *what* He is doing and *how* He is doing it. This glimpse we need, for we are easily discouraged by man's coldness toward, indifference to, and rejection of the Good News. Here we see Jesus rejoicing, content to know that the Father's divine plan was being carried out.

Are you discouraged by what you see around you, or by what you hear in the news? Go to the Father in prayer now, and ask for His strong, immovable assurance that all things are still in His hands, and are subject to His wise and holy permission.

June 23

"'While I was with them in the world, I kept them in Your name. Those whom You gave Me I have kept; and none of them is lost except the son of perdition, that the Scripture might be fulfilled.'" John 17:12

Judas Iscariot, *"'the son of perdition,'"* had attached himself to Jesus because he thought Him to be the Messiah, and he expected to receive reward and honor in the Messianic Kingdom. Gradually, the truth came home to Judas, and he discovered the vanity of his expectations. It became clear to him that what awaited Jesus was not a crown but a cross, and that now the wisest course of action was to come out of it on the best possible terms.

We observe for our benefit: *The journey into sin gains momentum; we never know where a path of wrong motives may end!* John was beheaded, Jesus began to withdraw both from enemies and from success, the Christ began to make references to things like shame, disaster, and death; plus other experiences such as the failure to heal the lunatic child – all of this bringing Judas disappointment, given his hopes and expectations. The mental and the moral alienation went on together down a slippery slope.

We observe humbly, and also for our benefit, two sins of Judas: his covetousness and his hypocrisy. His covetousness was the root sin. Eventually, his love of money affected him to the point where he sold his own master. His hypocrisy - of continuing the profession of an apostle and pretending to be zealous for the poor – yet all the while, hearing the perfectly delivered sermons and discourses of Jesus on the subject of repentance.

Imagine being Judas, and listening to *these* words from Jesus: **"'Did I not choose you, the twelve, and one of you is a devil?'"** and, **"'He who eats bread with Me has lifted up his heel against Me'"** and, **"'Woe to that man by whom the Son of Man is betrayed! It would have been good for that man if he had not been born.'"** And then, knowing full well that Jesus was speaking of *him*, replied, **"'Rabbi, is it I?'"** (see Matthew 26:25).

Are there times when you think you are hidden in your disguise? Dear friend, pray and repent of any known sin that causes you to pretend.

"*Your will be done on earth as it is in heaven.*" Matthew 6:10

The third petition of the Model Prayer emerges from the second petition, and is explanatory of it; God's kingdom will come when His will is done on earth as it is in heaven.

You can look around and see that God's will is not always being done on this earth. Things are very wrong and broken on earth; demonic powers are jumping all over the minds of men. So, to ask that His will be done **"on earth as it is in heaven"** is to stretch your expectations! Clearly, this prayer requires that you know something about how His will *is* being done in heaven.

In heaven, God's will is being done *happily.* You will want to do His will gladly. In heaven, doing God's will is *top priority.* You will want to give attention to making His will the first-place concern of your day. In heaven, God's will is done *energetically.* You will want to put your whole heart, your whole being into passionately accomplishing His will. In heaven, God's will is done *immediately.* You will not want to procrastinate carrying out His will for your life. And in heaven, God's will is being done *constantly.* You will want to focus on doing His will continuously, not occasionally. In heaven, God's kingship is a *reality.* Cherubim and Seraphim, saints and angels, delight to do His will there. It is in heaven where God speaks, and it is done!

But on earth, even His own people do not always obey, and His rule is not always recognized; multitudes of people rebel against Him and refuse to acknowledge His authority. Nature obeys God. In all God's universe, *man* is the only one who is disobedient. So remember, when you pray, "Your will be done on earth as it is in heaven," you are expressing the desire to learn to obey God *as the angels do. God wants your priorities to be heavenly priorities!*

In heaven, the angels never even consider saying, "God, I will do that, first thing tomorrow." Pray that you will do God's will cheerfully, completely, and immediately.

June 25

"'While I was with them in the world, I kept them in Your name. Those whom You gave Me I have kept; and none of them is lost except the son of perdition, that the Scripture might be fulfilled.'" John 17:12

We know that Jesus is referring to Judas Iscariot when He mentions *"the son of perdition"* in His prayer. This reference demonstrated that Christ had not been deceived by Judas and that God's hand and counsel was in the matter, *"that the Scripture might be fulfilled."* Jesus' watchword was not "you have seen," but rather, *"it is written."*

On one occasion when Jesus was having conversation with the Sadducees, He made a comment that the Holy Spirit still uses to convict Believers today. Jesus told them, *"You are mistaken, not knowing the Scriptures nor the power of God"* (see Matthew 22:29). What would the Church of Jesus Christ look like if only we took care of business in just those two areas? God help us to read, study, memorize and know the Scriptures. And may we increase daily in our awareness of and belief in the power of God.

Judas was not chosen because he would turn traitor, but because he had in him (at the outset) the possibility of higher things. But not long after Jesus chose him, He perceived what was in Judas and knew the part that he would play. To be sure, Judas is a strange character, and everything about his choice and conduct is mysterious. *Yet a greater mystery is, why did Jesus choose any of us to be His followers?*

Jesus said, *"You did not choose Me, but I chose you and appointed you that you should go and bear fruit, and that your fruit should remain"* (see John 15:16). Christ placed you in an important *position* when He chose you. He did not give you a task, or place on you a burden; He honored you and blessed you by choosing you. Yes, you may hesitate at the thought, and even fear your inability. But Jesus went on to say that the Father will give you whatever you may ask of Him.

Do not miss this truth! He chose you in order to bear fruit, and for you to do that, you must ask of Him in prayer, so that fruit may abound.

"'Your will be done on earth as it is in heaven.'" Matthew 6:10

While there are many parts of God's will that are *not* performed on earth as "in heaven" because of our sin, it is also true that there are parts of God's will which can only be performed on earth. For example, we are told in the Bible that it is His will that we believe on His Son whom He sent – but we cannot do this in the hereafter, because it is the will of God *for earth*. So while the "things" to be done in heaven and on earth may differ, the "manner" of doing them is to be the same in spirit – cheerfully, zealously, faithfully, and constantly.

In Psalm 103:20-22, we find these words: ***"Bless the Lord, you His angels, who excel in strength, who do His word, heeding the voice of His word. Bless the Lord, all you His hosts, you ministers of His, who do His pleasure. Bless the Lord, all His works, in all places of His dominion."*** The manner in which God's will is done in heaven is the manner in which we are to do His will on earth. God's will is to be done perfectly, with every creature being an agent of His will.

When you pray, ***"Your will be done on earth as it is in heaven,"*** *you are acknowledging that there is a huge difference in "atmosphere" between the two places!* That is because those who inhabit heaven don't ask questions about God's will; they just do it. It is the difference between "active" and "selective" obedience. Angels don't "pick and choose" among God's commands, as if they were strolling through the grocery store selecting what looks good. They look into God's face and obey out of pure love.

Scripture only gives you a glimpse into the angelic world – not to satisfy your curiosity – but to provide spiritual truths to stimulate your service as well as your hope. You are to imitate the obedience of the angels; their obedience is in humility and in perfect submission.

Pray that your heart will be more trainable to *their* kind of reverential obedience!

June 27

"'While I was with them in the world, I kept them in Your name. Those whom You gave Me I have kept; and none of them is lost except the son of perdition, that the Scripture might be fulfilled.'" John 17:12

Jesus refers to Judas as the son of *"perdition,"* a word that literally means, "perishing." The Greek word refers to "loss" or "waste" that eventually leads to ruin. Judas was *"the son of"* perdition in that he was akin to it, bound up in it. Interestingly, this is the same phrase for antichrist used in 2 Thessalonians 2:3, *"And the man of sin is revealed, the son of perdition."*

It is also important to understand the meaning of the phrase, *"that the Scripture might be fulfilled."* This does not mean that the ruin of Judas took place so that a "prediction" could be proven true. However, the Scripture was the written, prophetic expression of the all-righteous will of God – so, in effect, this phrase means, "that the declared judgment of the supreme Judge may be carried out." God foresaw all that Judas would become, in spite of all the grace given to him. Once the betrayal was accomplished, it was the fulfillment of the plan of anguish assigned to the Messiah.

We find the specific "Scripture" Jesus refers to in this prayer by turning to Psalm 41:9, *"Even my own familiar friend in whom I trusted, who ate my bread, has lifted up his heel against me."* Jesus had previously referenced that verse when speaking to the disciples (see John 13:18). Then we find Jesus' own "definition" of the Scriptures, by turning to Luke 24:44, 45, *"These are the words which I spoke to you while I was still with you, that all things must be fulfilled which were written in the Law of Moses and the Prophets and the Psalms concerning Me."* Jesus quoted the Scriptures, submitted to the Scriptures, and endorsed the Scriptures of the Old Testament.

What does Scripture *continuing* to be fulfilled have to do with you today? *You should count on every statement being infallibly accomplished, every promise being carried out to the letter, and every warning being perfectly fulfilled – according to the faithfulness of Him whose Word it is!*

Pray for your confidence, your trust, and your belief in the Word of God to deepen.

"Now it came to pass, as He was praying in a certain place."
Luke 11:1

On a day when Jesus was making His way toward Jerusalem, He stopped to pray while in the company of His disciples. When He finished praying, **"one of His disciples said to Him, 'Lord, teach us to pray, as John also taught his disciples.'"** It is unlikely that the inquiring disciple was one of the Twelve because Luke does not provide his name. It was probably one of the Seventy (see Luke 10:1, 17) or perhaps someone in the larger circle of disciples traveling with Jesus.

This inquirer had not been present when the Sermon on the Mount was delivered, during which Jesus first taught "The Model Prayer" in its entirety. So here the Lord responds with an abbreviated version of the Prayer because previously He had already given it in full.

Even though "The Model Prayer" was never prayed by Jesus (He who was without sin could not pray words like, "Forgive us our debts"), its words provide a sacred yet simple prayer pattern for His disciples to this day. Followers of Jesus love this prayer! When John Knox lay dying, he attempted to say this prayer aloud. But after he spoke the words, "Our Father," he paused, and said, "Who can pronounce words so holy?"

Notice how merely the response of Jesus to this disciple reveals the *importance* of prayer. Jesus answered the man immediately, provided explicit instruction, and gave His full attention to such a welcome request. *Surely it delighted the Lord that one of His followers recognized the value of prayer!* And so Christ took the time to provide a model prayer (verses 2-4), a parable (verses 5-8), and then a teaching lesson (verses 9-13) – all in response to this disciple's request.

On the other hand, "prayerlessness" is the act of ignoring or rejecting God! It is the attitude that we want things that God has to "offer" (peace, protection, salvation, mercy, forgiveness, eternal life), but we don't need *Him*.

Pray that your understanding of the importance of prayer will increase and that the continuous desire of your heart will be, "Lord, teach *me* to pray."

June 29

"'But now I come to You, and these things I speak in the world, that they may have My joy fulfilled in themselves.'" John 17:13

This entire prayer was, for the disciples, a divine summary of all that they had ever heard Jesus say about the Father, about Himself, about them, and about the Church that was to be. Certainly, this was a time of deep dejection for the apostles, and Jesus' desire was to turn their sorrow into joy. This He would do by permitting them to hear Him commending them and their cause to the Father.

The prayer was made with an "audible" voice, **"these things I speak,"** so that the disciples (and us) would hear the *quality* of prayer that would be in store for them. Jesus wanted them to be instructed and comforted by hearing the prayer, and He has caused it to be written down so that *we also* might know of His deep interest. Therefore, we should prayerfully read and meditate on this prayer for our own peace, edification, consolation, and happiness.

Martin Luther said that we should always be ready when God knocks, prepared to take our leave of this world like a Christian. It is strange that we will prepare for everything except death. The human heart beats about 100,000 times in the period of a day. One day, one of those beats will be our last. And moments later, we will either have had our first glimpse of heaven or our first experience of real horror and regret!

You can never approach death quite like Christ did. The words, **"But now I come to You"** express a brightness beyond your capability. *Jesus knew the glory, the rest, the songs, the light, the beauty that was beyond — but He especially longed to be with the Father once again!* What if *you* had similar views and thoughts of God? While you wait for His return, you should imitate this confidence Jesus had. Vance Havner wrote, "There is nothing morbid about getting ready to die. For a Christian, it is preparation for life's greatest adventure. (It) is but the end of a Prelude."

Pray that on the day you face death, you will have the confidence that Jesus had.

"'Your kingdom come.'" Matthew 6:10

If you are unsure over the reason why you as a Believer have been given another day to live, the answer is in some way connected to *this* petition of the Model Prayer. For this petition is "a trumpet-call to action" that points directly to what *should* be the very course and object of your life.

When you pray, be careful that you do not give the word "church" a narrow meaning only, by excluding all but your own local congregation where you are a "member." Aside from the seven *specific* churches described in the first three chapters of Revelation, Jesus mentioned **"the church"** (meaning the local congregation) only once (see Matthew 18:17). But He spoke habitually of the **"kingdom"** of God. *He wants you to be most concerned about the bigger picture!*

You should take time to study carefully His Sermon on the Mount. In that sermon, Jesus describes the kingdom of God, *the place where God rules*. The importance of that sermon to you includes the description of the "character" of the citizens of that kingdom – not arrogant, but meek and merciful; not destructive, but edifying; not condemning, but reconciling. In a sense, it is like reading your "spiritual job description."

When you pray, "Your kingdom come," you are asking that the King of kings, and the Lord of lords, will reign over your spirit and soul and body that He has redeemed. That requires the exposure and destruction of all corruptions, both outward and inward; and for truth and righteousness in all departments of life. When you pray for these things, you know that God will hear you, because you are praying according to His will. What you are really doing, is asking God for all that He has made to become as it was when He examined it after creating it, **"And indeed it was very good"** (see Genesis 1:31).

The leadership and attendees of the local church where you attend regularly need your faithful intercession. In addition, remember the bigger picture as you pray today, by pleading for His kingdom to come throughout the earth.

July 1

"'Father, forgive them, for they do not know what they do.'"
Luke 23:34

Someone once wrote, "It is right that man should love those who have offended him: he will do so when he remembers that all men are his relations and that it is through ignorance and involuntarily that they sin." This is a pleasant sounding statement until someone is breathing his last at the hands of abusive, cruel and violent men. C.S. Lewis wrote, "Everyone says forgiveness is a lovely idea until they have something to forgive."

Yet while hanging on the Cross, rejected and ridiculed, we find Jesus with no resentment, no anger, and no desire for punishment toward the men who were physically and verbally abusing Him. If we examine the original language, **"forgive"** is not expressive enough for an accurate translation. Words such as, "remit" or "send away" or "dismiss" with reference to the sins of these men, are closer to the true meaning. These more accurate translations reveal the Father's deep love for mankind that exceeds comprehension. Daniel 9:9 says, **"To the Lord our God belong mercy and forgiveness, though we have rebelled against Him."** May we praise Him!

Many dying men find themselves praying desperately, "Forgive *me*." It might be the most sincere expression of regret in their entire life, the moment when they realize that time has expired, and they have *missed* the countless previous opportunities to humble themselves and to repent. The dying Jesus, on the other hand, had no reason to ask forgiveness for Himself, but instead was thinking of *others* and of their eternal need. *Repentance is our offender's responsibility; forgiveness is our responsibility!*

When we consider how large an offense God forgave us, our gratitude to Him will motivate and enable us to forgive others. Grace is the good pleasure of the Father that moves Him to bestow benefits upon the *undeserving*. If you think God's grace is a reward for anything that you have done, you will be incapable of receiving it. All thanks be to God for grace abounding!

Pray now, to **"Be kind to one another, tenderhearted, forgiving one another, even as God in Christ forgave you."**

"'Your kingdom come.'" Matthew 6:10

It is difficult, if not impossible, to pray this prayer rightly without noticing the distance we are from its realization. Just look at our world! Is there divine discontent and passionate dissatisfaction over the conditions we see? We are face to face with passive godlessness all around us, are we not?

Gambling is breaking up marriages and families and has already become one of the strongest addictions among us. Terrorism is manifesting all over the globe. Violence continues to occur in the home and on the streets. Greed and the lust for money dictate decision-making, while the poor continue to starve and die. Churches are closing their doors, while too many new churches treat prayer as cosmetic. Political correctness pressures pastors to preach messages of comfort rather than of conviction.

If we are going to pray in the manner that Jesus taught us, if we are going to pray the words *"Your kingdom come"* sincerely, we must take care neither to hinder nor in any way thwart the advancement and interests of God's kingdom. However imperfectly, however feebly, however unworthily – we must endeavor to the clearest of our lights and to the best of our energies – to prepare the throne of that kingdom in our individual hearts and in the world.

Will you not only pray the words of this petition found in the Model Prayer, but also *fight* for it, and fight hard? Will you then wrestle mightily, and at all costs, against the corruption of its truth and against the adversaries of its holiness? Is there evidence to convict you, dear Believer, of doing any self-denying thing to promote the kingdom of God?

Ah! *How many of us, in God's sight, are doing anything except living and dying for ourselves?* Well then, let this prayer arouse us! Since our time on this earth is limited, let us pay no attention to what the spiritually uninformed may say or think, and let us do our duty! Expecting the opposition from a wicked world to increase, let us fix our eyes upon Jesus and pray to our Father, "Your kingdom come."

July 3

"'But now I come to You, and these things I speak in the world, that they may have My joy fulfilled in themselves.'" John 17:13

S hortly before Jesus prayed this prayer, He said, ***"These things I have spoken to you, that My joy may remain in you, and that your joy may be full*** (see John 15:11). Shortly after that, He made a couple of promises: ***"Your heart will rejoice, and your joy no one will take from you"*** and ***"Ask and you will receive, that your joy may be full."*** *Rich and gracious provisions are these that the Savior makes for the comfort of His disciples - and for us!*

When you lived in this world without knowing Christ as your Savior, you may have believed at times that you had real joy. Perhaps you laughed heartily and demonstrated a sense of humor, or you showed a happy enthusiasm watching a ball game. But as a Believer, you now have "His joy," and you easily distinguish *this* joy from any joy that this world can offer. Matthew Henry said it well in his *Commentary on the Whole Bible,* "We have no joy but in Christ."

It is important for all who belong to Jesus to know that He has these specific desires – that we should have *joy,* that this joy should be *His* joy, that this joy should dwell in us *fully,* and that this joy should be *permanent.* The joy of Jesus is none other than the joy of His salvation. It is the joy of justification from sin, perfect in Christ before God, fastened into the soul of the Believer by the indwelling Spirit and by the grace of God.

Just as light cannot exist where darkness reigns, joy cannot exist where sin reigns. If you choose to live in disobedience, you will become a fruitless and joyless Christian. But as soon as the power of sin is broken, and devilish strongholds are demolished – yes, when freedom from bondage is gloriously provided - joy everlasting begins to dawn!

If you have Christian friends or relatives that have lost their joy, pray for their joy to be restored. If it is *you* who has lost the joy of the Lord, pray for Holy Spirit conviction.

**"*And all Mine are Yours, and Yours are Mine,
and I am glorified in them.*'"** John 17:10

The disciples, like us, were always less than perfect. Yet in this prayer of Jesus, we find these remarkable words, **"*I am glorified in them,*"** or, "Glory has come to Me through them." How can this possibly happen? As we obey, serve, and trust Jesus, we vindicate His work as Savior and consequently bring honor and glory to Him. Yet another motive or incentive to our living for Jesus – that we, with all of our faults, may actually, *by His definition* - glorify Him through obedient living.

Brothers and Sisters, this is truly amazing! Here we are, living in the most elementary beginnings of our understanding of Him and of our faith in Him, yet we are prized and seen as beautiful by Him, to the point that we may actually glorify Him, as long as our faith and love for Him are set towards growth on the "upward road," as was the case here with the disciples.

In a similar way, the Church glorifies Him whenever it behaves obediently and biblically. **"*The church of the Laodiceans*"** was in the woeful condition of luke-warmness (see Revelation 3:16) because they desired the "man-pleasing blend" of being **"*neither cold nor hot.*"** This church was apparently moving in spiritual *decline* from heat to frost (not from frost to heat, which would have been moving in a God-glorifying direction).

Do you recognize any *spiritual* decline that is a consequence of political diplomacy? Back in 1946, Vance Havner wrote these words, "The political world is waiting for the sunrise. The politicians do not know it, of course. They would try to make the day dawn by their efforts around conference tables. But the hope of a better day rests with only One, the Lord of Glory. Only in Christ can you bring men together."

Only in Christ can we as individuals, we as the Church, and we as the United States of America, bring glory to God. *We are in a feeble condition because our prayer lives are feeble, even though He has taught us about prayer!* Pray for the United States to *glorify Jesus.*

July 5

"'But now I come to You, and these things I speak in the world, that they may have My joy fulfilled in themselves.'" John 17:13

*S*ince *Jesus has made such provision for our consolation of joy, why should we ever seek it elsewhere?* Are the consolations of God so "small" that they cannot overcome the afflictions of this world? A sour, complaining Christian is a dishonor to God and a grief to the Spirit because he is resisting the Spirit's work as the Comforter and refusing the Spirit's fruit (see Galatians 5:22).

You have *reason* to receive His joy. You will receive His joy when you remember your condition before you trusted Jesus for salvation. Hallelujah! What a change God made! 1 Peter 2:9 says, **"That you may proclaim the praises of Him who called you out of darkness into His marvelous light."** That light is "marvelous" because of the previous darkness in which you were helpless and hopeless. No man looks out upon the ocean with more comfort, than he that escaped a horrible shipwreck.

You have the *sources* from which to receive His joy. You will receive His joy *from His Word.* Jeremiah 15:16 says, **"Your word was to me the joy and rejoicing of my heart."** You will receive His joy *from His love:* **"We have known and believed the love that God has for us"** (see 1 John 4:16). And you will receive His joy *from the contentment in His perfect shepherding,* **"The Lord is my shepherd; I shall not want"** (see Psalm 23:1).

And you have the means to *maintain* His joy. First, by *faith.* It is the nature of faith to make things unseen, present. By faith, God is seen in action wherever He has promised, and this belief aids us in keeping our joy. Second, by *obedience.* **"The kingdom of God is not eating and drinking, but righteousness and peace and joy in the Holy Spirit"** (see Romans 14:17). Sin and disobedience *take away* joy and peace. You must walk so that you are in the condition capable of joy, **"walking in the fear of the Lord and in the comfort of the Holy Spirit"** (see Acts 9:31).

Pray that you will know and maintain *His* joy today.

"And do not lead us into temptation, but deliver us from the evil one"
Matthew 6:13

Basically, *"Deliver us from the evil one"* refers to two things. It can mean, "Deliver us from *falling into* this pit of destruction;" or, it can mean, "*Pluck us out* of this pit of destruction." In other words, keep us from sin; or, since we have already sinned, do not let this be our "resting place."

Since we are God's people and the sheep of His pasture, we are either sheltered in the fold, or we are wandering from it. This petition of the Model Prayer is asking that the wolf and the lion not leap into the fold, but, if they seize us, that God would save us from their fierce teeth and claws. We are praying for both protection *and* rescue because we are constantly in need of both.

Sin is a fearfully *cumulative* thing; once we take a sin by the hand, it leads to another. Once we are in a deep low, there may still be a *deeper* low! Therefore, *"You who love the Lord, hate evil!"* and pledge yourselves to the utmost to fight against it. We must not pray this prayer insincerely; we must not go to the tree - gaze at it, think of it, and reason with the evil one – and *then* ask God to deliver us! For rescue out of the power of evil, we need resolve and effort on *our* part.

Jesus spoke clearly to our part in being "delivered" from evil when He said, *"Strive to enter through the narrow gate"* (see Luke 13:24). We are to *agonize, struggle,* letting nothing deter us from entering through the narrow gate to the kingdom, while that door is open! We *"enter," by agonizing in constant, true repentance of sin!* Of course, *"many"* do not "like" a door that can only be entered by forsaking their sins.

Examine your heart thoroughly before praying this prayer. Is there *any* evidence of carelessness or false security? Do not wait until it is too late! Do not wait until the narrow gate is no longer open by grace! Agonize! Pray for *strength to forsake* unrepented sin.

July 7

"'But now I come to You, and these things I speak in the world, that they may have My joy fulfilled in themselves.'" John 17:13

Think of it: *"My joy."* The very joy of Jesus Christ! The joy of His is the joy that had been the portion of His heart through those thirty-three years while He dwelled among men. The joy of His is the joy of *victory*. The joy of His is the joy of *permanent satisfaction*. The joy of His is the joy of *fellowship with the Father*.

Just as Jesus places His disciples into the condition of peace, in order that from it they may draw the experience of peace, so He now places them into the condition of joy, in order that they may draw the experience of joy from it. In addition, *the measure of this joy is to be complete,* *"fulfilled"* – it is to be like a vessel that has been filled to the brim from which we may draw at any time. His joy is fulfilled in us in proportion as we consciously enter into it. *The trouble with many Believers is that they have just enough of Christ not to enjoy the world, but just enough of the world not to enjoy Christ!*

Therefore, when there are discomforts and troubles in the church, this prayer provides encouragement and consolation. We have also, *"And these things we write to you that your joy may be full"* (see 1 John 1:4), *"These things I have spoken to you, that My joy may remain in you, and that your joy may be full"* (see John 15:11), and *"Ask, and you will receive, that your joy may be full"* (see John 16:24). We are encouraged, then, that this is the *full measure* (not a temporary portion) of His joy that He provides.

This joy is fulfilled *"in themselves,"* in the hearts of His disciples, by their own feeling and experience, because they will *need* something divine and powerful "within," while operating in a world providing them with *"tribulation"* (see John 16:33). We are reminded that this intercession for our joy is what Jesus is doing for us *now,* in heaven!

Pray that you will experience His full "victory joy" today.

"Now it came to pass, as He was praying in a certain place."
Luke 11:1

The disciples knew about prayer; John the Baptist and some of the rabbis taught on the subject of prayer. Their culture was bathed in prayer – prayer in the morning, prayer in the evening, prayer before meals and special prayer for various occasions. The Jews were a praying people, but there was still a great deal to learn about this important subject.

When the disciples of Jesus saw and heard Him pray, their hearts were stirred. The Master taught them about prayer by *"praying"* in their presence. What a blessed experience that must have been for them! We cannot say for sure that the disciples always heard the "words" Jesus prayed. There may have been times when the Savior prayed silently in their presence, and there may have been times when the disciples simply could not hear the words He was saying aloud.

Prayer was Jesus' very breath and life! For Him, prayer was not an act of self-discipline requiring time management skills or gimmicks. It was neither forced nor artificial, but a very natural communion. He prayed with a thankful heart.

In addition to teaching about prayer by His example, Jesus answered the disciples' request to be taught on this occasion. On other occasions, He provided clear instruction on prayer and fasting (see Matthew 6: 5-18) and took advantage of teaching moments along the way (see Matthew 17:18-21). We who follow Jesus today are still learning from Him as we study God's Word, plus we have the supreme Teacher in the Holy Spirit living within us and guiding us *"into all truth"* (John 16:13).

Seeing the disciples' willingness to learn about prayer had to be a blessing to Jesus. We don't know for sure, but it is likely that Jesus had prayed for His disciples to have this desire because He knew how vital prayer would be in their lives and ministries. It is noteworthy that sometimes our Lord waits until such desires *arise* in our hearts so that we will more eagerly accept His instruction.

Pray for a desire, for eagerness, even a hunger, to learn more about prayer.

July 9

Jesus prayed, *"I have given them Your word."* The perfect tense indicates that the gift of the Word is *in the possession of* the disciples; Jesus is leaving them with this divine gift still in their hearts that they would continue to believe it, profess it, and preach it. The Word is the means by which the Father keeps His children from evil, fulfills the joy of the Lord in us, manifests Himself to us, guides us, warns us, teaches us, and comforts us.

God's Word is the testimony of the love of the Father, and of the Son, and of the Holy Ghost to us – and it is the testimony of the triumphs of the Son of God for us. It is the means for our sanctification, for in just a moment Jesus will pray, *"Sanctify them by Your truth. Your word is truth."*

Paul wrote boldly and clearly to the church at Thessalonica that this Word was not the word of man, but rather the Word of God: *"When you received the word of God which you heard from us, you welcomed it not as the word of men, but as it is in truth, the word of God, which also effectively works in you who believe"* (see 1 Thessalonians 2:13). *This declaration by Paul is one of the most delightful acknowledgments ever made to man!* The Word of God, so blessed and mighty to produce saving effects, *deserves* the most prompt and complete acceptance.

God hung the universe with words. You exist because God spoke. Dear reader, your heart should be stirred up to not only read but to *study* that Word. Why? Because it came down to you from such a Source, and because it has been given to you by such a Savior at such a cost.

May it happen to you as it did to the two disciples on the road to Emmaus – that Jesus Himself may walk with you and expound to you the things concerning Himself. Pray for a fuller understanding of God's holy Word, for yourself, and for the whole Church.

"For Yours is the kingdom and the power and the glory forever. Amen."
Matthew 6:13

If we live in God, then we are living in the world of reality. If we are living for the world and setting our affections on earthly things, then we are living in a world of fatal delusions. The world is near and present – something that we can touch. It has an alluring and seductive appearance, similar to how the crude apple appeared to Eve. A worldly life seems fascinating, but has anything ever come of it except misery and disappointment?

The word **"Amen"** means truth, reality. It means, "May this be fulfilled!" Therefore, it is the cry of the Believer's fervent hope. To pray "Amen," is a prayer in itself, a separate prayer expressing our expectation and our confidence. Still too often, we pray as those who mean nothing and expect nothing.

Errors and failures of popular religion spring up because men focus on the *forms* of worship rather than the Object of worship; they want to *make* religion and *display* religion, rather than "evidence" religion, through humble and loving lives. Even the preachers who remain and faithfully preach the Word today have to ask lazy congregations, "Can I get an 'Amen,'" because the audience is just that - an audience.

Prayers said by you but unfelt within you, worship in which you are present but in which you take no part, are empty. You might just as well patent a machine to do it for you. But when the heartfelt "Amen" puts the petitions that you have offered into the hand of God, and when your "Amen" is the expression of your belief in His love and wisdom, then, as Luther says, "As your Amen is, so has been your prayer."

May you come to the place in your prayer life where all things here below vanish, and where nothing seems important but holiness of heart and the salvation of others. *Pray like you are living in the world of reality!* Pray Scripture. Today may be the day the Spirit prompts you to *agonize* in prayer – for His kingdom to come on earth as it is in heaven.

July 11

"'I have given them Your word; and the world has hated them because they are not of the world, just as I am not of the world.'" John 17:14

2 Timothy 3:12 says, *"All who desire to live godly in Christ Jesus will suffer persecution."* Paul does not say, "All that *profess* Christ," in order to distinguish between those who are, in truth, lacking commitment. Professing Christians are changing. Some are worldly enough to "suit" the world, and not Christ-like enough to "offend" the world. Persecution in *"the world"* comes to those that "live godly in Christ" and are holy, obedient, and true to the Master.

Anytime a child of God has the world's respect, he should look to his conscience! Jesus said, *"Woe to you when all men speak well of you, for so did their fathers to the false prophets."* If you are living as though you are of this world, then there is nothing worthy of your new nature. Listen to yourself and see if the hopes of your heart are evident in your conversation. A person who is of this world should *"think it strange that you do not run with them"* (see 1 Peter 4:4). Oil and water will not mix, and when they seem to, it is because there has been a compromise.

If you are living as though you are of the world, there is nothing worthy of your expectation of God's blessing and favor. You are striving for a reward from this world. A Christian is satisfied with nothing but eternity. And finally, if you are living as though you are of this world, there is nothing worthy of Christ's example. The contents in a thousand worlds will not satisfy your desires. Jesus died to deliver you from this present world, and He ascended that you might follow Him with your whole heart while you still live in the world.

You cannot be good for the world *spiritually* if you get your priorities and message "from the world." This truth partially explains the failure of Christians to win "the world" to Christ. Sad but true, too often the world fails to see the difference or any gain by the change.

Pray that people "of the world" will see Jesus in you.

"And Jesus lifted up His eyes and said, 'Father, I thank You that You have heard Me.'" John 11:41, 42

On other occasions when He performed miracles, there were people who said Jesus was operating in partnership with Satan. They attributed His cure of a blind man to the work of a demon or to deception. On this occasion Jesus made it clear that what was taking place was due to His partnership with God, causing those who were present to face that fact – a fact He had consistently voiced on previous occasions.

It is not an acceptable explanation that this prayer was a request of the Father for the "power" and "authority" to raise Lazarus from the dead. Jesus is not functioning here as some mere "tool" of the Father, powerless for any type of work unless given help from above. Wholly *one* with the Father, Jesus raised Lazarus from the dead. The miracle these people were about to witness was performed in direct answer to Jesus' *prayer.*

John 11:42 explains that Jesus prays this prayer **"because of the people who are standing by."** This was a very unique situation, in which a prayer was spoken aloud *for the sake of those present* to receive an important truth. Not all prayer should be private; there are occasions when public or corporate prayer is appropriate. But definite precautions should be taken whenever we pray aloud in the presence of others (see Matthew 6:5-8).

Our "normal" circumstances of corporate prayer should have us praying to the *Father's* ear, rather than for the purpose of sending a message to the ears of those present. Unnecessary formality, wordy rambling, and altered voices – done for our glory – is unacceptable. *Jesus always prayed in the Spirit, and we must do the same, whether we are praying privately or publicly!*

Jesus knew Proverbs 3:6, which says **"In all your ways acknowledge Him."** Christ was being careful to honor the Father for the miracle that was about to be performed. He directed the attention to God when He could have easily drawn attention to Himself.

Pray that the Father will help you remember today to audibly give *Him* glory for whatever you may accomplish for His kingdom.

July 13

"'I have given them Your word; and the world has hated them because they are not of the world, just as I am not of the world.'" John 17:14

"Hate" is a strong word. There are many other words that communicate displeasure that are not as powerful. Referring to His disciples then and now, Jesus prayed, *"The world has hated them."* Today we will think about some of the reasons why this word is indeed appropriate.

"The world" is an alien environment to the true disciple of Jesus Christ. It is alien because it is actually managed by a curse, resulting in all manner of physical dangers to a Christian. And it is alien because the Christian is of such a nature that he does not belong to the world. Left in the midst of a hostile world, disciples are in desperate need of protection. They will be boycotted and persecuted. Jesus knew that the world would not change, so He prayed in this manner for those who remain in the world.

So we have "the world," the carnal mind, on one side; the Father's "word," the mind of Christ, on the other. They cannot be reconciled. This deep-seated antagonism, this warfare, this clash between God's light and the darkness of this world, can only be ended when the old man is crucified (see Romans 6:6) and when his thoughts are brought into captivity to the obedience of Christ (see 2 Corinthians 10:5).

Jesus said, *"If you were of the world, the world would love its own. Yet because you are not of the world, but I chose you out of the world, therefore the world hates you."* At the trial of "Faithful" in *The Pilgrim's Progress*, one of the Jury gives as his reason for hating the prisoner that, "He would always be condemning my way." *There, precisely, is the reason why the world "hates" the true follower of Jesus!* The true Believer, under the power and leadership of the Holy Spirit, *exposes* the errors and lies of those who are *"of the world."* The result is hurt pride that turns into anger.

Understanding *why* the world hates you is valuable information. Pray that this understanding will make you more compassionate toward those who are of the world.

"*Your will be done on earth as it is in heaven.*" Matthew 6:10

Today we will focus on the "will" of God. It is a *loving* will, for He is "our Father." His will is truly the "outcome" of His Fatherhood. And it is a *holy* will, for He is "in heaven."

How mysterious, how humbling – the examination of the will of an infinite God! We are hardly suited to dictate what His will *ought* to be, but, in the light of His own revelations, we confess that we know "something" of His will as revealed to us in His Word and by His Son. As we prayerfully study Jesus' earthly life and teaching, we learn the nature of His Father's will. Surely He who came to save us would not instruct us to pray for the accomplishment of a will that is opposed to His own mission!

Our part, then, is to concur with God's will and to be grateful that His power is supreme. Our desire is to be both willing and enabled to do what He wills to be done *by* us. We can either concur with His will, or we can dispute it; we can either perform His will, or we can resist it. Sun, moon, and stars unconsciously obey; only man stands within this loyal universe and dares to say "No" to Almighty God!

Jesus said to the Jews, **"You are not willing to come to Me that you may have life,"** and He said to the Pharisees, **"How often I wanted to gather your children together, as a hen gathers her brood under her wings, but you were not willing!"** The Son of God was saying, "I had the will to save you; you had the will to reject Me. Your will is opposed to Mine!" Paul wrote to the Corinthians, **"We implore you on Christ's behalf, be reconciled to God."** Harmony between our will and God's is brought about only by the Holy Spirit, **"For it is God who works in you both to will and to do for His good pleasure"** (see Philippians 2:13).

Pray for your will to be in perfect harmony with His.

July 15

"'I have given them Your word; and the world has hated them because they are not of the world, just as I am not of the world.'" John 17:14

Jesus prayed, *"I am not of the world."* Christ *never was* of the world. He was, *"holy, harmless, undefiled, separate from sinners"* (see Hebrews 7:26). But how is it also true of His disciples - that *they* are "not of the world?" Again, God's Word provides the answer.

2 Corinthians 5:17 says, *"If anyone is in Christ, he is a new creation."* Hebrews 3:1 says that Christians are, *"partakers of the heavenly calling."* Philippians 3:20 says a Believer's *"citizenship is in heaven." In view of all of this, the Christian is but a stranger and pilgrim here in this world, on a "journey" to his home in heaven to be with Jesus!* Grace has delivered Christ's disciples from this *"present evil age"* (see Galatians 1:4) so that they now have new affections, new interests, and a new Master. They have been separated from the world and their obedient lives "condemn the world" (see Hebrews 11:7).

We look now for application. What are the *characteristics* of a disciple who is "not of the world?" First, there is a difference in their *inward principles* - the difference between the spirit of the world and the Spirit of God (see 1 Corinthians 2:12). Second, they are under different *rulers* - the difference between *"the god of this age"* and Christ, whose *"kingdom is not of this world"* (see John 18:36). Third, there is a difference in their *path* - the difference between men of this world walking *"according to the course of this world"* (see Ephesians 2:2) and Christians walking according to the rule of God's Word.

Fourth, there is a difference in their *aims* - the difference between the child of the world who minds earthly things and the child of God who lives to glorify Him (see 1 Corinthians 10:31). And fifth, their *ends* are different – the difference between the carnal man moving downward (first to the earth and then to hell) and the Christian moving upward (to a place not made with human hands).

Pray that today you will demonstrate the characteristics of one who is *not* of the world.

> *"'Father, forgive them, for they do not know what they do.'"*
> Luke 23:34

Bible students have long debated the answer to the question concerning whom Jesus was referring when He said, *"forgive them.* For whom was the Master praying? Primarily, for the Roman soldiers who were blindly obeying the orders that they had received. But then they were just "tools" with no moral responsibility. What did they know? And then there were those people standing behind the soldiers, inspiring and directing them.

Possibly, "them" referred to the Jews, who by rejecting and slaying their Messiah, were smiting themselves with a mortal blow. They had treated Jesus as though He had no official authority to proceed as a public reformer of the established Jewish customs (see John 2:18-19). It was the evil will of the Jewish authorities that set this whole train of events in motion.

It is more likely that Jesus was praying here in a more *inclusive* way for those who *"do not know what they do"* in bringing Him to His death. This would include *"the people"* (Acts 3:11-17), plus those dwelling *"in Jerusalem, and their rulers"* (Acts 13:27; 1 Corinthians 2:8). Before we pass judgment on *specific* individuals, such as Caiaphas and Pilate, we should remind ourselves that God alone knows the hearts of men, and therefore, to what degree *we* sin against better knowledge. Truly, who of us can say assuredly to another person: "This you could and should have known?"

To "forgive" or to "dismiss" indicates that these were terrible sins – something grave and serious to dismiss. Even with consideration for ignorance, all the sinning connected with the Passion of Jesus was open, flagrant and deliberate. Are there sins *we* commit that are, in some way, related to the sins that put Jesus on the Cross? *Perhaps the behavior we display, or the words we speak, or the attitudes we hold, demonstrate to others that we are not paying attention, or that we do not know what we are doing!*

Pray today that the decisions you make will demonstrate, and will witness to the fact, that you know what you are doing as a child of the King.

July 17

"'I have given them Your word; and the world has hated them because they are not of the world, just as I am not of the world.'" John 17:14

Only a person who is "not of the world" can say rejoicing along with Paul, ***"For I consider that the sufferings of this present time are not worthy to be compared with the glory which shall be revealed in us."*** We need comfort not only when we suffer for Christ, but also (and often, much more) when we endure other types of suffering. Place *all* the sufferings into one pan of a scale, and the coming glory into the other pan; the pan with the former, flies into the air as if it were holding feathers! Beloved, this is not an overstatement, but simple fact.

It may be that the person of the world can more easily discern a counterfeit Christian than can a Believer. The *contrast* between Jesus and the world may be more vivid, more obvious, to the person of the world than to the person in the Church. Since the ways of the world have blended in with the ways of the Church, discernment of counterfeits can become more challenging for the Believer. Therefore, not only do the people "of the world" need to see Jesus in you, but also the people "not of the world."

The disciples are ***"not of the world;"*** they are the children of God. They have overcome the world and so ***"the world has hated them;"*** the grammar actually reads, "began to hate," meaning that the world began to recognize *Jesus* when observing the disciples. *Please pause to consider the importance of this matter as it relates to you!*

The opposition from the world comes as a manifestation of the fact that it has *recognized* the union of the disciples with the Lord Jesus! In other words, not only are the disciples "not of the world," but they are *of God*; God is their portion, His love is their home, His promises are their joy, and His everlasting arms are their security. Oh, that this can be said of each of us – that people "of the world" would see *Jesus* when they observe us!

Pray that others will see Jesus in you.

"'Your will be done on earth as it is in heaven.'" Matthew 6:10

Why should God's **"will be done?"** The simple answer: because it is *God's!* As Creator and Preserver, He has every right to rule. All things depend on Him for existence, and He has every right to expect obedience from all beings.

You receive so much when you do His will! You receive His *benefits* when you obey His commands. He *guards you from injury* when you walk in His ways. You have *unspeakable joy* as you perform His will. There is *peace* unlike any other when you lovingly obey Him. He completely *satisfies your heart* when you perform His will. And when spirits of evil plot to do you harm, there are *holy angels,* closely allied to you, in sympathy with you, and employed in helping you on earth.

But what do we know about how God's will is done **"in heaven?"** Jesus said, **"If you love Me, keep My commandments"** (see John 14:15). *No obedience is acceptable to God except obedience inspired by love!* Angels do the will of God *lovingly.* They are in the immediate presence of God, whose essence is love, and so they are under love's most potent influence. Therefore, angels are perfectly loyal, and they obey every command of God because it is His. (Imagine how the faith of loving angels must have been tested, when they saw their Lord insulted and tormented by His foes and were not allowed to rescue Him!)

"In heaven," obedience prompted by love is *cheerful.* Angels obey not because they must, but because they would. As it would bring pain to birds to be restrained from singing, so it would be a burden to angels to be spared loving service to God. Angels in heaven do the will of God *promptly.* They are compared to wind and to lightning in their swiftness of service. Angels do not wait for a more "convenient" time; Gabriel, **"being caused to fly swiftly,"** brought the reply to Daniel while he **"was speaking in prayer"** (see Daniel 9:21).

Pray that, like the angels, you will lovingly, cheerfully, and swiftly do the will of God.

July 19

"'I have given them Your word; and the world has hated them because they are not of the world, just as I am not of the world.'" John 17:14

By the time Jesus prayed this prayer, the Apostles had tasted from the bitter cup of threatenings. Surely by this point in time, people had called *"those of his household"* (see Matthew 10:25) cruel names. A few short months later in Jerusalem, they would all *"suffer shame for His name;"* a little later the record of martyrdom began, along with scatterings by persecution.

From the terror of violence to the terror of laughter, the world seeks to frighten off the Believer. The world secretly plots against you, inwardly curses you, says all manner of evil against you, opposes you and rejoices when evil falls on you. But why? Why does *"the world"* hate you just because you are a Christian?

First, *"I have given them Your word."* The Word of God is a transforming but *revealing* account, and those who are "of the world" do not appreciate much of what it reveals. Yet Jesus gave His disciples this Word to possess and to convey. Christ said, *"For everyone practicing evil hates the light and does not come to the light, lest his deeds should be exposed."*

Second, *"they are not of the world."* It is not that the Word *made* you socially repulsive, religiously arrogant, or aggressively hostile toward those of the world. The world hates you because your conduct and your character, developed by the Word, leave those who are of the world restless instead of comfortable with their plan of combining "the best of both worlds." You are giving them the Word that tells them to give God His right place in life: the *first* place. And that requires them to surrender the control they've worked hard for.

Christians, then, are the world's "rebels." *Sinful men do not appreciate it when people do not join them!* And when the disagreement is passionate and about "religion" (especially about which religion is the "true" religion), hatred develops easily. Of course, the devil is doing his part, promoting pride and envy.

So, do not be surprised when the world hates you. Surprise is for things "unexpected." Pray over Matthew 5:11, 12.

"And Jesus lifted up His eyes and said, 'Father, I thank You that You have heard Me.'" John 11:41, 42

The scene around the tomb of Lazarus was full of tension and excitement! What was Jesus going to try to do? Would this be the occasion when He would fail? The witnesses present dared not disbelieve, but they dared not believe. Jesus was well aware of the possible "consequences" of this miracle. Should He fail, His claims to be the Son of God would be discredited. Should He succeed, the rulers would be so enraged so as to plot His death.

Many call the raising of Lazarus our Lord's greatest miracle. Jesus prayed aloud so that the multitudes at the scene would hear that He was partnering with God in what He was about to do – He was not acting alone. Eventually, all eyes were fixed on the tomb. What a dramatic moment! And then, just three words spoken by the Master: ***"Lazarus, come forth!"***

The anticipation present at the tomb of Lazarus is in some ways similar to the anticipation at the contest on Mount Carmel, recorded in the eighteenth chapter of 1 Kings. After the prophets of Baal came up short, it was Elijah who prayed ***"Hear me, O Lord, hear me, that this people may know that You are the Lord God."*** And then the fire of the Lord consumed the burnt sacrifice, the wood, the stones, the dust, and the water in the trench.

Behold the faith of Elijah! Behold the faith of Christ! *On both occasions, God was glorified because of "unusual" faith!* Too often we cross our fingers when we pray. Too often we hope, but we do not believe. Just moments before calling forth Lazarus, Jesus said to Martha, the sister of Lazarus, ***"Did I not say to you that if you would believe you would see the glory of God?"*** It makes us wonder what we have *not* seen, due to our lack of genuine faith.

Have you reached the point in your life that you truly believe that God is who He *says* He is? Pray that today your faith will not merely increase, but that it will become *unusual* faith.

July 21

"'I have given them Your word; and the world has hated them because they are not of the world, just as I am not of the world.'" John 17:14

The gift of the *"word"* changed the spiritual nature of the disciples, making them foreigners to the world. Through their contact with Jesus, the world considers them traitors, "hating" them accordingly. This hatred will be intensified as the disciples preach and teach the Word and begin to make further inroads throughout the world.

This constant contrast between the mind of Christ and the spirit of the world fills the New Testament. Jesus had exposed its hypocrites, denounced its idols, repudiated its smile, and condemned its prince – and was now showing indifference to its curse. For the most part, the conflict is not between the disciples and people that, even the world, would refer to as "wicked" men. No, the hostility is coming from men whom the world would see as "good" (because they accept the world's standards).

The world hates the disciples of Jesus because *we do not belong to its system.* Jesus said, **"If the world hates you, you know that it hated Me before it hated you. If you were of the world, the world would love its own. Yet because you are not of the world, but I chose you out of the world, therefore the world hates you"** (see John 15:18, 19). And the world hates us because *we do not conform to its practices and standards.* Paul wrote, **"Do not be conformed to this world, but be transformed by the renewing of your mind"** (see Romans 12:2).

The Word reveals to us what the world is *really* like; the Word exposes the world's deceptions and dangerous devices. Without God's Holy Word, **"given by inspiration of God,"** Christians would be struggling to understand *why* the world hates them so. *But with the Word of God (provided we read, study, and pray over it), we have true understanding not available to men from any other source!*

Martin Luther said, "A man's word is a little sound, that flies into the air, and soon vanishes; but the Word of God is greater than heaven and earth." Pray that your love for God and for His Word will deepen today.

"Your will be done on earth as it is in heaven." Matthew 6:10

Obedience is easy when the will of God agrees with the requirements of our comfort zones. But for God's will to be done **"on earth as it is in heaven,"** there will need to be high exertion and painful self-sacrifice. Angels "in heaven" do *all* of God's will. *We do God's will as they do it in heaven when we obey without preference!* "Selective obedience" is a term that describes how too many Believers (and churches) obey God. These people obey primarily those commands that are convenient, appearance approving, or easy for them.

Even "lost" people often do good deeds for their fellow man. They just don't do it in the power and in the Name of Jesus. It is clear from Scripture that in most "benevolent" work we are doing God's will: protecting the weak, caring for little children, feeding the hungry, clothing the naked, visiting the sick and those in prison, tending to the dying, and caring for the elderly and for the widow - all of this is pleasing activity in God's sight. But the most *important* example of helping our fellow man is our effort to "rescue the perishing." We should stop here and be certain, that we see the connection between the salvation of souls "on earth" and the will of God "in heaven."

Jesus said, **"There will be more joy in heaven over one sinner who repents than over ninety-nine just persons who need no repentance"** (see Luke 15:7). Already experiencing the joy of heaven, angels would not burst forth into such gladness on account of some "trivial" event. Heaven understands how much is at stake regarding the salvation of one soul. And if the salvation of just one soul brings *fresh joy* to heaven, then what a satisfying reward we receive for this type of obedience!

Oh, for the time when earth will resemble heaven, in the doing of God's will! Are you contributing to *His* will being done on earth? What a *privilege* to make such a contribution! Thank God that you still have that opportunity. Pray for more doors to open.

July 23

"'I have given them Your word; and the world has hated them because they are not of the world, just as I am not of the world.'" John 17:14

"The world has hated them" as a consequence of the disciples having ceased to be conformed to the world. Specifically, the world hates the persons, the principles, the profession, and the presence of all true Christians. True Christians have a nature, a spirit, a worship, a character, and a conduct different from that of the world's. Since the world cannot bear their living testimony against itself, the world hates true disciples of Jesus. The teachings of the disciples are entirely opposed to the world's ways, principles, and pursuits. And because such teaching cuts at the "root" of the world's *pride*, the world cannot bear it.

Jesus came to earth to call guilty, lost sinners. This is Good News when a man comes to himself, and knows that *he is* a guilty, lost sinner. But to the proud, self-righteous spirit of the world, this news is very insulting. The world cannot endure teaching from the Word, which makes nothing of its good intentions, piety, good works, and churchgoing! ***The natural man does not receive the things of the Spirit of God, for they are foolishness to him.*** The truth is, it wounds proud human nature to be told that all the world's great wisdom goes for nothing!

The devil and unbelieving men try to impose substitutes for the Word of God. The Church has always been in danger of being corrupted by the world, but in these dark days in which we live, God help us if the world starts to be corrupted by the Church! We must judge all things and all men solely upon the Word of God, and not the Word of God by human systems. *By the Word of God, we stand or fall!*

"Has God indeed said" was, and is, the voice of the devil. We are living in an hour in which hell is let loose. The devil is still speaking and deceiving. One of his accomplices will likely put a counterfeit in front of you this day.

Pray for the supernatural ability to discern between the devil's voice and God's voice.

"*Your will be done on earth as it is in heaven.*" Matthew 6:10

Throughout His earthly ministry, Jesus made it clear that He came to obey, saying, *"For I have come down from heaven, not to do My own will, but the will of Him who sent Me"* (see John 6:38) and *"My food is to do the will of Him who sent Me, and to finish His work"* (see John 4:34). Then, at the close of His ministry, it gave Jesus satisfaction to say to the Father, *"I have finished the work which You have given Me to do"* (see John 17:4).

Agony intense, desire strong, submission absolute – this is the highest possible example of obedience, and it was perfectly lived out by the Lord Jesus! The example of Jesus Christ is the high mark at which we are to aim. We are not to aim at what other people or other churches do; we are to imitate only the obedience of the Master. To aim lower, to rest short of it, would make us untrue both to ourselves and to God. And so we pray this petition of the Model Prayer to be enabled to *submit* in the same spirit of trust.

It is with deep thoughtfulness and sincerity that we should make this petition! We are self-convicted if we offer it rightly. With every intention of imitating Jesus, we make this prayer putting the will of God above all else. We make this prayer asking, "Father, what is it that *You* want me to do?"

Have you ever thought that you were doing the will of God, when, in fact, you were only doing it *partially?* Is it possible that you sometimes feel that you are doing His will, when, in reality, you are acting mostly according to your own inclinations, interests, and will? The worst doom that can ever overtake you is being left to your own will! Refusal to walk in God's ways results in walking in your own. What a terrible description of the devil's victims this: *"Taken captive by him to do his will"* (see 2 Timothy 2:26).

Pray that you will know and do God's will.

July 25

"'I do not pray that You should take them out of the world,
but that You should keep them from the evil one.'" John 17:15

Many of Christ's disciples over the years, when facing the sorrows and sins of life, have desired to *"Wander far off, and remain in the wilderness. Selah"* (see Psalm 55:7) or have felt like Jeremiah, when he wrote, *"Oh, that I had in the wilderness a lodging place for travelers; that I might leave my people, and go from them"* (see Jeremiah 9:2). To take the disciples *"out of the world"* would appear to be the surest and easiest deliverance from frustration, hatred, and from *"the evil one"* – but they still had a critical part to play in the world. Jesus did not request such an escape for His disciples, because something far better was awaiting them – not a flight to the wilderness, but a flight to *Him!*

Like Jesus, the disciples had a mission. The world being a "hospital," their mission was to make their "rounds" by proclaiming the Good News and by demonstrating the compassion of Christ. Jesus said, *"I was hungry and you gave Me food; I was thirsty and you gave Me drink; I was a stranger and you took Me in; I was naked and you clothed Me; I was sick and you visited Me; I was in prison and you came to Me … Inasmuch as you did it to one of the least of these My brethren, you did it to Me"* (see Matthew 25:35, 36, 40). These services can be rendered to God only while we are *in* the world.

The importance of the mission of the disciples (and through them, of the whole Church) cannot be overstated. *Jesus is to depart from the world; the disciples are to go into the world!* The entire mission of Jesus while He was in the world, has, in reality, been the mission of the Father in and through Him. The mission of the disciples, sent into the world by the Son, is likewise not theirs, but *His through them.* Consequently, the mission of the Church is the continuation of the mission of its Lord.

Pray that you will know the *importance* of your mission.

July 26

"And when Jesus had cried out with a loud voice, He said, 'Father, into Your hands I commit My spirit.'" Luke 23:46

The Master *prayed* in all of the significant moments of His life on earth, so we should not be surprised that He met death in the same way that He met life. *If we would die in prayer, we must live in prayer!*

We have read of His long nights of devotion. We have read of His early morning prayers before the break of day. We have read of His prayers before He chose the Twelve. We have read of His prayer before He called forth Lazarus from the grave. We have read of His prayer in Gethsemane. We have read where, at least once, He sent the crowds away so that He could be alone in prayer. Jesus was a busy person, but He was *never* too busy to pray.

Prayer brings us many benefits. It *aligns* our will with God's will. Jesus knew God's will, and He prayed to accept it. There are times when Christians pray in order that we may *determine* God's will. Prayer gives us *direction* for doing God's will. Knowing God's will and doing it, are two entirely different things. Choices have to be made, and prayer gives us Holy discernment. And prayer allows us to continually commit *our* spirit to the Father's care. When this day is done, and we enter the nightly darkness of sleep, we have no charge over ourselves, and by faith, we peacefully commit our spirits to His **"hands."**

This third and final prayer of Jesus from the Cross was the evening prayer of Jewish children. The night Jesus was crucified, children in the homes of Jerusalem were praying the same prayer He prayed at Calvary. The spirit of this prayer is the same spirit represented by the prayer, "Now I lay me down to sleep; I pray Thee, Lord, my soul to keep."

God grant that, as life's shadows lengthen and the evening comes, as you finish the race and your work is done, you may have your child prayer again. But for now, as you pray to the Father, commit your spirit once again to His care.

July 27

"'I do not pray that You should take them out of the world, but that You should keep them from the evil one.'" John 17:15

What Jesus is asking here for His disciples demonstrates the fact that the "truest" life of the "true" saint is lived *abnormally;* that is to say, under the challenges and burdens of the normal day and the common life in the world. Only in these circumstances will the disciple know the "true" victory of the "true" Gospel, for only Jesus Christ can lead a soul *victoriously* along through the crowds, the confusion, the pain, and the distractions of life.

This may seem strange, the Believer's "platform" being **"the world,"** where he is constantly solicited by an evil heart of unbelief to do what he ought not to do, and to be what he ought not to be – a world filled with peculiar attractions suited to his fallen, corrupt nature, where he has to **"wrestle...against principalities, against powers, against the rulers of the darkness of this age, against spiritual hosts of wickedness in the heavenly places."**

In other words, here we are in the world – a world that hated Christ and crucified Him, where every sort of evil surrounds us, where every temptation suited to poor fallen nature is present on every side, a world where it is utterly impossible to pass through without being dirtied along the way – yet we are *sent* into this world by Christ Jesus, who prays that we would not be removed from it! How very little qualified are we to judge how God deals with His people! Certainly, we are in great danger of misunderstanding what He is doing unless we are students of His Word.

Here is the lesson: *a spiritual victory over evil is to be preferred before a total exemption from it!* Here we learn another truth regarding how we should pray. Our prayers should not be for deliverance from the world, but from the *evil of* the world – from *sins,* rather than from afflictions. Of all evil, sin is the greatest. **"And you shall call His name Jesus"** because He will save His people from their *sins.*

Pray that you will be delivered from the evil of the world.

"*Your kingdom come.*" Matthew 6:10

There are three "stages" in the coming of the kingdom. The first stage is when the kingdom comes to our own soul individually; the second stage is when the kingdom comes throughout the world by the spreading of the truth, and the third stage is when the kingdom comes universally in the Final Advent.

When does God's **"*kingdom come*"** to the Church? First, there has to be fidelity in the pulpit. For that to happen, the preacher must show Christ rather than himself, must teach revealed truth rather than human theories, and must shed light on darkness. This will produce the fruits of spirituality in worship, grateful praise, a departure from sin, and sinners asking, "What must I do to be saved?"

On the other hand, when we find a local congregation praying and laboring for "our" church rather than for **"*Your*"** kingdom, that congregation is not praying **"*In this manner.*"** That congregation resembles a regiment in battle breaking its line of connection and indifferent to the progress of the fight elsewhere, producing a hindrance rather than a help to the entire army. Earnest prayer for the kingdom of God must reprove church rivalries, controversies, and jealousies.

The *proactive* side of kingdom-focused praying means remembering to pray for the extinction of all tyranny (both in individuals and in multitudes), for the exposure and destruction of corruptions (inward and outward), and for the truth to manifest in all departments of government. In short, we are praying that whatever the enemy intends for harm may be overruled for good. Writes Maurice, "If God had not heard this prayer going up from tens of thousands in all ages, the earth would have been a den of robbers."

Be an **"*epistle ... known and read by all men*"** (see 2 Corinthians 3:2), and you will recommend His rule wherever you go. *May your behavior and your decisions say, "I want my God to reign over me because I love Him so much!"* Pray that you will compassionately and intentionally respond today, to the numerous opportunities before you to *promote* the coming of the kingdom.

July 29

*"'I do not pray that You should take them out of the world,
but that You should keep them from the evil one.'"* John 17:15

In a few more years and in God's timing and manner, you, the Lord's soldier, will be done with conflict, and will enter into the joy of your Lord! But for now, He wishes you to stay here. **"I do not pray that You should take them out of the world,"** because to abide in the world is needful for others, and profitable for you.

In times of great difficulty, Believers sometimes prefer to die so that they can "be with the Lord." But does this preference come from a true longing to be with Jesus, or from a desire to get rid of their troubles? If it comes from the former, they would have felt the same wish to die at other times when they were *not* in difficulty. The wish to escape from trouble by dying is a selfish wish. Moses, Elijah, and Jonah erred when they requested to be "taken out of the world," and their prayers went unanswered! Better to glorify God by your life here, *especially* when life is difficult, allowing *Him* to say when "it is enough."

Therefore, be content to pray for your *preservation* - not to prolong your time with loved ones, or to escape from disappointments and sorrow - but to fulfill the work God has given you to do for His glory. Do not run from the duty assigned by God, whether you understand His reasoning or not; **"For My thoughts are not your thoughts, nor are your ways My ways, says the Lord."** The soul is to be kept in the custody of the body until the One who gave it at the beginning gives the command. Yes, it is far better to be with Jesus, but you should not look for your wages until you have done your work.

Remember that your Father sees a much larger picture than you do. He knows everything you are feeling, plus a lot more! He understands when you grow weary. But His timing is *perfect.* Pray for your preservation, health, and protection – that He will continue to be glorified through you.

"'Father, forgive them, for they do not know what they do.'"
Luke 23:34

Ignorance is different from innocence, thus the *need* for Jesus' prayer from the Cross, **"Father, forgive them."** What, then, was the ignorance Jesus referred to? It is that they were ignorant of the fact that they were crucifying **"the Lord of glory"** (1 Corinthians 2:8), ignorant of the fact that they were fulfilling **"the voices of the Prophets which are read every Sabbath"** (Acts 13:27) and ignorant of the fact that they were killing **"the Prince of life"** (Acts 3:15-17).

Sin is always greater than it seems, whether at the moment of temptation or as time passes on! These soldiers thought that they were doing nothing more than executing a man. But it was so much more than that; they were murdering the Messiah, putting to death the Son of Man, killing the Savior of mankind. They, like us, did not recognize the extreme seriousness, the awfulness of their act.

We know not what we do when we hurt a human spirit by something that we say or do. While we may have meant to inflict only a momentary irritation on someone, our behavior may require a long time of healing. We know not what we do, when we start off on an evil course of some kind, imagining it to be only a very *slight* deviation. Instead, we have begun a slow, steady, spiritual descent.

We know not what we do when we dishonor the One we call *Master*, by choosing sin over obedience. It is unknown to us the fullness and the intensity of His feeling of disappointment and sorrow when we fail Him! We know not what we do when we hinder the cause of Christ through sins of omission or of commission. We have not put the kingdom of God **"first,"** and oh, the *consequences* of that!

We know not what we do when we do not surrender ourselves and our service, and we could continue – but perhaps the Holy Spirit has already begun to convict your heart! Seek His face. Bow before Him in prayer with sincere repentance, and humbly consider "what you do."

July 31

"'I do not pray that You should take them out of the world, but that You should keep them from the evil one.'" John 17:15

Why must we be left *here?* Because **"the world"** is the best place where we can learn the most important lessons that must be learned outside heaven. *Now is our chance!* What are those lessons?

First, we are here to learn *our own nothingness;* our weakness, our emptiness, our unworthiness, our corruptions, and our unbelief. Only in the world could we learn such lessons as these, and learn them so well. For it is not when we are enjoying Christ most that we glorify Him best; it is when we trust Him while our feelings are negative and depressed, when we are experiencing failure, when we walk through the darkness, and when the world hates us - that we truly glorify Him.

Second, we are here to learn *the strength, the motives, the tactics, and the number of our enemies.* Here on earth, we realize that, alone, we are no match for "the world, the flesh, and the devil." And third, we are here in the world to learn *the faithfulness, the patience, the love, the care, the keeping, and the goodness of our God.* Surely we would be swallowed up, if it were not for His holding us, sheltering us, and carrying us.

The world is the place where we experience His faithfulness, but it is also the place where He sees our loyalty. He commands that we **"Go therefore and make disciples of all the nations, baptizing them ... teaching them."** The kingdom of heaven is as leaven, and leaven works not from without, but from within. We must not take ourselves out of the world – for the world's sake, if not for our own.

Yes, there are sincere monks and nuns who are wholly cut off from the world and who spend their entire lives in meditation and prayer. John the Baptist was **"in the wilderness"** during the days of his short ministry. We should not criticize those who strive to renounce the world in ways we may not understand. Rather, humbly pray today that you and fellow Believers will be obedient to the will of God.

"Your kingdom come." Matthew 6:10

*I*t is hypocrisy to pray **"Your kingdom come,"** *if you are not helping to promote it!* What are some ways you can promote the kingdom of God? You may be able to help evangelize the multitudes in your community who are still outside the Church. You may be able to help circulate the Scriptures or copies of various religious literature. You may be able to teach the Bible to young people in a Sunday School or Bible class.

You may have the Spiritual Gift of Giving (see Romans 12:8) and be able to support kingdom-focused ministries. And *all* of God's people, if they, in fact, cannot for some reason participate in the activities mentioned above, can surely *pray* for the Holy Spirit to move specific lost people to repentance.

So when you pray this prayer sincerely, you understand that this petition involves *effort* of some kind to send the Gospel throughout the world. In the parable of the Faithful Servant, Jesus said, **"Blessed is that servant whom his master, when he comes, will find so doing;"** "so *doing"* your duty, making that effort, becomes part of the fulfillment of your prayer and gives you the posture in which your Lord desires to find you when He returns.

You understand that true Christianity is necessarily *aggressive* – not aggressive in the sense that you "overpower" an individual by "pounding the top of his head with a Bible" – but aggressive in a manner that demonstrates an *urgency* to reach the world with the message and the compassion of Jesus Christ. The Apostle Paul spoke with such urgency when he asked, **"How then shall they call on Him in whom they have not believed? And how shall they believe in Him of whom they have not heard? And how shall they hear without a preacher?"** (see Romans 10:14).

May this prayer ascend today from the workplace, from the home, from the church in the village and the church in the inner city, from the streets, and from the shopping malls. Join now with many thousands of Believers throughout the world, praying, "Your kingdom come."

August 2

"'I do not pray that You should take them out of the world,
but that You should keep them from the evil one.'" John 17:15

Sharing your *personal testimony* – the story told through your words and through your behavior about the incredible difference Jesus has made in your life – is one of the reasons you are still in **"*the world.*"** Your personal testimony gives glory to God for what *He* has done, and is still doing, *for you*. There never has been a testimony, there is not one now, nor will there ever be a testimony exactly like yours, because your life and your circumstances cannot be duplicated in its entirety. *Your personal testimony is like your DNA; it is uniquely yours, and therefore it is powerful!* It should be something you consider to be *precious*, like the pictures you may be displaying of family members.

Your personal testimony needs to be heard by your *lost friends and acquaintances*. It is a powerful seed that the Father wants to plant because, with His nurturing, it can mean that something of eternal consequence can "happen" in that person's life that you cannot produce. Because of the uniqueness of your testimony, there is an opportunity for *sincerity* in your speech that can be detected by the listener. And your testimony presents an opportunity to explain to the lost person that Jesus loves him.

Fellow Believers need to hear your testimony. They are encouraged and blessed when they hear what God has done and what He is doing now within His family. They rejoice when they hear how He is at work in their midst, particularly when they have been interceding in prayer for you. Your Brothers and Sisters in Christ who are in the world with you want God's best for you, and your personal testimony about the Father's goodness brings them joy. Read Psalm 34:3.

You may not have thought about this, but *your heavenly Father* wants to hear your testimony! It blesses Him and gives Him glory when you speak of His greatness and of His love toward you. **"You who fear the Lord, praise Him! All you descendants of Jacob, glorify Him"** (see Psalm 22:23).

Pray that your personal testimony will bless someone today.

"Then little children were brought to Him that He might put His hands on them and pray." Matthew 19:13

"Little children"** played a very special part in the ministry of Jesus Christ. On this occasion, the Savior communicated several important truths. First, Christ showed that children should be **"brought to Him"** at an early age. This places a responsibility upon family members and even neighbors, for little children cannot "bring themselves." And when the place to meet Jesus is at the church, the church must be *prepared* to receive, care for, and teach the children about the Lord.

Second, Jesus demonstrated that it is a "teaching moment" when we pray for little children. Sadly, parents often overlook the blessing their children can receive from hearing their name mentioned to *God* by a loved one. Such early impressions teach children that their heavenly Father cares about them personally and intimately. Praying with and for children teaches them that God loves them, and that prayer is how we "talk to God." From the womb to the bedside, we must pray fervently for little children.

Third, this act of Jesus showed that children are often "instruments" of God to carry out His purposes. Here, God used these children to teach the disciples an important lesson about **"the kingdom of heaven."** On another occasion, the indignant chief priests and scribes heard children crying out in the temple and saying, **"Hosanna to the Son of David!"**

In his *Book of Martyrs,* Fox tells how a valiant Believer by the name of Lawrence was burned at Colchester. When Lawrence was carried in a chair to the fire (because through the cruelty of the Papists he could not stand upright), several young children gathered around the fire and prayed, "Lord, strengthen thy servant, and keep thy promise." God answered the cry from the mouths of these little children, and Lawrence died firmly and calmly for his Master.

Making the necessary time to pray for children may be more important today than ever before! Not only do children today face strong temptations and multiple challenges, but they also face great dangers. Jesus set the example; take a child in your arms today and lead them in prayer.

August 4

> *"'I do not pray that You should take them out of the world,*
> *but that You should keep them from the evil one.'"* John 17:15

If God were to take His servants *"out of the world,"* the opportunity for the disciples to have a "salt" and "light" influence would be removed. Jesus said that we are *"the salt of the earth"* and *"the light of the world."* By using the images of "salt" and of "light," Jesus gave us insight into what it means to make a lasting and powerful difference in the world that will bring glory to the Father.

Since the world is decaying spiritually, it is in need of salt. Salt hinders corruption, and seasons whatever it touches. And since the world is dark spiritually, it is in need of light. Peter described this world, this place where God is denied and where man is exalted, as *"a dark place"* (see 2 Peter 1:19). Things are distorted in the dark. As salt, we need to have the kind of character that penetrates and purifies by contact; as light, we need to have the kind of conduct that points people to God when they observe us.

All of this connects to the fact that Christians *are* different, and that they should *be* different. The Greek emphatic pronoun, "you," or, "you and only you," begins the statements Jesus made about our being salt and light (see Matthew 5:13, 14). The Master was saying that we simply must not fail the world that we are called to influence. *The world does not know it, does not understand it – but the world's only hope is the influence of the Believer who introduces Jesus Christ!* Therefore, retain your saltiness and do not conceal your light through sin, compromise, laziness, or fear.

Here is a specific application; we should be more courageous in condemning evil. There are too many times in our communities when standards slip and slide for want of a clear Christian protest. Salt may bite, but the honey of "political correctness" hinders the true exposition and influence of the Word of God. My friend, may you *always* show the compassion of Jesus as you influence men.

Pray that you will be His salt and light today.

"'Give us this day our daily bread.'"   Matthew 6:11

The word *"Give"* is the wide opening of the mouths of baby birds hungering around the parent. It is the Father giving out of His hand directly into yours, and if it comes from Him, it is *good.* Because He gives so quietly and constantly, His giving is hardly recognized and appreciated. God is the only "Giver." Satan has no gifts; he just has "baits." The bread is *"our"* bread, the plural indicating an interest in the needs of the general body of Believers; we should expect it to be so, for He who gives all is Father of all – Father of *"us."*

In His amazing plan, God created people to have "needs" such as food, clothing, and shelter. When people stray away from the Father, their needs often remind them of their need for Him. *To ask God for* *"bread"* *is not out of place, because it has to do with your welfare!* In our affluent society, the average Christian may have difficulty taking this request for daily bread seriously. Why pray to God for food when I have a week's supply on hand? But whether you have little or much of this world's goods, this petition teaches you that God is your *source* of supply.

"I have been young, and now am old;" says Psalm 37:25, *"yet I have not seen the righteous forsaken, nor his descendants begging bread."* Yet, "give" does not expect God to place you above the working ways of men; you trust that He will also find labor for you that will win you bread. "We lift our empty hands to heaven, and God lays work upon them." So this petition does not mean that God will do for you what He expects you to do for yourself. An old proverb says, "God feeds the birds, but He does not throw the food into their nests!"

Nor does this petition give you any right to ask for wealth and luxuries, though God may give them. Jesus said ask for the *necessities* of life. As you pray, ask Him to provide you with *today's* needs.

August 6

"'I do not pray that You should take them out of the world,
but that You should keep them from the evil one.'" John 17:15

Today we are considering a very important truth that every Christian needs to know: we need to be "kept" by God. We *are kept by the power of God through faith for salvation ready to be revealed in the last time"* (see 1 Peter 1:5). The Father keeps us from the Devil that we would not come under his power, and from the world that we would not be deceived by its allurements. *That Jesus asked the Father to keep us shows that it is not within our power to keep ourselves!*

We are so weak; we are easy to consent to lusts or to faint under afflictions. We can no more stand against Satan alone than a lamb can against a wolf. That is why we need to be kept by Almighty God *"who is able to keep you from stumbling"* (see Jude 24), and who *"knows how to deliver the godly out of temptations"* (see 2 Peter 2:9). Always remember: *"The Lord is faithful, who will establish you and guard you from the evil one"* (see 2 Thessalonians 3:3).

While some Bible translations of John 17:15 read, "the evil one," and others read, "the evil," this is not a problem, because both objectives apply. We need to be kept from the power and snares of Satan and all of his accomplices until their course is run. The Father does not take us *"out of the world,"* because a spiritual victory *over* all of this evil is better than a total exemption *from* it.

Our reaction and response to the truth that we are unable to keep ourselves should work in us a spirit of conscious, daily *dependency.* Knowing and believing this truth should inspire in us confidence and assurance while filling us with praise! Most of the time, we do not know what to do. And so our prayer must become, *"Our eyes are upon You"* (see 2 Chronicles 20:12). We sing and speak of His faithfulness, and He is *able* to keep us.

Pray that you will be conscious throughout the day today of His keeping power.

"'Give us this day our daily bread.'" Matthew 6:11

The gospel of charity and helpfulness is in this petition. *"Give us this day our daily bread"* becomes a sham prayer if you are not ready, at the cost of sacrifice, to help to *provide* bread for those who lack. Basic human needs must be met while the kingdom of God is established. Do not forget - it is *Jesus* who is instructing you to pray this way! In Matthew 25:35, 36, Jesus described those who will *"inherit the kingdom,"* by saying, *"for I was hungry and you gave Me food; I was thirsty and you gave Me drink; I was a stranger and you took Me in; I was naked and you clothed Me; I was sick and you visited Me; I was in prison and you came to Me."*

When addressing the early Church, James said, *"Pure and undefiled religion before God and the Father is this: to visit orphans and widows in their trouble, and to keep oneself unspotted from the world"* (see James 1:27). Ezekiel described shepherds who only desired to care for themselves, saying, *"You eat the fat and clothe yourselves with the wool; you slaughter the fatlings, but you do not feed the flock. The weak you have not strengthened, nor have you healed those who were sick, nor bound up the broken"* (see Ezekiel 34:3, 4).

The lesson is clear: you are like the Israelites in the wilderness, in that you are careful to obtain more than you need today because you are uncertain that God will provide for you tomorrow! Since God has prospered you, the Christ-like response from you is *compassion*. Jesus said, *"For everyone to whom much is given, from him much will be required; and to whom much has been committed, of him they will ask the more"* (see Luke 12:48).

Never tell people you have been "lucky." Do not tell people you have been "fortunate." Regardless of your "accomplishments," avoid saying, "I have done well." Instead, tell people "God is good." Tell people "God has blessed me."

Pray that you will remember that He has given the bread.

August 8

"'I do not pray that You should take them out of the world,
but that You should keep them from the evil one.'" John 17:15

Understand that the more anyone – man or woman, clergy or layperson – tries to be in the world, the more he needs to guard his own spiritual life with the help of the Father's keeping. If you desire to be in the world but not of it, you need to pray to be kept *"from the evil one."* You need all of the Father's help that you may not be *"conformed to this world,"* but rather, *"transformed by the renewing of your mind."*

Just as it was necessary for Jesus to pray that Peter's faith should not fail under the sifting process of the evil one, it is just as essential to our safety that the same prayer should be offered in our behalf. We *need* to be kept; we *need* to be guarded. No one of us is safe, not even for one hour if the protecting power of God were to be withdrawn. *We should pray for His keeping every day of our lives!* For Satan's determination against Christians is just as bitter and undying in its hate, as it was in the days of Jesus.

The ruler of this world had nothing in Jesus but has much in each of His followers. To name only a few examples, we need His keeping for *the maintenance of our Christian integrity.* We need His keeping for *the preservation of our purity.* And we need His keeping for *the brightness of the shining of our spiritual lamp.* Oh, how we should thank and praise God for His much-needed keeping!

A child is truly blessed who has received the care of a loving parent. Yet God's love is so much more than mere parental affection. *"The Lord is your keeper. The Lord shall preserve you from all evil; He shall preserve your soul. The Lord shall preserve your going out and your coming in from this time forth, and even forevermore"* (see Psalm 121:5, 7, 8).

Be in awe of His power and grace! Tremble as you come to God in prayer, with the realization of your *need* of Him today.

"'Father, glorify Your name.'" John 12:28

No man can tell what next month or next week will bring. We do not even know what is in store for tomorrow, and we certainly cannot predict the mode, manner, or circumstances of our own death. With these facts in mind, Jesus stands absolutely alone in the human experience of knowing exactly what His last moments on earth were going to look like.

Preceding this prayer of Jesus comes a monolog recorded in verse 27, in which He is not addressing the disciples or the bystanders. Those words were, however, spoken audibly so that everyone present could hear His troubled cry: ***"Now My soul is troubled, and what shall I say? 'Father, save Me from this hour'? But for this purpose I came to this hour."***

His soul "troubled," meant that Jesus' heart was suffering torture, grief and dejection - all at the same time. All the dreadfulness of His impending death was fully revealed to Him; all that was awaiting Him was made clear. It is important to remember that He was free at this time to withdraw from the mission, had that been His desire. But no! Even with the frightfulness, the utter horror, the inconceivable and terrible death process before Him – Jesus thought of His purpose for coming into this world and continued on.

This matter of remembering who we are with consideration for God's purposes – especially at a time when we are troubled – is critical! The Apostle Paul put it this way: ***"And He died for all, that those who live should live no longer for themselves, but for Him who died for them and rose again."*** Such a verse is worthy of memorization! Self-centered living should have no place in the life of a person seeking the kingdom of God first.

It is always appropriate to stop, as Jesus did here, and ask, ***"And what shall I say?"*** Is this about *me* and about what *I* want, or is this about *God* and about what *He* wants? Pray that the decisions you make today will be made with the purposes of God in mind.

August 10

"'I do not pray that You should take them out of the world, but that You should keep them from the evil one.'" John 17:15

The history of the Church and the individual experience of every member of it is proof enough that Christians are not secured by themselves of outward tribulations, distresses, and even violent assaults from the world, the flesh, and the devil. We are not secured from spiritual conflicts, temptations, or humiliating failures in service. And Believers are not secured from bodily suffering, crushing bereavements, and pain. Yet "evil," to us, is in reality that which can hurt the *soul*; all these other things, which we may think and call "evil," will work together for our good (see Romans 8:28).

The Lord Jesus Christ prayed, Father, *"keep them from the evil one."* The disciples might feel the enemy's "blows" (*"a thorn in the flesh was given to me, a messenger of Satan to buffet me"*; *"the devil is about to throw some of you into prison, that you may be tested"*), but they were to be "preserved" outside the circle of his spell and power. They were to be spiritually detached from him, and thus enabled to be more than conquerors over him, through the strength of Him in whom we *"can do all things."*

Why do we need Him to keep us? Because the whole world is full of snares. Take, for example, the conditions of adversity and prosperity. Proverbs 30:8, 9 says, *"Give me neither poverty nor riches – feed me with the food allotted to me; lest I be full and deny You, and say, 'Who is the Lord?' or lest I be poor and steal , and profane the name of my God."* Temptations are like the wind; they can come from east, west, north, and south.

Why do we need Him to keep us? Because of our own weakness. *"Each one is tempted when he is drawn away by his own desires and enticed."* Satan could not prevail against us were it not for our own lusts. We *"watch"* that we may see when the enemy approaches; we *"pray"* that we may not be self-confident when tempted!

Pray a prayer of praise and thanksgiving that He keeps you.

*"**Give us this day our daily bread.**"*   Matthew 6:11

The Model Prayer is a *beautiful* prayer, like the most finished work of art. The words are plain, yet majestic. The thought of "substituting" other words for the words Jesus provided never enters the mind. No man can say that he is familiar with the heights and depths that this prayer reveals, or with the treasures of wisdom, it contains.

Yet many of the old church fathers and numerous Bible commentators refused to believe that this petition we are examining today was a request for ordinary food – for "mere bread." They could not be persuaded that a request for such a commonplace thing as *"**bread,**"* could possibly have a place in such a holy prayer as this. But actually, the Model Prayer becomes all the more beautiful because it *does* include this petition!

"Give us bread" is asking God to supply *primary physical needs.* It is not too trivial a request to bring to God, as though the Father is only concerned with helping in the great crises, or in the unexpected emergencies, or in the terrible tragedies. No, God is the God for all of the "common" events during *"**this day**"* and during *every* day. He notes the fall of a sparrow, and He counts the hairs of the head. No need, no event, is too small or insignificant for Him to notice or address.

This is a petition for *all* men – from the poor to the rich, from the pauper to the prince. Why? *Because all men are absolutely dependent upon God for everything!* Man depends upon God for his physical strength, for his very breath, and for life itself. People say that a certain person is "independently wealthy." Independent of *what?* Independent of *whom?* Even with the assumption that earned wealth can be "kept," of whom is a man "independent?" Man cannot make food; he cannot create bread. With all of his knowledge of science, he cannot *command a harvest.* Almighty God must give it!

This is a petition for *you.* As you consider your needs today, understand that God must give it. Ask Him for bread.

August 12

***"'I do not pray that You should take them out of the world,
but that You should keep them from the evil one.'"*** John 17:15

*T**his prayer gives us the opportunity to listen to Jesus pour out His heart!* It reveals how deeply He loved the disciples, and how fully He knew them. It shows how much it meant to Him that every need of theirs be met. Maybe Jesus was thinking, "I would like to take you with Me, but it is impossible. I would like to spare you all that you will have to go through; but as you go through life, remember how I interceded for you in My prayer."

One of the sweetest songs ever written about the mission of a true disciple of Christ is the hymn, "So Send I You." E. Margaret Clarkson wrote the hymn first as a poem. It appeared in a religious magazine and was eventually seen by John W. Peterson. He wrote, "One morning while improvising at the piano, with the lines of this poem before me, the melody came. Somehow I sensed in my heart that God was going to use this song." New stanzas were written in 1963. Read John 20:21, and then worship the Father as you read these words:

> *So send I you, by grace made strong to triumph*
> *O'er hosts of hell, o'er darkness, death, and sin,*
> *My name to bear, and in that name to conquer,*
> *So send I you, my victory to win.*
> *So send I you, to take to souls in bondage*
> *The word of truth that sets the captive free,*
> *To break the bonds of sin, to loose death's fetters,*
> *So send I you, to bring the lost to me.*
> *So send I you, my strength to know in weakness,*
> *My joy in grief, my perfect peace in pain,*
> *To prove my pow'r, my grace, my promised presence,*
> *So send I you, eternal fruit to gain.*
> *So send I you, to bear my cross with patience,*
> *And then one day with joy to lay it down,*
> *To hear my voice, "Well done, my faithful servant,*
> *Come share my throne, my kingdom, and my crown!"*

Pray for a deeper understanding of how much He cares for you.

August 13

"'Father, glorify Your name.'" John 12:28

As yet, no wounds had been inflicted on His body; no hands or instruments of violence had touched His physical frame. But bodily sufferings and mental sufferings are two entirely different experiences. What deep sorrow Jesus had to be feeling, what agony - that would prompt the Son of God to declare aloud, *"Now My soul is troubled!"*

Troubled in the center of His emotions (His *"soul"*), means that Jesus was deeply stirred and agitated. Profound emotions had been building up within the Savior's soul prior to this prayer. Yet, with the very next breath, came the words, *"Father, glorify Your name."* There was no pause for thinking the matter through. This declaration came quickly because Jesus' greatest desire was to glorify His Father in heaven. Christ shows us the Father, reconciles us to the Father, and teaches us to live all the way to the end for His glory.

If Bible scholars, commentators, interpreters, and students were to argue their cases for the "most revealing" of all of Jesus' prayers, this very short prayer would have to be part of that discussion. For this prayer reveals His heart, His devotion, His identity, His determination, His commitment, His desire, His priority, His purpose, His mission! Therefore, these four words of this prayer say quite a bit about the *focus* of the Savior of the world.

Having considered all of this, it is time now for self-reflection. What do *we* say when we face times of crisis and decision? We, who are called by His name, must seek the same state of heart, the same vision, the same identity, the same commitment expressed by this prayer. If we become too concerned about the length of our life or about the circumstances of our death, it is unlikely we will place ourselves in God's hands, and then rest in His perfect arrangement. To be sure, there are many things to do in life, accompanied by many impulses. *But this great principle must govern our will:* "Father, glorify Your name!"

Pray that your life focus will be to see the Father's name glorified.

August 14

"'I do not pray that You should take them out of the world,
but that You should keep them from the evil one.'" John 17:15

There are some translations that say, *"evil one,"* and some that just say, "evil." Which is correct? Both are! The "evil" deed and the "evil one" (Satan, or an evil man) are so clearly joined, that protection from the one involves protection from the other. Literally, the request is for the Father to keep the disciples "out of the hands of" or "clutches" of the evil one.

Here are two reasons why we need to be kept out of the hands of Satan. First, the devil prompts *our enemies*. Just prior to Jesus' arrest in the Garden of Gethsemane, He said to the chief priests, captains of the temple, and the elders who had come to Him, *"This is your hour and the power of darkness."* In Revelation 12:12 we read, *"Woe to the inhabitants of the earth and the sea! For the devil has come down to you, having great wrath, because he knows that he has a short time."* *If we could see the evil spirits with our bodily eyes, hanging on the ears of the leaders of the world as well as on the ears of common people, inspiring them against the saints of God, we would more appreciate and understand God's keeping for which Jesus prays!* Second, the devil prompts *us*. We read, *"Ananias, why has Satan filled your heart to lie to the Holy Spirit?"* (see Acts 5:3) and *"For we do not wrestle against flesh and blood, but against principalities, against powers, against the rulers of the darkness of this age, against spiritual hosts of wickedness in the heavenly places"* (see Ephesians 6:12). Jesus does not ask that we be kept from "trouble," but rather from the evil of sin. How grateful we are that our God is stronger than this Satan!

Jesus makes this request, however, because He was conscious of the fact that the devil does have power and influence among men. Therefore, in view of the task that He is committing to His disciples, Jesus wants the keeping power of the Father for them.

Pray for alertness from the Holy Spirit.

August 15

"'Give us this day our daily bread.'"   Matthew 6:11

The best skilled, the most able among us, must still wait on God for his *"bread."* Except in so far as God fills it with His goodness, the future is simply blank to us. We have learned over the years that what other people are receiving and even profiting by, could be a *disastrous* gift to us. And so we ask for *"our"* bread – for that which is suited for us in *our* present circumstances.

The One who taught us this prayer lived Himself one day at a time, not certain in the morning where the evening meal was to come from. Jesus did not know each evening where He would find shelter that night, and while He was on earth He had no home He called His own. Most of us would find these conditions undesirable, but there is blessing attached to such poverty.

Jesus anticipated the anxiety that we must provide for tomorrow as well as today. Therefore, He reminded us that He who clothes the lilies of the field, and who provides for the birds of the air, knows that our lives need to be maintained with "necessities." And so we are taught to ask the Father to take us through *"this day,"* and if tomorrow comes, He knows that we will be as dependent on Him then, as we are now.

The Bible says, *"And having food and clothing, with these we shall be content"* (see 1 Timothy 6:8). God's plan is for Christians to walk by faith and not by sight (see 2 Corinthians 5:7). We are to be content with what each day brings, but are permitted to ask our Father for what we believe we need. So we are to renew this petition *"daily."* *God often gives us far more than enough for the day, but even in the midst of plenty, our real satisfaction lies in the Father alone!*

Acknowledge that your time is in God's hands and that you do not know what a day will bring. Pray for both the realization and the understanding, that sufficiency is found in Him.

August 16

*"'I do not pray that You should take them out of the world,
but that You should keep them from the evil one.'"* John 17:15

The Lord Jesus had a perfect understanding of the role of the devil. He knew that all the hatred of *"the world"* that is against His disciples would be inspired by Satan. The disciples will war not only against flesh and blood but also against demon spirits with *"the wicked one"* at their head (see Ephesians 6:16). Christ left nothing out in His request. His knowledge of the devil and his role led Him to anticipate the need for the Father's "keeping."

Thorough knowledge of the enemy and a healthy regard for his uniqueness is a necessary preparation for victory in war. Similarly, if we underestimate our enemy, we will see no need to wear armor, and we will go out to the battle unarmed, or in our own puny strength. *What the sixth chapter of Ephesians is actually telling us, is that our real struggle is not with human beings, but with cosmic intelligences; our enemies are not human, but demonic!* That is why Jesus prayed for the Father to *"keep"* us.

We need to be "kept" because the forces arrayed against us are *powerful.* The *"principalities"* and *"powers"* and *"rulers of the darkness of this age"* have neither conceded defeat nor been destroyed, so they continue to exercise *limited but considerable* power. Secondly, we need to be kept because these forces are not only powerful, but they are *wicked.* The darkness of falsehood and sin is their natural habitat. They are utterly unscrupulous and ruthless in the pursuit of their malicious designs.

Finally, we need to be kept because these forces coming against us are *cunning.* They operate in a combination of tactical shrewdness and ingenious deception. Sometimes he roars like a lion, but more often Satan is as subtle as a serpent. David Martyn Lloyd-Jones wrote, "I am certain that one of the main causes of the ill state of the Church today, is the fact that the devil is being forgotten. All is attributed to us."

Pray that the greatest power, the power that raised Jesus Christ from the dead, will manifest in you today.

"'Father, forgive them, for they do not know what they do.'"
Luke 23:34

W e know that one man, in particular, heard this compassionate prayer, along with the other things Jesus said - the repentant criminal crucified next to Him. Jesus' heart, although He was bearing the intolerable burden of mankind's sin, was revealed not only through His lovely prayer to God but through His loving response to a man dying next to Him: **"Assuredly, I say to you, today you will be with Me in Paradise."**

Other things besides Jesus' prayer may have "contributed" to the repentant thief's conversion, such as the inscription over His head, **"This is the King of the Jews,"** or the Scriptures he may have known from himself being a Jew. The truth is, we can never know the secrets of a man's heart to find out *exactly why* he makes that glorious turn which the Bible calls repentance.

But this we know - nothing could have cheered the heart of Jesus, and taken His mind off of His own suffering – even for just a moment - as having someone appeal to Him in His last moments on earth, on whom He could pour out His mercy! In the Garden of Gethsemane, an angel strengthened Him. But here, it was a man nailed up at His side who understood who He was, and ministered consolation. This man believed when even the apostles doubted.

And, the thief prayed to Christ as having a **"kingdom."** He knew that Jesus would die before long, and yet he believed that He would come to a kingdom. We, too, must believe in Christ's kingdom, that He reigns in heaven, and that He will come a second time to rule over all the earth.

And so the Lord's perfect body was laid to rest in Joseph's tomb to await the third day of resurrection, and the thief's corrupting body was thrown on to Jerusalem's public rubbish incinerator called Gehenna. But the two had already entered into the heavenly realm called Paradise!

Pray a prayer of thanksgiving and praise that, because you have trusted Jesus, you are on your way to join the repentant thief in Paradise.

August 18

"'They are not of the world, just as I am not of the world.'" John 17:16

Jesus' tender heart for His disciples is so clear *throughout* this prayer recorded in John Chapter Seventeen. He prays for them like a mother dying might pray for her children – not that she is indifferent to all other interests – but that her family is the natural, primary interest of her attention. He prays for them as the precious fruit of His life-labor, the hope of the future, and *the missionaries of the truth to the whole world!* The disciples must abide in the truth, and they must abide in the world for the sake of the truth. On the occasions when they felt the hatred of the world most, they must understand that they were doing *the most good.* (Notice the repetition in this verse 16 of the words before, in verse 14; these are provided as an introduction to verse 17.)

Who are the "happy" people today, the men and women who actually "enjoy" life? Are they the people who have allowed the thought of God to pass out of their lives? Or are the people who truly enjoy life the ones who can say with conviction the words of St. Peter, **"Blessed be the God and Father of our Lord Jesus Christ, who according to His abundant mercy has begotten us again to a living hope through the resurrection of Jesus Christ from the dead, to an inheritance incorruptible and undefiled and that does not fade away, reserved in heaven for you"** (see 1 Peter 1:3, 4). *Surely **"the world"** has not been made any happier by discarding the old hopes and the old faith!*

It was the Holy Ghost who enabled the simple-minded apostles to give utterance to their thoughts and to proclaim what their Father taught them. They told the world what its true character, weighed in the balances of God, really was; consequently, the world hated them and persecuted them to death.

Today, if we were as outspoken and faithful as the apostles were, we would find ourselves in the same category. Pray that you will be honest with the world, and faithful to God.

"Give us this day our daily bread." Matthew 6:11

God wants us to continually remember our dependence on *Him* because that prompts us to rejoice in His loving remembrance of *us* on a *"daily"* basis. Not to do so is foolish – even sinful. Jesus devoted a huge portion of His Sermon on the Mount to this subject, and if the evil involved were not so significant, He would not have thought it necessary to emphasize the Father's provision with so many arguments. If Jesus asks any of us at the end of our journey, "Have you lacked anything?" we would have to answer, "The Lord was my Shepherd, I did not want."

"Bread" is what we are instructed to ask for, meaning the bare necessities of life. As T.T. Lynch put it, "This is a prayer for daily *bread*, not for daily cake." It is a prayer not for the necessities of a lifetime, but for the necessities that will sustain us *today*. Can you visualize how our appetite for wealth, our love for luxury, and our desire for comfort stand rebuked by this prayer? Because in our culture, we desire *more* than our portion, *more* than enough – even *more* than we can possibly use.

We should consider the trust of a small child. He unconsciously depends upon his parents for his daily portion. He *trusts* them to provide, based on his "experience" of his needs being met for as long as he can remember. *It does not even occur to him to "worry!"*

So how can you apply these truths? If you could "hoard up" all of your needs for a full year, you wouldn't have to use your *faith* again for another 365 days! You would not have to *believe* God, and you would not need to *study* His Word nor *hear* from Him! You could just "coast along" for a year. But as long as you are thinking just one day at a time, you will need to *operate by faith* tomorrow, and the next day. And in doing so, you will glorify God.

Pray that you will trust God for the portion you need *today*.

August 20

"'They are not of the world, just as I am not of the world.'" John 17:16

"*They are not of the world*" is a reference by Jesus not to the material world, but to the *people* of the world – their principles and practices, their pleasures and pursuits. The people of the world have their hopes, aims, desires, and even their religion. But they are not of the Father, and they have a fearful destiny awaiting them; **"*the earth and the works that are in it will be burned up*"** (see 2 Peter 3:10).

The enemies of the disciples' souls (the world, the flesh, and the devil) will be overthrown and confounded. Jesus pronounces these words of intercession before His Father in the hearing of His disciples and for our comfort. **"*Strangers and pilgrims*"** are *travelers*. They are known by their language and manner – a different language, a different manner from that which is spoken and lived around them.

The *unworldliness* of Jesus is our model; **"*I am not of the world.*"** The separating line that marked His life from the world's life is the line which is to mark our own. *It was not an outward separation from the world, but an inward separation from its spirit!* The separation arose from His life of holy consecration and His life of abiding prayer.

Our Lord showed a sincere desire to be alone with the Father, with regard to both time and place (see Mark 1:35, 6:45, 46; Luke 5:16, 6:12). Prayer was Jesus' very breath and life. For Him, prayer was not an act of self-discipline that required time management skills or gimmicks. His prayer life was neither forced nor artificial, but a very natural communion. And He prayed with a thankful heart (see Matthew 11:25, 15:36; Luke 10:21, 22).

Before He began His earthly ministry, before He cast out demons, before He chose His disciples, before He taught the multitudes, before He performed miracles, at every major crisis, and before He died on the Cross – Jesus prayed. Prayer was a necessity – not just an "important thing," but an *essential* thing!

Pray for the practice of private, kingdom-focused prayer, to become a high priority in your life.

"'Father, glorify Your name.'" John 12:28

H ere Jesus is victorious over the devil because the sacrifice of obedience to God triumphed over selfishness – which is the root of Satan's entire philosophy. The prince of this world has gained his place through self-seeking, trickery, deceit and cruelty. Jesus would have none of it, for what mattered most to the Savior was that the name of His Father would be glorified.

This prayer of Jesus is, in fact, the identical petition that begins "The Model Prayer," *"(Our) Father in heaven, hallowed be Your name."* The sanctifying of God's name, His being reverenced as the Holy One, and the doing of His will on earth as it is in heaven – are the essentials of glorifying God. This should always be our prayer motive: to glorify that "name," so that it will *stand out before men* in all of its truth, grace, and power. Only a few words make up this prayer, but oh, the importance!

The death, burial, and resurrection of Jesus displayed the glorious attributes and power of God more than any other event! Pause now to consider that truth. But then there is also the truth of the Judgment; it is all tied together.

Perhaps no other truth is so far removed from the thoughts of men than the Judgment. Someday we must all face God! But how often does that fact cross our minds? Not often, because we are so busy enjoying life and dealing with our pressing circumstances. Once again the urgent replaces the important in our thinking. Hebrews 9:27 says, *"It is appointed for men to die once, but after this the judgment."*

The Judgment: the pronouncement of a final decision by The Heavenly Judge! What awaits us at death is God's verdict. We will not need to wait until the Final Judgment at the end of the world to know where we will spend eternity. We will know at once - the verdict of heaven or hell - at the instant of death.

Pray rejoicing today over that blessed assurance that, because you have trusted Jesus, you are ready for God's verdict.

August 22

"Sanctify them by Your truth. Your word is truth."' John 17:17

We progress in sound living only as we progress in sound *understanding*. *"Your word is a lamp to my feet and a light to my path."* If we hold fast the truth, we will be sanctified by the Spirit of God. To be made holy is to be made like God as He is revealed in Jesus. This may sound bold and presumptuous until we recall the words of Jesus, *"Therefore you shall be perfect, just as your Father in heaven is perfect"* (see Matthew 5:48). God desires holiness in us, Jesus prays for it, and, if we will let Him, the Holy Spirit produces it. It has been said that there is no offering that we can bring to God so precious as personal holiness.

The word, *"sanctify,"* is constantly used in the Septuagint to express the dedication and consecration of both persons and things to God. Sanctification is the gracious work of God that sets the Believer apart for Himself and for service in the world. *It involves not only a cleansing from the filthiness of sin but also a preparation by the infusion of grace; not only the elimination of poison but also the filling of what is divine!*

A number of theologians divide sanctification into three categories: positional, practical, and perfect. *Positional* sanctification never changes, because, in Christ, we have been set apart to belong to God and to serve Him. In 1 Corinthians 1:2, Paul still addressed the inconsistent church at Corinth as, *"sanctified in Christ Jesus,"* a called-out people. *Practical* sanctification refers to our day-to-day lives; since we have a holy position in Christ, we should live like it. Lastly, *perfect* sanctification does not take place until we see Jesus at His coming (see 1 John 3:2).

In the case of the eleven disciples, all that Jesus had done for them previously was part of their sanctifying and setting apart unto God. Because they were to remain in the world, they needed this sanctification of the Father in order to keep them as a body separate from the world.

Pray for your own sanctification.

"'Give us this day our daily bread.'" Matthew 6:11

This prayer is clearly meant not only for the Disciples, but for all Believers, in all places, and at all times. There is no need to add anything to the Model Prayer, for nothing is left out. Using this devotional commentary daily will hopefully lead you to the point where you can speak to God with greater ease than you can speak to others. There is so much to learn from the Master about prayer, so let's listen again!

Jesus fed "physical" bread to multitudes of people when they assembled to hear Him teach. He did not forget the needs of the human body, for He loves man. Before feeding the four thousand, He said to His disciples, **"I have compassion on the multitude, because they have now continued with Me three days and have nothing to eat. And I do not want to send them away hungry, lest they faint on the way"** (see Matthew 15:32).

In addition, by teaching us to ask God for **"bread,"** Jesus is communicating that our desire for "worldly" things should be moderate. Clement of Alexandria once compared the right attitude of a man toward his possessions to be the same as his attitude toward a shoe – the most important thing is that it needs to *fit. Our desire should be to receive only enough to sustain our bodily life to the end that we are enabled to do God's will effectively!*

How wicked it would be if we begged temporal mercies so that we may be enabled to sin against God! It happens! James 4:3 says, **"You ask amiss, that you may spend it on your pleasures."** No, we are to desire temporal things for *spiritual* ends. For example, Hannah prayed for a child, but for what reason? Listen to her prayer: **"O Lord, if You will remember me, and give Your maidservant a male child, then I will give him to the Lord all the days of his life"** (see 1 Samuel 1:11).

Pray for a new awareness of how you can use what God has already given you for kingdom purposes.

August 24

"'Sanctify them by Your truth. Your word is truth.'" John 17:17

Since the devil offers a counterfeit for every major blessing and grace that comes from God, it is important to verify that something as vital as sanctification is *genuine*. A person can cultivate many excellent virtues and be known as a "good person," and yet have a heart that is without God's sanctifying grace. Socrates practiced and taught a strict morality, but he was ignorant of Biblical holiness. The Stoics, who were the most bitter of Paul's enemies (see Acts 17:18), were prominent among the moralized heathens. Paul, himself, wrote of those who had *"a form of godliness"* but who were *"denying its power."* We do not become holy by adopting clean habits.

Sanctification, then, is not merely an effort on the part of a Christian to "live a better Christian life." *It is actually not an effort by man at all, but rather a work of God!* It is God that sanctifies, which is why Jesus makes this request of the Father. Whether it be justification in the past tense, sanctification in the present tense, or glorification in the future tense – salvation is wholly of God, and it is God who sanctifies.

Are you aware of your present corruption? Does your heart cry out in anguish, as you consider how prone you are to wander from your Savior? Are you practicing selective obedience? Are you rebuking the devil? Are you growing in grace? Are you more faithful in your prayer life? Are you praying for others? Are you seriously studying the Word of God? Are you distinguishing between what only *you* can do, and what only *God* can do? Is the Holy Spirit bringing you under conviction?

Draw near to Him! Spend time with Him! Reach out in faith to Him! He is the altogether holy One. He can teach you to *despise* your sin, when only now you "regret" it. Pray Isaiah 6:5, *"Woe is me, for I am undone! Because I am a man of unclean lips, and I dwell in the midst of a people of unclean lips."* Pray this in the name of Jesus, Amen.

"'Give us this day our daily bread.'" Matthew 6:11

In the Model Prayer, we see concern for everything from the smallest things to the greatest things – everything from asking for our daily ration of bread to the coming of the kingdom of God. Small things and great things, inward things and outward things, material things and spiritual things, are all included in this prayer! Jesus might have taught us to speak to Him only about the "big" things, but had that been so, we would have been left terribly alone.

A father who does not listen to everything his child says is not a loving father. A father may smile when his child shows little knowledge or maturity, or when his child has so little understanding of the difference between small and great things. But a loving father listens, nevertheless.

This petition deals with the daily "support" for the trusting child of God. When He sent out His disciples, Jesus was explicit about the manner by which their needs should be met. He said, **"Provide neither gold nor silver nor copper in your money belts"** (see Matthew 10:9) and **"Take nothing for the journey, neither ... bread nor money"** (see Luke 9:3). Jesus assured them that the laborer is worthy of his meat and that their requirements would be met by heavenly provision. They were to have no anxiety about **"daily bread,"** because, **"Your heavenly Father knows that you need all these things"** (see Matthew 6:32).

When you are serving the Lord, you should look to the Father for your supplies. *He will give physical and mental strength for the task at hand, and He will provide all things needed for each day!* What you have a right to ask from God is what you *need* – no more, and no less. This divine instruction does not reduce all Believers to one "level," but simply leaves it to an *all-knowing* God to determine what is actually needed for the day.

In reality, you are a petitioner, coming with empty hands to your Father. Pray with strong confidence and trust, as you ask Him today to provide you with daily bread.

August 26

"'Sanctify them by Your truth. Your word is truth.'" John 17:17

God works in us through *"truth"* (see 1 Thessalonians 2:13). When we *know, believe, and act* upon God's truth, He is able to work powerfully in our lives. We are sanctified in and through God's truth by the Word of God, by Jesus Christ, and by the Holy Spirit. Therefore, any experience that helps us to learn the Word of God better, to love Jesus more, and to yield to the control of the Holy Spirit is an experience of sanctification. Faith, prayer, and even chastisement are also means of sanctification.

God's way of working is by light. *"Awake, you who sleep, arise from the dead, and Christ will give you light."* The power of grace breaks in upon the soul by the light of the Gospel. John 1:4 says, *"In Him was life, and the life was the light of men."* The Gospel works only when accompanied by the Spirit. *There is a huge difference between seeing things in the light of reason, and seeing things in the light of the Spirit!* Unfortunately, most men are content with a superficial belief and a human explanation of divine things.

Is there a "motive" for sanctification? The purpose for it is so that Jesus might send us into the world to share the truth of the Gospel and to declare what God has done for a lost world. *Serving others* is the mark of a sanctified Believer. When Jesus prayed, *"I sanctify Myself,"* He meant that, for *their* sakes, He was setting Himself apart to die on the Cross. While His disciples were continuously debating over which of them was the greatest, Christ humbled Himself and washed *their* feet!

Paul wrote, *"For all seek their own, not the things which are of Christ Jesus"* (see Philippians 2:21). In other words, men still let their own interests interfere with the interests of Christ. As you read these inspired words of Scripture, does the Holy Spirit bring you to repentance? Are your own interests interfering with those of the kingdom of God?

Pray that you will *"seek first the kingdom of God"* today.

August 27

"'Father, forgive them, for they do not know what they do.'"
Luke 23:34

During the Sermon on the Mount, Jesus preached these words recorded in Matthew 5:44, **"Pray for those who spitefully use you and persecute you."** Here on the Cross, in the midst of great suffering, Christ is literally praying for those who were using Him despitefully. Here we see our glorious Leader doing what the greatest generals and captains have proudly claimed, that they "never bade men to do that which they were not willing to do themselves."

When we pray *sincerely* for those who do us wrong, when we *honestly* want God's best for them and pray for their benefit, we do something **"more than others."** To do this requires motivation that comes from having the *compassion* of Jesus for people. When people abuse us, do we ask God to punish them, or do we ask Him to have mercy and pity upon them? When lost people affecting our lives behave like lost people, do we ask God to save their souls and to open their eyes before it is too late, or do we comfort ourselves by deciding that they are really of no value?

Whether or not we follow Jesus' example of His first of three prayers from the Cross, depends on the interest we have and the value we place on why Jesus came to earth in the first place. He came, says the Scripture, **"to seek and to save the lost."** We must keep *this* knowledge, *this* perspective before us at all times as we encounter people!

One last truth; the verb tense suggests that Jesus *kept praying, kept repeating* His request, **"Father, forgive them, for they do not know what they do"** – even while the iron spikes were being driven through His hands and feet! That fact should cause us to humble ourselves, should it not? *For our prayers for our enemies are often silenced by our pride, while feeling more highly of ourselves than we should!*

Pray now for the people who have abused you and wronged you, asking the Father to bless them and to draw them to Himself by the Holy Spirit.

August 28

"'Sanctify them by Your truth. Your word is truth.'" John 17:17

The sanctification of God's people is a very important matter. *All of the manifestations of God's grace in some way connect to sanctification!* For the disciples, sanctification meant a self-dedication to the work of preaching the Gospel, the renunciation of everything that would hinder their message, and a focus on showing the world the meaning of redemption.

As we voluntarily *read, study, and apply* God's Word to our lives, the sanctifying process is in progress. There are clear signs that sanctification is taking place in an individual's life. For one, a sanctified person lives as one *available for the service of the Gospel;* to be a disciple is to be a missionary! Paul wrote, **"And He died for all, that those who live should live no longer for themselves, but for Him who died for them and rose again"** (see 2 Corinthians 5:15). 1 Peter 1:16 says, **"Be holy, for I am holy."** Therefore, the sanctified person is *seeking to be like God in holiness.*

Another sign of sanctification is when we become *increasingly determined to follow Jesus all the way.* Paul wrote to Timothy, **"I have fought the good fight, I have finished the race, I have kept the faith"** (see 2 Timothy 4:7). Along the journey, the sanctified person is *demonstrating the fruit of the spirit:* **"love, joy, peace, longsuffering, kindness, goodness, faithfulness, gentleness, self-control"** (see Galatians 5:22, 23). The sanctification of the Old Testament is a *ritual process* of ceremonial observance; the sanctification of the New Testament is a *spiritual process* through the liberating work of the Holy Spirit. Corrie ten Boom wrote, "Sanctification is not a heavy yoke, but a joyful liberation."

Lastly, the sanctified person is *developing a hatred for sin,* not simply a regret of it: **"You who love the Lord, hate evil!"** (see Psalm 97:10). Based on the signs of sanctification listed above, do you recognize the sanctification process taking place in *your* life? Do you see yourself as a missionary of the Gospel truth? Pray that you, and every person with whom you come into contact, will see evidence of your sanctification.

> *"'Simon, Simon! Indeed, Satan has asked for you, that he may sift you as wheat. But I have prayed for you.'"* Luke 22:31, 32

"Martha, Martha." "Jerusalem, Jerusalem." And here, *"Simon, Simon!"* On each occasion, Jesus is showing deep emotion. The word *"you,"* the first time it is used here in connection with Satan, is plural - and so Jesus was applying this warning regarding "sifting" to *all* the eleven. They were present and could hear what Jesus was saying to Peter, and they understood that they were all being described as targets.

Jesus uses the proper name "Simon" in His address (not "Peter, Peter," which would apply to this disciple's rocklike nature). He addresses head-strong Simon because he is the one who would get into the greatest danger. Jesus prayed for the other disciples as well (see John 17:6-19), but the story of Peter's denial shows that he was far more vulnerable than the others, and more in need of the Master's help.

We all have places of vulnerability in our hearts, don't we? *The truth is, the devil has been observing our weaknesses and strengths since the time we were born!* Souls are that important to him! Satan and his accomplices have been listening to and watching everything. At the time of this writing, America's government is in the news regarding what "types" of information it gathers on individuals and the "methods" by which that information is gathered. Consider the fact that the devil has a current "file" about you and about each person on earth, and that he *uses this information daily* to our detriment!

Jesus prayed specifically that Peter's *faith* would increase because that was where he was vulnerable. Do you know where *you* are vulnerable to the devil? Do you easily become angry? Do you easily feel lonely? Do you easily become discouraged? Do you easily become discontent? Do you easily become proud? Do you, like Peter, lack faith?

As was true of His disciples, you are also in need of such warnings from our Lord. An attack may be coming that will require the intercessory prayer of Jesus. Pray for divine revelation of your vulnerable places, and thank Jesus today for His much-needed intercession when you are tempted.

August 30

By the power of His *"truth,"* God will provide words which recall the thought that the Father is the only *real* God – and that consequently, His word, as spoken by Jesus, is reality. The "quality" of this truth is emphasized by Jesus' use of the noun instead of the adjective ("truth" instead of "true"). Jesus is saying, "Your own word *is* truth, composed wholly of truth, without any mixture of falsehood." *This certifies the inerrancy and infallibility of the Word, without exception!* This includes the Word of the Old Testament (on which Jesus placed His approval repeatedly), and the revelation that Jesus added in person (with the promise of its perfect preservation through the Holy Spirit).

Satan corrupts you through lies; God sanctifies you through the truth. Only as far as you walk according to God's Word, will you be separated from evil. Notice the connection between the petition of Christ recorded in verse 15 (*"Keep them from the evil one"*) and this petition, *"Sanctify them by Your truth;"* the former is secured by the latter.

You are not sanctified through impressions, emotions, sacraments, traditions, or by visions. It is through the truth that the *love* of God is revealed. Love is a sanctifying principle; *"We love Him because He first loved us"* (see 1 John 4:19). *Faith,* which purifies the heart, is produced by the truth, *"Faith comes by hearing, and hearing by the word of God"* (see Romans 10:17). *Hope* is produced by the truth, for it is written in Colossians 1:5, *"The hope which is laid up for you in heaven, of which you heard before in the word of the truth of the gospel."*

Because the Word is *God's* truth, it is the "final authority!" And if the Word is truth, you should place the *highest* value, the *highest* priority upon it, as you live your life from day to day. Dear friend, is that what you are doing?

Pray that reading, knowing, and believing the Word of God will become more *essential* to you each time you hold the absolute truth in your very hands.

> *"'Simon, Simon! Indeed, Satan has asked for you, that he may sift you as wheat. But I have prayed for you.'"* Luke 22:31, 32

Imagine hearing the Son of God inform you that the same devil who harassed Job, is out to get *you!* And it gets worse! The word translated *"has asked"* actually implies *begging!* Satan wanted to bring down these men badly. Not content with only Judas, the devil desired the whole group!

While speaking directly to Simon, Jesus explained that a sifting process was upon them all. Satan is under God's authority, and so he cannot sift without gaining permission. And so here Jesus pulls back the curtain and reveals who is *behind* the ordeal through which the eleven would pass that night.

The devil is the enemy of everyone who puts his trust in God. The old Puritan commentator, Trapp, explained that Jesus uses a fan and sifts to get rid of the "chaff," while the devil uses a fan and sifts to get rid of the "wheat." Christian, our greatest enemy is determined to toss us about and cause friction and great harm in our lives. The devil is out to destroy our faith, our witness, our usefulness, and even our very life!

A great problem in the Church today is that we do not think of ourselves as "soldiers" (see 2 Timothy 2:3). A large number of believers continue to think that talk of "spiritual warfare" is silly, or that it is merely "symbolic" language in the Bible. The New Testament applies military terminology such as *fight, armor, warfare, weapons,* etc. to prayer. Jesus was reminding His disciples, as He reminds us right now, that the devil is not only real - but he is our *adversary.*

If we are going to be victorious over a real devil, we must take the reality of spiritual warfare more seriously! This involves recognizing the "movements" and "schemes" of the enemy, which is precisely what the Lord was revealing here to the disciples.

Pray that the Father will supernaturally enlighten you today as to the schemes and plans of the devil that are currently affecting your life, and that He will provide you with the discernment and power to overcome the enemy.

September 1

"'Sanctify them by Your truth. Your word is truth.'" John 17:17

"**Y**our *word*" refers to the Message about God in Christ when conveyed in any and every authentic form from the Father. Large parts of Scripture had not yet been produced at the time of this prayer, and two or three of the disciples who were listening that very night would later be contributors to Scripture as we have it today.

The truth needs to be kept because this evil world hates any truth that sheds light on darkness. D.L. Moody wrote in the front of his Bible, "This book will keep you from sin or sin will keep you from this book." Disciples of Christ must abide in the truth, and also abide in the world for the sake of the truth. An old Slovenian proverb says, "Speak the truth, but leave immediately after!" When Jesus' disciples feel the world's hatred most, is when they are doing the most good; the weight of their cross is the measure of their impact.

You cannot "invent" truth; you can only discover truth, because it exists apart from your knowledge of it! Therefore, truth stands above your opinions, your deductions, and your education. In a few hours from when Jesus prayed this prayer, Pilate would ask, **"What is truth?"** Pilate was not sneering; his tone was that of an indifferent man, who believed that anything in the nature of religious truth was useless speculation. The educated Roman world had many men like Pilate. They had no faith in their own gods, although they continued the usual idolatrous rites.

In 1986, Charles Colson wrote, "Taking our stand on biblical truth can be our only defense against our culture's penchant to reduce all issues to simplistic suppositions and glib answers." Men will say, "I have known plenty of good people who had no religion." But that is like saying, "I have known plenty of good knives which would not cut." Man is still made for union with God and for His service and glory. God is man's true home, and God's "word" is truth.

Pray that today you will live out your knowledge of truth.

"'Give us this day our daily bread.'" Matthew 6:11

The human body that God made dependent on daily bread is to be nourished and prayed for. The Father knows that man is capable of doing without various common human needs. But to any who may fanatically or proudly profess to be continuously "superior" to the needs of the body, Jesus said clearly, "Your heavenly Father knows that *you need* all these things" (see Matthew 6:32).

We are to make *God* (rather than what He "provides") the *priority* of our lives. The Model Prayer teaches us that only *after* we have asked that His **"name"** be hallowed, only *after* we have asked that His **"kingdom"** may come, and only *after* we have asked that His **"will"** may be done – is it appropriate to ask that our **"bread"** may be given.

There are six petitions in the Model Prayer; the first three petitions have to do with "heavenly" things, and the second three with "earthly" things. We are looking today at the fourth petition, which is located in that second grouping. When we pray rightly, there is no "sudden descent" from the first grouping to the second, from heavenly to earthly petitions, because we need to have our earthly life nourished to enable us to *do* heavenly things on earth. *The best reason why we ask for bread, then, is so that we will be equipped to serve in His kingdom!*

Jesus said, **"What man is there among you who, if his son asks for bread, will give him a stone?"** (see Matthew 7:9). It is a child's instinct to ask food from his parent, and it is the privilege and natural instinct of an earthly parent to provide food for his child. Our Heavenly Father is a *Giver!* He is the life of all that lives. The Psalmist wrote, **"You preserve man and beast"** (see Psalm 36:6). Jesus said, **"Look at the birds of the air, for they neither sow nor reap nor gather into barns; yet your Heavenly Father feeds them"** (see Matthew 6:26).

Pray that you will notice and be thankful for God's continuous gifts to you today.

September 3

"As You sent Me into the world, I also have sent them into the world."
John 17:18

When Jesus prayed to the Father saying, *"As You sent Me ... I also have sent them,"* what exactly did He mean? Christ was comparing the similarities between the reasons why *He* was sent and the reasons why He sends His *disciples.* Today we will seek to understand that comparison.

Jesus was sent to reveal and to show forth the glory of the Father; His disciples are sent to show forth Christ's glory, to the glory of the Father. Jesus was sent on an errand of mercy to seek and to save that which was lost; His disciples are sent as His instruments to tell a sinful world of One who is mighty to save. Jesus was sent as the Holy One to a scene of corruption; His disciples are sent to be *"the salt of the earth."* Jesus was sent as the Light; His disciples are sent to shine as lights in the darkness of this world. Jesus was sent to be about His Father's business; His disciples are sent to redeem the time, to be instant in and out of season, always abounding in His work.

This part of Jesus' prayer declares an important truth - the truth of *Jesus' pre-existence, "As You sent Me into the world."* Earlier in this very prayer, Jesus said, *"Glorify Me together with Yourself, with the glory which I had with You before the world was,"* and later in this prayer, *"You loved Me before the foundation of the world."* In Colossians 1:17, Paul describes Jesus as, *"before all things."* Christ shared in the creation of the world (see John 1:3; Colossians 1:16; Hebrews 1:2).

Jesus was sent into the world by the Father, because of the world's need. *God does not send messengers without a cause!* If human prophets had been enough, there would have been no need to send Jesus. Furthermore, Jesus was sent into the world that the Father would be glorified. The heart of Christ was in full harmony with the heart of the Father.

Pray for your heart to be in harmony with the heart of God.

> *"'Simon, Simon! Indeed, Satan has asked for you, that he may sift you as wheat. But I have prayed for you.'"* Luke 22:31, 32

First Judas, then Peter and the disciples, then Jesus will be the primary targets of Satan. See Jesus watching and praying over the disciples to ensure that the devil's blow will not be mortal; the enemy will only be permitted to see what in them was good corn and what was chaff.

The term *"sift"* was used by Jesus, not Satan, to illustrate what the coming ordeal would be like for the disciples. *Wheat must be sifted and cleaned because of its value!* The sifting is a violent and continuous shaking of the sieve that causes the solid wheat to fall through. The Father was giving His permission for the disciples to be put through the severest trials, to see whether they had the needed faith for when Jesus would be arrested and separated from them.

How humbling it is to look at this scene: the vain, self-confident, self-willed Simon son of Jonas - distinguished from the devoted, heroic, rock-like Peter. See the difference between the bad and the good, the vile and the precious – in the same man. And it does not take long before we recognize ourselves in this picture.

Should we not recognize that, what is right now going on all around many of *us*, is the same as what was taking place then with the disciples? Now comes to mind that He taught us to pray, **"But deliver us from the evil one."** There may be an ambush awaiting us at any time. We must always remember Peter's words of caution: **"Be sober, be vigilant, because your adversary the devil walks about like a roaring lion, seeking whom he may devour"** (literally, "swallow").

There are weaknesses, even in the most sincere. There is rebellion, even in the one who loves Jesus with all of his heart. There is error, even in the one who strives the hardest. There is unbelief, even in the very faithful. There is a tendency to wander, even in the most devoted.

Pray to be sifted under the careful supervision of Jesus, so that your faith will stand up to what awaits you.

September 5

"As You sent Me into the world, I also have sent them into the world."
John 17:18

Jesus came to bear witness that He was king, but He did not come to possess His kingdom and act as a king. Christ was sent to earth for the purpose of redeeming (1 John 4:10, ***"He loved us and sent His Son to be the propitiation for our sins"***) and instructing (see our verse today) the world. Consider how God demonstrated His love by the way He went about this. Rather than entrusting an angel or an archangel with our salvation, He sent His own Son. Jesus submitted to this sending by the Father; He was *ready* to be sent!

There were "similarities" between the sending of Jesus and the sending of the apostles, but not "equality." The apostles were not redeemers. But both Jesus and the apostles were authorized ministers and officers of the Church; Christ was authorized by the Father, and the apostles by Christ. Both Jesus and the apostles had the power to send others. To hear the apostles was to hear Jesus (see Luke 10:16) and to hear Jesus was to hear God.

Now as His disciple, you are Christ's ambassador; ***"We are ambassadors for Christ"*** (see 2 Corinthians 5:20). An ambassador is a person sent with *dignity and authority* to conduct affairs of the greatest importance. Jesus Christ, who is the King of kings and Lord of lords, has sent *you* into the world! And so how beautiful are your feet (see Isaiah 52:7)! In addition, an ambassador is a person sent with a *duty* – in his life and conversation, and in his ministry and calling – so as not to disgrace Christ. As His ambassador, you are to be faithful and sincere with men.

Read 1 Samuel 12:1-5. Samuel had demonstrated integrity before the people of Israel. *You do not want to lack integrity as an ambassador of Jesus Christ!* Webster defines "integrity" as, "The quality or state of being of sound moral principle; uprightness, honesty, and sincerity." As an ambassador of Christ, you want to be known by your truthfulness, trustworthiness, and character.

Pray for God to make you *ready* to be sent.

"'Give us this day our daily bread.'" Matthew 6:11

The word *"us"* forbids you to pray selfishly. When you ask bread for yourself, you are taught to ask it for others. The Model Prayer begins with the word *"Our,"* reminding you of God's family. We are all sinners, and we all share the same fallen nature. We are all God's prodigals, all brothers in the same great family; all equally guilty, all equally redeemed. We cannot separate ourselves even from the worst and lowest.

It would sound strange if a family gathered together and one of the members prayed, "Give *me* this day *my* daily bread." Instead, we are to have the mind of the early church, where *"The multitude of those who believed were of one heart and one soul; neither did anyone say that any of the things he possessed was his own"* (see Acts 4:32). There is always enough food, and some to spare, sent by the Father for the family "us."

The word translated *"daily"* occurs nowhere in Greek literature, and is found only here in the Model Prayer. The meaning is close to "seasonable, suited to our need." God does not limit your petitions to only sporadic occasions of great crisis; He wants to hear your voice each day that your faith would be nourished and that your relationship to Him would be intimate. Someone once said, "Carnal men are like swine, which ravin upon the acorns, but look not up to the oak whence they drop."

Daily *"bread"* refers to that which supplies and protects the temple of the Holy Ghost. God is glorified when you nourish the nature He gave as the clothing and instrument of your soul. What He gives, you may use in moderation and gratitude - but you are not instructed to ask for *more* than "daily bread."

Bread includes what is necessary! It comes to you day by day, as the manna came to Israel in the wilderness from heaven. They were not allowed to gather more than for the day; if they greedily and disobediently did so, it stank, bred worms, and grew corrupt.

Pray for increased contentment.

September 7

"As You sent Me into the world, I also have sent them into the world."
John 17:18

It is true that the Trinity are one in essence, in will, and in actions. All the persons in the Godhead are co-essential and co-equal in glory and honor. But the sending of Christ into the world is chiefly ascribed to God the Father, because *salvation* is His personal operation (see John 3:16) and because He is both judge and chief. Therefore, Jesus said, **"My Father is greater than I"** (see John 14:28).

There are occasions when we can compare ordinary ministers to the apostles – if their mission is compared to Christ's! Our verse today shows that they still must be **"sent;" "And how shall they preach unless they are sent?"** (see Romans 10:15). Ordinary ministers are sent by a power derived and delegated *from* Christ. They are to open the mind of God to men, and to pray – in Christ's name and authority – that men will be reconciled to God.

Therefore, both apostles and ministers of the Gospel, pastors, and teachers of the Church, are "sent" by Christ with the consent and blessing of all the Persons of the Trinity. Jesus Christ and God the Father "send," **"Paul, an apostle (not from men nor through man, but through Jesus Christ and God the Father who raised Him from the dead)"** (see Galatians 1:1); the Holy Spirit "sends," **"Take heed to yourselves and to all the flock, among which the Holy Spirit has made you overseers"** (see Acts 20:28, and see also Acts 13:2). One might say that ministers are *sent* by the will of the Father, *qualified* by the Holy Spirit, and *commissioned* by the authority of Christ as King of the Church.

Now for the application. Jesus carried the Father's mission to a certain point and then uses His disciples to carry that mission to completion. The first sending contemplated the second, according to the Father's will. Both sendings are **"into the world."** *That means you are here for the world's sake!* The Greek word that we translate to mean "sent" literally means, "on a mission."

Pray that you will be "on a mission" wherever you go today.

"'Father, forgive them, for they do not know what they do.'"
Luke 23:34

This is not our Lord praying for Christians. This is a prayer for sinners that their sins would be forgiven. And from the subsequent testimony of the Acts of the Apostles, we find evidence that many of them were forgiven and trusted Jesus for salvation.

Jesus modeled praying for the lost not only in this prayer but also in His prayer recorded in John 17:21 when He prayed, *"That they also may be one in Us, that the world may believe that You sent Me."* And He taught us to pray, *"Your kingdom come, Your will be done on earth as it is in heaven."*

Paul modeled praying for lost sinners when he shared, *"Brethren, my heart's desire and prayer to God for Israel is that they may be saved"* (Romans 10:1). In Romans 9:2, Paul testifies to having great sorrow and continual *pain* in his heart for the lost! When we pray for the salvation of lost people, we know that we are praying God's will because we read in John 3:17, *"For God did not send His Son into the world to condemn the world, but that the world through Him might be saved."* In 1 Timothy 2:1-6, we find this exhortation from Paul, *"that supplications, prayers, intercessions, and giving of thanks be made for all men"* because God *"desires all men to be saved and to come to the knowledge of the truth."*

How, then, should we pray for the lost? First, we must pray for them with a cleansed heart. *We cannot sincerely ask for God to rule in the heart of a lost person when we are unwilling for Him to first rule in our own heart!* Second, we must recognize that lost sinners are "perishing" (John 3:16), and allow that truth to become a burden to our hearts. Third, we must pray for the lost person to have a receptive heart to the truth of the Gospel. And fourth, we must pray for the convicting work of the Holy Spirit to draw them to Jesus.

Pray earnestly now for your lost friends by name.

September 9

"As You sent Me into the world, I also have sent them into the world."
John 17:18

"I *also have sent them into the world"* is a truly remarkable statement! Do you realize that you are not here on earth for the purpose of conducting your own business? As much as you love your family members, do you realize that you are not in the world for fellowship with them? The truth is, you are not here of your own choice, nor are you here to select the position or course you wish to take; Jesus selected it *for* you!

The One who sent you "into the world" could *remove* you from it any minute now, should it be His will to do so. But then you would no longer gain from the victories over the world's disappointments, temptations, and corruptions. Then you would not learn to live by faith or by hope - through *experience. So Jesus sent you into the same place where the Father sent Him, that you would become proven and strong for His glory!*

You have been sent to the same location where Jesus was sent, for the following reasons: to learn the power of His name, to prove His love, to triumph in His salvation, to learn to depend on Him alone, to be His servant, to know the Father intimately, to overcome the world (**"more than conquerors through Him"**), to be the light of the world, to be witnesses against the world, to bring Him glory, and to carry on His redemptive service.

Therefore, the question today is this: Do you know for certain that the daily work you are doing is what *He* has sent you to do? Examine your heart, and repent if you find pride or selfishness. For if the work you are doing daily is "outside" the work of His will and His calling, you will neither please nor glorify Him – and, when you leave this world, you will not be able to say as He did earlier in this prayer, **"I have glorified You on the earth. I have finished the work which You have given Me to do."**

Pray for revelation of your mission.

"And forgive us our debts, as we forgive our debtors."   Matthew 6:12

In Matthew's version of the Model Prayer, we find the word *"debts"* and later the word *"trespasses,"* while in Luke's version we find the word *"sins."* There are some minor differences between the three words, but they are not problematic toward understanding the prayer.

Every sin is a "trespass," a transgression, an overstepping of the bounds. Of course, the Bible considers sin from the viewpoint of God, which means sin is *disobedience*, or "debt." David reached the place where he saw the enormity of his sin in its true light; he lost sight of himself, Bathsheba, and Uriah, and cried, *"Against You, You only, have I sinned, and done this evil in Your sight"* (see Psalm 51:4).

When we sin, there is something in our act for which we become *liable* to God. Even the sins of our *past* history are included in this word "debt," because they are not yet done with us. The ink never fades in the eternal account books containing the long, black, damning list of all our sins that create that debt - our sins of *commission* (the evil words we have spoken, the evil deeds we have done, the evil thoughts we have had), and especially our sins of *omission*. *"Debt" is something we owe!* In relation to God, it is something we owe to Him but cannot pay.

There are certain things that even the most "mature" Christian owes to God, such as reverence, service, obedience, first place, complete surrender, and his best and deepest love. *"All have sinned and fall short of the glory of God."* We have given God less than His due; He has a claim against us, and we are "in debt" to Him. And before tonight comes, one way or another, we will have added to that debt.

Now the Good News! Your sin is met with His forgiveness, and your debt is met with His mercy! *"But where sin abounded, grace abounded much more."* Jesus cancelled your debt on the Cross. There is forgiveness with God! All that is required is that you should *ask* for it.

September 11

"'I pray for them. I do not pray for the world but for those whom You have given Me, for they are Yours.'" John 17:9

The words, "Nine-eleven," will have special meaning to Americans for a long time to come. On September 11, 2001, we began to pay closer attention to the activities of people referred to as "terrorists." Who were these wicked people? Were they mad? How could they do such horrible things? One thing is for certain: terrorists then and now, are *lost* people. *We should not be shocked when lost people behave like lost people!* And lost people need our prayers of intercession. Desperately.

This portion of Jesus' prayer, particularly the words, **"I pray for them,"** (referring here to the disciples) speaks to prayers of intercession. Jesus continues with the words, **"I do not pray for the world,"** but that does not mean He *never* prays for the world; it means that at that particular moment, His prayer focus was on the disciples. For today's devotion, let us join together and intercede with a focus on the salvation of terrorists. What is the biblical basis for doing so? Two particular passages come to mind.

First, we are instructed by the Apostle Paul writing these words to Timothy: **"I exhort first of all that supplications, PRAYERS, INTERCESSIONS, and giving of thanks be made for ALL men, for Kings and all who are in authority, that we may lead a quiet and peaceable life in all godliness and reverence. For this is good and acceptable in the sight of God our Savior, who desires ALL men to be saved and to come to the knowledge of the truth. For there is one God and one Mediator between God and men, the Man Christ Jesus"** (1 Timothy 2:1-5, capitalized words by the author).

Second, we are familiar with these instructions from Jesus Christ recorded in Matthew 5:44, **"But I say to you, love your enemies, bless those who curse you, do good to those who hate you, and PRAY FOR those who spitefully use you and persecute you"** (capitalized words by the author). Jesus is clearly referring to the *heart attitude* we are to have toward the unsaved.

Pray for the salvation of terrorists.

September 12

"As You sent Me into the world, I also have sent them into the world."
John 17:18

There are similarities between the mission of Jesus in the world and the mission of His disciples in the world. Both missions come with *divine authority;* the Father sent Jesus into the world, and Jesus sends the Church into the same world. Both missions have the same *motive;* the Father's love sent Christ into the world, and the Church must demonstrate His love toward men. And both missions have the same *objective;* Christ came **"to save that which was lost"** (see Matthew 18:11), and the mission of His disciples is to introduce Christ to men.

Disciples who are sent around the world into certain countries abroad - with the divine objective of preaching and teaching the Gospel - experience great danger and intense temptation. The measure of holiness that serves the ordinary Christian will not be enough for the missionary disciple. Today we will focus on the *type* of prayer needed to support the missionary who has been sent **"into the world."**

Praying the words, "God bless the missionaries," or even praying for missionaries on their birthday, is good - but not enough! Pray specifically for needs that you know; some of those needs are "obvious:" financial, acceptance and favor with men, political, social, physical health, patience, physical protection, and things that God's Word says that *He* wants for men. Be sure to include fasting if led, praise, and thanksgiving. Pray for specific requests that have been received from the missionary; if you do not know of any, investigate!

And then there are the "less obvious" needs of the missionary disciple that require fervent prayer: boldness, joy, compassion, humility, personal study and prayer time, discernment, a yielding to the Spirit, and the pulling down of demonic strongholds. If you use a "prayer list" to help you remember to intercede for specific people and circumstances, be certain to include the names of missionaries on that list. Find out all you can about the country in which they serve, and listen carefully to the news for any mention of that country that may prompt you to pray.

Pray specifically for the needs of a missionary.

September 13

"'Simon, Simon! Indeed, Satan has asked for you, that he may sift you as wheat. But I have prayed for you.'" Luke 22:31, 32

The words translated *"I have prayed,"* have at their root the thought of *binding*. Satan tripped the disciples up, but he was bound from entering *into* them. Therefore, the disciples clearly demonstrated "weakness" in the final crisis, but not wickedness.

No one knows how far you may fall if you lose faith in God. Without faith, even good men are weak. Peter was kept from falling away by special grace granted to him in answer to Jesus' prayers. The possibility exists that Jesus is praying for you right now, at this moment, that *your* faith will not fail, because He is now seated at His Father's right hand in glory praying for each of us who trust Him (see Romans 8:34, Hebrews 7:25 and 1 John 2:1).

What Jesus did for Peter, He does for you. How do you know, dear reader, but that the fiery trials through which you are now passing, or through which you are about to pass, may be allowed by Jesus at Satan's request? No man knows when or how He intercedes – this is a matter between the Father and the Son. But we do know that Jesus is still our Priest, who is active in the presence of the Father *for* us.

What joy should flood your soul over the fact that a stronger hand than yours is holding your life! For if the devil had the audacity to believe that he could shake loose the faith of Jesus' immediate disciples, are you of the impression that your own strength is sufficient for such an attack on your faith?

Jesus said we are to rejoice because our names are written in heaven, but how comforting to be reminded today that each of our names who trust Him are written on His "prayer list!" Just to know He is watching and praying for us is a source of tremendous peace as we travel through life in this world.

Pray that any attack of the devil and all of his demons against you today will be defeated through the intercession of Jesus Christ on your behalf.

September 14

"As You sent Me into the world, I also have sent them into the world."
John 17:18

Today we are considering the meaning of Christ's words, *"I also have sent them into the world,"* and our focus is on the three words, "into the world." To whom are Christ's disciples sent? We are sent to *all* who are in the world – without any distinction of nation, sex, race, culture, or background. Jesus said, *"Go into all the world and preach the gospel to every creature."* There was a time when Jesus first sent forth the Twelve, that He instructed them, *"Do not go into the way of the Gentiles, and do not enter a city of the Samaritans. But go rather to the lost sheep of the house of Israel"* (see Matthew 10:5, 6). But now, He sends them into the world to preach the Gospel to "every creature."

Before we go, we are to first listen to the promptings of the Holy Spirit! The *timing* by which we visit men is given to us by the Spirit. Acts 16:7 says, *"After they had come to Mysia, they tried to go into Bithynia, but the Spirit did not permit them."* And prior to that, the Spirit did not permit Paul, Timothy, and Silas to preach in Asia (see Acts 16:6). The timing on those occasions was not *first* confirmed by the Spirit, who had a purpose for them going instead to Macedonia (see Acts 16:9ff).

The important lesson for all of us as His disciples is this: even the preaching and teaching of the Gospel is governed by none other than God's special providence and care. It is not enough to simply do the "right things" for God, but also to do them *by the leadership and timing of His Spirit. We are not to be messengers of the Gospel following our own will or timing, but as Holy men of God* **"moved by the Holy Spirit!"** *(see 2 Peter 1:21)* Failure to learn this lesson has produced churches that are "busy," but not "fruit-bearing."

Pray that all you do for God today, and the timing in which you do it, is first confirmed by His Spirit.

September 15

"And forgive us our debts, as we forgive our debtors.'" Matthew 6:12

The Model Prayer shows that we should take care of the needs of our body, but we should take *even better care* of the needs of our soul. We should be more desirous to have our souls saved and nourished than to have our bodies fed.

Though the body dissolves into dust, the soul lives (see Luke 12:4). Again, because the **"body is the temple of the Holy Spirit who is in you"** (see 1 Corinthians 6:19), it is fitting that we take good care of it. But even if we follow a rigid routine of physical exercise along with a strict diet, if we starve our soul, we demonstrate that we do not understand the priorities of God.

Now we come to this little word **"and,"** to examine its meaning at this point of the Prayer. Notice that Jesus uses the word "and," to connect this petition for forgiveness of sin with the previous petition for daily bread – His revelation that, though we have daily bread, it is as nothing without forgiveness. Thomas Watson put it this way: "As a man that is condemned takes little comfort from the meat you bring him in prison, without a pardon; so, though we have daily bread, yet it will do us no good unless sin be forgiven."

Nothing can be called so clearly "yours," as sin! Your daily bread you have from God; your daily sins you have from yourself. That is the reason why, oftentimes, when you hear this part of the Model Prayer prayed aloud, you may notice a change in the *tone of voice* when the word "and" is spoken - for now, *sorrow* has been added to the mix.

Bread gives you the personal capability to do the "outward" things that please God; forgiveness gives you the "heart condition" you must have in order to do those things. Because of the fact that you are just as likely to take the provision of forgiveness for granted as you are the provision of bread, so you must remember to *ask.*

Ask God to show you how to forgive.

"'As You sent Me into the world, I also have sent them into the world.'"

John 17:18

E ver since the fall, there has been a quarrel between God and man. The reason Christ has sent us *"into the world,"* is to persuade men by the power of the Holy Spirit to lay down the weapons of their defiance, and to trust Jesus. Colossians 1:28 declares, *"Him we preach, warning every man and teaching every man in all wisdom, that we may present every man perfect in Christ Jesus."*

We are here, then, for the world's sake – to show forth the praises of him who has called us *"out of darkness into His marvelous light."* Christ leaves us in the world as His representatives, just as He came as the Father's representative. We must remember that the Lord's work is not *our* work for the Lord, but the Lord's own work *through* us and *through* others.

Philip Schaff, the great church historian, wrote, "Christianity once es-tablished was its own best missionary. And while there were no professional missionaries devoting their whole life to this specific work, every congre-gation was a missionary society, and every Christian believer a missionary, inflamed by the love of Christ to convert his fellow men. Every Christian told his neighbor the story of his conversion, as a mariner tells the story of his rescue from shipwreck."

Oh, to be so one with the Lord Jesus that His life may flow through your veins! May He borrow your eyes to show you the needy? May He borrow your lips to speak His messages? May He borrow your face to show men His looks of patience and love? May He borrow your hands to do His service? May He borrow your feet to take His Good News to the weary?

Does the Holy Spirit convict you today of your need to be more mind-ful that you are an ambassador of Jesus Christ in this world? Charles Spur-geon said, "If God has called you to be a missionary, don't stoop to be a king." Pray that you will take the opportunity that God provides you today, to tell someone the story of *your* "rescue from shipwreck."

September 17

"And I will pray the Father, and He will give you another Helper, that He may abide with you forever." John 14:16

This is not an occasion when Jesus prayed, but it is a reference to a prayer He *promised* to pray, so we will include it. The word translated *"pray"* here means to "ask" or to "request." Jesus will be requesting that the Father *"give"* the Holy Spirit. Notice that both the Holy Spirit and Jesus (see John 3:16) are *gifts* from God.

The giving of the Holy Spirit reveals *each* person of the Trinity at work for one purpose: The Son is requesting, the Father is giving, and the Spirit is coming. As is often the case with the Trinity, we trust in what God reveals and rest content - even when our understanding is lacking.

The translation *"Helper"* or "Comforter" (describing one who consoles) used in reference to the Holy Spirit, gives us only a partial understanding of His role. Jesus will be praying for *another* "Paraclete," who ministers in the same way as when Jesus "revealed" God to the disciples, "showed" them the Father, and "led" them to the Father. Jesus will be asking for *another* "Advocate," who will represent the Father to believers in the same way that Jesus represents believers before the Father (see 1 John 2:1). Thus, not one but *two* advocates have been appointed to us: Jesus on the throne, and the Spirit in our hearts!

Because of the vast amount of spiritual truth there is to learn (and because of our laziness and lack of concern to learn it), there is the need of the Holy Spirit to *"forever"* draw us and teach us. And then there is the glorious role of the Holy Spirit in the salvation of men! As the Spirit (not Nature) *interprets* Jesus, men find God. It is the role of the Holy Spirit to make the reality of the one, true, living God convincing to all men – in the same way that Jesus did to His disciples. *How wonderful, how precious, the Holy Spirit!*

Pray today that you will have a heart that is open wide to the work and ministry of the Holy Spirit in your life.

"And for their sakes I sanctify Myself, that they also may be sanctified by the truth." John 17:19

One definition of "sanctification" is, "The work of God's free grace, whereby we are renewed in the whole man, after the image of God, and are enabled, more and more, to die unto sin, and to live unto righteousness." The sanctification of which our Lord speaks in *this* prayer is the consecration of the whole being to the spiritual purpose of the service to our heavenly Father; to give up everything in order that His will may be accomplished, and to do that will to completion.

The first human ears these words ever fell on were the ears of the Eleven. As time went on, the words of this prayer that the Apostles may have remembered most as they went about their daily ministries were, **"For their sakes I sanctify Myself."** In a daily life of increasing holiness and of intercessory prayer, the disciples saw something of the meaning and value of Jesus' words regarding sanctification.

Literally, Christ's words read, "And in their behalf, I on My part sanctify Myself." Jesus is speaking of a sanctifying act in which He is engaged at that moment. Both Jesus and the disciples are sent, both have a mission, both missions are divine, both are holy, and so both need to be set apart, devoted in a holy sense to do their work. *But the complete sense of the emphatic phrase, "for their sakes," is that, unless Jesus sanctifies Himself, no sanctification and no mission of the disciples could be possible!* Jesus does not say that He and the disciples are sanctified "in like manner." Out of the one sanctification, the other is to proceed – and so the two are placed side by side. Christ now sanctifies Himself by voluntarily entering His sacrificial and atoning death.

Jesus "sanctifying Himself" is, therefore, a clear reference to the Cross. The great High Priest set Himself apart for you and devoted Himself as the Lamb of God to be slain for you. Hebrews 10:14 says, **"For by one offering He has perfected forever those who are being sanctified."**

Thank Jesus for sanctifying Himself for your sake.

September 19

"And forgive us our debts, as we forgive our debtors.'" Matthew 6:12

It is far easier to notice our sins of "commission" – those sins that we know we have done, said, or thought. But "debt" is also a way to describe a large classification of sins we refer to as sins of *omission*. The word "debt" refers to how much we "owe" someone; it represents an obligation. A debt arises when we fail to pay what is due; the Believer owes God his complete obedience, and not paying what is due Him places him in debt. A most consequential debt is sin, for it eventually brings the "non-paying," unrepentant, man to a fiery prison for eternity.

We are unable to determine how much we owe God for our sins of omission. The truth is, we have seldom *tried* to make a careful and honest determination of what is due Him for sins of omission. We had might as well compare the number of these sins to the pebbles of sand at the beach! Picture the man who begins to pray with the purpose of confessing, but he finds himself at a loss to recall anything *specific* to confess. *He must remember that there are multitudes of deeds that he either cannot recall, that he did not consider as sin, or that he left undone!*

When you ask forgiveness daily for your sins, Jesus teaches you to view your sins as **"debts."** Notice the plural form; sin is not a single but a multiplied debt. The Model Prayer teaches that you are not just a repeat sinner, but that you are also a "debtor." Your sins have been *affecting* God, in that you have abused the resources and blessings that He has furnished you for the doing of His kingdom work. Still, over and over, He has renewed or replaced these resources, rather than casting you off as "hopeless." Praise His name!

Pardon is one of the things that you can only have by *asking.* There is forgiveness with God. Praise Him for the countless "new starts" He has given you throughout your life, and ask Him to forgive you of your debts.

September 20

"*And for their sakes I sanctify Myself, that they also may be sanctified by the truth.*" John 17:19

For Jesus to pray, **"*I sanctify Myself,*"** can seem difficult to understand. How could the Son of God become *more* holy or *more* sanctified than He already was? He was *already* as pure and holy as *God* is pure and holy! But the meaning of what Jesus was praying is, "I dedicate, I set apart My whole self – My person, Godhead, Manhood, soul, body, My very existence – all **"*for their sakes.*"** Whatever the merit of My blood and the glory of My name, I dedicate to all that My people will need!"

What did Jesus hold back? Nothing! Here, just a few hours before His death, He is still sanctifying Himself, surrendering Himself, dedicating Himself, to fulfill and to finish His Father's will. His was a complete surrender, an absolute devoting of Himself, that He might be the sanctification of His people. And notice that this was done on His own, "I sanctify Myself." He had the right and the authority, He had the power and the love to do so. He prayed this prayer in the hearing of His disciples so that they would know what was *His* aim, *His* motive for sanctifying Himself.

But what does, "for their sakes," have to do with *you?* Throughout His life, Jesus had to train, discipline, and sanctify His *human nature.* That is why we read in Luke 2:52, **"*Jesus increased in wisdom and stature, and in favor with God and men.*"** It was of His Father's "free grace" that He, the man Christ Jesus, the carpenter's son, was what He was, and did what He did. *Yet this "increase" was for your sake because this human nature - which He trained, and hardened in the fires of temptation – is the nature which He prepared for you!*

Have you ever deliberately prayed, as Jesus did, to sanctify yourself? If not, pray today for all of you to be His alone, to suffer whatever seems good to Him, and to do whatever He asks you to do. Ask Him to write His name of ownership and authority upon your heart – as His forever.

September 21

"'Stay here and watch with Me.'" Matthew 26:38

We are at Gethsemane, and reverently our heads are bowed just to think that we are taking a glimpse of this scene. Even John, who leaned on His breast, could observe *this* picture only in part. There is more involved here than we can ever know, but we should remember privately that these events happened - and that they happened *for us.*

Jesus has brought Peter, James, and John to a place in the Garden just a little further than the other eight disciples, and then He says: *"Watch with Me."* What was the desire of the Master? Did He want these three disciples to physically guard His period of exceeding sorrow from any intrusion by man? Do the words "with me" reveal that He was asking for the support of sympathetic friends? Did He desire that these three men once again serve as witnesses of something extraordinary, as they had served on previous occasions? He may have desired all of these things, and more.

Christ *"went a little farther."* The literal translation of Luke's account describes Jesus as having to "tear Himself away from them" in order to withdraw this short distance. Someone said it well: "Our Lord has followers in His sufferings, but of equals He has none." The disciples could watch with Him, but they could not pray with Him. He will have them as near as possible, yet He must be alone. Before they slept, these three disciples needed to hear and see what their redemption has cost Him, and then record what they had heard and seen, that the world may know (see 1 Peter 5:1).

Notice the truth of His character! He had nothing to hide. Jesus desired His followers to see Him in His *weakness* as well as in His strength. Previously we saw His *zeal* as an Evangelist, His *compassion* as a Healer, His *wisdom* as a Teacher, His *faithfulness* as a Master. *Receive this important lesson: integrity, as both His witnesses and children, means that we avoid hypocrisy and falseness!*

We too, must watch with Him. Pray now that you will.

"And for their sakes I sanctify Myself, that they also may be sanctified by the truth.'" John 17:19

Jesus said in this prayer, that sanctification must be accomplished *"by the truth."* On a previous occasion, Jesus said, *"I am ... the truth"* (see John 14:6). We know that the "written" Word is truth, but He, the *living* Word, is *the* Truth. John said that Jesus is *"full of grace and truth"* (see John 1:14).

Christ was *devoted* to the truth. When the devil tempted Him, Jesus demonstrated that devotedness to the truth brings victory. And Paul said, *"take ... the sword of the Spirit, which is the word of God."* It takes a sharp, offensive weapon that will deal the death blow to the accomplices of Satan who teach the doctrines of demons. It was true in Jesus' day, and it will always be true – *there is great need for the Word of God to be spoken in the power of the Spirit* – even though men do not want to hear it. And we have the promise of God recorded in Isaiah 55:11: *"It shall not return to Me void, but it shall accomplish what I please, and it shall prosper in the thing for which I sent it."*

Jesus demonstrated His devotion to the truth by practicing it! During His entire lifetime on earth, Christ devoted Himself to both preaching *and* practicing the truth. Once again there is an important lesson here for *you*. Do you "practice what you preach?" How much *value* are you placing on "the truth?" If this matter of the truth is so close to the heart of your Lord, can you be "careless" with it? His honor and your happiness are involved here, for no child of God can be happy while walking carelessly.

Under conviction of the Holy Ghost, then, how should you *proceed* in your progressing sanctification? Lean unreservedly on the Lord Jesus Christ! *"The heart is deceitful above all things, and desperately wicked."* That is why God has to show you the truth about yourself by "degrees," because to see *that* truth all at once, would crush you!

Pray for the desire to repent of the wickedness He reveals.

September 23

"And forgive us our debts, as we forgive our debtors.'" Matthew 6:12

Are there two greater subjects in life than sin and salvation? The knowledge of sin is meant to drive us to the Savior. The love of Jesus is meant to deliver us from sin. Sin and salvation are the main two topics of Scripture. But men dread the Scriptures and Biblical preaching or teaching because the true disclosures of their wretched condition move them away from their carefree attitude toward sin.

For today's devotion, we are looking at *Jesus'* description of sin. Only He who died for us knows the greatness of sin. Only Jesus has seen sin at its *depths,* and therefore He alone fully understands why forgiveness of sin is necessary. **"Forgive us** (or, literally, "dismiss for us") **our debts"** means, "send our sins away, as far as the east is from the west so that they will never be found." ("Trespasses" is a mistranslation, found in the Church of England Prayer Book but not in the Model Prayer itself.) But thanks be to God, it is our *sin* that brings out the Savior!

In this Model Prayer, Jesus refers to sin as "debt," meaning, "that which is justly or legally due." An overdue obligation is a sin. Our sins against God are all debts overdue, and all of us are bankrupt. But what exactly is it that we *owe* God? We owe Him *ourselves!*

2 Corinthians 5:15 says, **"And He died for all, that those who live should live no longer for themselves, but for Him who died for them and rose again."** *All that we are - body, soul, and spirit – is His!* Yet our debt is growing daily, for God is continuously giving and we are continuously misappropriating His gifts. In addition, we suppose (or hope) that God does not *feel* our sin as a "personal wrong" against Him; we are more comfortable viewing sin in the abstract or analyzing it similar to a Rorschach test.

How seriously are *you* considering your sin?

Pray that today you will combine a deep sense of debt, a thankful assurance of forgiveness, and a resolute departure from sin.

September 24

"'Father, forgive them, for they do not know what they do.'"
Luke 23:34

How much more knowledgeable are we today, than those who did not *"know"* what they were doing when Jesus was crucified? Have all of the tools and resources available to us today for knowing the Bible, the sermons and CD's we have heard, the Bible studies we have attended, or the beautiful sanctuaries we have built - not made us more "aware" of our sinful behavior against the purposes of God?

If ignorance was the reason in Jesus' day, *what is our reason for not knowing what we are doing?* What is the reason why Good Friday does not strike our hearts like lightning? Through the number of days that have passed since our Savior's crucifixion, the knowledge of God in Christ has spread throughout the world. Yet, in many ways, God's people today react to what He is doing with no more interest than that of the soldiers raffling garments next to the Cross.

May the Church tremble! As He intercedes for us today, must Jesus continue to plead to the Father, *"they do not know what they do"?* Yes, He must. Because *only gradually*, the more the world runs to the end of its course, the nearer the Antichrist comes with his false prophet - the better will men learn to know what they are doing. *The great need of our day is to make it a priority to know, study, and believe the Holy Scriptures – so that we would know what we do!*

Here is what God's Word says; please turn to and read Joel 2:12-14. Is there a word from the Lord here for you? *"Turn to Me with all your heart, with fasting, with weeping, and with mourning."* Sincere confession with repentance will remove the sin barrier that blinds us from knowing what we do.

Make this your humble prayer today: *"Father, I am undone, and I am much in need of your forgiveness. Thank you for the blood that Jesus shed for my sins. May I live today in such a manner, that it cannot be said that I know not what I do."*

September 25

"And forgive us our debts, as we forgive our debtors.'" Matthew 6:12

Thankfully, God is not merely a "Giver;" He is also a "Forgiver." And when He is forgiving, that is when He gives *most*! Your sin prevents the true blessings and joys of heaven from coming into your life. That fact is one of many reasons why you ought to hate your sin. But when you receive His gift of forgiveness, that obstacle is removed, and all things are yours.

How easy it is to be led astray by the opinions of the world – including the opinions of Christians! The Bible speaks of various topics using words much more severe than what you may think "necessary." Many statements in Scripture may appear "exaggerated" when your mind is under attack by the devil. Peter came to Jesus one day and asked, **"Lord, how often shall my brother sin against me, and I forgive him? Up to seven times?"** Peter thought "seven times" sounded *extravagant!* Jesus answered him, **"I do not say to you , up to seven times, but up to seventy times seven"** (see Matthew 18:21, 22).

To be sure, Satan is *still* asking, **"Has God indeed said?"** (see Genesis 3:1). Has Jesus said, **"In this manner, therefore, pray?"** And does not every word of this Model Prayer reveal to you your sin? **"Our"** Father convicts you of your failure to intercede for the family of God, **"Your kingdom come"** convicts you of your lack of praying for the salvation of those who are lost, and so on. So that by the time you reach this petition, **"forgive us our debts,"** you are *already* burdened with awareness of your disobedience.

In order to sincerely pray this Model Prayer, you will have to conduct a *daily* survey of your heart – something the enemy will tell you is "unnecessary." But you are aware that you have sinned daily against others and against God. The devil will attempt to convince you that self-examination is necessary only on such occasions as prior to partaking of the Lord's Supper or in times of affliction.

Invite the Holy Spirit to do His convicting work in your heart.

> *"And for their sakes I sanctify Myself, that they also may be sanctified by the truth."* John 17:19

There is something you need to understand about your own sanctification – it is for the sake of *others*, and not just for your own sake. Jesus prayed, "***For their sakes*** I sanctify Myself." Similarly, you are to be a person of *intercessory* prayer, not simply a person of prayer. As Christ was in His life of holiness and constant intercession, so are you to be in this world. You must sanctify yourself for the sake of others, for all prayer is ineffective and fruitless in a life of known and allowed sin. *Sin and prayer cannot both live at the same time in the same heart!*

If you desire to be a blessing to your fellow man, you must begin by sanctifying yourself. You may not have heard this topic preached upon or taught in church, but it is absolutely necessary and, as we see here, Christlike. It is only by beginning within, by seeking to become what He was, and then by constantly abiding in Him - that it is *possible* for you to do the type of *holy* work that reaches the hearts of men. Look at it this way – if a surgeon, before he performs an operation, sterilizes his hands and instruments lest he should introduce some germ of infection into the body of the patient, how much more careful ought those to be who operate not on bodies, but on souls! "For their sakes ***I sanctify Myself.***"

Here we have the Lord Jesus Christ, distinctly stating in the hearing of His disciples, what was His "aim" and what was His "motive" for sanctifying Himself. "For their sakes," an expression of personal love for His people, runs throughout all accounts of His work and mission. You will find His unselfish motive expressed once again when you read, ***"For you know the grace of our Lord Jesus Christ, that though He was rich, yet for your sakes He became poor, that you through His poverty might become rich"*** (see 2 Corinthians 8:9). Clearly, Jesus is *for you!*

Pray with a grateful heart, because He will *never* refuse you.

September 27

"'My soul is exceedingly sorrowful, even to death. Stay here and watch with Me.' He went a little farther and fell on His face, and prayed."
Matthew 26:38, 39

Jesus seldom spoke of His sorrow, but here in the Garden of Gethsemane, He speaks of having *exceeding* sorrow. It is because He now realizes that the time has come to **"lay down"** His life (John 10:17), **"to give His life a ransom for many"** (Matthew 20:28), and **"to be sin for us"** (2 Corinthians 5:21). Who can imagine all of this happening to one individual on one occasion?

"Even to death" indicates the extremity of anguish Jesus is feeling, reaching even to the utmost limit of endurance – so that it seemed that anything stronger would be death itself. His soul was literally dying of grief. Just these three arresting words that Jesus spoke, "even to death" should have alarmed the disciples! They knew the Master's personality well enough to know He was not in the habit of being "overly dramatic." Yet they failed to provide Him with even the little human sympathy He desired.

It had been Satan's plan all along to prevent the crucifixion! The devil had offered Jesus the kingdoms of the world but without a Cross (see Matthew 4:8, 9). Satan had used Peter to tempt Jesus from going to the Cross (see Matthew 16:22, 23). Even while Jesus was *on* the Cross, Satan put it in the heart of men, who were either present or passers-by, to suggest that Jesus come down from the Cross (see Matthew 27:39-44)!

There are so many lessons for us to learn from an examination of Jesus praying at Gethsemane, and each lesson is an important one. Our focus today is on this: In the face of His excruciating sorrow and horrible agony, Jesus roused Himself to *pray!* If you, dear Believer, have any doubt as to how *essential* prayer is to you, the child of God, stop now to pause and consider the meaning of Christ's action under these circumstances.

You are to lay all of your wants before the Father. He really does care for you! Don't allow your faith to be shaken today, no matter what your circumstances. Fall on your face in humble prayer with gratitude.

September 28

"'I do not pray for these alone, but also for those who will believe in Me through their word.'" John 17:20

W e tend to *"pray"* about the things that are on our hearts. Here, Jesus has on His heart the eleven disciples who are with Him, as well as the disciples who are to follow Him in the future. The more He exercises Himself as Mediator in their behalf, the more His heart is drawn out to them and to their needs. *The blessing that is easy for the Bible reader to miss is that in this prayer, we are actually hearing some of the same conversation that had taken place between Jesus and His Father - before the world was!*

As we learn to intercede in prayer for one another, we should notice that Jesus was willing to ask the *very best* things for His disciples – not for worldly riches or things of enjoyment that this selfish world (and even some preachers!) encourages us to obtain with His blessing – but that they be *kept* in the Father's name, *sanctified* through the Father's truth, and *united* in the Father's love. Therefore, understand, dear friend, that *these* are the things that we should desire most for one another when *we* intercede in prayer.

While it is obvious that, thus far in this prayer, from Verse 6 through Verse 19, we have seen a primary emphasis on the needs of the Eleven – there has also been a secondary reference to *the disciple of Jesus in general.* In this and in the verses that follow, the Lord now prays more specifically with a view toward the whole host of believers in all the generations to follow. Our Lord's desires (and also His expectations) for the Eleven are meant for *all* of His followers and His entire Church.

Which means He includes *you* in this beautiful, loving intercessory prayer! Remember, the Father *always* hears Him (see John 11:42) when He speaks of you! You have His Word on it! You were provided for before you were born! You were not born too late to receive the blessing of the prayers of the Savior of the world!

Thank Him for placing such a high value on you.

September 29

"'And forgive us our debts, as we forgive our debtors.'" Matthew 6:12

"**Forgive us our debts**" does not refer to the "initial" forgiveness of your sins, which you received from God at the moment you were saved. That forgiveness in *regeneration* is a once-and-for-all experience. But the forgiveness of daily *sanctification* must be experienced as often as we *still* sin.

There are some who believe that this petition is proof that you have to be saved each day. But when you pray this prayer, you are a *Christian* who calls God **"Our Father."** You are praying as a child of the King who is *already* in the kingdom! When you sin, God does not "throw you out of the Family!" It is not your salvation that is endangered, but your *fellowship.*

This petition *is necessary* because as a child of God, you do not always do God's will. You *disobey* Him and break fellowship with Him. You *disregard* Him and break fellowship with Him. So you pray this prayer either to restore broken fellowship with the Father or to keep that fellowship "healthy" when you have not broken it. Paul explained, **"Godly sorrow produces repentance"** (2 Corinthians 7:10). When you have Godly sorrow, you mean what you are saying with all of your heart; you mean your confession of sin so deeply, that you never want to do it again.

The picture of the "Prodigal Son's" return home comes to mind. *Your Heavenly Father sees the first symptoms of your genuine repentance!* Jesus said, **"But when he was still a great way off, his father saw him and had compassion, and ran and fell on his neck and kissed him"** (see Luke 15:20). If you will ask for His forgiveness and confess your sin, **"He is faithful and just to forgive."**

Yes, when you sin against God, you incur an "obligation" upon yourself. But the pardon that God offers signifies that the past is abolished and that *suddenly you find yourself before God in an entirely new situation!* You are freed from your "debt!" How marvelous! How glorious!

Your Heavenly Father is watching and waiting for your return! Come home to Him.

"'I do not pray for these alone, but also for those who will believe in Me through their word.'" John 17:20

As parents provide for their children yet unborn, Jesus tenderly provided for future Believers through intercessory prayer. The Bible tells us of some of *"those who will believe"* in Jesus through the teaching of the apostles. Examples are the *"three thousand"* that were added on the day of Pentecost (see Acts 2:41), and the *"many myriads of Jews"* who believed some thirty years later (see Acts 21:20). The true glory of Pentecost was not in the mighty rushing wind or in the tongues of fire; it was rather in the multitude who believed when they accepted the testimony of the apostles. Later, these converts would be told how *Jesus had already prayed for them* because He was sure of what would happen!

And we cannot restrict His foresight to these, for it stretched all the way to your family members and to yourself – for all generations of the Church have received their knowledge of Christ ultimately from the word of these eleven men! This prayer needed an answer then, and it has always needed an answer because there have always been Believers to pray for. There have been martyrs, missionaries, bishops, scholars, preachers, and deacons in desperate need of His intercession – not overlooking the sincere and lowly in private life through the years.

Like a mountain hiker on a cliffside, gazing out across an expanding vista as range succeeds range into the distant horizon, so Jesus gazes out across the rolling centuries and sees His flock. Yet the prayer we are considering today is not the only time that Jesus had the future Church on His heart. We find these words of Christ in John 10:16, *"And other sheep I have which are not of this fold; them also I must bring, and they will hear My voice; and there will be one flock and one shepherd."* And Matthew 18:17 records His words of instruction regarding dealing with a sinning Brother, *"... Tell it to the church. But if he refuses even to hear the church ..."*

Here is the blessing: even *then*, He was praying for us! Praise Him.

October 1

"He went a little farther and fell on His face, and prayed."
Matthew 26:39

If we bring together all three of the accounts provided by Matthew, Mark, and Luke, it seems that Jesus first fell to His knees and then literally prostrated Himself while praying in Gethsemane. Apparently, the posture of prostration was not normal for Jesus when He prayed, prompting the noting of this posture by the disciples. Mark's words and verb tense to describe Jesus' posture in prayer on this occasion literally mean that He was *continuously* writhing in anguish upon the ground! It is difficult for us to even imagine this picture of our Lord in such anguish.

Of course, Jesus did not assume these positions in order to pray more "effectively," and definitely not "for show;" lying on the ground as twisted as any of those gnarled olive trees themselves, it was *the agony of His soul* that caused Him to fall on His face. All of us should consider it repulsive to assume a kneeling or prostrate prayer position *publicly* unless Spirit-prompted brokenness takes us there. These are prayer positions of *humility and submission*, and not for show.

The glory of the Lord appeared to Moses and to Aaron when humbly, **"they fell on their faces"** at the door of the tabernacle of meeting (see Numbers 20:6). Begging in desperation for God's guidance, that occasion marked a crucial point in the history of the wilderness wanderings.

In your private prayer times, do you find it easy to kneel, to bow, to bend, to become humble? Have you experienced prayer periods when the Spirit of God asked you to fall to your knees, and you could not resist because there was no doubt it was Him prompting you? In 2 Chronicles 7:14, God's people are told to **"Humble themselves, and pray and seek My face, and turn from their wicked ways."** What a timely word for us, for the Church, and for America today! *Notice that we are not instructed to ask God to humble us; we are to humble ourselves!*

In whatever posture the Spirit prompts you, pray now with a spirit of humility and submission. Seek His face.

> *"'I do not pray for these alone, but also for those who will believe in Me through their word.'"* John 17:20

Jesus prays now as the head of His body, the Church. As He prays, the concerns and benefits of all of His members were on His mind. In a few hours, He would lay down His life as their substitute. Not one situation, not one circumstance, did He overlook in His great heart. Therefore, if today's Church would only see Jesus as we see Him praying here, we would have the much-needed confidence and encouragement we lack.

Today we think of this prayer of Jesus with consideration for your unconverted friends and family. Christ prayed *"for those who will believe"* in Him, for those who did not yet know Him. *And this was not a "lumping together" of the unconverted; because only He could accomplish this kind of intercession, Jesus had every single possible individual person fitting this description in mind!* First, He prays for the people you know and care about in the condition of their unbelief – that they *may* believe; and then He prays for them when they *do* believe, as a result of the Holy Spirit's convicting work.

Isaiah said of the coming Messiah, *"He was numbered with the transgressors, and He bore the sin of many, and made intercession for the transgressors"* (see Isaiah 53:12). But why is it *necessary for us* to stand in the gap in prayer for our unbelieving friends? The Bible provides three answers that describe the horrible dilemma of the unconverted. First, *"the god of this age has blinded"* their minds (see 2 Corinthians 4:4). Second, your lost friends are literally in *"the snare of the devil, having been taken captive by him to do his will"* (see 2 Timothy 2:26). And third, they are hindered when *"the cares of this world, the deceitfulness of riches, and the desires for other things entering in choke the word, and it becomes unfruitful"* (see Mark 4:19).

Intercede now for your lost friends, for at this moment, the devil is using whatever devices he can to keep them from coming to a knowledge of the truth and from trusting Jesus for their salvation.

October 3

"Father, forgive them, for they do not know what they do."
Luke 23:34

This first of three prayers by Jesus from the Cross, was a fulfillment of the last verse of the great prophecy in Isaiah 53: ***"Therefore I will divide Him a portion with the great, and He shall divide the spoil with the strong, because He poured out His soul unto death, and He was numbered with the transgressors, and He bore the sin of many, and made intercession for the transgressors."***

But the uniqueness of this prayer is revealed through an additional observation. In the Hebrew, the word "seven" (*shevah*) comes from the root word "*savah*," which means, *to be full* or *satisfied* or *have enough of*. It was on the *seventh* day that God rested from the work of Creation. It was full and complete, good and perfect. Nothing need be added to it, nor taken from it.

This prayer of Jesus from the Cross is the first of *seven* things He said. With any series of words or actions in Holy Scripture, the number seven marks that series as conveying some important revelation of God to us. Thus, seven is about *completeness*. Chance, then, had nothing to do with the fact that there are seven sayings from Jesus at Calvary, and chance had nothing to do with the place or order of succession each saying occupies.

It was Jesus who had said, ***"Out of the abundance of the heart the mouth speaks."*** *We conclude, then, that this tender prayer was the first thing Jesus said from the Cross so that the overflow of His forgiving, compassionate heart would be revealed - even while the nails were entering His hands and feet!* This prayer, then, exposed the divine depths of His spirit while the hammers fell and the soldiers swore.

Are we able to sense the horror, the anxiety that made almost every spirit captive that day on the hill called Golgotha? Have we ever imagined that we were among those standing there witnessing that scene? In your mind's eye, try to picture Jesus on the Cross as you pray – and then give thanks that He died for you.

"'I do not pray for these alone, but also for those who will believe in Me through their word.'" John 17:20

There is a huge difference between believing "about" Jesus and believing "in" Jesus. In fact, a person could miss heaven over the difference! Christ does not pray, "those who will believe *about* Me," but rather, **"those who will believe in Me."** There is also an important difference between believing in "God" and believing in "Jesus." Christ said, **"You believe in God, believe also in Me"** (see John 14:1). *Dear reader, these are not petty matters concerning "semantics;" these are truths concerning eternity!*

"In" Jesus, we receive a mediator who is fit to go *between God and us*. The great "value" of Christ is in dealing with *God*. To believe "in" Jesus is to accept Him as Lord and Savior upon *God's* incredible offer and under *God's* conditions. That is why we read in Hebrews 10:19, **"Having boldness to enter the Holiest by the blood of Jesus."** When we believe "in" Jesus, we know that He is *ours*, and we trust Him.

When we believe "in" Jesus, we believe in God and in the Word of God for a different reason. *Now,* believing in God means His loving us when we were sinners and His giving His Son to die; *now,* believing in the Word of God becomes the unspeakable truth that *reveals* that fact! It changes *everything* when we believe "in" Jesus – the Savior who took our place and died, was wounded for our transgressions, and now stands before the throne as our Representative! Oh, many thousands of people have talked of believing that there "is" a God and that the Bible "is" a special Book – who have never taken refuge "in" Jesus for their salvation!

Looking further into God's Word, you will find Acts 13:39 saying, that **"by Him"** everyone who believes is justified from all things. Romans 3:25 says, that God set forth Jesus as a propitiation **"by His blood."** Yes and how many times have you read John 3:16, which clearly states that whoever believes **"in Him"** should not perish but have everlasting life?

Pray that you will never accept general "notions" or vague "ideas" about Jesus.

October 5

"'Father, forgive them, for they do not know what they do.'"
Luke 23:34

We can never be sinned against as Jesus was. Not even close. Still, He forgave, and He commands us to do the same.

Some of us have never been *deeply* wronged, but all of us have been hurt, abused or agitated numerous times along the way. Yet all of these experiences *combined* seem insignificant when we stand before the Cross of Christ.

Has anyone sinned against you? It is your *privilege* to imitate Christ and to forgive that person and to pray for him. Have you wronged someone? It is your *privilege* to humble yourself, turn from your pride, and seek reconciliation.

Looking at forgiveness from a different perspective, we might ask, "Would you prefer to imitate Jesus or Satan?" "Oh," you answer, "that is an easy question! I would *never* choose to imitate Satan!" But not so fast! When you refuse to forgive, do you not imitate **"the accuser of our brethren"** (see Revelation 12:10)? Have you ever sought sympathy by saying to someone, "Can you believe what *that person* did to me?" Or have you ever used the excuse, "That person doesn't *deserve* my forgiveness?"

Surely we all need to look regularly at the command found in Ephesians 4:31, 32, **"Let all bitterness, wrath, anger, clamor, and evil speaking be put away from you, with all malice. And be kind to one another, tenderhearted, forgiving one another, even as God in Christ forgave you."** *Here the Holy Spirit points to the "bottom line" of the matter of forgiveness, and reveals the weakness of our excuses!*

The Bible teaches that we cannot be right with God if we are wrong with our brother. This is not a stump that we can "mow around." There are believers who help themselves to forgive by writing down a list of names of people who have wronged them, and then praying blessing upon those people daily until the hurt disappears. Other believers select Scripture verses about forgiveness and commit them to memory. Do whatever it takes to imitate and obey the Savior regarding forgiveness!

Pray God's blessing on the people who have hurt you.

"'I do not pray for these alone, but also for those who will believe in Me through their word.'" John 17:20

The *benefit* of the *"word,"* is that it opens up to us the very heart of God. By it, we learn such things as the way of salvation and the manner in which God will govern the world. The word explains the reason why man is so unfulfilled and miserable apart from God. Praise be to God, that, in the books which we call the Scriptures, we find wisdom and truth that no man could possibly produce!

But in order for men down through the ages to believe in Christ *"through"* the word, God's *mercy* was required. Only our merciful Creator could *preserve* such a precious thing as His word over time – the record of the whole history of the world from the very creation! Of course, this word has been and continues to be, opposed by all of the powers in the world, but it continues to be miraculously preserved even to our time.

The word is a *living* word – a seed that has to grow and bear fruit before its full nature is known. Today, throughout the world, there is a missionary work taking place. *What is our interest in it?* The Church must *"contend earnestly for the faith which was once for all delivered to the saints"* (see Jude 3). God delivered His word to holy men chosen for that purpose, and with the intention that it be *kept*. For, to "deliver" something, implies that it is being left in the hands of another with *trust*. Therefore, it is the duty of the Church to *deliver* this word to the present age, and to *keep* it for ages to come, until the return of our Lord Jesus Christ.

Do you fully believe that this word is not the word of men, but that it is in truth, the word of *the living God? To be straightforward, "neglect" of God's miraculously preserved word is a sign of unbelief!* Today, invite the Holy Spirit to do His convicting work, by asking Him, "In what ways am *I* delivering Your word, so that men will continue to believe in Jesus?"

October 7

"'And forgive us our debts, as we forgive our debtors.'" Matthew 6:12

A person *already saved* makes this petition, asking that the daily transgressions of his still imperfect condition – sins both of omission and commission – may be graciously pardoned.

It is significant that this petition in the Model Prayer is the *only* one which Jesus saw the need to expand and enforce. *"As"* we forgive our debtors is sometimes misunderstood. It is not "because," "on the ground of," or "for the reason that" we forgive our debtors; it is "even as," "as also," or "like as" we forgive our debtors. In other words, the reference is to forgiveness that is similar in *kind* rather than in *degree*; "in like manner" rather than "in the same measure."

We should not lose sight of the immediate circumstances of the men into whose ears Jesus placed this petition. The friends and brethren of the first disciples disowned them, and those of their own household took on the attitude of foes (see Matthew 10:34-36). Therefore, the disciples learned to "forgive their debtors" in aggravated circumstances. It wasn't easy for them, just like it is not often easy for us, especially within our families.

The words of this petition must describe our own personal behavior before we can offer them with assurance of God's acceptance. *If we refuse to forgive someone, we cannot expect forgiveness from God!* If we retain an unforgiving spirit and judge someone, in like manner, we shall be judged.

You are to **"be kind to one another, tenderhearted, forgiving one another, even as God in Christ forgave you"** (see Ephesians 4:32). When you find this to be difficult to do, remember that forgiveness is so characteristic of the mind of Christ. Forgiveness means, "This will not separate us. Our bond of love is stronger than the separating power that wants to come between."

Is there a relationship in your life where forgiveness is needed? Does today's devotion bring divine encouragement for *you* to take further care of a strained relationship with someone? Ask God to search your heart concerning this. Allow humility to replace pride. Pray for the desire to *completely* forgive someone.

October 8

"'I do not pray for these alone, but also for those who will believe in Me through their word.'" John 17:20

The ***"word"*** communicated by the apostles, is the means for producing faith and for making believers. In reality, it is *God's* word; it is ***"their"*** word, not because they originated it, but because they were the special agents for its delivery and spreading. Apart from the word, there is no Church – because there is no *faith* apart from the word, and the Church is constituted out of only those who have faith.

Ephesians 2:19, 20 says, ***"You are no longer strangers and foreigners, but fellow citizens with the saints and members of the household of God, having been built on the foundation of the apostles and prophets, Jesus Christ Himself being the chief cornerstone."*** The word, as given to the Church through the apostles, is the foundation of the Church for all time. *Although a limited number of people physically "heard" the apostles preach and testify while they lived, they still speak "through their word" in the New Testament, and they still win new Believers!*

Notice in the passage above that the apostles are here placed on the same "level" with the Old Testament prophets. There is a sense in which the Eleven and Paul belong in the same class with Moses, Elijah, Isaiah, Jeremiah and the rest – because they exceed all others as the "inspired transmitters of the Word." To this day, we rightly believe, preach, and profess only what these apostles and prophets wrote. All of these *together* have contributed to the foundation of the Church.

But today, you have *this* opportunity to search your heart, and see if you agree with the words spoken by Peter, ***"Lord, to whom shall we go? You have the words of eternal life"*** (see John 6:68). Do *you* find in Jesus, "through their word," the Christ who is your Refuge, your Life, your Master? Do *you* find in Him, "through their word," the One to whom you gravitate as the only satisfying Answer to your needs?

Do *you* join today, at this moment, with those who pray saying, "I, too, am one of those who believe in You through their word?"

October 9

"'Father, forgive them, for they do not know what they do.'"
Luke 23:34

A t Calvary, we see the *physical pain* from hell on the Cross, and we also see the *mockery* from hell. The mockery that men inflicted upon Jesus Christ that day – yes, it was nothing less than the mockery and the defiance of hell! These were the greetings with which the demons welcome the damned. Christ heard Himself being mocked upon the Cross, coming to Him from the realm of darkness:

"You who destroy the temple and build it in three days, save Yourself!" "If You are the Son of God, come down from the cross." "He saved others; Himself He cannot save." "If He is the King of Israel, let Him now come down from the cross, and we will believe Him." "He trusted in God; let Him deliver Him now if He will have Him; for He said, 'I am the Son of God.'" "If You are the Christ, save Yourself and us."

Satan's true character and influence was exposed through the people connected to the events of the crucifixion. *The depravity of the human heart with its hatred of God, its ingratitude, its pride, its loving of darkness rather than light, was all on display!* Here the devil's power to put it into the heart of man to betray the Savior, was out front for all to see. The sights and sounds of rejection of the only sinless man to ever live were there around the Cross.

Witness the contest taking place at Calvary between the kingdom of God and the kingdom of darkness, between Jesus and Satan! Possibly only Satan and the fallen angels know fully the wickedness of their sin. They saw the light and rejected it. Scripture holds out no hope of forgiveness for them. But, He will forgive *you* if you turn to Him by faith. **"But there is forgiveness with You, that You may be feared"** (Psalm 130:4). Have you put your belief and trust in Christ for your salvation?

Make this your sincere and humble prayer today: **"Search me, O God ... and see if there is any wicked way in me."**

*"And at the ninth hour Jesus cried out with a loud voice, saying ...
'My God, My God, why have You forsaken Me?'"* Mark 15:34

This prayer is the only one of the seven sayings of Jesus on the Cross that is recorded by Matthew and Mark. The other six sayings are found in Luke and John. But this prayer best illustrates His deep suffering of soul from being regarded as sin while being sinless, or as Paul put it, **"He made Him who knew no sin to be sin for us."** And, of all the statements Jesus made from the Cross, this one is far and away the most difficult and profound.

Just about everything that has to do with the suffering of Jesus Christ is difficult to explain completely and fully. A well-known saying has it that those who would understand the poet must go to the poet's country. As we come to Golgotha, we listen to the Poet par excellence; Jesus is speaking. Yet these words of His prayer transcend our comprehension. For in the entire Bible there is possibly no other sentence so difficult to explain.

Even the witnesses at the foot of the Cross were confused by this fourth statement by Christ. People standing by the Cross imagined that Jesus had called for Elijah at the beginning of His prayer. Non-Jewish soldiers would have misunderstood the prayer because their understanding of who Jesus was came from statements made by His accusers and by angry mobs. And no Jew would have mistaken "Eli" for the name of Elijah.

Having said all of that, we can certainly know what this prayer *teaches*, even if we fail to understand completely all that it *means. It is important to remember that strange impressions come to ears that have not been opened by the Spirit of God!* Strange misunderstandings come to those who have not been enlightened by the same Spirit. When one is not guided by the Holy Ghost, strange misinterpretation and strange misapplication of divine truth come easily. It is not enough to be merely a "sincere" Christian, as important as that is.

"The Spirit of truth has come." Pray for understanding that comes from the Holy Spirit as you interpret the Scriptures.

October 11

"'And forgive us our debts, as we forgive our debtors.'" Matthew 6:12

These words from the Model Prayer mean much more than just an acknowledgment that we are indebted to God. This is a petition of the soul for all that we need and can *only* have from the Father. The words *"forgive us"* are to be prayed neither mechanically (as is true of *all* prayer), nor insincerely, nor with double-mind, nor flippantly; no, these words are to be prayed with an earnest, abiding and sincere desire for pardon.

"As we forgive our debtors" are words meant to encourage us to *do just that*, and not just occasionally, but faithfully. The "appended" petition, as it has been called, creates a check to our conscience. God's forgiveness is a great gift that we seek, and we should pray these words from the deepest sense of our need. Do we really understand the *magnitude* of what we ask God to do when we ask for His "forgiveness?" These words of the Model Prayer make us think about how great a gift we seek!

How suitable, then, to check your conscience as you make this petition, for it is so easy to become a careless hypocrite during prayer. The truth is, a man humble before God, is impressed to be charitable toward his neighbor. For how can you have the heart to challenge another person with his offences against you, when your own sin against God is pressing upon your soul? *In proportion as your own sin against God appears great to you, so will the offenses of others against you appear small!*

When you consider your sins, the mind of God and your mind, view very different objects; *"'For My thoughts are not your thoughts, nor are your ways My ways,' says the Lord"* (see Isaiah 55:8). If the wrong done to you by others seems greater than you can forgive, then *your own* wrongdoing is affecting you less than it should.

Jesus has given you these words – not to make your prayer "impossible" – but so that you may receive what you ask from the Father, when you pray today, "Forgive us our debts."

October 12

"'I do not pray for these alone, but also for those who will believe in Me through their word.'" John 17:20

Just like Jesus, we, as intercessors, have people on our hearts for which we pray *first*. In this prayer, Jesus began by praying for Himself, and then He prayed, *"for these alone,"* referring primarily to the Eleven, and finally for future Believers. In our case, parents may begin by praying for their children, or pastors may begin by praying for their church members. The order may vary depending on the circumstances, but intercessory prayer, as we see here with Jesus, should be *personal, compassionate,* and *definite*.

When we pray for others, our first concern should be that they would *receive the Word of God*. We should also pray, following Jesus' example, that they should be sanctified through that Word and kept from the evil one. As our intercessory prayer continues, we should pray for the unity of the Church. With the Holy Spirit prompting us, our intercession will at times include people who may not have been on our "list" when we began to pray, but who are in need of the Master's touch.

Even if the Bible contained no examples of intercessory prayer – even if Jesus had not taught you by word and by example to pray for others – then the very Spirit of your faith would constrain you to plead for others. Do you enter into the presence of God not thinking of anyone but *yourself?* The Cross of Christ was not uplifted for you alone! Charles Spurgeon said, "Intercessory prayer is the sweetest prayer God ever hears. Do not question it, for the prayer of Christ is of this character."

Dear friend, someone prayed for your salvation! It may have been your mother, your father, your grandmother, your grandfather, your child, your pastor, your Sunday School teacher, your friend. It may have been a prayer warrior in a church that was given your name. And, if none of these, then *Jesus* prayed for your salvation in this very prayer you are considering today! For *you* are among those for whom He prayed would *"believe in Me through their word."*

Join Jesus, and intercede for your unconverted friends.

October 13

"And at the ninth hour Jesus cried out with a loud voice, saying …
'My God, My God, why have You forsaken Me?'" Mark 15:34

When Jesus was born, there was an extraordinary light that guided the feet of the wise men to the manger in Bethlehem. But at His crucifixion, there was an extraordinary *darkness* that covered the face of the whole earth.

Only the night before, Jesus had said to the chief priests and elders and captains of the Temple: ***"This is your hour, and the power of darkness."*** And now at the Cross, these men are assembled and behold, an awful darkness falls upon the earth, blotting out the noonday sun. God darkened the sun's light by means of His own, just as He shook the earth and split the rocks.

So, *this was supernatural darkness.* The darkness gave the meaning of the cry, and the cry gave the meaning of the darkness, which was that Jesus had taken the place of guilty, lost sinners. God is Light, and the darkness is the sign of His turning away. The darkness lasted three hours, "three" being a number that represents "completeness" in Scripture. This darkness signified the blinding of the Jews' spiritual eyes, but more than that, it represented judgment; a sign that was wrought in the sun by God. Darkness and judgment go together in Scripture (see Joel 2:1, 2, 31; 3:14, 15; Isaiah 5:30; 13:9; Matthew 24:29; Mark 13:24; Luke 21:25).

If there is one thing that we can be sure of about sin, it is the fact that it separates us from God. That was the one human experience through which Jesus had never passed because He lived His life without sin. Jesus had never known the *consequence* of sin. In these three hours of darkness, Christ "completely" identified with the sin of man.

Therefore, God's claims against us have been met in full! Jesus was forsaken of God temporarily, that we might enjoy His presence forever! Christ endured the awful darkness that we might walk in the Light! He was forsaken, that we might be forgiven! Oh, what a Savior!

Pray now a prayer of praise and thanksgiving for what was accomplished for *you* on "the skull-shaped hill."

> ***"I do not pray for these alone, but also for those who will believe in Me through their word.'"*** John 17:20

Andrew Murray has said, "If we will but believe in God and His faithfulness, intercession will become to us the very first thing we take refuge in when we seek blessing for others, and the very last thing for which we cannot find time."

This "High Priestly Prayer" of Jesus is the model intercessory prayer. "Petition" is prayer relating to *our* personal need, and "intercession" is prayer that relates to the need of *others*. You do not intercede on your own behalf. And so there are three principles to all intercession: (1) a *need* on the part of the one spoken of (2) *power* on the part of the one spoken to, and (3) *contact* with both of these persons on the part of the one who speaks. Therefore, at least three persons are always involved in intercessory prayer. This fact can be illustrated easily through the Scriptures, for example, ***"And the LORD restored JOB'S losses when he prayed for his FRIENDS"*** (see Job 42:10, italics used by the author to identify the three aspects just mentioned).

W. Graham Scroggie said, "Every great intercessor has been a student of the map." *You may discover that there is no better way to study world history or geography than through intercessory prayer!* The earth is the field of God's redemptive operations, the place where we are pleading for His kingdom to come and His will to be done ***"as it is in heaven."*** William Carey and John Hyde agonized over India, Hudson Taylor over China, and David Livingstone over Africa. Have you agonized over your country in intercessory prayer?

Perhaps you would begin this Godly practice by making a rough sketch of the neighborhood or of the dwellings that exist *in the area surrounding your house.* You might pray for a different family each day, asking that the Spirit of God would draw that family to Himself. If you work outside the home, you might pray daily for the businesses that are located around your place of employment. What might God do?

Pray for God to make you a powerful, compassionate intercessor.

October 15

"'And forgive us our debts, as we forgive our debtors.'" Matthew 6:12

How can you know for sure that you have forgiven someone? Are there any signs? There are a few indications of genuine forgiveness. One indication is when you no longer *think* about how you might *punish* or *seek revenge against* the wrongdoer. Keep in mind that the devil plays the major role in the process of keeping you in a *state* of unforgiveness. The "battlefield" where the devil most often fights is your *mind*. When it comes to forgiveness (as in all temptation to sin), whoever runs the mind runs the show.

In addition to winning the battle of the mind over whether or not to forgive someone, there is a second indication of genuine forgiveness – you will sincerely *pray* for the offender. The Holy Spirit will introduce "prompts" to you, such as prayer for his health, his welfare, his family – maybe even his salvation.

A third indication of genuine forgiveness is when you are *ready and willing to seek reconciliation*. Is the Holy Spirit prompting you to take the initiative toward reconciliation? Genuine forgiveness is willing to do that, rather than waiting for the other person to take the first step. It becomes a matter of obedience to Jesus, who said, **"If your brother sins against you, go and tell him his fault between you and him alone. If he hears you, you have gained your brother"** (see Matthew 18:15).

You have probably heard people say, "But if you only knew what he did, you would understand why I cannot bring myself to forgive him." That is the devil's excuse. The truth is, that by not forgiving him for his terrible deed you are committing an even greater wrong than his. For by hurting you, he has merely offended man; but by refusing to forgive him, *you are offending God!*

To **"forgive our debtors"** *means that you no longer consider them as debtors!* Once you see the enormity of your own sins against God, the hurts that others have placed upon you appear very small by comparison. Pray to be forgiven, and pray for the will to forgive others.

"'I do not pray for these alone, but also for those who will believe in Me through their word.'" John 17:20

Man, by nature, is a selfish creature; yet the Bible says, *"None of us lives to himself."* Prayer, therefore, must not, it cannot stop at our own personal need. Who can measure the work, the impact, of those whose ministry is that of laboring – even agonizing – in prayer for others? In this prayer, our great prayer Teacher prays first concerning Himself, and then He puts His focus on the Eleven, followed by *"those who will believe in Me through their word."*

Today we are considering the value and sufficiency of having *Jesus Christ* intercede for us on a daily basis. As we begin, let's remind ourselves of that truth as declared in the Bible, *"He always lives to make intercession for them"* (see Hebrews 7:25). Only the Son of God could accomplish such a task when you consider the number of people for whom He is praying! This is such an easy fact to forget in the busyness of our daily lives.

Surely you feel truly blessed and very thankful when men take time to pray for you! God hears and often acts in response to, their prayers. But let's take a moment to consider how the intercession made for you by Jesus is *different* from the intercession made on your behalf by men. Spiritually and emotionally, Jesus is the *only* One who can actually say in truth, "I know how you feel" when He intercedes for you. For example, think about the occasions when you are tempted to sin. Hebrews 4:15 says that Jesus, *"was in all points tempted as we are, yet without sin."* One of the reasons why He was tried in every point that you are, was so that He could pray effectively for you!

Jesus can identify with the challenges of living at home because *He* lived at home. Jesus can identify with the challenges of working with the public because He worked in a carpenter's shop. And He can identify with the feeling of being misunderstood because He was *"despised and rejected by men."*

Pray with thanksgiving that Jesus Christ intercedes daily for you.

October 17

"And at the ninth hour Jesus cried out with a loud voice, saying ...
'My God, My God, why have You forsaken Me?'" Mark 15:34

Never was such a sorrowful soul expressed in any sound! Never has there been, nor ever will be, a cry from earth as *this* loud, long, lonely cry from the Cross, caused by the agony Jesus is now enduring. After hours of suffering, Jesus exerted Himself to raise His voice, because He meant those words to ring out over the crowd that had gathered around the Cross. We are all still learning what sin really is. But a couple of facts we do know about sin, as we listen to and watch Jesus at Calvary: sin is *deadly* to have caused such suffering, and sin is *hateful* to the sight of God.

Without this cry, we would never have realized the awfulness and the wickedness of sin, or the gravity of Isaiah's statement: **"Your iniquities have separated you from your God; and your sins have hidden His face from you, so that He will not hear."** Clearly, the **"darkness"** mentioned in Mark 15:33 and this agonizing cry of Jesus, go together.

And if this cry from Jesus had never been uttered, we might never have known that He had been **"forsaken."** The word "forsaken" has to be one of the most tragic words in existence! A man forsaken of his friends, a wife forsaken by her husband, or a child forsaken by his parents, are all terrible for sure – but a man forsaken of God has to be the most frightful condition of all! It was because Jesus bore our sins that a Holy God could not look on Him, turned His face from Him, forsook Him.

There are those who try to "explain away" God forsaking Jesus on the Cross. It does not sound to them like something that God would ever do to His Son. But the forsaking was necessary! Christ Himself had to work out our redemption without any help, even from His Father in heaven. And that is why God the Father had to stand aside, as it were, forsaking Him.

Jesus was forsaken, that you might *never* be forsaken. Pray today with a grateful heart.

> *"'That they all may be one, as You, Father, are in Me, and I in You;*
> *that they also may be one in Us, that the world may believe that*
> *You sent Me'"* John 17:21

The life and death of Jesus Christ was a prayer, and His current life in heaven is a *continuous* prayer. In this prayer, He summed up the desires of His heart into its highest and noblest issue. He prays here for a perfect and universal union among believers, for a historical continuity between the church of the first century and the church of subsequent centuries, and that the church's faith may not change. Therefore, as Jesus prayed, He was sure that although His last day in the world was only hours away, this was only the *beginning* of His reign.

Thomas Manton said, "This prayer is a standing monument of Christ's affection to the Church." He prays for its *unity* three times in the prayer: **"that they all may be one"** (verse 21), **"that they may be one"** (verse 22), and, **"that they be made perfect in one"** (verse 23).

The first aspect of the Church's unity is *unity with the apostles.* We are clearly told in Scripture that the very first converts (the 3,000 who were converted on the day of Pentecost) **"continued steadfastly in the apostles' doctrine and fellowship"** (see Acts 2:42). And the same apostle John, who recorded this prayer of Jesus, also wrote, **"that which we have seen and heard we declare to you, that you also may have fellowship with us; and truly our fellowship is with the Father and with His Son Jesus Christ"** (see 1 John 1:3).

Secondly, the Church is in *unity with the Father and the Son.* The manner in which the Father lives "in" the Son (**"You, Father, are in Me"**) is by making Jesus the object of the Father's supreme affection; the Son lives "in" the Father (**"I in You"**) by abiding in the light of His glory and in the power of His name. *A staggering request this, that as there is a mutual indwelling between the Father and the Son in the Godhead, so there is a mutual indwelling between the Church and the Godhead!*

Pray for a deeper commitment to the unity for which Jesus prayed.

October 19

"And forgive us our debts, as we forgive our debtors.'" Matthew 6:12

You need continual repentance and cleansing from sin, even though the debt of sin is already and finally settled to the extent that sin cannot take you to Hell. This daily restoration and cleansing that allows intimate *fellowship* with the Father will not be yours unless you forgive others who sin against you. The difficulty with forgiving others comes when you fail to realize that however inexcusable a person's sin against you has been, it is not even a *fraction* as wicked as your sin against God!

When you choose to hold on to an unforgiving spirit against another person, God says you not only make yourself ineligible for His forgiveness of your continued sin – but you also forfeit fellowship with the Father. No matter how many hymns you sing, no matter how many ministries you perform, no matter how many times you attend church – until that relationship to that person has been made right in your heart, your sins will not be forgiven by the Father.

The reason God shows mercy to you is not only that you would be forgiven, but that the mind of Christ Jesus may be in you. *You have obtained mercy in order that you may be merciful!* God's will is done on earth as it is in heaven when mercy reigns here below in our hearts and lives, as it reigns on the throne above.

When you forgive your **"debtors,"** you must do it because of the fact that God has already done "His part." In other words, forgiveness *begins* with God. He forgives first, and then you follow His example, demonstrating that you have been forgiven.

But *why* forgive? Consider these five answers from God's Word. First, that you may receive forgiveness from God (see Matthew 6:15). Second, that you may prosper spiritually (see Matthew 18:32-35). Third, that you may follow the example of Jesus (see Luke 23:34). Fourth, that you may obey the Scriptures (see Romans 12:14-19). And fifth, that you may be a testimony (see Colossians 3:12, 13).

Pray that the Holy Spirit will change your heart about forgiving someone.

"'That they all may be one, as You, Father, are in Me, and I in You; that they also may be one in Us, that the world may believe that You sent Me'" John 17:21

Just as there is a unity between Christ and the Father, so there is a unity between Christ and the Believer; therefore, there is a spiritual unity between these individual Believers because of their faith in Christ. **"That they all"** may be one, stresses the great *number* of Believers involved. Even though there are so many in number, all Believers are to be one unit, one body, one spiritual whole. Included in this large group are the apostles themselves.

Absolutely the highest type of oneness that exists is the oneness between the Father and the Son. *And this oneness is to be the model and pattern for the oneness of Believers!* Such a high model and pattern as this is needed for our oneness because the unity we are more familiar with is a *human* unity - such as what we face in the areas of racial or political relations. Believers can be *perfectly* one with each other only as they are one with the Father and Jesus.

The *Word* of God plays a huge role in the oneness for which Jesus prays. We know no Christ and no God without the Word, and no oneness among ourselves without the Word. In addition, the more we have of the Word in our hearts, and the more we allow it to rule in our lives, the more perfect is our oneness. We are as much one with each other, one with God, and one with Christ – as we believe, teach, live, and confess all that is contained in the Word.

We are all to **"be one"** in spite of "space," for we inhabit different countries on earth. We are to be one in spite of "time," for some are of the past, some are of the present, and some are of the future. And we are all to be one in spite of "differences," such as physical, mental, social, and circumstantial deviations. Although gradually attained, *perfection* is the goal of this union!

Pray that your union with the Father and the Son will deepen your relationships in the family of God.

October 21

"'Watch and pray, lest you enter into temptation. The spirit indeed is willing, but the flesh is weak.'" Matthew 26:41

Temptation is coming, so watch and pray for the beginning of it, says Jesus to His disciples at Gethsemane. We must not **"enter into"** anything that we have reason to believe, or suspect may soon become, temptation to sin. We must be knowledgeable of how a thing *becomes* temptation, **"watch"** for those signs, and **"pray"** for readiness and divine strength to overcome. Unfortunately, the disciples did not follow the Lord's instructions on this occasion, and the consequences of their disobedience are well documented in God's Word.

The subject of temptation affects every true Christian every day. John Bunyan described the Christian life as a journey through a very dangerous country. Augustine said that a saint's whole life is temptation. Today we consider a very important truth we must remember concerning how we "enter into" temptation, and it is this: *Whoever runs the mind runs the show!*

In the Old World, the gates to the cities had "keepers" who would open or close the doors depending upon who was seeking admission. We must call upon the Holy Spirit to be the gatekeeper at the door to our minds. He will then guard against the evil guest seeking entry. It is easy to understand why Satan makes the mind his primary target. In wartime, one of the first targets that comes under attack is the "communications center." The purpose of attacking that location is to create confusion.

From a *spiritual* warfare perspective, your mind is "communications headquarters." The Apostle Paul said that we are to bring **"every thought into captivity to the obedience of Christ"** (2 Corinthians 10:5). Paul's use of the military term, "captivity," further underscores the truth that wrestling with temptation is a war that is taking place in the mind.

The more satisfied we are with Jesus, the easier it is to reject the devil and his offers. Satisfaction with God is "basic training;" it is one of the conditions we must meet in order to be holy. Someone once said, "God is most *glorified in us* when we are most *satisfied in Him.*"

Watch and pray right now.

"'That they all may be one, as You, Father, are in Me, and I in You;
that they also may be one in Us, that the world may believe that
You sent Me'" John 17:21

What is "Church unity?" Let's begin by stating what it is not. Christ does not refer here to a complete, perfect *uniformity* among Believers. If He did, His prayer has been unanswered, for no such uniformity exists. Nor does He pray for a union between the different denominations of the Christian church, for again, if He did, His prayer has been unanswered. Sects and denominations are ultimately the result of the devil's attempt to amplify our own spiritual pride and selfishness. What, then, *is* Jesus asking for?

"That they all may be one" refers to the union that all Believers have with one another as members of the same family, as living stones in the same spiritual temple where Jesus is the foundation stone. This family is identified in Ephesians 3:15, where we read, **"from whom the whole family in heaven and earth is named."**

The Bible names five types of union that bind the children of God to each other: (1) **"The unity of the Spirit in the bond of peace"** (Ephesians 4:3) – everyone wanting a unity that only the Holy Spirit can produce; (2) **"The unity of the faith"** (Ephesians 4:13) – everyone maturing together in the faith; (3) being **"of one heart and one soul"** (Acts 4:32) – everyone wanting to be faithful and obedient; (4) **"being knit together in love"** (Colossians 2:2) – everyone holding together tightly through the tests and trials; (5) being **"in the same mind and in the same judgment"** (1 Corinthians 1:10) – everyone desiring a scriptural understanding of their circumstances.

Notice that Jesus was looking ahead for His Church! Many churches today wait until the "circus" comes to town, and *then* think to pray for unity. It should be clear to us by now, that the devil accomplishes a huge amount of destruction by relentlessly ambushing church unity. Therefore, effective prayer for church unity must be "proactive" rather than "reactive." Since the unity of Believers was so heavy on the heart of Jesus just hours before His death, that should set off a prayer alarm in the Church!

Pray that we all may be one.

October 23

"And forgive us our debts, as we forgive our debtors.'" Matthew 6:12

In the Model Prayer, the High Priest who intercedes above, teaches us how to intercede here below. Receiving our instructions from none other than the Son of God, we pray, ***"Forgive us our debts"*** to a Father who pities His children and who calls them to Himself. Today we are looking at what acceptable prayer for *pardon* includes.

The first step is to *welcome Holy Spirit conviction.* Put away all the fallacies and rationalizations by which you have tried to persuade yourself that you can proudly plead "not guilty." Do not call it your "weakness," your "personality quirk," or your "bad habit;" call it your consent to rebel against God and to sin.

The next step is to *be genuinely sorry* for not only the consequences of the sin but the sin itself. This is when you cry out, "God be merciful to me a sinner." Read through the Psalms and you will find the groanings of contrite hearts. The third step when sincerely praying for pardon is to *confess* your sin. If you wish to be healed, you must show your wound to the Physician. Proverbs 28:13 says, ***"He who covers his sins will not prosper, but whoever confesses and forsakes them will have mercy."***

Confession leads you to the fourth step, which is *true repentance. Biblical repentance involves a change of mind about both sin and God; it would be contrary to God's holiness to pardon sins that you intend to repeat.* This is a step so important that not a day should be lost without it. Every day's delay increases the "debt," lessens the opportunity of pardon, and weakens your desire to seek it.

There cannot be any genuine prayer for pardon unless you are cultivating a forgiving spirit. It is a prayer of the child of God. In the Model Prayer, Jesus has undoubtedly connected the duty of forgiveness with the prayer for it. One way to overcome an unforgiving spirit is to *stop looking back on the injuries that provoked it.*

Review the four steps mentioned above. Ask God to give you a forgiving heart.

"'That they all may be one, as You, Father, are in Me, and I in You;
that they also may be one in Us, that the world may believe that
You sent Me'" John 17:21

W e can't make *this* kind of unity "happen!" Jesus was not concerned here with our "mechanical" attempts at union through the coordination of organizations; He was praying about the *spiritual* unity of His people – a Church within the churches - when Believers would see and understand the same things. The life we share as Christians is nothing less than a participation in the life of the Godhead! And when *this* kind of unity exists, **"the world"** takes notice, for a unity among Believers that is not *apparent* can have no effect on the world.

It is possible that Jesus prayed this prayer with Psalm 133:1 on His heart, which says, **"Behold, how good and how pleasant it is for brethren to dwell together in unity!"** Most of us have learned by now (some of us the hard way) that Believers do not always "get along" with each other. *In fact, the disciples argued with one another right in front of Jesus!*

"As You, Father, are in Me, and I in You" refers to the highest union that can ever exist – the union between *the Man Christ Jesus* and *the Son of God*. This is the union between the human nature complete in all its fullness, and the divine nature complete in all its attributes. Jesus' desire is for the union between Himself and His followers to correspond in every way to this union between Himself and the Father.

Here is the application. Given your knowledge of this divine union, and given your knowledge of the importance that Christ Jesus places on it – how ought you to walk, having *received* the Lord Jesus Christ? Colossians 2:6 says, **"As you therefore have received Christ Jesus the Lord, so walk in Him."** What a new outlook arises regarding your sin as a Believer, when you consider your sins to be *against* such a divine union as this!

Praise God for His patience and forgiveness! Yes, praise Him for never leaving you or forsaking you! Pray that your walk with Him today will demonstrate to the world the divine union for which Jesus prayed.

October 25

"Then they came to a place which was named Gethsemane; and He said to His disciples, 'Sit here while I pray.'" Mark 14:32

"**G**ethsemane" was one of Jesus' favorite places to pray. It was a secluded, quiet place, just over the hill from the home where He had found sheltering love. When He was in Jerusalem, He visited this garden frequently. Luke 21:37 tells us: *"And in the daytime He was teaching in the temple, but at night He went out and stayed on the mountain called Olivet."* And once more, in Luke 22:39, we read: *"Coming out, He went to the Mount of Olives, as He was accustomed, and ... When He came to the place."*

"And Judas, who betrayed Him, also knew the place; for Jesus often met there with His disciples" (see John 18:2). Judas' plan to capture Jesus was based on his knowledge of the fact that the Master spent the nights sleeping in Gethsemane – in fact, Judas had slept there too, along with Christ and the other disciples. But there was no need to "hide" from Judas; the hour had arrived for Jesus (knowing the plans of Judas), to *deliberately* place Himself into the hands of His enemies in that garden.

Gardens are special places. A garden is often a place of rest, but it is also a place where things *happen*. It is interesting to note that it was in a garden, the Garden of Eden, that man had *lost* his battle with Satan. Now the second Adam *wins* the battle back in another garden, the Garden of Gethsemane. No other garden ever meant so much as these two!

This private garden on the hillside of Olivet was a place where Jesus had often found a quiet atmosphere for prayer. Understandably, He now returns to that sanctuary for the last time, to face this incredible hour.

The human heart is touched by certain "places" that remain in our memories – sometimes often-visited, sometimes long-unvisited, yet long-remembered and still soothing to the soul. *Dear reader, prayer is worthy of a special place!* If you have not already done so, establish a favorite place today where you will regularly go to meet with the Father.

As you pray now, worship Him.

"that they all may be one, as You, Father, are in Me, and I in You; that they also may be one in Us, that the world may believe that You sent Me" John 17:21

When we consider church unity, our responsibility lies in maintaining and expressing it – *not* in attempting to "create" it through uniformity of practice or through union of visible organization.

The only possible way to have unity among believers is when all of them *first* find unity with God in Christ. *That* unity leads a believer to cherish the Holy Spirit's healing and harmonizing influence and to keep the example of Jesus before him. The union of believers with one another in the Father and the Son is essentially spiritual, and not visible or external. But it ought to *result* in a visible union that will appeal to a world that cannot see the purely spiritual.

The unity of the church causes the world to believe that Jesus was sent by the Father and that the Father loves the church. Therefore, church unity has a huge impact upon the world. Jesus revealed an unseen God to the world by becoming flesh (see John 1:14), and the church will be a visible revelation of the unseen Father and His love. There is clearly an evangelical purpose in church unity, **"that the world may believe that You sent Me."**

Now let us be completely honest. The Christian Church today lacks in nothing so much as unity. No virtue is so absent from it as real spiritual union. So a trend has emerged to do away with church "business meetings" in order to preserve church unity, but that decision merely *hides* selfishness, self-seeking, and pride that is still present!

We must instead, each of us, be a *real* unity completely in accord with Jesus, even as He was completely in accord with His Father. *As the Father was seen in Jesus, so Christ should be seen in us!* And when that happens, that small part of the world which has to do with us may indeed believe that One has been sent from heaven to make men into a happy, united family.

Pray that the unity that you already have with Jesus will become real enough and deep enough to affect those around you.

October 27

"And do not lead us into temptation, but deliver us from the evil one"
Matthew 6:13

In His high priestly prayer, Jesus said, **"I do not pray that You should take them out of the world, but that You should keep them from the evil one"** (see John 17:15). Believers will remain in a state of "siege," and consequently will never be free from the many dangers and snares of life. Therefore, Jesus teaches His disciples to pray that nothing would *become* a temptation to them, for everything and anything in this life has the potential to become a temptation.

When you pray this petition of the Model Prayer, you are not praying, "Don't allow me to *ever* be tempted," even though you have experienced the destruction of sin and you do not want to *continue* experiencing the devastation sin brings. You are asking God to lead you not "into" (for the Bible states clearly that God tempts no one) but "through" the experience if He should permit the temptation for your good. You are asking Him to "steer you clear" from what has previously ruined you because you realize that you are not as strong as you think.

"Do not lead us into temptation" *is really a confession that you need a divine leader when it comes to the matter of temptation!* Even *prior* to the arrival of a temptation, you need supernatural intervention in three specific areas: to see where you are vulnerable to the enemy's attack, to detect the enemy when he is lurking or approaching, and to recognize where the enemy is already at work. The Master warned, **"Watch and pray, lest you enter into temptation. The spirit indeed is willing, but the flesh is weak"** (see Matthew 26:41).

Only Jesus has measured the *total* force of temptation. The devil tempted Him by every possible avenue to all types of sin, but with absolutely no success. That is what you are after today, and every day – the desire for holiness above all! Trust in God's upholding hand today when the moment of temptation arrives.

Pray that when you are tempted today, you will rely on supernatural intervention to enable you to overcome.

> *"'That they all may be one, as You, Father, are in Me, and I in You;*
> *that they also may be one in Us, that the world may believe that*
> *You sent Me'"* John 17:21

Oh, to *be* "in Him," and also to *know* that we are "in Him!" Does being "in Him" mean the same thing as being in "what is His" – such as in His church, in His family, or in His kingdom?

How does a Believer know when he is *"in"* Jesus? To be "in Christ" is Paul's characteristic description of the Christian. But John uses that word, too. 1 John 2:5 says, **"But whoever keeps His word, truly the love of God is perfected in him. By this we know that we are in Him."** And John speaks of one who **"abides in Him"** (see 1 John 2:6). We can conclude that being a Christian consists of a personal relationship to God in Christ, knowing Him, loving Him, and abiding in Him as the branch abides in the vine (see John 15:1-5).

Just think of some of the "benefits" of being "in Him:" you are covered with His wings, His own divine perfections are wrapped around you, you are identified with Him and His interests, you share in His triumphs and His joys, His grace is connected to your guilt, His strength is applied to your weakness, His glory is attached to your salvation! Yes, **"He who dwells in the secret place of the Most High shall abide under the shadow of the Almighty,"** and, **"As the mountains surround Jerusalem, so the Lord surrounds His people from this time forth and forever."**

God's *love* has brought you to this union with Him. You are "in connection with" (fellowship with) God when His light, His truth, His Word, is in you. God's Word is always the "means," for without the Word there is no connection with God. To repudiate the means is to lose the *result* (the fellowship) – the goal that God's love would attain.

So the keeping of His Word is the proof that you are "in Him!" For in the keeping of His Word, His love is truly perfected in you. Listen, as He speaks to you through His Word. Then pray, as did Samuel, **"Speak, for your servant hears."**

October 29

"And He said to His disciples, 'Sit here while I pray.' And He took Peter, James, and John with Him " Mark 14:32, 33

At the entrance to Gethsemane, Jesus instructed eight of the eleven disciples accompanying Him to *"Sit here"* (He probably pointed to the place) *"while I pray."* The word translated "pray" here means more than just "to be in the act of prayer;" it means "to make a definite prayer and to complete it." It is possible that these eight disciples may have been serving as "guards" to watch by the gate for the coming of Judas.

Then three of the disciples, *"Peter, James, and John,"* were instructed to continue further with Jesus. These are the same three disciples, you will remember, who were witnesses on the occasions when Jesus raised the daughter of Jairus, and on the Mount of Transfiguration. But is that fact the only explanation for why these particular three were permitted to get closer at Gethsemane? There are a number of possibilities to consider.

Some say that these are the three disciples who loved Him best. They were also among the first group of four selected among the Twelve (see Matthew 10:2). For some reason, Jesus took these men a little further along than the rest on more than one occasion. Many say that these three were like Jesus' "inner circle," and that He trusted them more than the others. Not all believers are in the same place in their relationship to Jesus.

All of that said, these three men did have their flaws like the other eight who were told to stay behind. We are quick to think of Peter, for example, as being impulsive, vulnerable, and the one who denied the Lord. We are sometimes harder on Peter than we are on ourselves! Yet we can find encouragement as we see Peter, James, and John move closer to Jesus praying at Gethsemane, by considering this: No one of us has a perfect record, far from it! *But we can still be permitted to fellowship with Him and to draw close to Him!*

Pray that your love for Jesus will deepen to the place where He trusts you and permits you to see more of Him.

"'That they all may be one, as You, Father, are in Me, and I in You;
that they also may be one in Us, that the world may believe that
You sent Me'" John 17:21

In this verse and in the subsequent verse 23, we are told not only the *consequence* of church unity but also the very *object and purpose* of it. Jesus prays that those who believe in Him may so live in unity, **"that the world may believe"** that God sent Him. People do not observe us and glorify us; they see Jesus and glorify Him. So faith begets faith, and believers multiply, through the unity that they enjoy with the apostles, with the Father and the Son, and with each other. This unity need not be "uniformity;" in fact, the truest and deepest manifestation of *this* unity is shown in diversity!

Within the fellowship of those who are bound together by personal loyalty to Christ, the relationship of love reaches an intimacy and intensity *unknown elsewhere* – and that, if for no other reason, is why we should *desire* church unity. When *this* unity is experienced, without such "barriers" as race, nationality, or language, it is one of the most convincing evidences of the continuing activity of Jesus among men. But where it is *not* apparent, unbelievers remain in their unbelief. Thomas Manton said it well, "Divisions in the church breed atheism in the world."

Our "unhappy divisions" as they are sometimes called, do not make us as unhappy as they should! They are a chief cause of weakness in today's church. Far more emphasis is placed on style, methodology and on *how* we do church today than on *being* the church. The result? Large churches that are packed with immature Believers.

How often do you pray for this unity? Do you think about unity as something that may happen if everyone joins the "denomination" or the "type" of church to which *you* belong? Or do you think of church unity as a coming together of **"all those who love our Lord Jesus Christ in sincerity."** Understanding this prayer that Jesus prayed, understanding His heart's desire, will allow you to *agree* with Him in prayer for unity in His church.

Pray that you will desire the same unity for which Jesus prayed.

October 31

No one can teach you as well as Jesus. To teach *perfectly* on the subject of prayer, two things are required: a perfect knowledge of God's character, and a perfect knowledge of your condition and needs. Jesus had them both. The fact that the Father sent His Son to deliver these petitions demonstrates how willing He is to hear you.

Jesus does not tell you to pray for removal from the battlefield; He instructs you to pray for protection as you fight! As John A. Shedd put it, "A ship in harbor is safe – but that is not what ships are built for."

"Do not lead us into temptation" does not mean that God will lead you into sin if you forget to ask Him not to do so. Rather, He is teaching you to pray, "Don't lead me into the exam room if I don't need to be there." Even though you know that times of trial and testing are inevitable throughout your life, it's not something you "look forward to," because the devil often turns "tests" into *temptations* in areas where you are apt to receive a failing grade.

Today we are living in and witnessing an increasingly poisonous atmosphere throughout the world around us. "Evil" refers to anything that even *appears or promotes* wickedness, which would include "Halloween," yet this is a day about which sincere Christians still disagree regarding its observance and so-called "harmless fun." The most important thing to remember is this: if the devil were not so intrusive, deceitful, and dangerous, Jesus would not have taught us to pray for *deliverance* from him!

The words, **"Deliver us from the evil one,"** make up what some Bible commentators call the "seventh" petition of the Model Prayer. But it is a petition so closely connected to the one previously made in the same sentence, that the majority of scholars see the two requests as one. When you pray, "Deliver us from the evil one," you are trusting God for your protection from anything that interrupts your fellowship with Him.

Pray for deliverance from the evil one.

"that they all may be one, as You, Father, are in Me, and I in You; that they also may be one in Us, that the world may believe that You sent Me" John 17:21

Notice that the people living in *"the world"* are not going to "automatically" believe that God sent His Son to them. *They are going to have to be convinced!* The word "world" spoken here by Jesus in prayer, refers to a society that is organized not only *without* God but also *against* God; in other words, it is the world of the ungodly.

Jesus is referring to the world as a "system" of things, that *you* used to belong to before you were saved. The Bible says, **"You once walked according to the course of this world"** (see Ephesians 2:2). This world system is a powerful force on people's lives. Therefore, it takes a more powerful force to convince the people whose pleasures, understanding and satisfaction come from the world. To accomplish this, amazingly, God chose *unity among Believers!*

Today we are looking at two things that you are "up against," as a Believer who desires to reveal the truth about God *within this world system.* First, this world system is *dangerous.* People living within it, even Christians, are deceived into thinking that this world is actually a pleasing and comfortable place overall. But the Bible warns otherwise, saying, **"Do not be conformed to this world," "Do you not know that friendship with the world is enmity with God?"** and **"Do not love the world or the things in the world."** With Satan as its "prince," this world is *anything but* comfortable!

Second, this world system is *deceived.* In spite of all the world's ideas for how to obtain lasting peace and unity among themselves, the world cannot make sense of things apart from God, because **"the god of this age"** (Satan) has blinded their minds. 1 John 5:19 says, **"We know that we are of God, and the whole world lies under the sway of the wicked one."**

Yet, even with all its danger and deception, this world can *still* be persuaded by God's love! Pray in agreement with Jesus.

November 2

"And do not lead us into temptation, but deliver us from the evil one"
Matthew 6:13

The daily pardon of sin that we seek should not diminish our "dread" of sin. When God forgives us, it should deepen our repentance and increase our hatred of evil. A forgiven soul fears God and dreads sin. The same Jesus who said, **"Be of good cheer; your sins are forgiven you"** also said, **"Go and sin no more."** Yes, God can turn Satan's temptations into benefit, as He did with Job. God can also "overrule" Satan when temptation is successful and bring good from it, as He did with Peter. *But the more we live, the more we learn, and the more we know - the more a child of God absolutely dreads sin and temptation!*

The Believer who loves God deeply distrusts himself, dreads sin, and therefore prays, **"Do not lead us into temptation."** He prays, "Do not lead us where there are snares and strong enemies, for we are weak." Solomon, speaking of the immoral woman, said, **"Remove your way far from her, and do not go near the door of her house"** (see Proverbs 5:8). As children of God, we do not offer up this petition sincerely, unless we *spiritually discern* and then *avoid,* the dangerous borderlines.

Twice this petition uses the word "us" rather than "me." The entire family of God is in danger of temptation! Moving from childhood to youth, from youth to adulthood, or from adulthood to old age does not eliminate temptation to sin. There is no pause in the battle; the road remains narrow. Therefore when you pray for your Brothers and Sisters in Christ, come to their *rescue* instead of considering their guilt. Regard them with sympathy, as you should wish to be regarded – as a wounded soldier lying on the battlefield. It is *our common enemy* who has injured them.

Yet Satan is not *your* enemy as much as he is *God's* enemy. Therefore, when the devil tempts you to sin, it is your Father's honor he attacks. Pray that you will regard temptation as an opportunity to defend God's honor, instead of an opportunity to gain fleshly satisfaction.

"'That they all may be one, as You, Father, are in Me, and I in You;
that they also may be one in Us, that the world may believe that
You sent Me'" John 17:21

The challenge of Jesus' prayer is inescapable because the *local congrega-tion* is where **"the world"** most immediately encounters the Church. Relationships within the local church are to be such that the watching world will come to recognize that, **"God so loved the world that He gave His only begotten Son."** Relationships between church members are to be a persuasive reflection of the mutually supportive, completely loyal, and eternally accepting love of the Father and the Son.

Whether these relationships are between men with women, young with mature, laity with clergy, rich with poor, socially upper with socially lower, leadership with membership, skin of this color with skin of that color, new converts with established members – and whatever other polarities may exist within the fellowship – Jesus is praying for a supernatural unity among them that is so genuine **"that the world may believe"** that God sent Him.

But in addition to the "challenge" of Jesus' prayer, there is *encourage-ment.* We are encouraged that we, as Believers, do not have to "create" this amazing unity! All of our attempts to create it have failed miserably. Thankfully, this unity for which Jesus prays is a reality which *God Himself* gives. Therefore, *our* duty is to give authentic expression to that which God has already worked in our midst. Our churches are *already* one in God. We need to allow that supernatural unity to find expression both *in* the local church and *between* the churches.

And so despite all appearances, the church is one and will be one. Yes, we still must prayerfully work at the *expression* of that unity, but at least we know that there is no reason to despair when we see the spiritual health and condition of congregations across our land. *Jesus has prayed for this unity!*

When you pray in agreement with Jesus for this supernatural unity, you are praying with a kingdom focus. Jesus taught you to pray, **"Your king-dom come. Your will be done on earth as it is in heaven."** Take time to pray now with a desire to see *His* unity expressed in your church.

November 4

"And do not lead us into temptation, but deliver us from the evil one"
Matthew 6:13

God has always led His people into certain circumstances and sur-roundings. *"Do not lead us into temptation"* is a request that no hostile attack be made upon that course of life that is pleasing to God for you. It is a petition that your path today will not involve you in any moral or spiritual danger and that you will not come under the influence of people who do not know God or who do things contrary to His holy will for your life. *You do not want to be overcome by temptation and drawn into sin!*

2 Peter 2:9 says, *"The Lord knows how to deliver the godly out of temptations."* And when He considers it wise *not* to deliver, even then, He is gracious not to leave you. Temptation has two scenarios. One scenario is when you are given an occasion to show your fidelity. This is similar to when *"God tested Abraham"* (see Genesis 22:1) or to when He tested the children of Israel in order to do them good (see Deuteronomy 8:16).

The other scenario of temptation is when the devil tempts you to sin against God, with the intent to corrupt or defile. This is what took place when the devil *"tempted"* Jesus in the wilderness (see Matthew 4:1). When James writes, *"God cannot be tempted by evil, nor does He Himself tempt anyone,"* the Apostle is referring to this second scenario. Actually, all trial and temptation may be shrunk from, even when you understand that the result could be good.

What, then, is the lesson here? When you pray this petition, and you should pray it often, you are asking for safety and defense in *all* dangers – that they may not *become* temptations to you. While this petition will not always be granted, it is still the cry of your heart, because you understand your personal weakness against the powers of evil. Cultivate the mind of Jesus, so that in all circumstances, you will say with Him, *"Nevertheless, not as I will, but as You will"* (see Matthew 26:39).

Pray those very words now.

> *"'That they all may be one, as You, Father, are in Me, and I in You;*
> *that they also may be one in Us, that the world may believe that*
> *You sent Me'" John 17:21*

"*That the world may believe that You sent Me*" refers to the fruit which is to follow from the spiritual unity just mentioned; Christ's Word is to break forth more and more and be accepted in the world as God's Word. The greater *our* oneness in the Word, the greater our victories in the world. The world is still the object of Jesus' love, and His saving efforts still extend to it by the Church bearing His Word. It makes a great difference how the Church *behaves* in bringing the Word to men. The saving impact of the Word brought to men by the Church is *reduced*, when great parts of the Church "pervert" parts of the Word.

Additionally, there is fruit when the world is convinced of the intensity of the Father's *love*. The world will be convinced of Divine love through love from Believers. The perfect unity of Believers will produce this realization. The lost world cannot see God, but they can see Christians. What the world sees in us, is what they will believe about God. If they see love and unity among Believers, they will believe that God is love. Just as the Church's lack of unity is a huge stumbling block to non-Christians, so will her unity be the chief argument for the Divine character of Christ's mission.

Therefore, some would conclude that the only "Bible" that the world reads is *the character of Christians.* If that is true, we have the explanation why we are not seeing more baptisms than we are seeing throughout the world. To the Church today, unity is more of a "breath of fresh air," a luxury, a convenience – than it is a *witness* to a lost world. *We want unity for the benefit it is to ourselves, more than we want it for the benefit it is to "the world!"*

May God forgive us for our divisions! May God help us to remember what is written, **"By this all will know that you are My disciples, if you have love for one another."** May this be your prayer today.

November 6

"And do not lead us into temptation, but deliver us from the evil one'"
Matthew 6:13

We are still short of enjoying the *security* of that home not made with human hands. And when we look forward and see what lies between that home and us, we are reminded that sin has not only stained but has poisoned us; the sense of our weakness grows, as we reach the realization that we cannot allow evil to have its way with us.

We have been not only wearied but weakened by our sin. Jesus says to us what He said to the adulteress, **"Go and sin no more,"** but that word "go" launches us into a bleak and dangerous world. Such possibilities of disaster and hurt; such likelihood of utter ruin is out there ahead! The appetite that is in us for evil finds food in unexpected and unlikely places, for the world is still pressing in its offers of easy help to sin. Our flesh still clamors to be satisfied in the world's way.

In addition to sinning deliberately, we have continued to sin through ignorance, weakness, and habit. We fear being placed again and again in these predicaments, and so we pray, **"Do not lead us into temptation, but deliver us from the evil one."** Some Believers see this as two distinct petitions rather than one (making seven petitions rather than six in the Model Prayer), but "temptation" and "evil" are too closely joined together to separate them.

Let's be clear about *what we are asking* when we pray this petition. Just as fire must have fuel (must be fed and active in order to be living), so the life of evil must be fed in order to remain alive. When we pray this petition, then, we are asking that God would not permit the "nourishment" suitable to our fleshly and natural desires. We are asking Him to order our circumstances, that we may have the least possible temptation to sin.

Loving Him with all of your heart, combined with this acute awareness of what sin can accomplish, leads you to make this request! Pray this petition because you need to take precaution against yourself.

"And the glory which You gave Me I have given them, that they may be one just as We are one.'" John 17:22

What is *"the glory"* that Jesus is praying about? The glory of God is His nature, what He is – pure, selfless *love*. Romans 5:8 says, **"But God demonstrates His own love toward us, in that while we were still sinners, Christ died for us."** This is the "glory" that the Father gives to the Son and that the Son gives to us, that we too, may be one, as the Father and the Son are One.

The grammar in Jesus' prayer literally reads, "And I the glory," with an emphasis on the word, "I." It is the glory of the Incarnate Word, which He *acquired* as the reward for His perfect work here on earth. Isaiah said, **"Therefore I will divide Him a portion with the great, and He shall divide the spoil with the strong, because He poured out His soul unto death."** Christ's glory is His eternal Sonship, and believers in Him have the privilege of becoming sons of God. **"The Spirit Himself bears witness with our spirit that we are children of God, and if children, then heirs – heirs of God and joint heirs with Christ"** (see Romans 8:16, 17).

So absolutely *certain* is your future glorification, that Jesus refers to it as a thing already accomplished, **"I have given them."** If you are having difficulty understanding all of this, perhaps there is another way to explain it. *Your union with the Father* is the "subject" of this portion of Jesus' prayer. As He prays, Jesus is telling His Father (in your hearing) the fact that He has bestowed on you the glory given by the Father to Him, thus "qualifying" you for union and communion with the Father Himself. *As a believer in Jesus Christ, you are united to God as closely as it is possible for a creature to enjoy!* This is the *love* of God accomplished, and the *love* of God revealed to you!

There are *so* many things that God wants to reveal to you about Himself. Today, He wants you to understand that you are *forever* His child. Praise and thank Him.

November 8

"And do not lead us into temptation, but deliver us from the evil one'"
Matthew 6:13

As He did in the case of both Abraham and Job, God exposed Jesus to a very critical and precarious position where sin is easy, and holiness is difficult. It was *"by the Spirit"* that Jesus was led up into the wilderness to be tempted by the devil (see Matthew 4:1). It is noteworthy that when He gave this prayer to His disciples, Jesus had just passed through His own trial - and He remembered what it had cost Him. His holy nature was violently driven within sight of sin, and Jesus knew that if similar temptation came to the disciples, the result might well be different.

As a disciple of Jesus the Christ, you do well to pray that God will so guide your path that you may escape from those more violent and seductive temptations. If given the choice, you would rather avoid the tougher temptations altogether, than to take your chances at overcoming them. Perhaps within your occupation or profession, there is some temptation that seems to conspire with some weakness in your character – making sin easier for you than elsewhere. The devil has seen to it!

The harder you purpose in your heart to live to God, the more clearly you see ways you displease Him! There are certain conditions, certain circumstances, in which you discover you invariably give way to sin, despite all your resolve to be obedient. At times you become disgusted, because only a few hours ago you asked forgiveness for a particular sin, and now you have yielded to that same sin again!

Yes, loving God like you do, you will pray daily, *"Do not lead us into temptation, but deliver us from the evil one."* Because so suddenly do you find yourself in the presence of temptation, it often seems as though there is little time to resist. Therefore, your only real security is through an appeal to God for divine intervention, such as this very petition.

Pray that God, in consideration of your frailty, will order your life today that you will be exposed as little as possible to temptation.

"'I in them, and You in Me; that they may be made perfect in one, and that the world may know that You have sent Me, and have loved them as You have loved Me'" John 17:23

Today we consider the meaning of the words Jesus prayed, *"I in them."* The least as well as the greatest, the least educated as well as the most instructed, the youngest as well as the oldest – *all* are His portion forever. Jesus is *in* His Believers as the Father is *in* Him. The soul that trusts the Lord Jesus has Him working *in* the man according to Galatians 2:20, *"It is no longer I who live, but Christ lives in me."*

It is important to recognize that this unity neither requires compromising the truth nor overly sensitive diplomacy. That is because it is a unity bound up in *Him.* "I in them" explains how Believers have the glory of Jesus - how it was given them. "You in Me" explains how the Father gave this glory to Jesus – how He now has it. With Jesus dwelling in the Believers, His glory is made theirs, even as the indwelling of the Father in Jesus makes the Father's glory His.

If you are going to do anything for God, you must do it in and through Jesus, in whom God is *"well pleased."* Colossians 3:17 says, *"Whatever you do in word or deed, do all in the name of the Lord Jesus."* But Christ is not only to be the "cause" of what you do, He is also to be the "means" by which you do it, for He said, *"Without Me you can do nothing."*

Light cannot have communion with darkness. Never overlook the fact that sin still creates a distance between you and God in all of this! The truth stated in Isaiah 59:2 still remains, *"Your iniquities have separated you from your God; and your sins have hidden His face from you, so that He will not hear."* *The more you allow sin to operate in you, the more it hinders the perfection of the union Jesus prayed for in this prayer!*

Is sin in the way of *your* enjoying this divine union for which Jesus prayed? As you pray, welcome the Holy Spirit to convict your heart of sin.

November 10

"And do not lead us into temptation, but deliver us from the evil one'"
Matthew 6:13

It is easy enough to fall into temptation after praying, but to fall into temptation *without* prayer, is an inexcusable thing!

All men have a basic knowledge that there are some things that are desperately wrong about this world and that our condition here is not completely satisfying. We see no possibility of "accidental deliverance" from the effects of sin, or of sin merely "disappearing gradually." Therefore, we need to be asking God to deliver us from that evil which is *within* us. But tragically, we often work on the "branches" of evil, instead of on the root.

This petition, **"Do not lead us into temptation, but deliver us from the evil one"** must be prayed *honestly*. Have you not asked God to deliver you from evil, while a little deeper in your heart, there was this *intention to give in* should a particular temptation arise? *This petition goes to the very core of your heart and exposes your true purposes!* Just how desirous are you to be cut off from all chance of enjoying your "favorite sins?"

This is a petition that you will not even venture in the direction of danger to your heart. It expresses your desire to avoid even the "beginning stages" of temptation. It means you want to be put on guard against the "earliest movements" of sinful inclination. To "flirt" with temptation, is to have lost strength already. The devil will whisper that you have already gone too far to turn back.

Yet there is hope! We make this petition to the One who *has* delivered us, *still* delivers us, and *will* deliver us from the evil one. You will be happiest today, living truly in the joy of your salvation, if you can sincerely pray, "Today, I desire to be *far* from everything which may nourish evil within me, and I desire the presence of such things only as my Father will use it to mature me."

If you can't see the devil's tricks, you can't avoid them. Pray for spiritual discernment of any deceit the devil is using against you in temptation.

> *"'I in them, and You in Me; that they may be made perfect in one, and that the world may know that You have sent Me, and have loved them as You have loved Me'"* John 17:23

All God's creatures were created *perfect*. When God created man, He created him perfect, but when temptation came man fell because he was not **"made perfect in one."** And so divine grace was provided that there would be no *future* "fall." Made perfect in one, God's children cannot fall unless God Himself fails! Understand, that this union about which our Lord Jesus Christ prays has God for its "center," Christ and His fullness for its "supply," and the indwelling Holy Spirit for its "power." This is the only way by which we can be made perfect in one.

Jesus is praying that His people would *divinely* see eye-to-eye and face-to-face and that they would *divinely* understand the same things. This happens through personal union with the Lord so deep and so real as to be comparable with His union with the Father. If this union happened instantaneously at the moment of conversion, Believers would have a much different appearance and fewer divisions. But self-will (the result of pride), coupled with a lack of love, is unwilling that *any* person would think differently from us!

And so we are examining a union that is a *process. Jesus' prayer is for Christians to grow in grace and knowledge, and to become stable, mature, Spirit-led Believers!* If we deviate from the Word of God, or if we do not accept it as we should, we will hinder the consummation of the oneness and the fulfillment of this prayer. Knowing this, even now, Jesus continues to intercede for our completeness and our spiritual growth. The *ultimate* unity, then, must be postponed until at last, it comes to consummation.

Do you recognize the *emphasis* that Jesus places on this unity as He prays? Do you see how important this is to Him, how He reiterates it three times within just a few moments of this prayer? That very observation should lead you to make the "preservation" of this unity a priority in your life, in your church, and in your prayers.

Pray for God to show you ways in which you can preserve His unity.

November 12

"And do not lead us into temptation, but deliver us from the evil one'"
Matthew 6:13

Has man reached the point yet where he realizes the catastrophe ahead if he does not take the biblical point of view? Has he come to himself with the awareness of the truth, that there really is such a thing as a devil who can lead him around by the ear by simply showing him the right bait? Has man not yet grown tired of being the great poker player, whose dangerous gamble quickly leads to the tragedy of losing his own soul? Does pride still keep him from calculating in the factor that is "God" in his plans?

This particular petition, **"Do not lead us into temptation,"** *proves that life is dangerous!* Luther actually threw his inkwell at the devils he believed were bothering him. Before we laugh at him, it is important to remember that just because we do not "see" something – sometimes because we have not been *taught* how to see spiritually – does not prove that it does not exist.

Temptation, among other things, leads us to be torn away from our *relationship* to God. It is not about the particular "act;" it is about the relationship. In just a "moment" we decide against God. In addition, things compete with God that should never compete, such as our possessions, our reputations, and our family members (who sometimes wear the most harmless-looking sheep's clothing).

In the final analysis, there is *nothing* and *no one* the devil does not know how to use for the purpose of hindering individuals and even nations from God's care. *That* is why life is dangerous if you do not have a biblical understanding of things. *That* is why the sixth chapter of Ephesians describes the life of a Believer as a soldier's experience. We are tempted to rejoice and rest when we should be fighting a battle!

Jesus is teaching you something about **"the evil one"** by instructing you to *pray* against him. It would be much more simple and convenient if you could just "wave him off." But you are not contending against flesh and blood. Pray as He has taught you.

"'I in them, and You in Me; that they may be made perfect in one, and that the world may know that You have sent Me, and have loved them as You have loved Me'" John 17:23

There are two specific concerns about the world that Jesus has on His heart in this portion of His prayer. First, He knows that people in *"the world"* do not automatically believe that it was *God* who sent them Jesus; second, He knows that people in the world do not automatically believe that God *loves* them as He loves Jesus. These two dilemmas can only be solved, says Jesus, by the world's recognition of a divine oneness among God's people. But what *hinders* the world from seeing the truth concerning these things?

The world is hindered from knowing the truth by the temporary but permitted power of Satan and his accomplices. *The devil's influence extends to the minds, bodies, and characters of all men – including God's people!* Another factor to consider is that God is long-suffering; *"Because the sentence against an evil work is not executed speedily, therefore the heart of the sons of men is fully set in them to do evil"* (see Ecclesiastes 8:11).

Several additional hindrances can be named to this fragmented world receiving the truth. There is a sad lack among God's people to conform to the image of their heavenly Father, and divisions caused by weak Believers provide an excuse for unbelief. Sad, often painful or tragic circumstances exist in the lives of God's people, that would appear to the world as contradictory. Sometimes the world only hears the sighing and the murmurings of the struggling, and questions how a loving God can permit so much pain.

Furthermore, the Bible speaks of a *blindness* that affects the beliefs of men. 1 Corinthians 2:14 says, *"But the natural man does not receive the things of the Spirit of God, for they are foolishness to him,"* and 2 Corinthians 4:3,4 explains, *"The god of this age has blinded"* the minds of *"those who are perishing."*

Considering all of the above-named hindrances that exist to men believing the truth, you can understand why Jesus revealed the critical *role* of divine unity in His prayer. Pray that your contribution to this unity will be a testimony to the truth.

November 14

"And do not lead us into temptation, but deliver us from the evil one'"
Matthew 6:13

What comes next after forgiveness? A life of struggle and conflict against the world, the flesh, and the devil! After forgiveness comes sanctification and "working out our own salvation" as Paul put it. **"Do not lead us into temptation"** is a prayer for protection in the future. If you have truly repented of your sin, you want not only your "past" to be blotted out – you also want grace to overcome temptation in the days ahead.

You are always in danger, because of the freeness of forgiveness, of being led to think lightly of sin. In the early days of he Church, there were some who interpreted this freeness of forgiveness as a "license" to sin. Their attitude was, "What does it matter? God will forgive." They sinned (so they said), "that grace might abound." Holding that attitude, sin was seen as light, cheap, even trivial!

You should measure the enormity of sin by the sacrifice of the Cross. *It cost God the life of His only Son to deliver you from it!* Your life in Christ is not a pattern of sin and pardon, sin and pardon, sin and pardon – day after day, week after week. Rather, the pattern of your life in Christ is pardon, sanctification, and holiness. You are to obey and live out the words, **"Go and sin no more."**

And so He has taught you to pray for pity on your weakness. You are to cry to God that He will not permit the world to overcome you, dragging you down once again to sin. Admit it – you are very prone to sin, and that is why temptation is such a terrible thing. It is easier for you to do wrong than it is for you to do right. To do evil is quite easy, but to do right is difficult and requires that you swim against the current.

A mature Believer reaches the place where he understands that he is a **"wretched man"** (see Romans 7:24). The Believer who discerns his own natural carnality is becoming a mature Christian. Pray for maturity in Christ.

> *"'I in them, and You in Me; that they may be made perfect in one, and that the world may know that You have sent Me, and have loved them as You have loved Me'"* John 17:23

Just as *love* among Believers would be a proof of their true discipleship (see John 13:35), so *oneness* would be a proof of Jesus' true Messiahship. The world will then have such a clear demonstration of God's power and grace toward His people, they will know that the One who died to make this divine union *possible* was indeed the One sent by the Father, and that they have been loved by the Father as He loves the Son. In other words, the world will know that the Father loves the Believer in the Lord Jesus Christ, even as He loves the Lord Jesus *Himself!* This being so, we should learn to depend upon our Father's love at all times and under all circumstances.

Large numbers of today's church leaders look at such things as outdated methods, overcrowded rooms, and worship styles as the barriers to effective evangelism. But Jesus, in this very prayer, reveals that the worst barrier to evangelism is the gossip, insensitivity, unjust and negative criticism, jealousy, backbiting, selfishness, and unforgiveness that accompany *disunity* among Believers. *The Gospel that has been committed to our trust is being openly contradicted and veiled by sinful relationships within the Church that has been commissioned to communicate it!*

This kind of unloving behavior must rip open the very heart of Jesus, who desires that the world be persuaded to come to Him! The heart of Jesus is as wide and broad as the heart of the God who so loved the world as to send His only Son. Jesus prays that ***"the world may know"*** (keep on knowing) who sent Him, and the *means* of answering His prayer is the mission of His people.

What an opportunity, what a moment you have right now – to praise Him and thank Him for the love He has for the world – that saw the plight of sinners like yourself, and purposed to save them (see John 3:16)! This saving love blessed you with everlasting life, and with all the divine gifts that apply to your life here on earth. Give Him praise and glory!

November 16

"Now in the morning, having risen a long while before daylight,
He went out and departed to a solitary place; and there He prayed."
Mark 1:35

W e need to talk to God about men before we talk to men about God. On this occasion we see the Savior of the world doing just that. He had a clear understanding of the Father's will for that day, *"Let us go into the next towns, that I may preach there also, because for this purpose I have come forth."* But He knew that prayer for compassion and divine discernment must *precede* the encounters ahead.

Are we guilty in the Church of Jesus Christ of neglecting to pray fervently before we set out to do the work we call ministry? Are we satisfied doing work that appears spiritual, but that lacks the *power* of God that comes from seeking His face? Are we satisfied with a "quick word of prayer" before we go forth?

The "towns" Jesus spoke of would have been smaller, village towns scattered throughout Galilee. The people in the country towns needed to hear Him, too. But there would be hindrances, thus the need for preparatory prayer. One hindrance being that the people He would be addressing would be more excited about "seeing the miracles" they had heard about, than about "receiving His teaching."

Another ongoing hindrance to His work was the presence and influence of the devil and his accomplices. Jesus would be dealing with demons and unclean spirits later that day. None of us can afford to be surprised or overtaken by the enemy. Far better to have lost some sleep for the purpose of prayer, than to have been unprepared for the manifestations of Satan's hatred for the work of God's kingdom.

Not long before, the Spirit had led Jesus into the wilderness to be tempted by the devil. Jesus was prepared for Satan's temptations because He had been *praying.* This is war! We are at war for the souls of men. *And we are not prepared for any battle on any given day unless we have been praying regarding our assignment!*

Pray now, that you will be obedient and victorious − to the glory of God - in the kingdom assignments before you.

"'I in them, and You in Me; that they may be made perfect in one, and that the world may know that You have sent Me, and have loved them as You have loved Me'" John 17:23

It was the prayer of Jesus that two convictions would be awakened in *"the world."* First, the conviction that the Father had, in fact, sent the Son, and that Jesus was God's perfect Manifestation and Representative to man; and second, the conviction that God loved man as He had loved His Son. Jesus said, *"The Father Himself loves you, because you have loved Me, and have believed that I came forth from God"* (see John 16:27).

We should notice that the reason *why* He loves us is found "outside" of ourselves. We are sure that there is nothing in us that could attract the love of One so holy. *It is incredible that although we are so sinful, we should be a part of such love!* He loves us unconditionally, and for His own reasons. God's love is like Himself – *infinite!* The love of God is the Father in the midst of His Church, "singing" over His children.

God could not love us and bring honor to Himself if His *wisdom* had not found this way of loving us *in Christ* – for if God loved us for our own sakes, it would be a very imperfect love - our graces being so weak and our service so lacking. The Father's love was "demonstrated" by sending Jesus (see John 3:16), and is "proven" by the way Christians love one another.

Let this truth comfort you today – that when the world hates you, the Father loves you *"as"* He does the Son! Because God is unchangeable, you can be sure that if ever He loved you, He loves you now! *Meditate* on this! *Worship Him* for this! For if God gave Jesus, who was so dear to Him, then what can He "withhold" from you? If He had a "greater" gift for you, He would have given it!

Romans 8:32 says, *"He who did not spare His own Son, but delivered Him up for us all, how shall He not with Him also freely give us all things?"* Pray that you will believe the *intensity* of the love that has found you.

November 18

"And do not lead us into temptation, but deliver us from the evil one'"
Matthew 6:13

Still yet to be discovered are heights and depths of treasure and wisdom in the Model Prayer. Satan, **"the evil one,"** is not mentioned "by name," so as to not disrupt the calmness of the prayer. The Model Prayer is short, making it easy to learn and remember. It mentions every need associated with life and righteousness; it expresses every desire of a prayerful heart. All of the prayer petitions that you will ever bring to the Father should agree with the petitions of the Model Prayer. Through that agreement, you will both avoid error and obtain mercies.

That said, this prayer was meant to be an "aid" to disciples desiring maturity in prayer, rather than a "binding" method for approaching God. It was *not* given to become a "liturgical formula" for the Church. The words were never designed for mere repetition, although they have been prayed by many a soldier in war. This Prayer is only a "vehicle" – a *model* - of the prayer life, not the prayer life itself.

By sanctification, the filling of the Spirit, and maturity in spiritual understanding, you should, by God's marvelous grace, be able to pray as Jesus prayed! Yet, even the most "advanced" Believer still finds relief and rest, by falling back on these divine words. Today, we are examining the final petition of the prayer.

"Evil" is everything that disturbs your communion with God. Unfortunately, "sin" is not a visitor; it is an *inmate*, a persistent enemy that has established itself. **"Evil is present with me,"** confessed Paul. No Believer is immune to **"temptation,"** which is why Paul also warned, **"Let him who thinks he stands take heed lest he fall."**

When you ask God to **"deliver"** you from Satan and his accomplices, you are asking Him to "snatch you up" from *all forms* of evil, as a mother snatches up her child from the approach of an angry dog. Whether from disease or hatred, terrorism or hypocrisy – from *all* of it we pray – "Good and merciful Father, *deliver* us!"

Using your own words, pray in agreement with the Model Prayer.

"'Father, I desire that they also whom You gave Me may be with Me where I am, that they may behold My glory which You have given Me; for You loved Me before the foundation of the world.'" John 17:24

This portion of Jesus' prayer has been called, "the most remarkable prayer ever prayed." Without a doubt, it is quite unlike any prayer that *we* have the liberty to pray! For all of our prayers are but variations on the theme, "Not my will, but Yours, be done." Jesus seems to pass beyond the realm of prayer with these words because His will is identical with the Father's will. Therefore, here, Jesus prays, *"I desire,"* or, more accurately translated, "I will."

Christ is not "demanding" anything; Jesus came to execute His Father's will, so He is not irreverently insisting that the Father execute His will. The Father and the Son are in perfect accord. As Believers, we must remember that to **"come boldly to the throne of grace"** does not mean to "order God around." *Notice the sweet spirit with which Jesus prays – here and always!*

Later that very night in the Garden, Jesus prayed, **"Not My will, but Yours, be done."** But here, there is no such reservation in His prayer, because He *knows* that the Father wills what He wills – that those who have been given to Him shall be with Him. And He adds the reason *why* He wills to have them with Him – that they may behold His glory with the eyes of the *spiritual body* that they did not have there and then. It is the final bliss of His disciples – forever in the heaven of His own unveiled presence!

The verb included in the phrase, "they also whom You gave Me," refers to a past act with a continuous present effect. God gave all Believers of all ages to Jesus, and they are His, even if they are as yet unborn. Dear reader, if this is His will, who can doubt that it will be accomplished?

When you die, you might have a sweet meditation using these very words of Jesus, "Father, I desire that they also whom You gave Me may be with me where I am." Pray a prayer of thanksgiving, that this desire of Jesus includes you who have trusted Him.

November 20

"'For Yours is the kingdom and the power and the glory forever.'"
Matthew 6:13

There is a sense in which praying the petitions of the Model Prayer causes us to focus on our desperate need for help, but there is also the need to know that our prayer is not in vain. We reach the end of the prayer and find this assurance from the little word **"for."** It is *because* **"the kingdom and the power and the glory"** belongs to *God*, that we can pray this prayer with confidence. It is because of the truth found in these final words of the Model Prayer, that "the future" will not turn out to be vague, unpredictable, and unverifiable.

It can also be said, that this doxology is an "argument." When we pray that little word "for," we plant our foot and take our stand! We argue, "Our sure and only hope is in *God*, in His character, in His name, and in His promise. **"Yours"** is the kingdom, and *altogether* Yours; it is certainly not ours. *"You"* prepared it from all eternity. And You made Your own Son the king. And that is why all history and all future has meaning.

Because affairs and behavior throughout the world appear to be far from God, we are tempted to believe that He is remote from it; we suppose that He is not in any way affecting the nations and their rulers and their politics. The temptation is to think that the kingdom belongs only to blind fate or chance, or maybe that the kingdom is our own. This is an evil and demonic lie.

We belong to God's "kingdom," and Jesus is our King. It is by God's "power" that we live on earth and stand free from Satan's control. And it is for the furtherance of God's "glory," that all has been done for us, and that all of the petitions of the Model Prayer are made.

The devil enjoys working in an atmosphere of uncertainty. Don't give him that opportunity. *The most important matters of life are things about which you can be absolutely certain!* Speak the promises of God as you pray.

> *"'Father, I desire that they also whom You gave Me may be with Me where I am, that they may behold My glory which You have given Me; for You loved Me before the foundation of the world.'"* John 17:24

Each time that a Believer's soul leaves this earth and enters heaven, it is an answer to Jesus' prayer. Someone once said, "Many times Jesus and His people *pull against* one another in prayer. You intercede in prayer for the sick saying, 'Father, I will that my Brother remain with me where *I* am;' while Christ prays, **'Father, I desire that they also whom You gave Me may be with Me where I am.'"** Thus you are at cross-purposes with your Lord, for the Brother cannot be with Christ in heaven and on earth with you, too; the soul cannot be in both places.

This prayer "conflict" happens more often than you may think! Thousands upon thousands of churches have a mid-week prayer service, in which the primary focus of the praying is for the physically sick saints to stay alive. It is false and presumptuous to believe that, just because God has the *power* to heal, He will heal *everyone* who experiences an illness. When our friends and loved ones become ill, it is right to pray for them. But we must pray *rightly!* We must pray, "Father, not my will, but Yours be done," even when it is very difficult to do so.

There have been, and will continue to be occasions when, although you do not understand it at the time, it pleases Jesus to call people home to be with Him in heaven when you are not ready to "let them go." Jesus understands what it means to love someone. *But you would give up your prayer for your Brother's life if you realized that Jesus is praying in the opposite direction!* You would instead pray, "Lord, please take him! By faith we let him go, that he might receive his *permanent* healing!" Remember, permanent healings are not a rationalization for times when we do not receive what we have asked; God knows *exactly* what He is doing.

What, then, shall we say? *Praise God* for hearing the prayer of our Lord Jesus, and for hearing *your* prayers, as you desire His will over your own.

November 22

"'For Yours is the kingdom and the power and the glory forever.'"
Matthew 6:13

"Power"** belongs to God. He is able to do anything that pleases Him. *We have only to think of the incarnation or of the resurrection to be in total awe of His incredible power!* But if "might" did not exist in perfect harmony with the "attributes" of God such as wisdom, grace, mercy, and holiness, then "power" would just be overwhelming and crushing.

It is by God's power that we can even live on earth and can stand free from the clutch of Satan and his accomplices. God is the cause (either by His power or His permission) of all *changes* – physical, circumstantial, or otherwise.

The end, the purpose of all His works and ways, is God's **"glory."** When we consider the glory of God, we must do so differently than when we consider the glory of man. Man seeks glory because he is selfish; God, on the other hand, is *love* – and His glory is the manifestation of Himself. Man seeks glory in order to make himself the center of attention; God, by contrast, *actually is* the only center of life and light.

For His own glory, God will save, bless, and sanctify all who call upon His name. It is for the *furtherance* of God's glory that we make all these six petitions in the Model Prayer. Throughout the Bible, it is clear that all things are for the greater glory of God. When we say that He does all things for His glory, we mean that He does all things so that we may know His character and know Him as He is, **"That I am the Lord, exercising lovingkindness, judgment, and righteousness in the earth"** (see Jeremiah 9:24).

We pray this benediction from the desire for the world to be guided right and kept safe, for whatever is true and good to rule. In spite of all evil, there is Hope invincible! Because He is our Father, He will deliver us! He will found His universal kingdom and receive the glory due His name!

Rejoice as you pray, for your Father is still in control.

*"Jesus took bread, blessed and broke it ...
then He took the cup, and gave thanks."* Matthew 26:26, 27

Jesus expressed thanksgiving to God during the meal and so the Supper has been called the Eucharist, which is the form of the language He used both on private occasions and on this occasion. In the Jewish tradition, a giving of thanks preceded each individual "course" of the meal. Some churches today depart from this example of how Christ administered the Supper, in that they pronounce only one prayer at the beginning of the meal with a reference to both the bread and the cup.

In Jesus' day, the two traditional prayers offered prior to the distribution of unleavened bread were, "Blessed be thou, O Lord, our God, King of the Universe, who bringest forth from the earth" or, "Blessed art thou, our Father in heaven, who givest us to-day the bread necessary for us." The blessing over the cup was, "Blessed art thou, O Lord, our God, King of the Universe, who hast created the fruit of the vine."

None of the four accounts of the Supper provide the actual words of the *prayer* of blessing and thanksgiving that Jesus spoke over the bread and wine. It is entirely possible that when Jesus prayed at the Supper, He was mindful that the disciples needed to be enlightened to intelligently receive the bread and cup with regard for what each element was to convey. Therefore, the Lord may have departed from (or added to) the traditional prayers mentioned above.

The Gospels tell us that Christ had a thankful heart. *Notice that when all the forces of hell were gathered together to destroy Him, still - Jesus gave thanks!* It is more appropriate to "give thanks" than to "say grace." Jesus was not speaking a blessing on the elements themselves – He gave thanks for them. We should do as He did, and acknowledge the goodness of God through praise and thanksgiving at mealtime and *all* times. Often we are "in a hurry" when we pray, and being grateful does not cross our minds.

1 Thessalonians 5:18 says, *"In everything give thanks."* As you prepare to pray, have a *thankful* heart.

November 24

"He took the seven loaves and gave thanks ... they also had a few small fish; and having blessed them. " Mark 8:6, 7

There are numerous accounts in Scripture where Jesus "said grace" before meals. In this case, when Jesus *"gave thanks"* for the loaves and then *"blessed"* the fish, He was pronouncing the prayer that was usual at a meal – He said grace. If Jesus' words had varied between the two prayers, it is likely Mark would have called attention to it.

Thanksgiving was always connected to meals. The Talmud (which means "to study, to learn") is the written story in Hebrew and Aramaic of biblical interpretation, of the making of bylaws, and of wise counsel covering a period of almost one thousand years. In Jewish eyes, it ranks second only to the Hebrew Scriptures as a religious possession. It is in the Talmud that we find the statement, "He that enjoys anything without an act of thanksgiving is as one that robs the Almighty."

Today, children are still taught to say their prayers at bedtime and to say grace at meals. While young children may not fully understand *why* they are asked to say these two prayers, it is an important exercise for them in learning to talk to God. There is a time to pause and to remember that God is good and that He is the giver of all good things.

It is safe to suppose that all of us, at one time or another, have started eating a meal without remembering to thank God. Sometimes we forget to say grace because we feel very hungry and we are in a hurry to satisfy that need. Sometimes we are distracted and just begin to eat. Sometimes we remember to pray after we have started eating. Sometimes we just forget. It does not appear that Jesus ever failed to pause and give thanks before a meal.

Pausing to give thanks before a meal follows Jesus' example, and therefore is important. *It demonstrates the attitude of the heart!* The person who is truly grateful to God for providing exceedingly more than he could ever deserve is more likely to understand the reason for "saying grace." Pray today with a grateful heart.

"In that hour, Jesus rejoiced in the Spirit and said, 'I thank You, Father, Lord of heaven and earth.'" Luke 10:21

"*In that hour*" refers to when Jesus had told the Seventy in what to rejoice (see Luke 10:17-20). ***"The Spirit"*** had already been poured out upon Jesus (see Luke 4:18), and it was the same Holy Spirit that prompted this outburst of praise.

"*Jesus rejoiced.*" God being present is the source of true joy, and Jesus was always aware of His Father's presence. He was rejoicing here, over the disciples' service. He was rejoicing over the vision of continuing and completing the Father's work – that this first success of the disciples was "only the beginning" of a triumphant campaign over the forces of evil and sin. He was rejoicing over the fact that, even though there are setbacks, God is good, and He is in control. Therefore, whether in success or in setback, we rejoice!

"*I thank You, Father*" teaches us to pray rejoicing whenever we see the powers of Satan and his accomplices fall by the power of God. We should remember to thank Him for every such victory – whether large or small, whether in our circumstances or in the circumstances of others – for He alone is worthy of all praise and glory! Actually, this word means much more than just to "thank." There is an *intensification* present, that says more accurately, "I openly confess (or acknowledge) *to your honor.*"

After an angel visited Mary and told her she would be the mother of the Messiah, **"*Mary said: 'My soul magnifies the Lord, and my spirit has rejoiced in God my Savior. For He has regarded the lowly state of His maidservant.'*"** *So it is, and so shall it ever be; there is rejoicing when the pure in heart come into contact with the living God!* Therefore, you may rejoice in your contact with Him through His Holy Word, you may rejoice in your contact with Him through worship, and you may rejoice in your contact with Him through prayer.

Are you overwhelmed by the incredible goodness of God today? Follow the example of Jesus shown here, by giving way to prayerful thanksgiving, praise, and rejoicing in the Spirit.

November 26

Certain Bible passages receive more attention than others, and perhaps that is inevitable. This occasion, this moment in the life of our Lord, may be worthy of more attention than it has received. For here we are considering a "turning point" that affected eternity.

What a terrible temptation to experience, and what a choice for the Savior of the world to make! Jesus was free at this moment to withdraw from the path He knew would lead to a dreadful death. He considered the possibilities. Jesus then put His emotions into the form of a question to Himself, as to what He should do. The answer came quickly, a supreme moment of temptation overcome. He had come to suffer, and He was resolved to suffer. The hour had come that would crown all of His previous life and work.

Jesus' human nature was, understandably, reluctant to endure the agony of Golgotha. But let's take a moment now to consider a most horrible thought: What if Jesus had prayed to be delivered from that hour – to be brought safely out of the conflict? Such a prayer for deliverance, if answered, would have meant *the ruin of the world!* So much was at stake!

But Jesus wanted His Father to be recognized as a lover of sinners. **"For God so loved the world that He gave His only begotten Son."** That would be the point of, the need for, suffering on the Cross. That is why He prayed that His Father's name would be *glorified*. Continuing forward would ensure that, **"The ruler of this world"** would be deposed from his present ascendancy by the perfect obedience of Jesus at Calvary, thus giving God all glory and honor forever!

How easy it is for us to go from day to day, business as usual, and not even give a thought to the things we are considering here! And yet, this is *everything!* This is the greatest story, as well as the greatest outcome.

Pray a prayer of thanksgiving that this choice Jesus made, meant that you could be forgiven and have eternal life.

"'Father, I desire that they also whom You gave Me may be with Me where I am, that they may behold My glory which You have given Me; for You loved Me before the foundation of the world.'" John 17:24

Clearly, Jesus is expressing a very strong desire that His disciples be *with Him where He is.* He had expressed this desire previously, when He said to them, **"I go to prepare a place for you. And if I go and prepare a place for you, I will come again and receive you to Myself; that where I am, there you may be also"** (see John 14:2, 3). Jesus promised the dying thief, **"Today you will be with Me in Paradise."** The Head and the members must be together.

It is the Believer's heaven on earth to see (through a glass darkly) and enjoy (through a heart of faith) even a little of Jesus and have Him with us in spirit. Christ is "with us" now, but *then* we will be "with Him!" Paul said, **"Having a desire to depart and be with Christ, which is far better"** (see Philippians 1:23). Let us long to be with Him – whether by communing with Him in the present or by communing with Him in heaven!

Those of you who have not believed in Jesus need to understand that the Son of God came down to *where you are!* Jesus left heaven and came to this world, and now He invites you to be among those who will come to be with Him *where He is,* to claim His precious blood as the ground of your acceptance. Why continue to reject Him? Why continue to say, **"Go away for now; when I have a convenient time I will call for you?"**

We are listening here to His tender heart; **"with Me"** *is the language of love!* Our Lord gazes to the future as He prays, anticipating the embrace of His beloved bride in the glory that is to be. He spans the centuries with His piercing eye, and catches a glimpse of *you!* And understanding your needs lifts up His voice in earnest petition and prays that, ultimately, you might be with Him where He is.

Pray that your love for Him will deepen as you reflect on the meaning of this prayer.

November 28

"'For Yours is the kingdom and the power and the glory forever.'"
Matthew 6:13

"**Forever**" is an incredible word! Whenever we use that word in prayer, we find peace and rest in the infinite power, wisdom, and love of our Father in heaven. "Forever" reminds us of the truth that in hell, one moment is as a thousand years; but in heaven, a thousand years are as one moment.

Moses declared, *"From everlasting to everlasting, You are God"* (see Psalm 90:2). Only God can say, *"I am God, and there is no other; I am God, and there is none like Me, declaring the end from the beginning, and from ancient times things that are not yet done"* (see Isaiah 46:9, 10). His attributes, His perfections, are "forever." Our hope is grounded upon the *character* of Him to whom we pray.

This doxology of praise at the conclusion of the Model Prayer is the result of *attempting* to contemplate the magnificence of God. He is able to do far more abundantly than all that we ask or think. To praise God means to see things from the perspective of their end, which is why Paul and Silas after they received a severe beating could sing midnight praises to God (see Acts 16:25). *Prayer and praise should always go together!*

Has Jesus done *less* for you than what He did for the man with the unclean spirit who came out of the tombs? If not, then consider what Christ said to that man after setting him free, *"Go home to your friends, and tell them what great things the Lord has done for you, and how He has had compassion on you"* (see Mark 5:19, 20). "Go ... and tell!" Tell them what Jesus has done for you, and how He has had compassion on you!

Pause now to consider some wonderful things God has done for you. Praise Him for each of those things in prayer. Then listen for the Holy Spirit to confirm to you the names of specific people who need to hear about the great things the Lord has done for you. Now make the *commitment* to go and tell.

"'Father, I desire that they also whom You gave Me may be with Me where I am, that they may behold My glory which You have given Me; for You loved Me before the foundation of the world.'" John 17:24

The subject of heaven is not brought up suddenly in this prayer. The entire prayer has led up to it, beginning with the theme of the glory of the Father and of the Son. Then Christ prayed regarding the necessities of the Church – for preservation, for sanctification, for unity – and all for a divine influence upon the world. Only now, near the completion of His prayer, are we hearing Jesus mention heaven, that they *"may be with Me where I am."* The Lord's *work here*, before the Lord's *joy there*.

This will, this desire of Jesus expressed here, lifts the whole Church from earth to heaven, from the lowliness here below, to the exaltation above. Heaven will complete the process of revelation begun by Christ on earth. Examining the text, in the phrase, *"that they may behold,"* the stress is on the verb – "to gaze upon as a spectator." *It refers to looking at objects that are extraordinary!*

In heaven, Believers will see with unspeakable delight, all the wonders of the glory of Jesus. Furthermore, the present tense indicates *continuous* beholding of all of His attributes. Only glorified eyes can behold in blessedness the glory of the exalted Redeemer, so our own glorification also takes place.

Although we know that heaven is *an actual place ("I go to prepare a place for you")*, its location is unknown, and it is useless to speculate about the location of a place "large enough" where *all* Believers of *all* time can be where He is. But Scripture teaches us that Heaven is a place where Jesus and the redeemed will be, and where Christ's glory will be fully seen. If you, dear reader, know Jesus Christ, then there is only one possible prospect that can make you forever content – to be *with Him*, to be so with Him as to see Him, as to behold His glory. Oh, the hope of an endless Heaven!

As you rejoice over these truths, pray for the ability to let go of the things of this world in exchange for the opportunity to gaze forever at Jesus.

November 30

"'For Yours is the kingdom and the power and the glory forever. Amen.'"
Matthew 6:13

It seems that this doxology of praise in the Model Prayer was "added" when the prayer came to be used in the church and that it was inserted into copies of Matthew's Gospel, with some variations. A doxology was used when the Model Prayer began to be included in public worship as a liturgy to be recited or chanted. These words do not appear in the similar prayer given on another occasion and recorded in Luke 11:1-4. Without question, the benediction fits the prayer well, even though it does not appear in the oldest and best Greek manuscripts.

Therefore, it is safe to say that it is "likely" that this benediction was *not* part of the Model Prayer as Jesus gave it. It does bring to mind 1 Chronicles 29:11, which says, **"Yours, O Lord, is the greatness, the power and the glory, the victory and the majesty; for all that is in heaven and in earth is Yours; Yours is the kingdom, O Lord, and You are exalted as head over all."**

"Amen" is the test of your *sincerity* when you pray. For example, praying **"Hallowed be Your name"** demonstrates your desire to meditate on the attributes of God; **"Your kingdom come"** demonstrates your desire to see laborers sent into the harvest; **"Give us this day our daily bread"** demonstrates your desire to be content with God's provisions; **"Forgive us our debts, as we forgive our debtors"** demonstrates your desire to love your enemies; and **"Deliver us from the evil one"** demonstrates your desire to keep yourself unspotted from the world. *Adding "Amen" to a prayer, then, expresses your willingness to be the answer to your own prayer!*

In many churches, saying "Amen" has weakened into a cue that we can open our eyes after a prayer or into encouragement for the preacher during his sermon. But in the Jewish tradition, "Amen" literally meant a vow of commitment to actually do what had been prayed, in partnership with God.

Ask the Father to reveal how you can partner with Him by "living out" the petitions of the Model Prayer.

December 1

"'Father, I desire that they also whom You gave Me may be with Me where I am, that they may behold My glory which You have given Me; for You loved Me before the foundation of the world.'" John 17:24

Heaven is a major theme of the Scriptures. It is mentioned 550 times in the Bible by that name alone. Jesus once referred to heaven as His Father's "house" (see John 14:2).

"With Me where I am" does not describe a "state of mind." Right now, Jesus is in an *actual place* called heaven! The Greek word for "place" is *"topos,"* from which we get the word "topography" – the study of places. Our Lord taught us to pray, ***"Your kingdom come, Your will be done on earth as it is in heaven."*** Both earth and heaven are real, literal, physical places.

The only information we have about heaven is in the Bible. Heaven is not necessarily "up" in terms of location from the earth, although the Bible says that the earth is God's footstool. Revelation 21 and 22 give the measurements of the Holy City in cubits. Obviously, we could not "measure" heaven unless it was an actual place. If we could get a *full* appreciation of what heaven is, we Believers would be very homesick! But to Jesus, heaven is simply where His Father has His *home.*

Home is a place where love is supreme. It is the place where you grew up as a boy or as a girl, playing around the yard with siblings and neighbor children, sitting around the fireside on a wintry night with Mom and Dad. As far as you are concerned, there are things about that old home place that are not true about any other spot on earth.

The most marvelous thought that can occupy the mind of man is heaven, and how to go there. So, the real question, the most important matter is not, that a "place" has been prepared for you, but *are you prepared* for that place? Are you going to heaven? If you are a Believer, then heaven is *your* home. And if, by the pure unmerited grace of God, heaven is your destination, do you ever *long* for it? *Would you rather be here, or there?*

Pray for a deeper longing to be home with Jesus.

December 2

"'For Yours is the kingdom and the power and the glory forever. Amen.'"
Matthew 6:13

Martin Luther once said, "As your Amen is, so has been your prayer." To be sure, **"Amen"** is a word frequently used but without very much thought. Today we will focus on the meaning and the use of this word. May we learn to say, "Amen," rightly.

The root meaning of this word has to do with "confirmation" and "support." Literally, "Amen" means, "So be it! So may it be! So shall it be! What I just heard is *trustworthy* and *sure!* I recognize the truth!"

The psalm of praise which Asaph and his brethren sang when the ark of God was brought from Obed-Edom, concluded with these words, **"Blessed be the Lord God of Israel from everlasting to everlasting! And all the people said, 'Amen!' and praised the Lord"** (see 1 Chronicles 16:36). David concludes a song of praise with the words, **"And let all the people say, 'Amen'"** (see Psalm 106:48). And when Ezra the scribe gathered the people together and opened the Book of the Law and blessed the Lord, everyone stood up and answered, **"'Amen, Amen!' while lifting up their hands"** (see Nehemiah 8:3-6).

Jesus is "the Amen of God." All of God's thoughts and purposes of peace concerning us are fulfilled in Christ. And all of our desires and longings toward God, find their fulfillment in Jesus. As the Amen of God, Jesus Christ reveals to us the God of truth and the truth of God. We *begin* our prayer by lifting up our hearts to the Father in heaven, and we *conclude* our prayer by "sealing" our petitions with Jesus.

Notice that when the disciples asked Jesus to teach them to pray (see Luke 11:1), He gave them "petitions" instead of "rules." The disciples (like us) were not as ignorant about "how" to pray, as they were about "what to pray for." *The lesson here is that praying in Jesus' name, the Amen of God, is impossible without self-examination, reflection, and the aid of the Holy Spirit!*

Do not be in a hurry as you begin to pray. Seal your petitions by saying, "Amen."

> *"'Father, I desire that they also whom You gave Me may be with Me where I am, that they may behold My glory which You have given Me; for You loved Me before the foundation of the world.'"* John 17:24

Jesus prayed, *"I desire that they ... may be with Me where I am."* It is amazing to hear Christ pray these words, that He *must* have us – frail, finite creatures, once mortals and rebels at that – there *with Him* in order to satisfy His heart! Yes, He wants *us*, everlastingly close to Him, where He is. He desires *our* everlasting fellowship. Such is the *love* of Jesus, that He finds it *necessary* for us to be with Him there in heaven forever! We cannot understand it, we do not deserve it, but we can believe it.

By making sure His disciples heard this prayer, Jesus is letting us understand that we will be perfectly satisfied being with Him and beholding Him. Praise and thank Him for this wonderful request! Thank God for the assurance of a heaven! For it is written, *"Today you will be with Me in Paradise" Lord Jesus, receive my spirit;"* and *"To depart and be with Christ."*

Thank God that to *"behold"* Jesus' glory means both a *mental* beholding and a *visual* beholding. There will be a glorified mind as well as a glorified eye that beholds Him. The mind must be satisfied in heaven, or else we cannot be happy. The mind must be satisfied with the sight of God. And so it will be the endless joy ("that they may keep on beholding") of seeing Jesus in heaven *"As He is"* (see 1 John 3:2). *Not only will our eyes see the beauty and the inhabitants, our eyes will see the glorious face of the Lamb!* Wicked men will see Christ, but they will see Him as a Judge to their terror; Believers will see Him who laid down His life for them. Our best and beloved Friend – to know Him through the Word is lovely and glorious, but oh, to *see* Him! Does that thought thrill your soul?

As you think about what the future has in store for you, lift up your heart in prayer and praise to your Master, who has given you everything for this world *and* for eternity!

December 4

"'For Yours is the kingdom and the power and the glory forever. Amen.'"
Matthew 6:13

The very last word and the very first word of the Model Prayer have great significance. Every time we sincerely pray this prayer, we pray with and for all Christians, to *"Our"* Father. Every Believer is our Brother or Sister. The body has many members – young and old, mature and immature, rich and poor. If you have trusted Jesus Christ to be your Savior, then the Holy Spirit has united you as one with many millions of people who are the Lord's.

Prayer and faith are very similar, in that prayer is your "vocal" faith. Faith puts wings to your prayers. When you pray, you must believe that God hears you; you express that faith by saying, *"Amen."* When your prayers are not simple and childlike, it is usually the result of a *weak* faith that supposes God needs more information from you, to help Him understand. *"Amen" is the expression of your confidence and expectancy that "it will be so!"*

The prayers of God's saints are "excellent" because they are prayers of faith; they express the feelings rather than the "views" of the one praying. "Amen" sees the final *fulfillment* of prayer – when Jesus, the Amen of God, will repeat what He said on the Cross, *"It is finished."* "Amen" expresses faith in His *purposes:* **"For the Lord of hosts has purposed, and who will annul it?"** (see Isaiah 14:27), and faith in His *promises:* **"For all the promises of God in Him are Yes, and in Him Amen, to the glory of God through us"** (see 2 Corinthians 1:20).

Think about the Amen of your life on earth. Said David Wilkerson, "The hardest part of faith is the last half hour." Do you want to be scrambling about during that last half hour, trying to get your thoughts together, praying frantically about business left undone with God? No, you will want to have a confidence and expectancy that everything God has said, will be so. You will want "the last half hour" to be the most *peaceful* time of your entire life.

Pray that it will be so.

December 5

> *"'Father, I desire that they also whom You gave Me may be with Me where I am, that they may behold My glory which You have given Me; for You loved Me before the foundation of the world.'"* John 17:24

Jesus prayed, *"I desire,"* meaning, "I will, I determine – that they will have fellowship with Me, in the glory of the Cross, and so in the glory that *results* from the Cross, in the ages to come." The word "glory" is used in a variety of ways throughout this prayer. Even the "boundaries" of the prayer are statements regarding the glory of God; at the opening, *"Glorify Your Son, that Your Son also may glorify You,"* and toward the closing, *"That they may behold My glory which You have given Me."*

Jesus often revealed the glory of God. One example is the incarnation, *"And the Word became flesh and dwelt among us, and we beheld His glory, the glory as of the only begotten of the Father, full of grace and truth"* (see John 1:14). Another example is His miracles and signs, which, according to John 2:11, *"manifested His glory."* And another example is the crucifixion, Jesus praying beforehand, *"Father, glorify Your name"* (see John 12:28).

What is the application? As a Believer, everything that God permits to happen in your life can and should be used for *His glory*. If you live your life for the glory of God, *it will be costly*. But it will be much more costly *not* to. The command is clear, *"Whether you eat or drink, or whatever you do, do all to the glory of God"* (see 1 Corinthians 10:31). We do all things for "God's glory," when the *excellence* of God's many glorious attributes shines forth by our actions, so that men may see His excellence.

You are to behave in a manner that gives *"no offense."* You should not act in a foolish, rude, or inconsiderate manner that places a stumbling block in someone's path in regard to Christ and to the Gospel. People may "take" offense, and you cannot avoid that. But you are not to "give" offense. *No action of yours should prevent a Christian from "drawing nearer" to Jesus, or an unbeliever from "coming" to Him!*

Pray that everything you do will be to the glory of God.

December 6

"For Yours is the kingdom and the power and the glory forever. Amen."
Matthew 6:13

Much of the misery and ruin of life comes to us because we refuse to take to heart the most obvious and every-day truths. It is a tragedy that so many Believers hold very superficial views about time and eternity! Do we expect too much, that men would at least be *serious* about their short journey on this earth, and do justly, and love mercy, and walk humbly with their God?

Instead, we occupy ourselves like children chasing bubbles. Life is but a fading flower; we are reminded of that truth from Scripture, nature, and life. We see death in nature – when the leaf falls, and when the flower fades. We see death in the living of life – when there are vacant chairs in our homes during the holidays, and when wrinkles begin to appear on faces. Yet only occasionally do we pay attention to this fact that life on earth is passing us. And even worse, we lose our vision of *why* we are here.

And so today, please carefully consider this word, **"forever."** If you worship a "forever God," then you are yourself, forever. All of your interests are, therefore, lifted up into the great future. Consequently, when you pray this prayer, it is not merely for the "present" that you pray. The kingdom that you seek to promote is forever, and the will that you wish to be done is forever. *When you pray in the manner of the Model Prayer, all things that you pray about are "linked to" the forever!*

Death is near all of us – it is just that no one of us knows *how* near. But near it is, even to those to whom it seems furthest. Yet even the reality of death cannot weaken the wings of fervent prayer to a forever God. Today comes a call to awaken spiritually!

"Gray hairs are here and there on him, yet he does not know it" (see Hosea 7:9). The danger is not in *having* spiritual gray hair; the danger is in *not seeing* the gray hair!

Pray for spiritual awakening in your heart.

"'O righteous Father! The world has not known You, but I have known You; and these have known that You sent Me.'" John 17:25

As He comes to the end of this remarkable prayer, Christ addresses His Father as, **"*righteous.*"** Throughout Scripture, "titles" of God are suited to the matter at hand. "Righteous" in a *legal* sense, means that God rewards men according to the merit of their actions. And "righteous" in an *evangelical* sense, means that God judges men according to what they have received rather than what they have done.

God is just, though men remain in blindness. Yet the truth is, God has done enough to reveal Himself; the lost have more means to find Him than they use well, and the same is true of the carnal Christians within the Church. The spiritually blind cannot endure a truthful guide. Isaiah 65:2 declares, **"I have stretched out My hands all day long to a rebellious people, who walk in a way that is not good, according to their own thoughts."** It is evil "that we do not know;" it is especially evil "that we desire *not* to know."

Jesus is declaring, "My Father is absolutely in the right, and is wholly kind. I am not free to tell you about His *reasons* yet, but I know Him perfectly, and you can rely on Him." As we listen to Jesus address His Father in this way, we listen with a deep peace. The glorious news is, when we pray, we can rely on this same righteous God, too. *Here we rest our confidence; here Christ Himself rested!*

The fact that God is righteous and just means that **"He is faithful and just to forgive us our sins and to cleanse us from all unrighteousness"** (see 1 John 1:9). Why is that? Jesus has suffered in our place, and it would be injustice to Christ if God did not forgive our sins. Having declared His will that His people might be with Him where He was, He now seals and crowns that claim by an appeal to His *righteous* Father. Justice *required* that His requests should be granted.

Praising God for His righteousness and mercy, pray for an increased hatred of your sins.

December 8

"'Father, forgive them, for they do not know what they do.'"
Luke 23:34

Behold Jesus, as He is being crucified by the most heartless and cruel mob ever assembled. He had done no evil, neither had He harmed anyone. And for no other reason than for religious prejudice, malice and envy – they seized Him, put Him through a mock trial, and subjected Him to the most dishonorable and disgraceful execution known in the world. And what did Jesus do? He prayed for their forgiveness! This is so far beyond and above what mere man would do (he would place his enemies in the worst light), that we cannot explain it on any other ground than to declare the truth: "God is love."

But wait! Due to our amazement over this compassionate prayer from the Cross, we may have overlooked something. *Not only did this sinless Lover of souls pray for His enemies, He died for them!* Jesus begins to use His own Cross, that those who nailed Him to it, might be saved!

It is true of every sinner, to some degree, that he knows not what he does. Jesus was not only "aware" of but was burdened for, the spiritual needs of others. It is unimaginable that a man being crucified would pray about issues he considered trivial. With nails in His hands and feet, Christ was praying and dying for *souls*, because He came **"to seek and to save that which was lost."** Hear the Savior's heart: "Father, give them *time* to repent. Give them the *desire* to repent."

This is how we must pray for our lost loved ones and friends. Time does not remind us each day of how fast it is passing. If we want to be reminded of how fast the moments are fleeing, we have only to stare at the second hand of a clock, and consider the fact that those particular seconds we just witnessed are *gone forever*, never to be repeated again!

May God place within your heart a new *urgency* to pray for the salvation of your lost loved ones and friends, and for those who mistreat you! Pray for them *now*.

"'O righteous Father! The world has not known You, but I have known You; and these have known that You sent Me.'" John 17:25

The two final verses of this prayer (verses 25 and 26) cannot be separated, for they provide a summation of the *themes* of the entire prayer – a "coda," as a musician might say. And when we consider the *timing* of this prayer, only hours before the agony of the Cross, it is all the more remarkable. Such an astonishing contrast, yet with deep harmony; such serenity in the midst of conflict; such a divine victory, yet counted upon as already won!

The **"righteous Father"** now becomes the focus of the prayer; the righteousness as seen in its eternal beauty, and in its divine love. This righteousness is too often *left out*, however little we may mean to or realize it, in much of our preaching, teaching, and praying. We forget too easily that His thoughts are not our thoughts, and that His ways are not our ways (see Isaiah 55:8). Therefore, we would rather hear sermons about His love than about His justice, and we would rather ask Him for what we want than for what we need.

Our righteous God must be the way and the goal of all our thinking; if we start from anything else, we will lose our way. A.W. Tozer has written, "The vague and tenuous hope that God is too kind to punish the ungodly has become a deadly opiate for the consciences of millions. It hushes their fears and allows them to practice all pleasant forms of iniquity, while death draws every day nearer and the command to repent goes unregarded."

You should love God for His justice and righteousness! His judgments are true. As you place your trust in God, your *safety* is guaranteed by His righteousness. His *compassion* for you flows out of His goodness, and goodness without justice is not goodness. *Mercy* does not become effective toward you until righteousness has done its work. The many *needs* of your life are not completely met until God's righteousness is applied to your circumstances.

Pray now with perfect peace to your righteous Father, thanking Him that His ways are not your ways.

December 10

"Now in the morning, having risen a long while before daylight, He went out and departed to a solitary place; and there He prayed."

Mark 1:35

Well-meaning people can distract us from obeying God, and selfish people can be a distraction, too. Here is a situation in the life of our Lord when a large number of people wanted His attention – some, if not all of them with legitimate, urgent needs. But Jesus did not hesitate with His response when the disciples informed Him of the needy crowd, saying, *"Let us go into the next towns, that I may preach there also, because for this purpose I have come forth."*

This discernment from the Spirit meant there would be lots of disappointed people! Luke records that the crowd actually came to the place where He was praying *"and tried to keep Him from leaving them."* They had seen Jesus do some unbelievable things the previous day, and they were excited about the possibility of Him being in their midst again.

Perhaps they felt rejected by Jesus' response. But what this crowd did not understand was that Jesus was on a mission to accomplish God's will that would necessitate covering lots of territory. Obedience to His Father would constantly require discerning between the "urgent" and the "important."

If you have the Spiritual Gift of Service, or *"ministry"* (see Romans 12:7), you can identify with the need to distinguish the urgent from the important. Persons with this Spiritual Gift have a strong desire to meet the needs of people anytime, anywhere - and as quickly as possible. If they are not *prayerful* in their use of this Gift, they soon realize how easy it is to be so busy responding to or meeting "needs," that they miss what *God* is saying.

Notice how Jesus succeeded in His life and work. Because He did not address every urgent need that men brought to His attention, Jesus had time to finish the important tasks *God* gave Him to do. *There are times when legitimate-sounding cries of man can actually distract you from accomplishing God's will!*

Pray that you will not be distracted - in any way or by anyone - from knowing and doing God's will for you today.

"'O righteous Father! The world has not known You, but I have known You; and these have known that You sent Me.'" John 17:25

Christ refers here to **"the world"** as He had met it and dealt with it **"in the days of His flesh,"** now about to close. Tragically, when He appeared in the world, men saw **"no beauty"** in Jesus (see Isaiah 53:2). He was only a name, and **"their heart was far"** from Him. This reminds us that it is all too possible to have around us a wealth of revealed truth and spiritual privilege, and yet to be quite ignorant of God.

That ignorance explains why Jesus prayed, **"but I have known You."** It must have been an effort, even for the man Jesus, to retain God in His knowledge while living in such a corrupt world! Yet Christ was Light in the midst of darkness, Love in the midst of selfishness, and Holiness in the midst of depravity.

One of the purposes Jesus had for coming down from heaven and into our nature, was to teach us how the Father could be known and trusted - because the Creator of the world was *unknown* by the world. And not from want of evidence, because **"the heavens declare the glory of God; and the firmament shows His handiwork,"** and because **"God, who at various times and in various ways spoke in time past to the fathers by the prophets."**

It is easy to read about those who have neither recognized nor known God over time, but may we, with your permission today, ask with compassion, "How great is *your* knowledge of God?" *You are surrounded with light, you have abundant privileges, you have endless resources – but, what do you know about God, given all of this light?* Some readers may answer, "Well, compared to the majority of Believers I have met, I believe I am doing quite well with my knowledge of God." How quickly they miss the point, for God will not compare their knowledge of Him using that standard!

Among the numerous benefits to prayer is the opportunity to have *intimate relationship* with God. Examine your prayer life! Pray for a more intimate relationship with your heavenly Father.

December 12

"And do not lead us into temptation, but deliver us from the evil one"
Matthew 6:13

The slave who has been set free after tasting the bitterness of bondage strives hard to avoid recapture. The more we have been forgiven, the more gratitude we feel. Pardon is a deterrent from sin; *"There is forgiveness with You, that You may be feared."* After Jesus said to the woman caught in adultery, *"Neither do I condemn you,"* He immediately said, *"Go and sin no more"* (see John 8:11).

Prayer is more than a Mobile Army Surgical Hospital (MASH) for the "wounded." It is also an arsenal to *equip* the soldier for the fight. The most valuable soldiers are not those who have merely marched on parade, but those who have been in real battles. Similarly, the strength of a ship is tested by the fierceness of the storm it encounters.

The Master teaches us to pray, *"Do not lead us into temptation."* We are never "tempted" by God in the sense of *allurement* to sin (see James 1:13). Allurement to sin takes place when we are *"drawn away"* by our *"own desires and enticed"* (see James 1:14). "Afflictions" or "trials," however, can be seen as temptations in the sense of being "tests" of faith – and these can either be *sent* or *permitted* by God. The Father's motive for "testing" is to benefit (not injure) the Believer, which is why James says, *"Count it all joy when you fall into various trials, knowing that the testing of your faith produces patience"* (see James 1:2, 3).

God presides over all of our circumstances. *The Father has a bountiful table for His children, but He spreads it within sight of the foe!* It is the Father's *plan* that we will have difficulties and temptations; He wants us to experience just enough conflict (and no more) as may make us good soldiers of Jesus Christ. A mountain guide carefully leads the Alpine climber through existing danger; otherwise, the summit cannot be reached.

As you think about the more difficult times you have experienced as a Christian, did you maintain a Biblical perspective? Pray that you will remember why God permits difficult circumstances.

December 13

"'O righteous Father! The world has not known You, but I have known You; and these have known that You sent Me.'" John 17:25

Jesus simply lays the facts before His *"righteous Father." "The world"* did not then (and does not now) know God. The Bible says, however, that the world *should have* known the Father, *"because what may be known of God is manifest in them, for God has shown it to them. For since the creation of the world His invisible attributes are clearly seen, being understood by the things that are made, even His eternal power and Godhead, so that they are without excuse"* (see Romans 1:19, 20). Yet the greater part of the world lies in ignorance; men are born in darkness, live in darkness, love darkness more than light, and are under the powers of darkness. Satan has a large territory that includes all the nations of the world. In our day, one hour spent watching a world news network provides verification of that fact.

Christ came to earth because of the world's ignorance of God. The world had no conviction of God's *righteousness*. The gods men worshiped were, for the most part, lacking in moral quality; the lack of righteousness in men themselves was reflected in their gods. In addition, the world had no conviction of God's *Fatherhood*. A father wants a family, and the knowledge of God as a "Father" is distinctive to Christianity.

Jesus prayed, *"I have known You."* *Christ knew the Father not by a process of inquiry, not by listening to sermons and teachings, but through direct knowledge!* He said, *"I and My Father are one."* By *"these,"* Jesus refers to the Eleven, but what applies to them applies to all Believers – that they "know" what Jesus says with a "full realization," even in a world of scoffing unbelievers.

We cannot be thankful enough that Jesus came to this earth, not to call men out of the world, but to teach them how to live "in" this wicked place. Today, you will live your life in a very wicked world – even if you spend the day all by yourself. Pray and ask, "Father, what is on *our* agenda today, that will further *Your* kingdom?"

December 14

"And do not lead us into temptation, but deliver us from the evil one'"
Matthew 6:13

As you have discovered, Believers are passing through a region partially occupied by the enemy. You have discovered that he and his accomplices often lurk in places where you least expect them. And you probably understand by now, that the work of God's kingdom involves encountering danger. *But take heart – it is the work of God (and not the devil) to choose where, when, and how you are to be exposed to danger!* We must be exposed to it, for now. Our safety is not in some temptation-proof cell, nor is it to dwell in a building on top of an impenetrable mountain. Our safety is rather in *having God for our shield* while following His guidance where fiery darts are coming from all directions.

So we pray, *"And do not lead us into temptation,"* and ask God to guide us to where outward circumstances may not connect with our fleshly tendencies, and in such a way that any resulting temptation might overpower us. In so praying, we are not praying to escape being tempted, but to overcome it to the end that endurance and victory are the outcome. But how will that happen?

"The Lord knows how to deliver the godly out of temptations" (see 2 Peter 2:9). He does this by using two methods: by leading us *out of its reach*, or by leading us *through it* while providing supernatural strength to conquer it. Luther said, "After God has forgiven us, there is nothing that we have so earnestly to pray for as that we fall not again into the same filth." Perhaps it is the prayer of Jehoshaphat that is most needed today, even more than the prayer of Jabez, when he appealed to God saying, *"We have no power against this great multitude that is coming against us; nor do we know what to do, but our eyes are upon You"* (see 2 Chronicles 20:12).

May you overcome any temptation to doubt today, that *God is!* He is the Author of good and not of evil, and He will deliver you! Praise His Holy Name forever!

> *"And I have declared to them Your name, and will declare it, that the love with which You loved Me may be in them, and I in them."*
>
> John 17:26

The verb *"declared,"* used here, implies a more detailed and explicit description of the Father's *"name;"* it is better translated, *"explained* to them." Jesus had articulated God's name to the disciples, through numerous utterances to them and through the presentation to them of Himself. Repeatedly, He had shown them His Father's character. Yet His revealing work at that time was not done; it had only begun! The disciples were *yet* to learn such things about the name, making even their present knowledge dim and elementary by comparison.

And even today, is not this same Jesus, with the Holy Spirit, making known that same name, by leading the individual and the Church *further* into a believing insight? Jesus does not teach His disciples "all at once." We could not handle that! Instead, we have a Teacher who will carry us further from one degree of knowledge to another, as waves pour in from a boundless ocean. Therefore, we *"grow"* in the grace and knowledge of our Lord and Savior Jesus Christ (see 2 Peter 3:18). It is not a good sign if we are content with just a little; we must grow until we come to heaven, and then there will be no more growth.

By declaring, manifesting, or explaining God's nature, the Atonement persuades sinful men to return to a loving God. As this sums up Christ's work, so it sums up ours, too – for all true mission preaching and work reveals that *God is love.* Is not the power of the Cross the fact that it is the supreme proof of God's love? So it is, that all true ministry, all true kingdom work, has one purpose and end – to declare God's nature and name as Love.

You were created to share this perfect life of love, which the Three Blessed Persons of the Trinity had *"before the foundation of the world."* *What a responsibility, what a task - but what a privilege!* You will be helpless to accomplish such a work without divine intervention! Pray, then, that God will empower and enable you today to share His love.

December 16

"And at the ninth hour Jesus cried out with a loud voice, saying ... 'My God, My God, why have You forsaken Me?'" Mark 15:34

Between the third and this fourth saying of Jesus from the Cross, a long interval elapsed of about three hours during which Christ was silent. During this interval of silence, **"there was darkness over the whole land"** (Mark 15:33). What was taking place in the mind of Jesus during those three hours? Our best answer to that question comes from the cry we are examining today – the second of three prayers from the Cross.

What a lonely experience this was for our Lord! Even the contour of the ground looks like a "skull," and now - total darkness! During the three hours of darkness and silence at Calvary, it is likely Jesus was repeating to Himself, for His strength and consolation, some of the psalms out of the "hymn book" of His people. Psalm 22 begins with the words, **"My God, My God, why have You forsaken Me?"**

Throughout His life on earth, Jesus found Himself forsaken! The members of His own household rejected Him, as did His fellow-townsmen in Nazareth. The nation at large eventually did the same. The multitudes that had once followed Him wherever He went, eventually got offended and went away. And at the end, one of His closest followers betrayed Him, and the rest forsook Him and fled. Yet in all of these disappointments, He knew that what He was doing or suffering was the will of God.

And here is the only record we have of Jesus addressing His Father using the word, **"God,"** when He prayed. "Father" was His normal prayer address, but the *closeness* between Father and Son was still expressed here by the word, **"My."** The reason Jesus does not use the word "Father" on this occasion is because a wall of separation has risen between the Father and the Son at this moment, namely the world's sin and its curse as they now lie upon the Son.

Even though God had to temporarily turn from Jesus and leave Him, Christ still cried to God as *His* God. As you pray today, thank God you can use words like "My" and "Father."

> *"'And I have declared to them Your name, and will declare it, that the love with which You loved Me may be in them, and I in them.'"*
>
> John 17:26

There is both a love of God "toward" us and a love of God *"in"* us. God's love "toward" us is from all eternity. Though we neither felt it nor knew it, God loved us in Christ before the foundation of the world. Jeremiah 31:3 says, *"I have loved you with an everlasting love; therefore with lovingkindness I have drawn you."* God did not love us because we loved Him; He loved us before we had an ounce of love for Him. And it was a *"great love with which He loved us"* (see Ephesians 2:4). So, before we know God as a Father in Christ, the love of God is *toward* us, but not in us.

But once we are "drawn" to Him and trust Him, God's love is "in" us at conversion, as soon as we begin to live in Christ. The precious Holy Spirit brings *assurance* that God's love is in us, for *"The love of God has been poured out in our hearts by the Holy Spirit who was given to us."* The result is that our hearts are stirred with joy, and thankfulness, and hope. And so God delights not only in loving us but in assuring us that He loves us!

Today, will you humbly consider the hardness of your heart? Will you confess, asking the Holy Spirit for a revelation of your true heart, the coldness of your love to Him who first loved you? Robert McCheyne wrote, "The only cure for a cold heart is to look at the heart of Jesus."

And then, after that time of confession and repentance spent with Him, rejoice over this fact: there is a day coming for you, on which the desire of this prayer is fulfilled! A day when God's own love to Christ will be "in you." A day when you will love Jesus with the love with which His Father loves Him. *"At that day you will know that I am in my Father, and you in Me, and I in you"* (see John 14:20).

Pray rejoicing, for that day is coming.

December 18

"And at the ninth hour Jesus cried out with a loud voice, saying ...
'My God, My God, why have You forsaken Me?'" Mark 15:34

This second of three prayers from the Cross was a quote from the Worship-book of the Hebrew people. In Psalm 22:1, David is prophetically describing the suffering Messiah. Jesus did not "quote" David, but David prophetically quoted the words of Jesus. The author of the Scriptures is the Logos through His Spirit. As a human being, Jesus referred to a statement in the Scriptures; as God, He once Himself announced the very statement He prays from the Cross.

Martin Luther wrote, "This Psalm ought to be most highly prized by all who have any acquaintance with temptations of faith and spiritual conflicts;" Spurgeon called Psalm 22 "the photograph of our Lord's saddest hours." Jesus does not recite the entire Psalm as He prays. He simply states the "theme" of the Psalm, quoting its first verse. Dominant in Psalm 22:1 is not an explanation of what the devil does, but rather a declaration of what God does *not* do. *Notice that Jesus does not "complain" about what the devil is doing - something we sometimes do!*

Since Jesus *"cried out with a loud voice,"* He showed Himself to be the very Being to whom the words of the Psalm refer – so that the Jewish scribes and people might ponder and understand the reason *why* He would not descend from the Cross when challenged to do so. This very Psalm declared that it was appointed that He should suffer these things. But mainly He prayed aloud because there are times when prayer must be verbal in order to make the expression complete. A complete prayer is a "speaking prayer" – whether spoken publicly or privately.

No doubt, there are occasions for "silent" prayer. But we should not be afraid to pray aloud, never attempting to "impress" anyone, but only to become lost in the desire, joy, and privilege to speak to and listen to our Heavenly Father. A mature prayer is put into language and is expressed in words, however feebly those words may be spoken or arranged, and without concern for the evaluation of men.

Praise your Heavenly Father *aloud* in prayer today.

"And I have declared to them Your name, and will declare it, that the love with which You loved Me may be in them, and I in them.'"

John 17:26

Jesus is just about to pass from the exercise of intercession to His Passion and to His propitiation for our sins. But He first directs this expectant gaze toward His followers. The last word He utters in this prayer is, "them."

It is striking that the *close* of this magnificent prayer is about **"love!"** Other topics were certainly worthy of attention, such as eternal life, or glory, or faith, or hope. No wonder Paul wrote, **"And now abide faith, hope, love, these three; but the greatest of these is love"** (see 1 Corinthians 13:13). We must observe here that the love of the Father dwells in us only through the mediation of the Son, and so the final words of the prayer are, **"I in them."**

"I in them" means, that no "exterior" contact, however close, will content Jesus; that is how *deeply* He loves His disciples. Christ must have His personal abode in the very "sanctuary" of the human personality. Within that sanctuary, He becomes the Inhabitant, the perpetual resident, of the surrendered and believing heart. Into that sanctuary, He carries with Him **"the love"** that was His own possession "before the foundation of the world." Therefore, His life will be so identified with their life and so repeated in their experiences, that He will be "in" them.

Jesus had now made His last address to the disciples and His final report to the Father. He had brought His followers to the point of professing belief in Him and had commended them to the Father's care. As He interceded then, so He intercedes now. To Him be glory!

This entire prayer reveals the priorities of Christ's heart: the glory of God, the sanctification of God's people, the unity of the Church, and the necessity of sharing the Gospel in a world of darkness! As you grow in your personal prayer life, remember to pray about these same priorities. When you pray, make His agenda your agenda. Do this, and you will pray according to the will of God.

Pray that your prayer priorities will reveal the heart of Jesus.

December 20

*"And at the ninth hour Jesus cried out with a loud voice, saying …
'My God, My God, why have You forsaken Me?'"* Mark 15:34

"**W**hy?" All *we* can answer based on our limited understanding is that only by God actually forsaking Jesus could the full price of our redemption be paid. During those three hours the penalty for our sins was paid completely; after that had been done, the Father turned back to His Son. What we witness here is the mystery of sin, sin's consequences, and God's method of dealing with sin.

God cannot look upon sin, nor can He condone sin. Sin is the exact opposite of everything that God is; there can be no common ground between the two. There is no "neutral zone" between God and sin, no overlap, no compromise. God will not have fellowship with sin in any fashion. Sin was not *in* Jesus, but it was *on* Him: **"And the Lord has laid on Him the iniquity of us all."** And so now that Jesus has our sins *on* Him, God must turn away – even from His Son.

The forsaking is sometimes combined with the death, but actually the two are distinct. The forsaking had been completed *before* the death set in. Before Jesus died, He first placed His soul into the hands of His Father (see Luke 23:46), something He could not have accomplished if He was still forsaken.

"Why" really means, "for what purpose" did you forsake me. Most Bible scholars believe that Jesus knew perfectly well "why" He was forsaken of God: because **"You are holy, enthroned in the praises of Israel."** *But men needed to know their own personal response to this action of God, which is why the "why" still demands attention today!*

What do *you* say? If you, knowing all these things about the seriousness of sin, cherish any favorite sin in your life, how can you expect God to use you? For if you are allowing any known, unrepented sin to find a resting place, you are grieving the Holy Spirit. This plea is now written to you with the compassion of Jesus: surrender your *all* to Christ!

Confess and turn from your sins, praying for the Father's merciful forgiveness.

"And I have declared to them Your name, and will declare it, that the love with which You loved Me may be in them, and I in them."

John 17:26

Life. Looking from the *outside*, Jesus' life on earth was, and ours is and will be, always a battle and often a sorrow. But looking from the *inside*, Jesus' life was an unbroken abiding in the love of God and a continual impartation of the *"name"* of God. The name refers not to His various "titles," but to His *manifested character*.

Our lives should be an ever-growing knowledge of God, leading to and being a fuller possession of His *"love,"* and of a present Christ. Jesus *"declared"* God's name to the disciples. When He looked back over His life, He had *no* flaw or incompleteness to report. There was *nothing* to see in His life of weakness, error, or sin. There were *no* defeats to remember. We forget how enormous this is! When Christ prays, "I have declared to them Your name," He is simply stating the facts that His life confirmed. He had learned God from no one.

We, on the other hand, as we look back on the example of our lives, see the imperfections. We see our own hypocrisies, as well as the excesses. Even considering our best efforts, we have distorted God's character through our decisions and behavior. We have consulted other sources of knowledge that are ambiguous and that lack authority, without the interpretation of Christ's life and His Cross. Often we allow ourselves to be persuaded by the words "maybe," when *our Lord* said, "Verily, verily."

Today's lesson is that Jesus Christ is the sole Source of certainty as to whether or not there is a God, and to what sort of a God He is! And what a comfort that is to *you*, as His present-day disciple! Your consciousness of God's love is meant by Jesus to be like His own. If Christ dwells in you, then God's love to Him falls upon you – not by "transference," but by your incorporation into Him.

As long as the Father loves His Son, He must love you, and *cannot cease* to love you. Pray and thank God for these assuring words of Jesus.

December 22

"And at the ninth hour Jesus cried out with a loud voice, saying ... 'My God, My God, why have You forsaken Me?'" Mark 15:34

The story is told of a man who had thought for a long time about this second of the three prayers from the Cross, and who finally concluded in desperation: "God forsaken by God; who can say anything about *that?*"

Of course, God did not forsake God. It is Man that is being forsaken by God at Calvary; the Man Jesus, as the sacrifice for sin – *He* is being abandoned, and only temporarily, and only by necessity. Now that His Father's face is turned away from Him, it is more than He can bear, and He cries out with a loud voice.

Why have **"You"** forsaken Me? It almost sounds like Jesus could be saying, "Just last night an angel appeared to strengthen Me; why is there no response from heaven *now?* I can understand how the Pharisees and Sadducees would have nothing to do with Me and would utterly reject Me; I can even understand how the disciples would forsake Me, but that You, My Father and My God should forsake Me, I cannot understand! Why have *You* forsaken Me?"

And then, we could understand if the emphasis of this prayer was on the word **"Me."** Jesus could have thought, "I have sought all my life to do nothing but Your will. Did I not hear Your voice at My baptism saying, 'This is My beloved Son, in whom I am well pleased?' Was not Your approval repeated at the transfiguration? Why, then, are You leaving me alone *now?* Why am I being left completely alone when I *most* need help and comfort?" Yet this cry, this prayer was not in the form of a complaint.

All of this said, we have not yet come to the end of the crucifixion of Jesus Christ. This was not the last word from Calvary. *Jesus did not die in despair, but rather with the shout of a Victor in triumph!*

Take heart, dear believer! God has not forsaken you, nor has He abandoned His watch over you. "It is no secret what God can do." Thank Him for His loving watchcare.

"And when Jesus had cried out with a loud voice, He said, 'Father, into Your hands I commit My spirit.'" Luke 23:46

This third prayer from the Cross, like the second one, is from the Psalms. *"Into Your hands I commit My spirit,"* from Psalm 31:5, had been uttered centuries earlier by the Spirit of prophecy. Jesus added the word, *"Father."* Rabbinical literature prescribed these words as a short evening prayer of commitment.

Pupils in the schools had to pray this prayer before they went to bed. This was the first prayer every Jewish mother taught her child to say when he lay down to sleep at night. It is likely, then, that Mary had taught this prayer to Jesus when He was a child. Thus when He was dying, Jesus prayed the prayer He had prayed as a little boy. Many millions of Believers have pillowed their heads with these words, or words very similar while learning to pray.

Throughout His days, Jesus had been a diligent student of the Bible. He listened to the Scriptures being read in the home of His childhood and in the synagogue. He knew the Scriptures through and through. Therefore, He knew where to go in His heart to call up Scripture for every circumstance of life. Whether He was preaching or in conversations with those who tried to trap Him, His language was saturated with Scripture, and He used it aptly.

But not only did Jesus rely on the Scriptures in His public life, He relied on them in His personal life. In the wilderness against the enemy and in His dying hour, the Scriptures were a present help to Him in every kind of need. And here is the lesson for us: *you can't quote what you don't know!* You can't fight off the attacks of the enemy with a "general idea" of what the Bible says.

One might ask, "Why did Jesus need to pray the Scriptures, instead of just using His own words?" It is because the Scriptures *are* God's words. The Father chose words of Scripture for His Son to use. As you prepare to pray, turn to your favorite Bible verse and speak those words to your Heavenly Father.

December 24

"And when Jesus had cried out with a loud voice, He said, 'Father, into Your hands I commit My spirit.'" Luke 23:46

Today let us observe the *manner* in which Jesus Christ faced death. His last cry, *"with a loud voice,"* was not like that of one dying. Mark 15:39 notes, *"So when the centurion, who stood opposite Him, saw that He cried out like this and breathed His last, he said, 'Truly this Man was the Son of God!'"* Jesus encountered death, not as the conquered, but as the Conqueror! His death was His last *act*; death did not take Him by surprise. He came to *give* His life a ransom for many.

Secondly, Jesus faced death victoriously. Although He was dying of wounds and intense suffering, in a brief period He rallied His final strength to die with a victorious shout! There are those who have tried to explain away this shout as physically impossible, but we do better to simply abide by the recorded facts. The difference here is that the body, mind, and soul of Jesus were unhurt by sin, as ours are.

Thirdly, Jesus faced death peacefully. The words of this prayer are the same as those of a little child falling asleep in his father's arms. John 19:30 says, *"And bowing His head, He gave up His spirit."* *The grammar of this statement describes a man peacefully letting his head sink back upon his pillow to go to sleep!* After His long battle, a sense of completion and peace came to Jesus.

Someone once wrote, "Blessed are they who die not only *for* the Lord as martyrs, not only *in* the Lord as all believers, but likewise *with* the Lord, as breathing forth their lives in these words, 'Into Thy hands I commend my spirit.'" We have all wondered at some point in life, what the circumstances will be when we face our last moments on this earth. How will we handle it? What will be on our minds, if there is even time to think?

Jesus died peacefully, with Scripture on His lips. Pray that today, and when the moment arrives for you to leave this world, you, too, will know the peace of God.

December 25

"'But now I come to You, and these things I speak in the world, that they may have My joy fulfilled in themselves.'" John 17:13

"**B**ehold, I bring you good tidings of great joy which will be to all people. For there is born to you this day in the city of David a Savior, who is Christ the Lord." *Joy accompanied the greatest announcement ever made to the world, and joy accompanies all who believe in and know the Subject of that announcement!* Today we come to a prayer of Jesus that contains an abundance of hope for us all, the words, "that they may have My joy." It was Jesus' desire that we would make our way through life fully realizing that He *is* all, that He has *done* all, and that He has *said* all that is necessary for our joy.

Notice that this joy is "fulfilled" in them (not merely "proposed" to them), meaning it is joy apprehended, realized, entered into, complete, satisfying, and sustaining *"in themselves!"* We possess it, but it is Christ's joy, *"My* joy." This joy is His to bestow because He *purchased* it for us, and He is the Author of it. His is a joy that brings rest from all of our fears and anxieties. It is a joy that is full, complete, abiding, and unchanging. We often think of Jesus as *"A Man of sorrows"* (see Isaiah 53:3), and certainly, He was. But we should not picture Him going about with a sad face or a melancholy countenance, for Christ was a Man of deep, abiding joy that came from His perfect accord with the Father.

There is nothing in the joy of Jesus that resembles joy originating from earth. Peter wrote, *"Though now you do not see Him, yet believing, you rejoice with joy inexpressible and full of glory"* (see 1 Peter 1:8). Because this joy is "full of glory," we could never describe *everything* about it. *This* joy is supernatural – indeed, *"joy of the Holy Spirit"* (see 1 Thessalonians 1:6).

Is your joy dependant upon the accidental occurrences of life, or is it drawn from the knowledge that whatever happens, the Father will take all responsibility for you? Pray to know *His* joy.

December 26

"And forgive us our debts, as we forgive our debtors.'" Matthew 6:12

A friend of any kind is something special to have in this cold and lonely world. But to have a friend who has the ear of God, a friend who calls out our name to the Father and asks for His blessing upon us – how many of these friends exist in our lives? Are we being such a friend to others?

We do not treat our friends as well as we may think. There is a sense in which we are shortsighted, thoughtless and inconsiderate toward them! During the Christmas season, we may send them gifts, cards, notes, and pictures of our family. We may send them an e-mail or call them on the phone. But have we *prayed* for them? If not, we have done everything for our friends but the *best* thing.

We *"forgive"* better, when we pray for our friends. We are to live in the atmosphere of mercy if we want to see earth be like heaven. Perhaps we have removed someone this year from our Christmas card or gift list, because we have felt hurt, forgotten, or wronged by them. *The Unforgiveness Prison is overcrowded!* Wouldn't it be wonderful if, this Christmas, we became part of a "jail-break" of unforgiving Believers?

Is not our forgiveness all too often grudging and half-hearted? Do we not often actually *cherish* the memory of the offences? So, instead of thinking, "I'll forgive you, but I'll never forget what you did," or "I'll forgive you this one time, but never again," or "I'll say I'm sorry if you will say you're sorry" – ask yourself, "What measure of forgiveness do I want God to use when I stand before His throne? Do I want Him to use the same measure that I have applied to others?"

Sometimes, when praying this petition of the Model Prayer, the words die on our lips because they require a forgiving spirit to be in us *before* we ask forgiveness of God. What a solemn warning there is with this petition! Ask God to rebuke you, and to change your heart concerning the forgiveness of others.

December 27

"And when Jesus had cried out with a loud voice, He said, 'Father, into Your hands I commit My spirit.'" Luke 23:46

To the beginning of the Psalm from which we find the words of this third prayer of Jesus from the Cross, He adds the word, ***"Father."*** That word is not found in the Psalm because in the Old Testament, individuals had not yet begun to address God by this name (although God was called the "Father" of the nation as a whole). Jesus introduced to the world a new and more intimate consciousness of God, which is embodied in this very word.

Stephen, the first martyr of Christianity, closely imitated Jesus on the occasion of his death, repeating a prayer similar to Christ's for His enemies, ***"Lord, do not charge them with this sin."*** Also, Stephen imitated this third and final prayer of Jesus from the Cross, praying, ***"Lord Jesus, receive my spirit,"*** addressing Christ with the dying prayer which Christ Himself had addressed to the Father.

The word, "Father," was continuously upon the Savior's lips. You will remember that His first words ever recorded were, ***"Why did you seek Me? Did you not know that I must be about My Father's business?"*** During "The Sermon on the Mount," Jesus spoke of the "Father" seventeen times. In Christ's final discourse to the disciples (recorded in John chapters 14-16), the word "Father" is found forty-five times. And throughout the "High Priestly Prayer" recorded in John 17, we see Jesus speaking to and of the "Father" six different times.

Today, you can look up to the great and living God and say, "Father!" Because God is your Father, He *loves* you as He loves Jesus Himself (see John 17:23)! Because God is your Father, He *cares for* you. Because God is your Father, He will ***"supply all your need."*** Dear reader, we need to enter more deeply into the blessedness of this relationship, so that we can join with the apostle and *shout,* ***"Behold what manner of love the Father has bestowed on us, that we should be called children of God!"***

As you take time to pray, enjoy the comfort of speaking to *and* listening to your Heavenly *Father,* and worship Him.

December 28

"And when Jesus had cried out with a loud voice, He said, 'Father, into Your hands I commit My spirit.'" Luke 23:46

Seven times Jesus spoke from the Cross. This was the seventh and final time. In Scripture, seven is the number of *completeness, perfection,* and the number of *rest in a finished work.* The subject of completeness brings us to a remarkable fact about this seventh saying, as well as the previous six. *In each one of the seven times Jesus spoke from the Cross, a prophecy was fulfilled!*

Prophecy number one is found in Isaiah 53:12, **"And He ... made intercession for the transgressors."** The fulfillment came from Jesus' first statement from the Cross, **"Father, forgive them, for they do not know what they do."** The second prophecy, made by the angel to Joseph, is found in Matthew 1:21, **"And you shall call His name JESUS, for He will save His people from their sins."** The fulfillment came from Jesus' second statement from the Cross, made to one of the criminals beside Him, **"Today you will be with Me in Paradise."**

A prophecy of Simeon to Mary is the third prophecy, found in Luke 2:35, **"Yes, a sword will pierce through your own soul also."** The fulfillment came from Jesus' third statement from the Cross, addressing His mother, **"Woman, behold your son!"** The fourth prophecy is found in Psalm 22:1, **"My God, My God, why have You forsaken Me?"** These were the words of Jesus' fourth statement from the Cross, His second prayer.

The fifth prophecy is found in Psalm 69:21, **"And for my thirst they gave me vinegar to drink."** The fulfillment came as Jesus spoke for the fifth time from the Cross and said, **"I thirst."** Prophecy number six is found in Psalm 22:31, **"He has done (finished) this"** referring to the work of Atonement. It is fulfilled by the sixth statement made by Jesus from the Cross, **"It is finished."** And lastly, the seventh prophecy is found in Psalm 31:5, **"Into Your hand I commit My spirit"** the fulfillment of which comes with the prayer we examine today.

The fulfilling of these prophecies demonstrates, even further, what a wondrous God we serve. Give Him praise and glory!

December 29

"And when Jesus had cried out with a loud voice, He said,
'Father, into Your hands I commit My spirit.'" Luke 23:46

W e come to the third prayer of Jesus from the Cross. For more than twelve hours, He has been in the hands of *men*. He had warned the disciples of this once when He said to them, **"The Son of Man is about to be betrayed into the hands of men, and they will kill Him"** (Matthew 17:22, 23). A second time, in Gethsemane, He said to the disciples, **"Behold, the hour is at hand, and the Son of Man is being betrayed into the hands of sinners"** (Matthew 26:45).

Jesus chose the plural of the word, "hand" when praying this prayer, while Psalm 31:5 uses the singular. This does not indicate an "error," as Christ was not "quoting" the Psalm. Yes, Hebrews 10:31 says, **"It is a fearful thing to fall into the hands of the living God."** *But it is the height of blessedness to commit oneself into these hands!*

Christ could have easily avoided arrest in a variety of ways, but He did not do so in the Garden, because the appointed hour had struck. The time had arrived for Him to be led as a lamb to the slaughter. And my, how the sinners took advantage of their opportunity, giving full vent to the hatred in their carnal hearts! With **"lawless hands"** they crucified Him.

We understand that *voluntarily* Jesus delivered Himself into the hands of sinners, and *voluntarily* now, He delivers His spirit into the hands of the Father. Never again will He be in "the hands of men" and at the mercy of the lawless. One day the tables will be turned, the situation reversed. There was a time when He was in *their* hands, but there will come a Day when they will be in *His!* Once they cried, **"Away with Him,"** but the Day is coming when *He* will say, **"Depart from Me!"**

Dear reader, as you pray today, remember that the one, true, living God has the last word. Have you surrendered your life to Jesus Christ? Rejoice as you pray, that in Christ, you are eternally secure in *His* **"hands."**

December 30

"And when Jesus had cried out with a loud voice, He said, 'Father, into Your hands I commit My spirit.'" Luke 23:46

The keywords necessary to understand in this prayer are the words, *"I commit"* and *"spirit."* Jesus is not petitioning the Father to "take" His spirit. He is "giving over" His spirit to the Father, in an act of dedication. The word actually means to make a "deposit" for safekeeping. This is a prayer of faith that the Father will provide governance for the next three days.

According to Zechariah 12:1, God *"forms the spirit of man within him."* It is the spirit that "distinguishes" man from the beasts, and it is the spirit that "links" man to God and to eternity. Ecclesiastes 12:7 says that at death, the spirit returns to *"God who gave it."*

Scripture reveals man to be *"spirit, soul, and body"* (see 1 Thessalonians 5:23). The spirit is thought to be the highest, most sacred part of our being, The spirit of man is distinguished from his "soul," in that the spirit is the most lofty part of the inner man. It is also true, however, that it is the spirit that sin seeks to corrupt and that our spiritual enemies seek to destroy. Therefore, there is quite a bit of activity taking place in the spiritual realm at death; Satan's last chance arrives to seize the spirit.

What an amazing moment this was! Jesus snatches His spirit away from those hostile hands, and places His spirit into the safe, strong, and secure hands of God! With what passion and tenderness must the hands of God have received the spirit of Christ!

Now to the point of today's devotion: Have you as a *sinner* committed your spirit into the hands of God? If you have not, please, do so today! Are you as a *Christian* living for the glory of Him who loved you and gave Himself for you? Are you walking in daily obedience to Him, knowing that without Him, you can do nothing? *For to die the death of the righteous, you must live the life of the righteous!*

Yield yourself into the hands of the Father, as you take time now to pray.

"And when Jesus had cried out with a loud voice, He said,
'Father, into Your hands I commit My spirit.'" Luke 23:46

In this seventh and last statement, as with His fourth statement from the Cross, Jesus is turning Scripture into prayer. His second prayer at Calvary was from His knowledge of Psalm 22:1, and this third prayer is from His knowledge of Psalm 31:5. Today we want to consider a beautiful habit that can be ours of turning Scripture into prayer, or as many call it, "praying the Scriptures."

As we have just noted, turning Scripture into prayer was demonstrated by our Lord Jesus from the Cross. Remember, Jesus had already explained the vital connection between prayer ("ask what you desire") and Scripture ("My words") when He said, *"If you abide in Me, and My words abide in you, you will ask what you desire, and it shall be done for you"* (John 15:7).

All of us will admit that there are times when we pray out of our own will, instead of out of God's will. Turning Scripture into prayer (saying back to God what He has already said to us) assures and confirms to the children of God, that their prayers are *in the will of God*. There is, however, this caution from Psalm 66:18: *"If I regard iniquity in my heart, the Lord will not hear."* The man who turns Scripture into prayer - but who proudly cherishes unrepented, unconfessed sin in his heart – is only reciting!

Turning Scripture into prayer brings with it a number of aids and blessings, that include determining the will of God, the avoidance of blind or selfish praying, the application of God's promises to our circumstances, and the strengthening of our faith. *God is raising up a people who, instead of praying "to" God, will pray "from" God!* They are a people who pray having already been in His presence, who know His Word and turn Scripture (His will) into prayer. Is the Father inviting you to make this prayer discipline a primary habit of *your* prayer life?

Using a favorite Scripture verse or perhaps a verse from the Psalms, take time now to make a Scripture verse become your personal prayer.

ABOUT THE AUTHOR

RICK ASTLE is passionate about teaching Christians how to pray biblically and powerfully. He has previously ministered as a local pastor and as a missions director and currently is the President of Rick Astle Ministries, Inc. Rick has conducted prayer ministries in Haiti, Africa, and in over 30 U.S. states, and has published five Christian books related to prayer, overcoming temptation, and God's will for our lives.

Born and raised in Oklahoma, Rick was saved as a high school student after his parents moved to Louisville, Kentucky. He is a graduate of The University of Kentucky and of The Southern Baptist Theological Seminary. Rick and his wife currently reside in Lumberton, North Carolina.

ABOUT THE MINISTRY

RICK ASTLE
-MINISTRIES-

RICK ASTLE MINISTRIES is devoted to equipping and encouraging the local church to prepare and to pray for spiritual awakening. This nationwide ministry comes alongside the local church by providing biblical teaching and books on a variety of prayer-related topics.

OTHER BOOKS BY RICK ASTLE

The Priority of Kingdom-focused Prayer
What Motivates God? – Encouraging the Church to Express the Father's Heart
The Believers Guide to Overcoming Temptation
Post-Event Prayer

**To learn more about Rick Astle, Rick Astle Ministries,
and to purchase books,
please visit www.RickAstle.com**

Index of Scripture References

Old Testament

Genesis
1:31	Jun 30
3:1	Jul 23; Sep 25
14:19	Mar 10
22:1	Nov 4
24:3	Mar 10
32:26	Feb 6

Leviticus
16:6, 33	Jan 14

Numbers
20:6	Oct 1

Deuteronomy
8:11, 15, 16	Jan 17
8:16	Nov 4

1 Samuel
1:11	Aug 23
2:2	May 21
3:10	Oct 28
12:1-5	Sep 5

2 Samuel
7:18	Jan 15
15:23	Mar 22

1 Kings
8:27	May 10
8:30	Mar 10
18:37	Jul 20

1 Chronicles
16:36	Dec 2
29:11	Nov 30

2 Chronicles
7:14	Mar 12; Oct 1
20:12	Aug 6; Dec 14

Nehemiah
8:3-6	Dec 2

Job
42:10	Oct 14

Psalms
2:7	Jan 11
2:11	May 25
5:2	May 10
16:11	Apr 27
19:1	Apr 24; Dec 11
22	Dec 18
22:1	Feb 10; Dec 16, 18, Dec 28, 31
22:3	Dec 20
22:7, 8	Apr 3
22:16	Apr 3
22:23	Aug 2
22:31	Dec 28
23:1	Jul 5
23:4	Mar 26
24:1	May 6
24:10	May 6
27:1	Feb 10
31:5	Dec 23, 28, 29, 31
34:3	Mar 24; Aug 2
36:6	Sep 2
37:25	Aug 5
39:3	Jan 20
40:8	Jun 17
41:9	Jun 23, 27
43:4	Apr 20

Psalms

44:4	May 6
46:1	Feb 10
47:7	May 10
50:21	Apr 20; May 25
51:4	Sep 10
51:5	Feb 28
51:15	Apr 8
55:7	Jul 25
57:7	May 26
63:1	May 13
66:18	May 9, 10; Dec 31
68:18	Mar 7
69:21	Dec 28
73:25, 26	Mar 17
73:28	Mar 17; May 29
86:11, 12	Apr 8
89:35	May 19
90:2	Nov 28
91:1	Oct 28
95:3	May 10
96:8	Mar 28
97:10	May 21; Jul 6; Aug 28
103:19	Jan 20
103:20-22	Jun 26
104:1	Mar 14
106:48	Dec 2
110:1	Mar 7
115:3	Mar 14; May 10
119:18	Feb 15
119:105	Aug 22
121:3-5	May 27
121:5, 7, 8	Aug 8
125:2	Oct 28
130:4	Oct 9; Dec 12
133:1	Oct 24
139:23, 24	Oct 9
143:10	Jun 17

Proverbs

1:8	Mar 27
3:6	Jul 12
5:8	Nov 2
18:10	Jun 16
28:13	Oct 23
30:8, 9	Aug 10

Ecclesiastes

5:2	Jan 20; Feb 4
8:11	Nov 13
12:7	Dec 30

Isaiah

1:11-15	Jan 31
5:30	Oct 13
6:3	May 25
6:5	May 23; Aug 24
6:8	May 14
13:9	Oct 13
14:27	Dec 4
26:3	May 26
27:2, 3	May 27
30:21	Jun 16
40:18	Mar 9
40:21	Feb 10
42:1	Jan 11
42:7	Jan 30
46:9, 10	Nov 28
50:6	Apr 3
52:7	Sep 5
53	Jan 11
53:2	Dec 11
53:3	Apr 13; Oct 16; Dec 25
53:5	Apr 3
53:6	Dec 20
53:12	Oct 2, 3; Nov 7; Dec 28
55:8	Jan 22; Jul 29; Oct 11; Dec 9

Isaiah
55:11	Sep 22
59:2	Oct 17; Nov 9
59:16	Jan 12
65:2	Dec 7

Jeremiah
9:2	Jul 25
9:24	Nov 22
15:16	Jul 5
17:9	Sep 22
23:24	May 2
29:11	Jan 24; Jun 9
31:3	Dec 17
31:34	Feb 11
33:3	Feb 15

Lamentations
3:23	Feb 6

Ezekiel
33:31	Mar 25
34:3, 4	Aug 7
34:11-16	May 27

Daniel
9:4	Mar 20
9:9	Jul 1
9:21	Jul 18
11:32	Feb 17

Hosea
Hosea 7:9	Dec 6

Joel
2:1, 2, 31	Oct 13
2:12-14	Sep 24
3:14, 15	Oct 13

Micah
2:10	May 13

Habakkuk
1:13	May 25

Zechariah
12:1	Dec 30

Malachi
2:10	Feb 28

New Testament

Matthew
1:21	Jul 27; Dec 28
1:23	Apr 17
3:17	Nov 9
4:1	Nov 4, 8
4:8, 9	Apr 13; Sep 27
4:11	May 9
4:19	Jun 7
5:11, 12	Jul 19
5:13	Aug 4; Sep 3
5:13, 14	Aug 4
5:14	Aug 4
5:16	Feb 25; Mar 1
5:44	Aug 27; Sep 11

Matthew
5:47	Aug 27
5:48	Aug 22
6:5	Jan 15; Feb 8, 12, 16
6:5-7	Feb 16
6:5-8	Jan 15; Feb 4, 12; Jul 12
6:5-18	Jul 8
6:6	Jan 19, 23, 27; Feb 12
6:7	Jan 10, 31; Feb 12, 16
6:8	Jan 13; Feb 16, 20
6:9	Jan 7, 9, 13, 15, 19, Jan 23, 27, 31; Feb 4, 8, 12, 16, 20,

Matthew

6:9, cont.	Feb 22, 26, 28; Mar 2, 6, 10, 14, 18, 20, Mar 24, 28; Apr 1, 8, Apr 15, 18, 20, 22, 24, Apr 25, 28; May 2, 6, May 19; Aug 21; Sep 25, 29
6:9-13	Mar 18
6:10	May 6, 10, 12, 16, 20, May 22, 26, 28; Jun 1, Jun 5, 9, 13, 17, 20, 24, Jun 26, 30; Jul 2, 14, July 18, 22, 24, 28; Aug 1; Sep 8, 25; Oct 14; Nov 3; Dec 1
6:11	Aug 5, 7, 11, 15, 19, 23, Aug 25; Sep 2, 6
6:12	Sep 10, 15, 19, 23, 25, Sep 29; Oct 7, 11, 15, Oct 19, 23; Dec 26
6:13	Feb 13, 18; Mar 18; Jul 6, 10; Sep 4; Oct 27, 31; Nov 2, 4, 6, Nov 8, 10, 12, 14, 18, Nov 20, 22, 28, 30; Dec 2, 4, 6, 12, 14
6:15	Oct 19
6:26	Apr 26; Sep 2
6:32	Aug 25; Sep 2
6:33	May 6
6:33	Jul 30; Aug 26
7:9	Sep 2
7:21	Jun 13
7:21-23	Jun 21
7:28, 29	Feb 23
8:27	Apr 17
9:2	Nov 2
9:8	Feb 23
9:38	Apr 15; May 14

Matthew

10:2	Oct 29
10:5, 6	Sep 14
10:9	Aug 25
10:25	Jul 19
10:32	Feb 25
10:34-36	Oct 7
11:25	Aug 20
11:28	Feb 6
11:29	Mar 6
12:34	Jan 14; Oct 3
13:23	Mar 27
14:22	Apr 26
14:23	Jan 1; Feb 2; Apr 26, 30; May 4
14:25	Apr 30
15:8	Dec 11
15:32	Aug 23
15:36	Aug 20
16:17	May 24
16:22, 23	Sep 27
17:18-21	Jul 8
17:22, 23	Dec 29
18:11	Sep 12
18:15	Oct 15
18:17	Jun 30; Sep 30
18:20	Jan 27
18:21, 22	Sep 25
18:32-35	Oct 19
19:13	Jan 21; May 14; Aug 3
19:14	Aug 3
20:28	Sep 27
21:13	Jun 25
21:15	Aug 3
22:29	Jun 25
23:14	Feb 8
24:26	Jan 23
24:29	Oct 13
24:46	Aug 1
25:35, 36	Aug 7

Matthew

25:35, 36	Jul 25
25:40	Jul 25
25:41	Dec 29
26:24	Jun 23
26:25	Jun 23
26:26, 27	Nov 23
26:38	Sep 21
26:38, 39	Sep 27
26:39	Apr 3, 10; Sep 21; Oct 1; Nov 4
26:41	Apr 9, 11; Oct 21, 27
26:44	Jan 31; Feb 12
26:45	Dec 29
27:39-44	Sep 27
27:40-43	Oct 9
27:51	Jan 22
28:19, 20	Feb 25; Jul 31
28:20	May 17

Mark

1:3	Jul 31
1:35	Jan 29; Feb 2, 6, 14; Aug 20; Nov 16; Dec 10
1:38	Jan 29; Nov 16; Dec 10
4:19	Oct 2
5:19, 20	Nov 28
6:45, 46	Aug 20
6:48	May 4
6:52	Mar 29
7:32	May 8
7:34	May 8
8:6, 7	Nov 24
8:17, 18	Mar 29
8:27	May 24
10:51	Feb 15
13:24	Oct 13
14:32	Oct 25
14:32, 33	Oct 29

Mark

14:33	Apr 6
14:33, 35	Apr 13
14:35, 36	Jun 18
14:36	Apr 13
15:33	Oct 17
15:33	Dec 16
15:34	Feb 10; Oct 10, 13, 17; Dec 16, 18, 20, 22, 28
15:39	Jan 28; Dec 24
16:15	Sep 14

Luke

1:27	Apr 17
1:46-48	Nov 25
2:10	Dec 25
2:35	Dec 28
2:47	Apr 2
2:49	Dec 27
2:52	Sep 20
3:21	Jan 11
3:22	Jan 11
4:16	Feb 2
4:18	Nov 25
4:42	Feb 2; Dec 10
5:5	Feb 11
5:16	Feb 2, 24; Mar 4; Aug 20
6:12	Feb 2; Mar 8, 12; Aug 20
6:12, 13	Mar 19
6:26	Jul 11
8:15	Mar 27
8:25	Jan 2
8:51	Jun 7
9:3	Aug 25
9:18	May 24, 30
9:28, 29	Jun 3, 7
9:35	Jun 3
10:1, 17	Jun 28
10:16	Sep 5

Luke

10:17-20	Nov 25
10:21	Jun 22; Nov 25
10:21, 22	Aug 20
11:1	Mar 18; Jun 28; Jul 8; Dec 2
11:1-4	Nov 30
11:2-4	Mar 18; Jun 28
11:5-8	Jun 28
11:9-13	Jun 28
11:24	May 26
11:27, 28	Mar 25
12:4	Sep 15
12:48	Aug 7
13:24	Jul 6
13:34	Jul 14
15:7	Jul 22
15:20	Sep 29
18:15	Jan 21
19:10	Aug 27; Dec 8
21:25	Oct 13
21:37	Oct 25
22:24	Jun 6
22:28	Jan 2
22:31, 32	Jan 2; Apr 16, 19; Aug 29, 31; Sep 4, 13
22:35	Jan 2
22:39	Oct 25
22:39, 40	Apr 21
22:40	May 5
22:42	Feb 20; Apr 3, 5; May 18; Nov 19
22:43	Mar 30; Apr 3; May 9
22:44	Apr 12
22:45	Apr 4
22:53	Jan 26; May 5; Aug 14; Oct 13
23:34	Jun 14, 15; Jul 1, 16, 30; Aug 17, 27; Sep 8, 24; Oct 3, 5, 9, 19; Dec 8, 28

Luke

23:38	Aug 17
23:39	Oct 9
23:42	Aug 17
23:43	Aug 17; Nov 27; Dec 3, 28
23:46	Jan 25; Jul 26; Dec 20, 23, 24, 27, Dec 28, 29, 30, 31
24:16	Mar 16
24:30	Mar 16
24:31	Mar 16
24:44, 45	Jun 27
24:50, 51	Jan 4

John

1:1	Mar 7
1:3	Sep 3
1:4	Aug 26
1:12	Jan 22; Feb 28
1:14	Feb 21; Apr 17; Sep 22; Oct 26; Dec 5
1:18	Mar 9
2:4	Jan 26
2:11	Dec 5
2:18, 19	Jul 16
2:22	Jan 18
3:3	Feb 13
3:16	Feb 9, 19; Apr 29; May 31; Jun 17; Sep 7, 8, 17; Oct 4; Nov 3, 15, 17, 26
3:17	Sep 8
3:20	Jul 19
4:34	Jan 25; Jul 24
5:40	Jul 14
5:43	May 29
5:44	Jan 28
6:11	Jan 17
6:38	Jul 24

John

6:38-40	Jan 11; Jun 17
6:48	Mar 13
6:64-71	Jun 19
6:66	Mar 21
6:67	Mar 21
6:68	Mar 21; Oct 8
6:70, 71	Jun 23
7:17	Mar 31
7:30	Jan 24
7:39	May 13
8:11	Nov 2, 6, 14; Dec 12
8:12	Mar 13
8:20	Jan 24
8:29	Jan 9
8:43	Apr 2
8:44	Feb 28
8:46	Feb 23
8:58	Apr 17
9:4	Feb 25
10:11	Mar 13
10:16	Sep 30
10:17	Sep 27
10:18	Feb 27
10:30	Dec 13
10:36	Jun 11
11:11	Jan 3
11:40	Jul 20
11:41, 42	Jan 3; Jul 12, 20
11:42	Apr 19; Jun 4; Sep 28
11:43	Jul 20
12:6	Jun 19
12:16	Jan 18
12:27	Jan 26; Aug 9, 13
12:27, 28	Apr 8
12:28	Aug 9, 13, 21; Nov 26; Dec 5
12:31	Nov 26
12:32	Jun 17
12:43	Jan 28
13:1	May 15

John

13:11	Jun 19
13:18	Jun 19, 27
13:34	Jan 16
13:35	Jun 10; Nov 5, 15
14-16	Dec 27
14:1	Oct 4
14:2	Jan 16; May 13; Nov 29; Dec 1
14:2, 3	Nov 27
14:6	Feb 11; Sep 22
14:8, 9	Apr 28
14:9	Feb 3, 21
14:15	Mar 23; Jul 18
14:16	Sep 17
14:20	Dec 17
14:23	Mar 23
14:26	Jan 16, 18
14:27	Jan 16
14:28	Feb 23; Mar 2; May 17; Sep 7
15	Mar 3
15:1-5	Oct 28
15:1-17	May 7
15:5	Feb 11; Mar 3; Nov 9
15:7	Dec 31
15:8	Jan 16; Feb 25
15:11	Jul 3, 7
15:16	Jun 25
15:18	Jan 2
15:18, 19	Jul 21
15:19	Jul 13
16:12	Mar 9
16:13	Jul 8; Oct 10
16:21	Jan 26
16:22	Jul 3
16:24	Jul 3, 7
16:27	Nov 17
16:30	Mar 31
16:32	Mar 21
16:33	Jan 16; May 15; Jul 7

John

17	Jan 8, 12; Dec 27
17:1	Jan 6, 8, 10, 12, 14, 16, Jan 18, 20, 22, 24, 26, Jan 28, 30; Feb 1, 3; Dec 5
17:2	Jan 10; Feb 3, 5, 7, 9; Apr 14
17:3	Feb 11, 13, 15, 17, 19
17:4	Jan 10; Feb 21, 23, 25, Feb 27; Mar 1, 3; Apr 14; Jul 24; Sep 9
17:5	Jan 10, 30; Mar 5, 7; Sep 3
17:6	Feb 7; Mar 9, 11, 13, Feb 15, 17, 19, 21, 23, Feb 25, 27; Apr 14, 18; May 1
17:6-8	Jan 6
17:6-19	Aug 29
17:7	Mar 29, 31
17:8	Jan 10; Apr 2, 7, 14, Apr 17; Jun 8
17:9	Feb 7; Mar 15, 20; Apr 19, 23, 25, 27, 29; Sep 11
17:10	May 1, 3, 7; Jul 4
17:11	Jan 10; Feb 7; Mar 15, Mar 26; May 11, 13, May 15, 17, 19, 21, 23, May 25, 27, 29, 31; Jun 2, 4, 6, 8, 10
17:12	Jan 2; Feb 7; Mar 15, Mar 21; Jun 12, 16, 19, Jun 21, 23, 25, 27
17:13	Mar 7; Jun 29; Jul 3, 5, Jul 7; Dec 25
17:14	Jun 8; Jul 9, 11, 13, 15, Jul 17, 19, 21, 23; Aug 18

John

17:15	Mar 22; Jul 25, 27, 29, Jul 31; Aug 2, 4, 6, 8, Aug 10, 12, 14, 16, 30; Oct 27
17:16	Aug 18; Aug 20
17:17	Mar 22; Jul 9; Aug 18, Aug 22, 24, 26, 28, Aug 30; Sep 1
17:18	Mar 15; Sep 3, 5, 7, 9, Sep 12, 14, 16
17:19	Jan 14; Jun 11; Aug 26; Sep 18, 20, Sep 22, 26
17:20	Jan 5; Sep 28, 30; Oct 2, 4, 6, 8, 12, 14, Oct 16
17:20, 21	Jun 6
17:21	Jan 3; Sep 8; Oct 18, Oct 20, 22, 24, 26, 28, Oct 30; Nov 1, 3, 5
17:22	Apr 14
17:22	Oct 18; Nov 7
17:23	Oct 18, 30; Nov 9, 11, Nov 13, 15, 17; Dec 27
17:24	Feb 7; Jun 19; Sep 3; Nov 19, 21, 27, 29; Dec 1, 3, 5, 15
17:25	Dec 7, 9, 11, 13
17:26	Dec 9, 15, 17, 19, 21
18:1	Mar 22
18:2	Oct 25
18:36	Jul 15
18:37, 38	Apr 29
18:38	Jan 28; Sep 1
19:15	Dec 29
19:26	Dec 28
19:28	Dec 28
19:30	Dec 4, 24, 28
20:17	Feb 26

John

20:21	Aug 12
21:25	Feb 24

Acts

1:9, 10	Jan 4
1:14	Jan 27
1:15	Mar 15
1:16, 17	Jun 16
2:23	Dec 29
2:32, 36	Mar 5
2:41	Sep 30
2:42	Jan 27; Feb 22; Oct 18
3:11-17	Jul 16
3:15-17	Jul 30
4:32	Jun 6, 10; Sep 6; Oct 22
5:3	Aug 14
5:41	Jul 19
6:4	Jan 27
7:54-60	Jun 14
7:55	Apr 27
7:56	May 17
7:59	Dec 3, 27
7:60	Dec 27
9:11	Jan 13
9:31	Jul 5
12:5	Jan 27
13:2	Sep 7
13:27	Jul 16, 30
13:29, 30	Apr 16
13:39	Oct 4
16:6	Sep 14
16:7	Sep 14
16:9	Sep 14
16:13	Jan 27
16:25	Nov 28
17:18	Aug 24
17:28	Feb 28
20:28	Sep 7

Acts

21:20	Sep 30
24:25	Nov 27

Romans

1:4	Jan 28
1:16	Jan 5; Apr 7
1:19, 20	Dec 13
3:23	May 25; Sep 10
3:25	Oct 4
5:2	Jun 1
5:5	Dec 17
5:8	Mar 13; Nov 7
5:12	Feb 28
5:20	Sep 10
6:6	Jul 13
7:19	Apr 6
7:21	Nov 18
7:24	Nov 14
8:15	Mar 20; Jun 18
8:16, 17	Nov 7
8:18	Jul 17
8:26	Feb 20; Mar 16; Apr 23
8:28	Aug 10
8:32	Nov 17
8:34	Apr 19, 27; Sep 13
8:37	Sep 9
8:38	Feb 5
9:2	Sep 8
10:1	Sep 8
10:8-13	Jan 5
10:10	Apr 14
10:14	Jan 5; Aug 1
10:15	Sep 7
10:17	Apr 7; Aug 30
11:36	Mar 1
12:1	May 31
12:2	Jul 21; Aug 8; Nov 1
12:7	Dec 10
12:8	Aug 1

Romans

12:14-19	Oct 19
12:18	Jun 4
14:7	Oct 16
14:9	Feb 7
14:17	May 16; Jul 5

1 Corinthians

1:2	Aug 22
1:10	Jun 6; Oct 22
1:21	Jan 5
2:8	Jul 16, 30
2:12	Jul 15
2:14	Jul 23; Nov 13
3:9	Jan 17
3:23	Mar 19; May 31
6:9	Sep 15
6:19	Mar 17
10:12	Nov 18
10:31	Mar 1, 18; Apr 8; Jul 15; Dec 5
10:32	Dec 5
13:13	Dec 19
15:3, 4	Apr 3
15:6	Mar 15
15:17	Feb 7
15:28	Feb 3

2 Corinthians

1:20	Dec 4
3:2	Jul 28
4:3, 4	Nov 13
4:4	Jul 15; Oct 2; Nov 1
4:6	Feb 21
5:7	Aug 15
5:15	Feb 21; May 31; Aug 9, 28; Sep 23
5:17	May 29; Jul 15
5:20	May 10; Jul 14; Sep 5
5:21	Sep 27; Oct 10
7:10	Sep 29

2 Corinthians

8:9	Sep 26
9:15	May 1
10:5	Jul 13; Oct 21
12:7	Aug 10
12:9	May 11

Galatians

1:1	Sep 7
1:4	Jul 15
2:20	Nov 9
3:26	Feb 28
4:6	Jun 18
5:17	Apr 10, 11
5:22	Jul 5
5:22, 23	Jun 12; Aug 28
6:14	Jan 30

Ephesians

1:6	Jan 22
1:17	Feb 17
1:18, 19	May 19
1:22	Feb 5; Mar 19
2:2	Jul 15; Nov 1
2:4	Dec 17
2:4-6	Apr 27
2:6	Jan 28
2:19, 20	Oct 8
3:15	Oct 22
4:3	Jun 6; Oct 22
4:13	Jun 6; Oct 22
4:18	Feb 13
4:31, 32	Oct 5
4:32	Jul 1; Oct 7
5:14	Aug 26
5:27	Feb 9
6:12	Apr 10; Jul 27; Aug 14, 16
6:16	Aug 16
6:17	Sep 22
6:24	Oct 30

Philippians

1:23	Nov 27; Dec 3
1:23, 24	May 17
2:7	Mar 3
2:8	Feb 27
2:9	Mar 5
2:11	Feb 1
2:13	Jul 14
2:21	Aug 26
3:8	Feb 17
3:10	Feb 17; Apr 10
3:20	Jul 15
4:13	Aug 10
4:19	Dec 27

Colossians

1:5	Aug 30
1:13	May 12
1:16	Sep 3
1:17	Sep 3
1:28	Sep 16
2:2	Jun 6; Oct 22
2:6	Oct 24
2:9	Feb 21
2:10	Mar 19
3:12, 13	Oct 19
3:17	Nov 9

1 Thessalonians

1:6	Dec 25
1:9	Feb 19
2:13	Mar 27; Jul 9; Aug 26
5:17	Mar 10
5:18	Nov 23
5:23	Dec 30
5:25	Apr 23

2 Thessalonians

2:3	Jun 27
3:3	Aug 6

1 Timothy

2:1-5	Sep 11
2:1-6	Sep 8
2:4	Jun 15
2:5	Feb 28
6:8	Aug 15

2 Timothy

1:12	Feb 17
2:3	Aug 31
2:26	Jul 24; Oct 2
3:5	Aug 24
3:12	Jul 11
3:16	Jul 21
4:7	Mar 1; Aug 28

Hebrews

1:1	Dec 11
1:2	Sep 3
1:3	Feb 21, 23
2:9	May 9
3:1	Mar 19; Jul 15
4:13	Mar 14
4:14	Apr 19
4:15	Jan 1; Oct 16
4:16	May 2; Nov 19
5:7	Mar 30; Dec 11
7:25	Mar 16; May 4; Sep 13; Oct 16
7:26	Jul 15
9:27	Aug 21
10:7-9	Jun 27
10:13	Jun 5
10:14	Sep 18
10:19	Oct 4
10:31	Dec 29
11:7	Jul 15
11:13	Aug 20
12:2	Jan 26

James

1:2, 3	Dec 12
1:2-4	Feb 18
1:12	Feb 18
1:13	Nov 4; Dec 12
1:14	Aug 10; Dec 12
1:27	Aug 7
2:7	Apr 8

James

4:3	Feb 20; Aug 23
4:4	Nov 1
4:7, 8	May 29
5:16	Jan 12

1 Peter

1:3, 4	Aug 18
1:5	Aug 6
1:8	Dec 25
1:15, 16	May 23
1:16	Aug 28
2:9	Mar 17; Jul 5; Sep 16
4:4	Jul 11
4:12, 13	Feb 18
5:1	Sep 21
5:6, 7	Feb 6
5:8	May 15; Sep 4

2 Peter

1:2	Feb 17
1:3, 4	Feb 15
1:8	Feb 17
1:19	Aug 4
1:21	Sep 14
2:9	Aug 6; Nov 4; Dec 14
3:10	Aug 20
3:18	Dec 15

1 John

1:3	Oct 18
1:4	Jul 7
1:9	Sep 29; Dec 7

1 John

2:1	Apr 23; Sep 13, 17
2:4	Mar 27
2:5	Oct 28
2:6	Oct 28
2:15	Nov 1
2:15, 16	May 21
3:1	Mar 2; Dec 27
3:2	Aug 22; Dec 3
4:2	Mar 7
4:3	Apr 17
4:10	Sep 5
4:14	Jun 11
4:16	Jul 5
4:19	Aug 30
5:13	May 3
5:19	Nov 1

Jude

3	Oct 6
24	Aug 6
24, 25	Feb 5

Revelation

1-3	Jun 30
2:10	Aug 10
3:16	Jul 4
5:12	Jan 30
12:10	Oct 5
12:12	Aug 14
15:3	Mar 19
15:4	May 21
21	Dec 1
22	Dec 1
22:20	May 6; Jun 1